p-Source

p-Source

A Guide to the Apple Pascal System

by Randall Hyde

DATAMOST™ INC
8943 Fullbright Ave.
Chatsworth, California 91311
(213) 709-1202

RESTON PUBLISHING COMPANY, INC.
A Prentice-Hall Company
Reston, Virginia

ISBN 0-8359-5410-2

Acknowledgements

A technical manual like this one wouldn't be possible without a lot of "inside" information. I would like to thank Roger Sumner and Keith Shillington for helping me understand the early I.4 and I.5 systems. Several tools were employed while deciphering the Apple Pascal System. DISASM/65, a program I wrote for the LISA v2.5 Interactive Assembler, was used extensively for disassembling the Apple Pascal p-code interpreter. The Pascal Tools I and II packages from Advanced Business Technology were a tremendous help as was the PDQ Package from DATAMOST. The p-code disassembler used in this manual is a program called "DECODE" written by Thomas Brennan. I have no idea whether this program is commercially available but in my opinion it's the best p-code disassembler available. If Mr. Brennan makes this package available it would be a good investment if you're interested in the internals of the Apple Pascal System.

This manual was written on an Apple II computer system using the Apple PIE (PIE Writer) word processing system available from Hayden Book Company. The original illustrations and drawings were created on Apple's LISA machine using LISADRAW. Without these two computer systems this project would not have been possible.

Randall Hyde

Table of Contents

SECTION 1: Programming Techniques in Apple Pascal **13**

Chapter 1 — Shared Allocation in Apple Pascal **15**
- Games People Play with the Case Variant 20
- An Overview of the p-System Run-time Environment 28
- Using the Case Variant with the Pointer Data Type 35
- Overview of the Pascal Run-time System Part Two 37
- Turning off the Range Checking Option 42
- When Not to Pull Tricks 44
- Program Listings 47

Chapter 2 — Improving the Performance of Apple Pascal Program ... **59**
- General Information About the USCD p-Machine 60
- Tools Required for Optimization 60
- Optimizing for Compactness 61
- Optimizing REAL Variable Accesses 64
- Optimizing String Accesses 65
- Optimizing Array and Subrange Accesses 66
- Optimizing I/O Instructions 67
- Optimizing IF and CASE Statements 67
- Using FILLCHAR to Initialize Arrays 69
- Optimizing for Speed 70
- Dynamic vs. Static Optimization 70

Chapter 3 — Using LST Files to Debug and Optimize Pascal Programs **73**
- Debugging Run-time Errors 76
- Program Listings 79

Chapter 4 — Examining Computer-generated Code **83**
Integer Variable Allocation 83
Real Variable Accesses 84
Array Allocation 85
Set Operations 86
Accessing Record Elements 88
Accessing String Variables 88
Pointer-Variable Usage 89
Code Generator for a FOR Loop 90
While Loops 91
The REPEAT . . UNTIL Loops 91
The IF . . THEN . . ELSE Statement 92
The CASE Statement 93
Expressions in Apple Pascal 94
String Handling Functions 95
Procedure Definitions and Calls 98
Program Listings 99

SECTION 2: Internal Operation of the p-Machine **149**

Chapter 5 — An Explanation of the p-Code Instructions **151**
Instruction Formats 152
Constant (Immediate) Loads 154
Local Loads and Stores 160
Global Loads and Stores 168
Intermediate Loads and Stores 176
Indirect Loads and Stores 184
Extended Loads and Stores 190
Multiple-Word Loads and Stores (Reals and Sets) 196
Byte Array Handling 202
String Handling Instructions 206
Record and Array Handling Instructions 212
Dynamic Variable Allocation 224
Top of Stack Arithmetic 232
Integer Operations 232
Integer Comparisons 250
Non-Integer Comparisons 251
REAL Operations 252
REAL Comparisons 276

STRING Comparisons 276
Logical Operations 276
Logical Comparisons 282
Set Operations 282
Set Comparisons 294
Byte Array Comparisons 294
Record and Word Arrays 294
JUMPS 296
Procedure and Function Calls 304

Chapter 6 — Inside the p-Code Interpreter 307
Zero Page Variables 307

SECTION 3: Modifying Apple Pascal 349

Chapter 7 — Modifying the Apple Pascal p-Code Interpreter 351
Program Listings 357

Chapter 8 — Attaching Your Own Devices to the Pascal BIOS 375
Modifying the Apple Pascal BIOS 375
I/O Overview 376
Creating Driver Using the "SYSTEM.ATTACH" Method 378
Replacing the CONSOLE: Driver 380
Replacing the PRINTER: Device (Unit 6) 387
Replacing the REMOUT: and REMIN: Drivers (Units 7 & 8) 389
Attaching Drivers to Block Structured Devices (Units 4, 5, 9...12) 390
Attaching User Defined Devices to the BIOS (Units 128-143) 392
Attaching Your Drivers to the System 392

Appendix: ATTACH-BIOS Document for Apple II Pascal 1.1 397

Index 453

Preface

This manual is intended to be a guide to the internal operation of the Apple Pascal System. It describes the operation of the Apple Pascal p-Machine, the operating system, and various systems utilities such as the SYSTEM.ATTACH program. It explains how to patch the system for improved performance as well as additional utility. It describes how to hook up nonstandard peripheral devices (such as a clock card or arithmetic processing unit) to the Apple Pascal System. Finally, it will attempt to provide a partial "road map" to the system explaining how memory is used and what it is used for. In short, it is intended to provide a strong "p-SOURCE" of information for the advanced Apple Pascal user.

The manual is divided into three main sections: Pascal program examples, a "road map" to the p-code interpreter, and a designer guide for peripheral manufacturers and assembly language programmers. The first section provides information on hints and various "tricks" available to the Apple Pascal programmer. The road map details how memory is used by various portions of the Apple Pascal p-code interpreter. The last section describes how to interface peripherals and machine language programs to the Apple Pascal System.

Section One
Programming Techniques in Apple Pascal

1

Shared Allocation in Apple Pascal

Introduction

This section will not show you how to become a better Apple Pascal programmer. On the contrary, it will teach you bad programming practices, poor programming style and non-portable techniques. While some of you may call these techniques abhorrent and label any program using them as poorly written, a simple fact remains: a poorly written program that works is much better than a well written program that does not.

This first section of *p-Source* discusses three main topics: the use of shared allocation in Apple Pascal (allowing you to implement the famous PEEK and POKE instructions as well as perform "bit-tweaking"); optimizing compiler generated code by rearranging declarations and program statements; and an easy method for debugging your Pascal programs using facilities built into the Apple Pascal compiler.

This manual assumes that you are a competent and experienced Apple Pascal programmer. The optimization hints and techniques described herein should *not* be utilized by the novice, nor should they be incorporated into a program from the outset. In most cases, a better algorithm or data structure will completely remove the need to use the machine dependent techniques described here. The optimization techniques presented make the program less maintainable, machine-dependent and harder to understand. Therefore they should only be used as a last resort to speed up or shrink your program.

Overview

While Apple Pascal provides several useful data structures for representing high-level objects, the need to access data in a low-level fashion is often required. Low level manipulation of a data object is easily accomplished by treating a memory location as one type of data under certain circumstances and as another type of data under other circumstances. The traditional solution has been to resort to machine language subroutines in order to perform these operations. Performing programming tricks in Pascal offers several advantages over using machine language. Machine language is difficult to learn and makes the program even less portable.

Apple Pascal provides variant records, a mechanism by which a record can vary in composition depending upon the environment. For example, you could have a record type PERSON that contains various fields depending upon whether the person was married or not.

Example:

```
TYPE
  MARITALSTATUS = (SINGLE,MARRIED);
  CASE MARITALSTATUS OF

   SINGLE: (NAME:STRING;
            AGE:INTEGER;
            SOCSEC:STRING;
            SEX:BOOLEAN);

   MARRIED:(NAME:STRING;
            SPOUSE:STRING;
            AGE:INTEGER;
            SOCSEC:STRING);

  END;
```

The purpose of a variant definition is to allow you to view a data structure differently depending upon several external cases. In the example above, the data types vary depending upon whether or not the person is married. The single person has an extra SEX component while the married person has an extra SPOUSE component.

Whenever a variant is defined, Apple Pascal allocates enough storage for the largest *variant* present in the variant part of the record definition (see Figures 1-1 and 1-2). Since (by using the case variant form of the RECORD definition) you have agreed to use fieldnames from only one variant in the variant part, Apple Pascal will reuse the same memory space for single and married people. That is to say, at one time the 248 bytes reserved for the structure above are used to hold the information associated with the married person; at a different time those same 248 bytes are used to hold the information associated with the single person. You are not supposed to use the fieldnames from the married variant field when dealing with a single person; likewise you mustn't use the fieldnames from the single person when dealing with a married person.

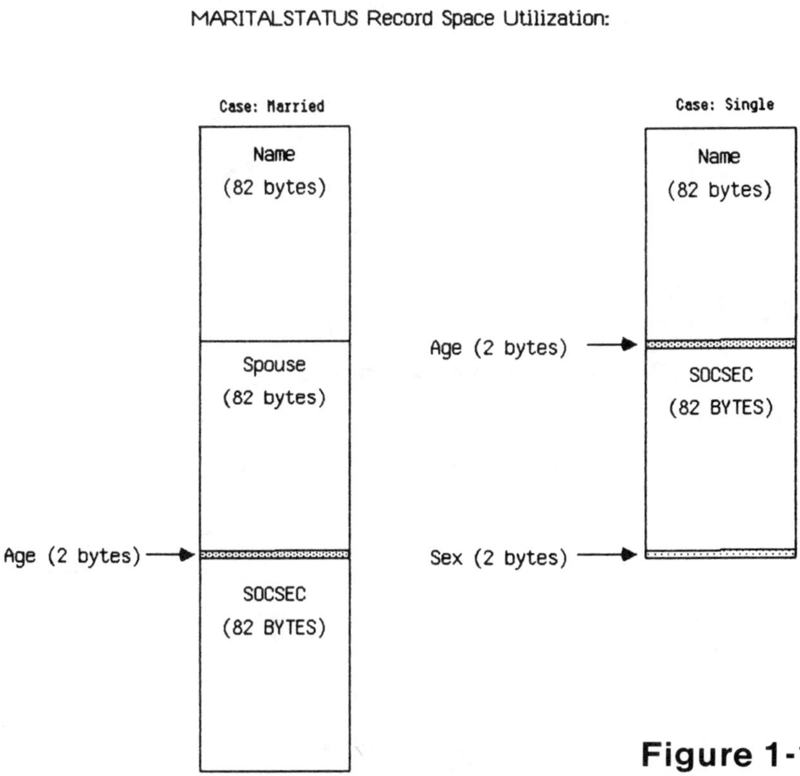

Figure 1-1

MARITALSTATUS Record Space Utilization:
(Without Case Variant Records)

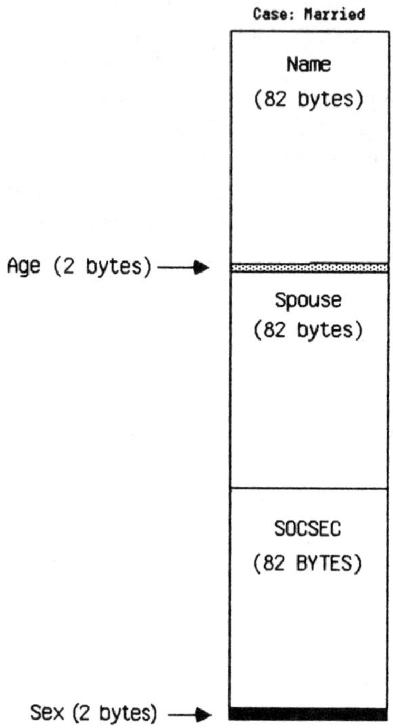

Figure 1-2

You will notice that 82 bytes are wasted when dealing with a record containing a single person. This, however, is much better than using the following record definition since this wastes space for both married and single people:

```
PERSON = RECORD

           NAME:STRING;
           AGE:INTEGER;
           SPOUSE:STRING;
           SOCSEC:STRING;
           SEX:BOOLEAN;

         END;
```

This discussion applies only to data structures which are defined as VARiables. Dynamic variable allocation (via the NEW procedure) has provisions for allocating the exact number of bytes required. If you declare PEOPLE to be a pointer to the data type PERSON, you could allocate storage using the command NEW(PEOPLE,SINGLE) that allocates only the number of bytes required by the SINGLE variant. NEW(PEOPLE,MARRIED) allocates the same amount of storage as NEW(PEOPLE) since the MARRIED variant requires the maximum amount of storage. In the discussion that follows I assume that pointers and dynamic allocation *are not* being used.

Before describing the various "tricks" you can play with the case variant part, a discussion of the case variant's purpose may be helpful. A good example where you would use a variant record is in a mailing list program. Many mailing list programs keep track of the number of records in a file by storing the record count as part of the file (usually in record number zero). Without the case variant part you would have to use a separate file, or worse yet include the count field in every record. With the case variant only the first record of the mailing list file need contain this information, e.g.,

```
TYPE

RECTYPE = (REC0,ALLOTHERS);
MAILLIST= RECORD CASE RECTYPE OF

           REC0:(NUMRECS:INTEGER[6]);
           ALLOTHERS:( {Normal record data goes here} );
          END;
```

As you can see, the variant portion is actually *useful* on occasion.

Games People Play with the Case Variant

Now we come to the whole purpose of this discussion — by bending the rules behind Pascal's back we can perform some really neat tricks. Before discussing these tricks a word of warning is in order: many of these techniques are non-portable, which means they will work fine on an Apple II but may not work on any other machine running Pascal (including the Apple ///).

The main idea behind all the neat and nifty tricks that follow is summed up in a statement made earlier: the programmer *should not* access fields in different variants when operating on the same datum. Note that we said *shouldn't*, not *can't*. The Pascal compiler has no way of knowing which variant the program is using so it will allow you to use mixed fields without complaining. After all, you agreed not to, if you do it's your own fault ("With freedom comes responsibility" — *Pascal MT+ Manual*). You can pull some very interesting tricks by breaking the rules and going ahead and accessing fields from the different variant fields.

For the purpose of discussion consider the record:

```
UNDO = RECORD CASE BOOLEAN OF

         FALSE:(I:INTEGER);
         TRUE :(B:PACKED ARRAY [0..1] OF 0..255);

        END;
```

Both variants require the same amount of memory, namely two bytes (see Figure 1-3). If a variable (say A) is declared to be of type UNDO, you could treat A.I as an integer in a fashion as though you declared an integer variable A.I. Likewise, you could treat A.B[0] and A.B[1] as the two elements of a packed array of 0..255 just like any other variable declared to be a packed array of 0..255 with two elements. A problem (and, in our case, the advantage to this scheme) occurs if you try to use A.I and A.B *simultaneously*. Consider the program segment:

```
A.I := 255;
A.B[0] := 0;
WRITELN(A.I);
```

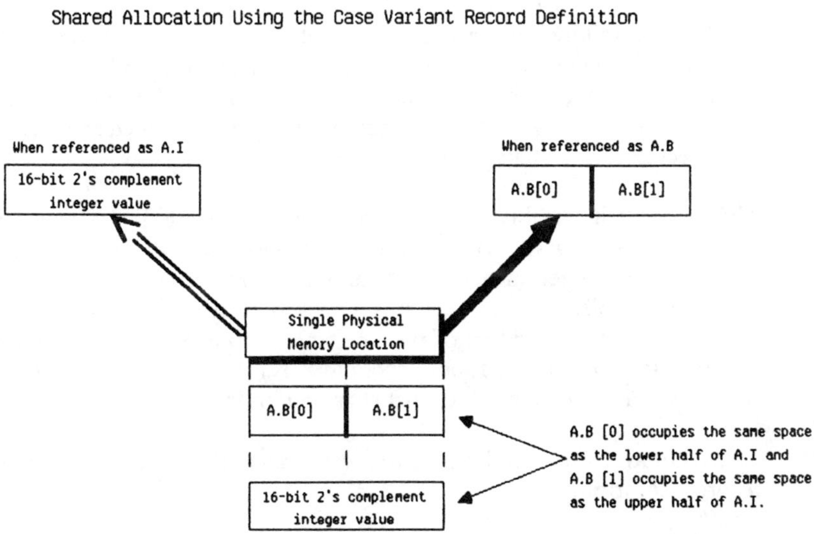

Figure 1-3

If you run this code you'll probably be quite surprised, it prints zero instead of 255 as the value for A.I! The reason zero is printed is that the variable A.I and the array A.B share the same two bytes in memory storage (see Figure 1-4). As a result, storing data into the array A.B modifies the contents of A.I as well. In this case it assigned zero to the low-order byte of A.I, which contained the only 1-bits of the integer 255.

This phenomenon is due to the fact that A.I and the array A.B share the same physical memory locations. Storing a value in A.I affects the contents of the array A.B and storing data into one of the elements of A.B affects the integer A.I. Exactly how they interact provides the basis of this chapter. A.B[0]'s storage corresponds to the storage of the low order byte of the integer A.I and A.B[1]'s storage corresponds to that for the high order byte of A.I (see Figure 1-3). This means that it is possible to disassemble an integer into its low-order and high-order components!

While this is mildly interesting, you're probably thinking, "Big deal, of what use is this?" Well, suppose you wanted to print the integer I as a four-digit hexadecimal value. While it could be done from Pascal without using any tricks (see Listing 1–1), the program in Listing 1–2 is much more compact and executes faster than programs using standard methods.

The piece of incredibly opaque code found in listing 1–2 will print the integer variable passed to it as a four-byte hexadecimal value. It starts by copying the integer into the A.I variable so that I can be disassembled nibble-by-nibble. The A.N array is a packed array of nibbles, each nibble corresponding to four bits of the integer A.I. Starting with the most significant nibble (there are four of them in A.N) the FOR loop converts each successive nibble to a hexadecimal character and writes it.

This technique can even be used to access data at the bit level. Consider the record definition:

```
GETBITS = RECORD CASE BOOLEAN OF

            FALSE:(I:INTEGER);
            TRUE :(B:PACKED ARRAY[0..15] OF BOOLEAN);

          END;
```

Accessing two cases in a variant record simultaneously:

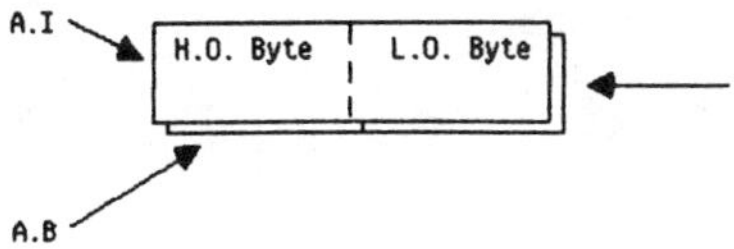

A.B[0] occupies the same space as the low order byte of A.I and A.B[1] occupies the same space as the high order byte of A.I

1) "A.I := 255" (note: $00FF is hex equivalent of decimal 255)

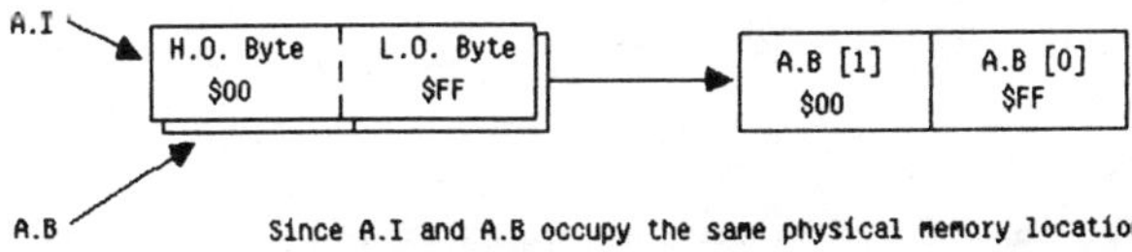

Since A.I and A.B occupy the same physical memory locations, storing $00FF (255) into A.I also stores $00FF into A.B. In this case the high order data byte ($00) is stored into A.B[1] and the low order data byte ($FF) is stored into A.B[0].

2) "A.B [0] := 0;"

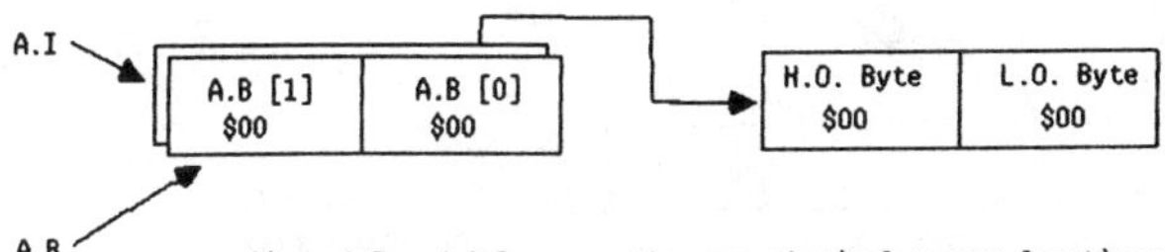

Since A.I and A.B occupy the same physical memory locations, storing zero into A.B [0] also zeroes out the low order byte of A.I. Since the high order byte of A.I already contained zero, A.I now contains the value zero.

3) "WRITELN(A.I);"

Since both the low order and high order bytes of A.I contain zero, zero will be printed.

Figure 1-4

In this example, a variable of type GETBITS (say A) has access to each of the individual bits in the integer portion of the variable (see Figure 1-5). For example, if you executed the code:

```
A.I := 0;
A.B[0] := TRUE;
A.B[2] := TRUE;
```

and printed A.I you would get the value 5 displayed on your terminal. This is due to the fact that you've set bits two and zero to one, which is the binary value %0000000000000101 (decimal five). For setting, resetting and testing bits this method works great. For other logical operations (such as AND and OR) there's a better way. . .

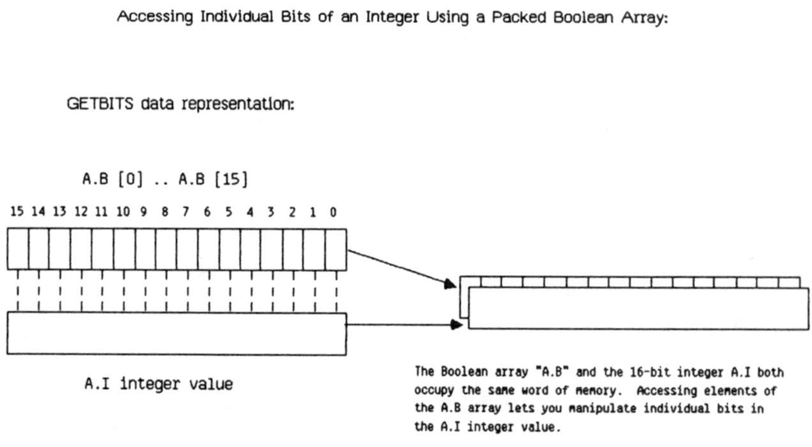

Figure 1-5

The Apple Pascal language implements set types using bit arrays. If you declare a variable to be of type "SET OF 0..15" Apple Pascal reserves a 16-bit array with one bit corresponding to each integer value. Bit zero corresponds to the value zero, bit one corresponds to the set element one, bit two corresponds to the set element two, etc. If you were to declare the variable A to be of type:

```
MAGICSET = CASE BOOLEAN OF

            FALSE:(I:INTEGER);
            TRUE :(S:SET OF 0..15);

           END;
```

Then an assignment of the form "A.S := [15,10,7,3,1];" sets bits one, three, seven, ten and fifteen to one and sets all other bits to zero (see Figure 1-6). This allows you to set multiple bit patterns with one assignment instead of the several required by the Boolean array method.

Better yet, the set construct allows you to selectively set or clear any particular bit(s) without affecting other bits. By using the Pascal set union and intersection operators you can emulate the logical AND and OR functions. The set union operator lets you emulate the logical OR function. Assuming you have three variables A, B and C of type MAGICSET, you could store the logical OR of A.I and B.I into C.I using the code:

```
C.S := A.S + B.S;
```

To perform the logical AND operation you would use the set intersection operator. To place the logical AND of A.I and B.I into C.I you would use the code:

```
C.S := A.S * B.S;
```

Apple Pascal Set Type Data Representation

Assuming you have a variable "S" defined by the statement:

```
S: SET OF 0..15;
```

The elements of S are represented using the bit array:

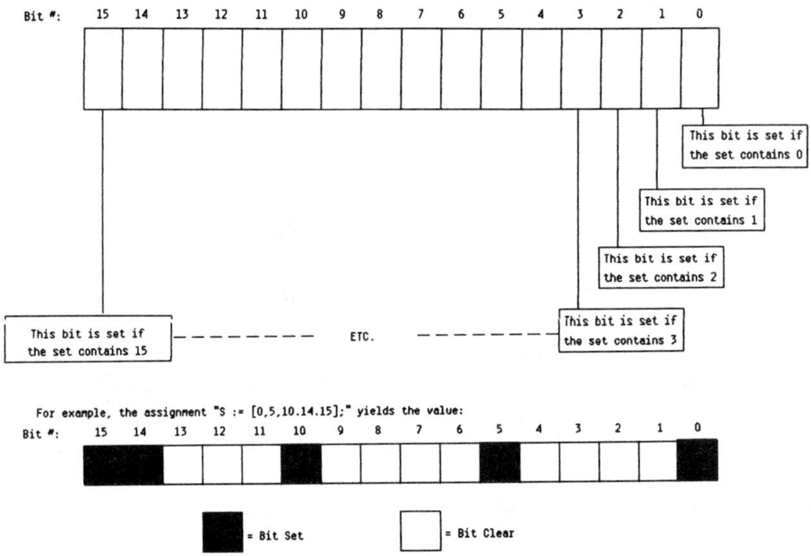

Figure 1-6

The set difference, (in)equality, set inclusion and set membership operators may also prove helpful every now and then.

Sometimes it's handy to treat a bit string as an element of a set; sometimes it's better to treat it as an element of a packed array of Boolean. In these situations use the type definition:

```
TRINARY = Ø..2;
BITSTRING = RECORD CASE TRINARY OF

                 Ø:(I:INTEGER);
                 1:(B:PACKED ARRAY [Ø..15] OF BOOLEAN);
                 2:(S:SET OF Ø..15);

             END;
```

This allows you to reference A in three modes (A.I, A.B and A.S) yet operate on the same data without having to make spurious assignments (see Figure 1-7).

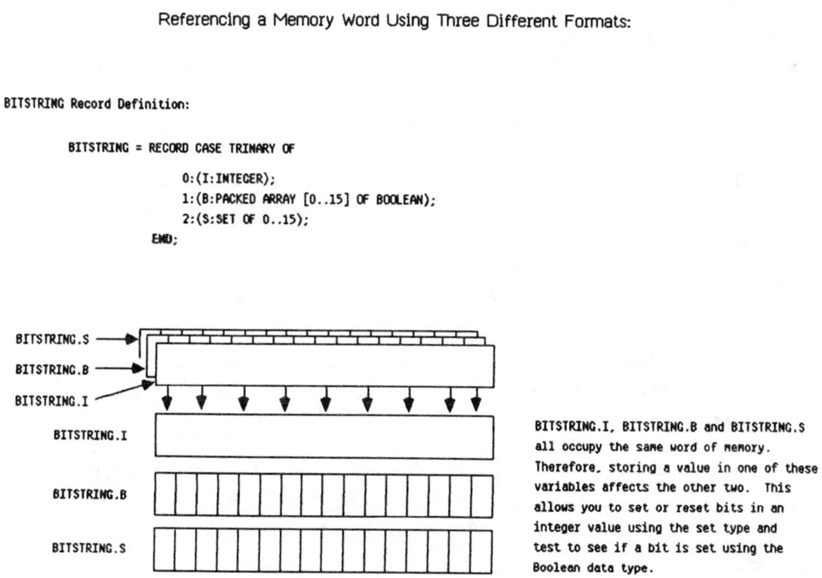

Figure 1-7

An Overview of the p-System Run-Time Environment

Before continuing, I must digress and discuss Apple Pascal's memory allocation scheme. Additional information concerning the Apple Pascal run-time environment can be found in the Appendix.

Figure 1-8 provides a schematic of what the system is like during the execution of a typical program. Since the Apple's architecture and 6502 microprocessor chip force certain constraints on the software, you will notice certain similarities between Pascal's memory map and BASIC's memory map. Like BASIC (or DOS), the lower memory locations (in this case locations $0 through roughly $1000) are reserved for the system software, the video screen, the hardware stack and for other purposes requiring data in a fixed location. Just like BASIC, the p-System's interpreter sits in the 16K language card freeing up space in main memory for the operating system and user programs and data. By placing part of the operating system into the 16K card, almost 40K of space is available for user programs and data.

In order to use space as efficiently as possible, the Apple Pascal system dynamically allocates storage on two *stacks* while the user program executes. The *program stack* starts at the top of memory (just below the operating system) and grows downward. Whenever you eX)ecute a program from the Apple Pascal command level, space is allocated on this stack for the program code and for any variables you declare in your program. When a program is invoked, first the code is loaded onto the program stack then any room required for permanent variables is allocated just below the program code. Figure 1-9 gives you an idea of what the stack looks like during the execution of a specific program.

With the exception of Apple Pascal's SEGMENT PROCEDUREs, the amount of memory required for program code remains constant throughout the execution of the program. SEGMENT PROCEDUREs are only loaded into memory when they are called. For bulky initialization code and other rarely called procedures, using Apple Pascal's SEGMENT PROCEDURE feature can save some space at the expense of greater execution time. Figure 1-10 demonstrates memory utilization during the execution of a SEGMENT PROCEDURE. You can see that the code for the SEGMENT PROCEDURE gets loaded onto the stack below the variables allocated by the calling code.

Apple Pascal Memory Map

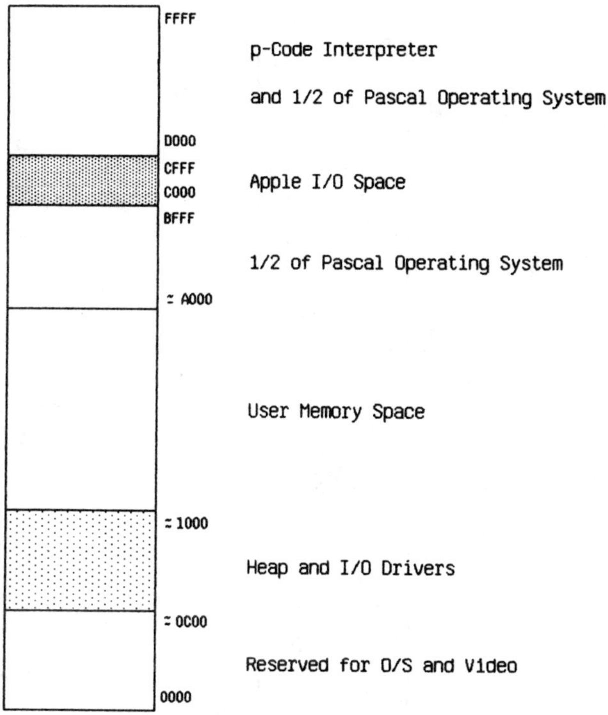

Figure 1-8

Memory Allocation During the Execution
of a Typical User Program

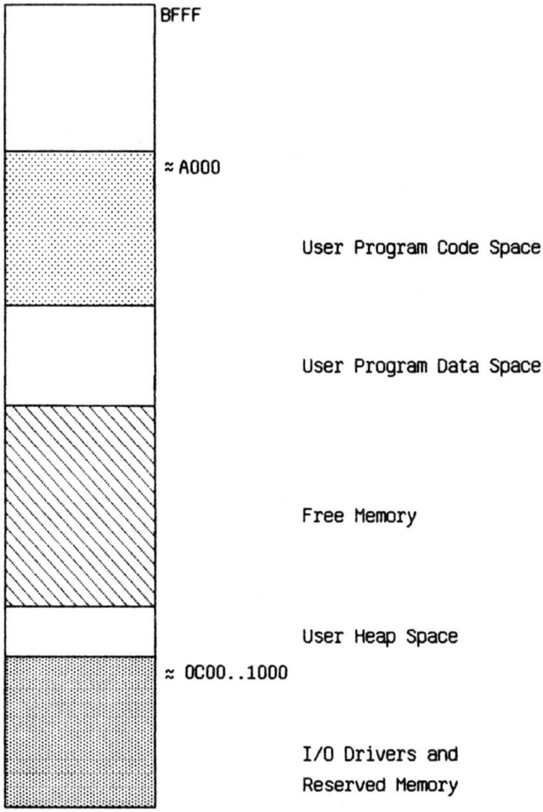

Figure 1-9

Memory Utilization During the Execution
of a Segment Procedure.

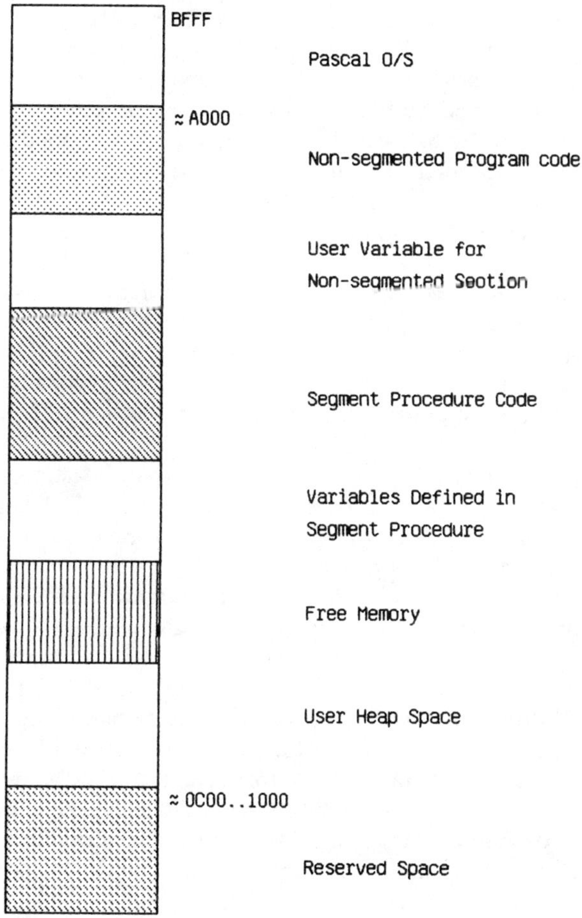

Figure 1-10

While the program stack is busy growing downwards, another stack is growing upwards. This second stack (referred to as the 'HEAP' in the Apple Pascal literature) is where space for Pascal's *dynamic* variables are allocated. Dynamic variables in Pascal are allocated with the NEW procedure. To allocate storage on the heap you must declare a *pointer* variable and then execute the NEW procedure passing the pointer variable as a parameter. A pointer variable requires two bytes of storage (enough to hold the 16-bit address used by the Pascal system) and is allocated on the program stack along with other variables. Whenever you execute the NEW procedure, the HEAP pointer is copied into the specified pointer variable and then the HEAP pointer is incremented to make room for the variable being allocated on the HEAP. Figure 1-11 diagrams how this allocation takes place.

Once the space is allocated and the address is copied into the pointer variable, the pointer variable can be treated almost like any other variable of the specified type. The major advantage of using a pointer variable is that you can completely change the data in a large record by simply changing the address the pointer variable contains (see Figure 1-12).

A minor problem with dynamic variable allocation in Apple Pascal is that pointers are always allocated automatically. The UCSD p-System was designed to run on almost anyone's hardware. In order to achieve this goal the system was designed to prevent machine dependent constructs from creeping into UCSD Pascal programs. While this situation is ideal when you're interested in creating portable programs, it creates some problems when you're interested in optimizing your programs by taking advantage of existing hardware in your machine. For example, the Apple's keyboard port is located at address $C000 in the memory space. It would be nice if you could override Pascal's automatic initialization of dynamic variables and load $C000 directly into the pointer. If you could do this, then you could access the Apple's hardware directly, without the need for special drivers and without the need for using 6502 assembly language. With this thought in mind I'll end the digression and return to the discussion of variant records (HINT: integers and pointers both require two bytes of storage).

Dynamic Memory Allocation Using NEW

"NEW(IP)" (Where IP is a pointer to an integer)

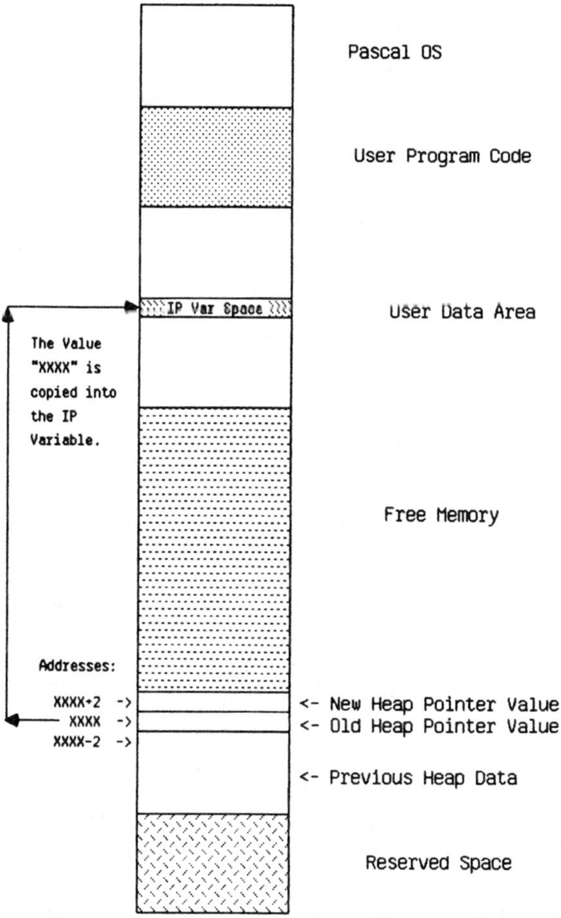

Figure 1-11

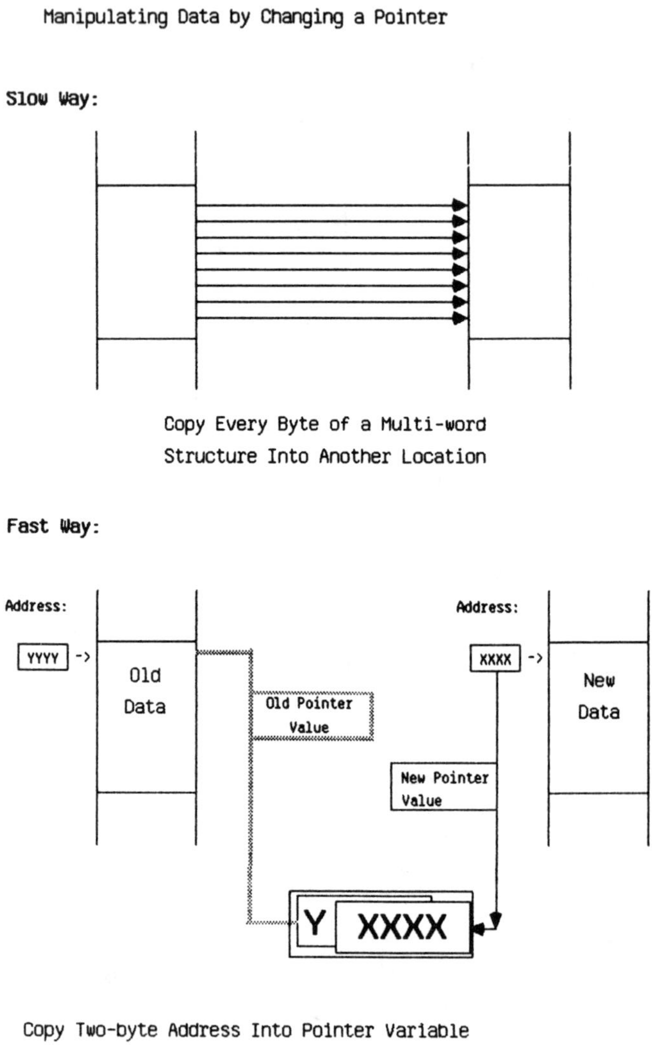
Manipulating Data by Changing a Pointer
Slow Way:
Copy Every Byte of a Multi-word
Structure Into Another Location
Fast Way:
Address:
YYYY ->
Old
Data
Old Pointer
Value
Address:
XXXX ->
New
Data
New Pointer
Value
Y
XXXX
Copy Two-byte Address Into Pointer Variable

Figure 1-12

Using the Case Variant with the Pointer Data Type

A pointer variable consists of a two-byte value that contains the address of the desired data type. For example, a pointer to an integer contains not the integer itself, but rather the address in memory where the integer can be found. Normally Pascal initializes the pointer to point somewhere on the heap whenever you execute the new procedure; you have no control over the address in memory that the pointer points to. But consider the record definition:

```
BYTE = 0..255;
TRIX = RECORD CASE BOOLEAN OF

        FALSE:(P:^INTEGER);
        TRUE :(I:INTEGER);

       END;
```

A variable (say A) declared to be of type TRIX will have exactly two bytes reserved for it. When referenced as A.P these two bytes correspond to the pointer to an integer (i.e., A.P); in the other case these two bytes can be an integer value (i.e., A.I). You can use this form of the case variant record definition to observe the actions of the Pascal NEW procedure using the code:

```
FOR J := 0 TO 99 DO BEGIN

        NEW(A.P);
        WRITELN('A.I= ',A.I);

        END;
```

By running this program you can observe A.I being incremented by two each time you pass through the loop, this demonstrates how Pascal allocates sequential memory elements during dynamic allocation.

While this may seem instructive, but impractical, there is one interesting use of this form of the case variant form: it can be used to tell you where a free block of memory lies in the Apple memory space. By using this case variant with the MEMAVAIL function you can determine the bounds of memory in use by the Apple Pascal System. The MEMAVAIL function returns the number of words (not bytes!) available to the system at any given moment. This value is computed by subtracting the value in the heap pointer from the value in the stack pointer and dividing by two. Since executing the NEW command loads the current value of the heap pointer into a pointer variable, this value plus two times the MEMAVAIL gives you the stack pointer value (see Listing 1–3).

The real power you get from pointers and the case variant is not their ability to determine the address a pointer contains, but rather you gain the ability to modify the address contained within the pointer. This is accomplished by *writing* to the integer instead of just reading from it. By writing to A.I you overwrite the pointer value that was originally stored there. For example, if you store -16384 into A.I and then use the pointer A.P you will access location $C000 (the Apple keyboard) in the Apple's memory space. This function gives you a built-in PEEK and POKE command all rolled into one! In fact, the BASIC PEEK and POKE commands could be easily simulated with the Pascal routines:

```
FUNCTION PEEK(ADDRESS:INTEGER):BYTE;
TYPE BYTE = PACKED ARRAY [0..1] OF 0..255;
     MAGIC = RECORD CASE BOOLEAN OF

                 FALSE:(I:INTEGER);
                 TRUE :(P:^BYTE);

             END;

VAR A:MAGIC;

BEGIN

    A.I  := ADDRESS;
    PEEK := A.P^ [0];

END;
```

```
PROCEDURE POKE(ADDRESS:INTEGER; VALUE:BYTE);
TYPE BYTE = PACKED ARRAY [0..1] OF 0..255;
     MAGIC = RECORD CASE BOOLEAN OF

                FALSE:(I:INTEGER);
                TRUE :(P:^BYTE);

             END;

VAR A:MAGIC;

BEGIN

    A.I       := ADDRESS;
    A.P^ [0] := VALUE;

END;
```

There is one very important difference between this Pascal version of PEEK and POKE and BASIC's PEEK and POKE: BASIC is limited to handling data 8 bits at a time; the Pascal structure lets you PEEK and POKE any data structure you wish. For example, if you wished to peek and poke integers instead of bytes you would change each occurrence of "BYTE" in the previous programs to "INTEGER". In fact, to peek or poke any data type (including arrays, sets and even pointers if you are so inclined) you need only replace "BYTE" with the name of the data type you wish to peek or poke. Listing 1–4 demonstrates how to read the Apple's keyboard by accessing the hardware directly.

Overview of the Pascal Run-Time System, Part Two

The Apple Pascal compiler generates storage for variables in a linear fashion. Starting with an offset of zero, variables are assigned an "address" that corresponds to the size (in words) of all the variables previously declared in the current procedure. If you declare three variables; I, J and R; using the declaration:

```
    I:INTEGER;
    R:REAL;
    J:INTEGER;
```

then the address zero is assigned to I, the address one is assigned to R (since I requires one word of storage) and the address three is assigned to J (I requires one word of storage and R requires two words of storage — see Figure 1-13). The exact amount of storage required for any Apple Pascal variable except for PACKED ARRAYs and long integers is outlined in Figure 1-14.

Pascal Variable Storage Memory Allocation

```
VAR  I:INTEGER;
     R:REAL;
     J:INTEGER;
```

Yields:

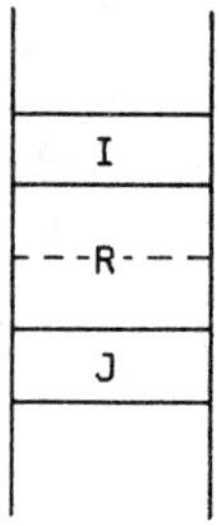

Figure 1-13

Storage Requirements for Apple Pascal Data Types

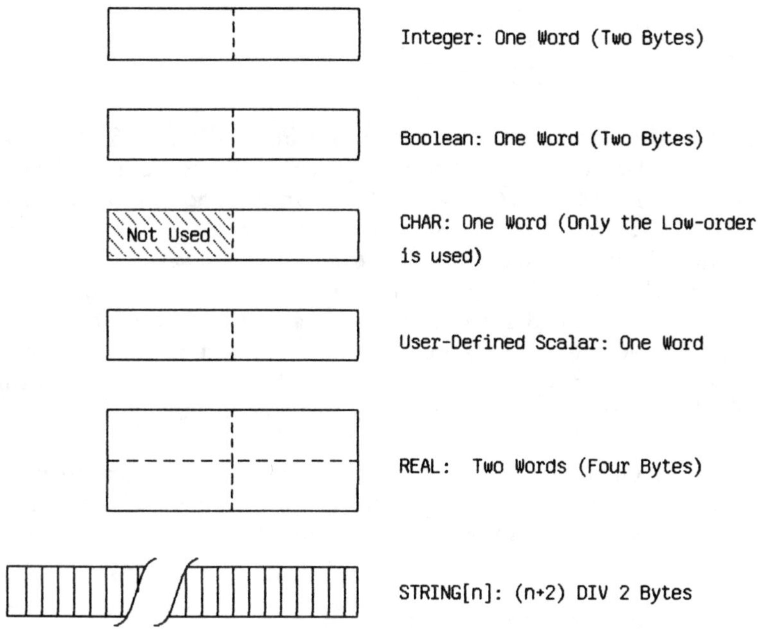

Figure 1-14

There is one instance where the assignment of a run-time address does not correspond to the appearance of a variable within a program. If you declare several variables of the same type in a Pascal statement, i.e.:

```
    I,J,K:INTEGER;
```

then storage for K is allocated first, then J and finally space for I is allocated. If this declaration was the first to appear in a procedure then K would be assigned the address zero, J would be assigned the address one and I would be assigned two. Whenever several variables are assigned the same type in a single Pascal statement, ***backwards address allocation*** is performed. The variable closest to the type identifier is allocated storage first. Arrays and records are allocated space in an identical fashion except, of course, the required number of words are reserved for the structure instead of simply reserving one or two words. Figure 1-15 shows what a stack frame might look like during the execution of a simple procedure.

If you are defining a procedure or function with parameters, then space is allocated on the stack for the parameters before space is reserved for the local variables. For example, the procedure:

```
PROCEDURE EXAMPLE(PARM1:INTEGER);
VAR R:REAL;
    I:INTEGER;

BEGIN
END;
```

allocates word zero to PARM1, word one to R and word three to I. For additional information on variable allocation in Apple Pascal see Chapters Two, Three and the Appendix.

Stack Frame During the Execution of a Typical Procedure

```
Procedure Simple;
Var I,J,K:Integer;
        L:Integer;
        R:Real;
        B:Boolean;

Begin

End;
```

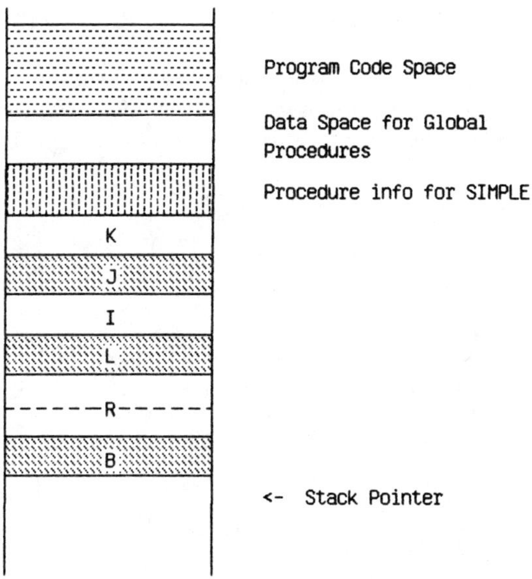

Figure 1-15

Turning Off the Range Checking Option

Whenever you declare a variable that is not an array, the Apple Pascal compiler emits code to reference the memory location associated with that variable. Whenever an array variable is referenced, the Pascal compiler must perform several steps to access the array element you specify. First, the *base* address of the array (the address of the first element of the array) is pushed onto the evaluation stack. If the array is a multi-dimensional array then a computation must be performed to convert the various indices into a single index. If the array is a one dimensional array the single dimension's value is used as the index into the array. The index is then multiplied by the size (in bytes) of an element of an array (i.e., multiplied by two for scalars, by four for reals, or by some other value for arrays of sets, records and other multi-word structures). Finally, the index is added to the base address to obtain the address of the element you're interested in accessing.

Before blindly accessing the memory location specified by this computation, the Pascal run-time system checks the index to make sure that it is a valid one. For example, consider the short little program:

```
PROGRAM JUNK;
VAR X:ARRAY [Ø..5] OF INTEGER;
    I:INTEGER;

BEGIN

  I := 6;
  X [I] := 2Ø;


END.
```

Since the X array doesn't contain a sixth element this program makes little sense. In practice, however, since variables are allocated sequentially in memory, storing data into the sixth element of X is the same thing as storing data into I (see Figure 1-16). To prevent little disasters like this from occurring, the Apple Pascal compiler emits a special CHK p-code instruction whenever you access an array element to check the array index and make sure it is in the specified bounds. If you've ever gotten a "value range error" then you've experienced this type of problem. While this range checking does prevent some unexpected problems from arising, by turning the range checking off and purposely accessing out of range array elements, you can perform some useful tricks.

Luckily the range checking in Apple Pascal can be turned on or off at will using the two compiler options "{$R+}" and "{$R-}". The "{$R+}" option (which is the default when you begin compiling a program) turns the range checking on and the "{$R-}" option turns it off. By interspersing these two options in a program, you can selectively turn the range checking off for a few statements and then turn it back on after those statements.

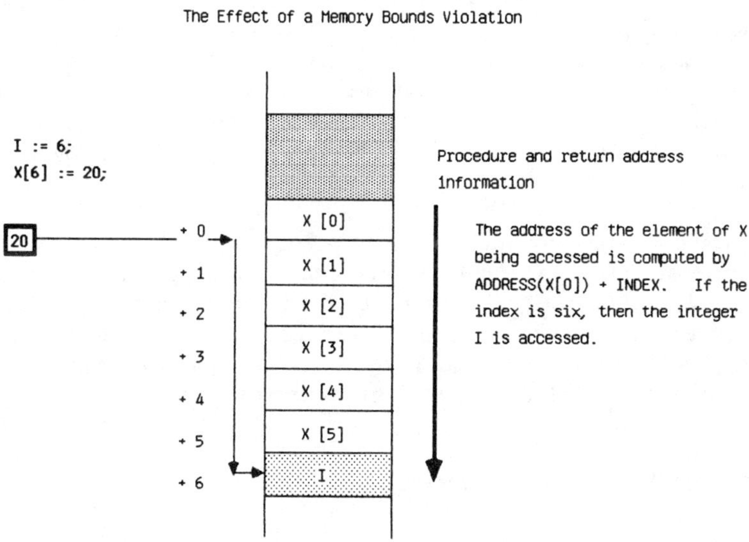

Figure 1-16

While the range checking is turned off, the Pascal run-time system will not detect an array index that is out of bounds. We can use this feature to fiddle around with memory locations adjacent to an array. Listing 1-5 demonstrates the effects of turning off the range checking and accessing non-existent array elements. Listing 1-6 performs the same demonstration, except it shows you how to access parameter values by turning off the range checking.

One rather useful task that the {$R-} option can be put to is determining the address of a structure in Apple Pascal. The ability to obtain the address of an object and reference that object strictly with pointers is very powerful. Any "C" programmer will immediately tell you one of Pascal's greatest shortcomings is its inability to obtain the address of some variable. By using the "{$R-}" option, however, it is possible to obtain the address of any structure in Pascal. Listings 1-7 and 1-8 present two possible alternatives for accomplising just that. Both programs rely on the fact that the "Y" parameter is passed to the ADDR function *by reference* (i.e., a VAR parameter). Whenever a parameter is passed by reference, the *address* of the parameter, not the value of the parameter is passed to the function. Normally, references within the function would take this into account and load the value pointed at by "Y" instead of the value contained in Y. By turning off the range checking and declaring an array of pointers immediately after the Y's declaration, you can obtain the address passed to ADDR by using an index of -1 for the array "P".

If you're wondering what this could possibly be used for, I suggest you obtain a copy of a "C" language programming manual. The "C" programming language relies heavily on the use of pointers and almost any "C" programming tutorial will spend a lot of time discussing how to use pointers. There's not enough space in this book to properly treat pointers so I will bow out gracefully and leave this function to other authors.

When Not to Pull Tricks

In this chapter I've described various techniques for accomplishing certain tricks by mis-using Apple Pascal. Nine times out of ten there will be a better way to accomplish a given task than to use the tricks presented here. These tricks were intended to be used that small 10% of the time when Pascal doesn't offer any alternatives. Program listing 1–9 demonstrates some alternatives to the tricks presented in this chapter. Mind you, the techniques in listing 1.9 are still tricks and in many cases they are still somewhat implementation dependent, but in most cases they are much more portable and more acceptable to the programming community at large.

Any time you use a trick the program becomes that much harder to understand. Maintaining programs using the programming techniques presented in this chapter is much more difficult than maintaining programs using standard Pascal constructs. If you know 6502 assembly language you're probably better off implementing many of the solutions presented here in assembly language rather than using Pascal to implement them. At least when reading an assembly language listing you're prepared for programming tricks. The problem with incorporating the tricks directly into Pascal is that Pascal's structure may hide the fact that you're performing a trick. Which brings up the last but most important issue: if you use a programming trick in Pascal make sure that you comment it well. Always state that tricky code follows (this puts out the red flag). Always explain exactly what's going on so that later you, or someone else, can figure out exactly what you did. An undocumented program containing these programming tricks will be hard to maintain later on.

Listing 1-1

```
(***********************************************************************)
(*                                                                     *)
(*  Program listing 1-1: Normal way to handle hex output routine.      *)
(*                                                                     *)
(***********************************************************************)


program TESTPRTHEX;



  procedure PRTHEX(I:INTEGER);
      var J: INTEGER;
          WASNEG:BOOLEAN;
          CHRS: packed array [0..3] of char;
          HCR: packed array [0..15] of char;


  begin

      HCR := '0123456789ABCDEF';
      WASNEG := I < 0;
      if WASNEG then I := I + 32767 + 1;
      for J := 3 downto 0 do begin

          CHRS [J] := HCR [ (I MOD 16) ];
          I := I DIV 16;

      end;
      if WASNEG then CHRS [0] := CHR( ORD(CHRS [0]) + 8);
      if CHRS [0] > '9' then CHRS [0] := CHR( ORD(CHRS [0]) + 7);
      write(chrs);

   end; { PRTHEX }

begin {MAIN}

   writeln;
   prthex(25);
   writeln;
   prthex(255);
   writeln;
   prthex(-2);
   writeln;
   prthex(-1);
   writeln;
   prthex(-512);
   writeln;

end.
```

Listing 1-2

```
(************************************************************************)
(*                                                                      *)
(*  Program listing 1-2: Tricky form of hexadecimal output routine.    *)
(*                                                                      *)
(************************************************************************)


program TESTPRTHEX;

type NIBBLE = 0..15;
     TRICK  = record case BOOLEAN of

                FALSE:(I:INTEGER);
                TRUE :(N:packed array [0..3] of NIBBLE);

              END;

var  HEXSTR: packed array [0..15] of char;

  procedure PRTHEX(I:INTEGER);
  var A:TRICK;
      J:INTEGER;

  begin

      A.I := I;  {Move I into special variable}
      for J := 3 downto 0 do
          WRITE( HEXSTR [ A.N [J] ]);

   end; { PRTHEX }

begin {MAIN}

   HEXSTR := '0123456789ABCDEF';
   writeln;
   prthex(25);
   writeln;
   prthex(255);
   writeln;
   prthex(-2);
   writeln;
   prthex(-1);
   writeln;
   prthex(-512);
   writeln;

end.
```

Listing 1-3

```
(**********************************************************************)
(*                                                                    *)
(*  Listing 1.3:  This short program demonstrates how you can de-    *)
(*  termine the address of the heap pointer, the stack pointer, and *)
(*  the amount of user space available.  All values computed are in *)
(*  words, so you must multiply by two to get byte addresses.        *)
(*                                                                    *)
(**********************************************************************)

PROGRAM MEMORY_AVAILABLE;
TYPE TRIX = RECORD CASE BOOLEAN OF

                TRUE :(I:INTEGER);
                FALSE:(P:^INTEGER);

            END;

VAR I:INTEGER;
    X:TRIX;

BEGIN

   I := MEMAVAIL;
   NEW(X.P);
   WRITELN('HEAP POINTER: ',X.I);
   WRITELN('STACK POINTER: ',X.I+I);
   WRITELN('MEMORY AVAILABLE: ',I);

END.
```

Listing 1-4

```
(********************************************)
(*                                          *)
(*  Listing 1.4:  This program reads the    *)
(*  Apple's keyboard directly by peeking    *)
(*  at location $C000 and poking at loc-    *)
(*  ation $C010.                            *)
(*                                          *)
(********************************************)

program listing_1_4;

type chrdata = packed array [0..0] of 0..255;
     magic   = record case boolean of

               FALSE:( data:^CHRDATA);
               TRUE :( adrs:integer);

            end;



var  I       :INTEGER;
     PAC     :PACKED ARRAY [0..79] OF CHAR;
     kbd     :magic;
     kbdstrb:magic;

begin

    kbd.adrs := -16384;       (* $C000 IN DECIMAL *)
    KBDSTRB.ADRS := -16368; (* $C010 IN DECIMAL *)
    I := 0;
    FILLCHAR(PAC,80,' ');
    repeat

       (* WAIT UNTIL A KEY IS PRESSED *)

       while (kbd.data^ [0] < 128)  do;


       IF (I < 80) AND (KBD.DATA^ [0] <> 141)
          THEN PAC [I] := CHR(KBD.DATA^ [0]);

       I := I+1;

       (* CLEAR THE KEYBOARD STROBE *)

       kbdstrb.data^ [0] := 0;

    UNTIL KBD.DATA^ [0] = 13; (* RETURN *)

    WRITELN('THE STRING WAS: ',PAC);

END.
```

Listing 1-5

```
(*****************************************)
(*                                       *)
(* Listing 1.5: accessing different vars *)
(* by turning the range checking off.    *)
(*                                       *)
(*****************************************)

program test_R_minus;

  VAR y:integer;
      x: array [0..0] of integer;

begin

    y := 25;
    writeln('Y, at point 1, contains ',y);

    {$R-}

    x [-1] := 10;

    {$R+}

    writeln('Y, at point 2, contains ', y);

end.
```

Listing 1-6

```
(*******************************************)
(*                                         *)
(* Listing 1.6: accessing different vars  *)
(* by turning the range checking off.     *)
(*                                         *)
(*******************************************)

program tstparms;


  procedure test_R_minus;

  VAR y:integer;
      x: array [0..0] of integer;

  begin

    y := 25;
    writeln('Y, at point 1, contains ',y);

    {$R-}

    x [-1] := 10;

    {$R+}

    writeln('Y, at point 2, contains ', y);

  end;

begin

  test_R_minus;

end.
```

Listing 1-7

```
(*********************************************************************)
(*                                                                   *)
(*  LISTING 1.7: How to obtain the address of an array in Pascal.    *)
(*                                                                   *)
(*  This program demonstrates the ADDR function, a function that     *)
(*  when passed and array returns the address in memory of that array *)
(*                                                                   *)
(*********************************************************************)

PROGRAM TEST;

TYPE PACKED_ARRAY_OF_CHARS   = PACKED ARRAY [0..7] OF CHAR;
     PAC_POINTER             = ^PACKED_ARRAY_OF_CHARS;
     ARRAY_OF_PACPTRS        = ARRAY [0..0] OF PAC_POINTER;

VAR X:PACKED_ARRAY_OF_CHARS; (* Array that we wish to obtain the address of. *)
    Z:PAC_POINTER;           (* Pointer that will be set to the address of X *)
    P:ARRAY_OF_PACPTRS;      (* Dummy required in the ADDR function list.    *)

        (*****************************************************)
        (*                                                   *)
        (*  ADDR must be passed two parameters, the array    *)
        (*  that you're interested in finding the address of *)
        (*  and a dummy parameter that is an array [0..0]    *)
        (*  of pointers.  The second array's type must be a  *)
        (*  pointer to the same type as the first array.     *)
        (*  The function value must be a pointer to the same *)
        (*  type as the parameter.                           *)
        (*                                                   *)
        (*****************************************************)

        FUNCTION ADDR(VAR Y:PACKED_ARRAY_OF_CHARS;
                          P:ARRAY_OF_PACPTRS):PAC_POINTER;
        BEGIN

           (**********************************************************)
           (*                                                        *)
           (*  The following bizarre code turns off the compiler range *)
           (*  checking so that a programming trick can be performed.  *)
           (*  By accessing array element P [-1] the function obtains  *)
           (*  the word on the stack just prior to the P [0] element.  *)
           (*  This corresponds to the address of the Y parameter      *)
           (*  (since Y was passed by reference) hence the address of  *)
           (*  the first paramenter is obtained in this fashion.       *)
           (*                                                        *)
           (**********************************************************)

           {$R-}

           ADDR := P [-1];

           {$R+}

        END;
```

Listing 1-7 (continued)

```
BEGIN

    (* Initialize X to all blanks and print it *)

    FILLCHAR(X,8,' ');
    WRITELN('The X array should contain blanks: ''',X,'''');


    (* Get the address of the X array and place it in Z *)

    Z := ADDR(X,P);


    (* Store stuff into the array pointed at by Z.  Since Z points *)
    (* at the X array, this stores data into X.                    *)

    Z^ [0] := 'A';
    Z^ [1] := 'B';
    Z^ [2] := 'C';
    Z^ [3] := 'D';
    Z^ [4] := 'E';
    Z^ [5] := 'F';
    Z^ [6] := 'G';
    Z^ [7] := 'H';

    (* Print X to verify that storing data into the array pointed at by *)
    (* Z stores data into X (since Z points at X)                       *)

    WRITELN('Now the array contains: ''',X,'''');

END.
```

Listing 1-8

```
(*************************************************************************)
(*                                                                       *)
(*  LISTING 1.8: How to obtain the address of an array in Pascal.        *)
(*                                                                       *)
(*  This program demonstrates the ADDR function, a function that         *)
(*  when passed and array returns the address in memory of that array    *)
(*                                                                       *)
(*************************************************************************)

PROGRAM TEST;

TYPE PACKED_ARRAY_OF_CHARS    = PACKED ARRAY [0..7] OF CHAR;
     PAC_POINTER              = ^PACKED_ARRAY_OF_CHARS;
     ARRAY_OF_PACPTRS         = ARRAY [0..0] OF PAC_POINTER;

VAR X:PACKED_ARRAY_OF_CHARS; (* Array that we wish to obtain the address of. *)
    Z:PAC_POINTER;           (* Pointer that will be set to the address of X *)

        (****************************************************)
        (*                                                  *)
        (*  ADDR must be passed the array that you're inter- *)
        (*  ested in finding the address of.                *)
        (*  The function value must be a pointer to the same *)
        (*  type as the parameter.                          *)
        (*                                                  *)
        (****************************************************)

        FUNCTION ADDR(VAR Y:PACKED_ARRAY_OF_CHARS):PAC_POINTER;
        VAR P : ARRAY_OF_PACPTRS;

        BEGIN

           (***********************************************************)
           (*                                                         *)
           (*  The following bizarre code turns off the compiler range *)
           (*  checking so that a programming trick can be performed.  *)
           (*  By accessing array element P [-1] the function obtains  *)
           (*  the word on the stack just prior to the P [0] element.  *)
           (*  This corresponds to the address of the Y parameter      *)
           (*  (since Y was passed by reference) hence the address of  *)
           (*  the first paramenter is obtained in this fashion.       *)
           (*                                                         *)
           (***********************************************************)

           {$R-}

           ADDR := P [-1];

           {$R+}

        END;
```

Listing 1-8 (continued)

```
BEGIN

    (* Initialize X to all blanks and print it *)

    FILLCHAR(X,8,' ');
    WRITELN('The X array should contain blanks: ''',X,'''');


    (* Get the address of the X array and place it in Z *)

    Z := ADDR(X);


    (* Store stuff into the array pointed at by Z.  Since Z points *)
    (* at the X array, this stores data into X.                    *)

    Z^ [0] := 'A';
    Z^ [1] := 'B';
    Z^ [2] := 'C';
    Z^ [3] := 'D';
    Z^ [4] := 'E';
    Z^ [5] := 'F';
    Z^ [6] := 'G';
    Z^ [7] := 'H';

    (* Print X to verify that storing data into the array pointed at by *)
    (* Z stores data into X (since Z points at X)                       *)

    WRITELN('Now the array contains: ''',X,'''');

END.
```

Listing 1-9

```
(****************************************************)
(*                                                  *)
(*  PROGRAM LISTING 1.9: Alternate ways of per-     *)
(*  forming tricks in Apple Pascal.                 *)
(*                                                  *)
(****************************************************)

PROGRAM LISTING_1_9;
VAR I,J,K:INTEGER;


   (*************************************************)
   (*                                               *)
   (*  The XOR function computes the logical ex-    *)
   (*  clusive-or of the two integer parameters     *)
   (*  passed to it.                                *)
   (*                                               *)
   (*  Note: the other primitive logical operations*)
   (*  (AND, OR, and NOT) can be sythesized using   *)
   (*  the AND, OR, and NOT operators.              *)
   (*                                               *)
   (*************************************************)

   FUNCTION XOR(A,B:INTEGER) :INTEGER;
   BEGIN

      (* The "odd" function is a type transfer function, it lets *)
      (* you treat an integer value as a boolean value.  The ord *)
      (* function does just the opposite, it lets you treat any  *)
      (* scalar value as an integer.                             *)

      XOR := ord( (NOT (odd(A) AND odd(B))) and (odd(A) OR odd(B)) );

   END; (* XOR *)
```

Listing 1-9 (continued)

```
begin

(* Demonstration of logical operations in Apple Pascal *)


      (* Logically AND two integer values *)
      (* The following code places the    *)
      (* logical AND of the two integers  *)
      (* J and K into the integer I.      *)
      (* The ODD function lets you treat  *)
      (* an integer value as though it    *)
      (* were a boolean value.  A call    *)
      (* to the ODD function doesn't gen- *)
      (* erate any code, it simply relaxes*)
      (* the Apple Pascal compiler's type *)
      (* checking momentarially.          *)
      (* The ORD function lets you treat  *)
      (* the resulting boolean value as   *)
      (* though it were integer.          *)

      I := ORD ( ODD(J) AND ODD(K) );



      (* Logical OR function- see above   *)
      (* for details.                     *)

      I := ORD ( ODD(J) OR ODD(K) );


      (* Logical negation function        *)

      I := ORD ( NOT (ODD(J)) );


end.
```

2

Improving the Performance Programs of Apple Pascal

Overview

Although Apple Pascal is a semi-compiled language there are times when it could benefit from a boost in execution speed. And even though Apple Pascal generates compact p-code, it is an axiom of computing that a program will always take at least one more byte than is available to the programmer. This section describes several techniques that can be used to increase performance and shrink the size of a Pascal program.

Before attempting to improve the performance of a program it is imperative that the operation of the Pascal p-machine is understood. Before reading this section read pages 223-264 in the Apple Pascal Operating System's manual to familiarize yourself with the terms and mnemonics presented in this section.

Before discussing how to improve the performance of an Apple Pascal program it would be wise to point out exactly what needs improvement. Traditionally compiled program performance has been divided into two categories: the speed of the compiled package and the amount of code generated for the compiled program. In general, a given program can be made to run faster at the expense of a larger codefile and it can be shrunk somewhat at the expense of execution speed. Luckily, the structure of the Apple Pascal system often allows us to speed up and shrink the program at the same time. Obviously there are thousands of ways to optimize a program in one fashion or another. Most techniques are based on using better algorithms. Such techniques are beyond the scope of this section. Instead, this section will concentrate mostly on mechanical optimizations which do not require much information about the algorithms in use.

General Information About the UCSD p-Machine

The UCSD p-Machine version II.0 (upon which Apple Pascal is based) was designed so that the p-code generated by compiling the Pascal operating system was minimized. The rationale behind optimizing for the operating system was that the operating system must always be in memory. By making the operating system as small as possible the designers maximized the amount of user memory. Furthermore, the operating system contains the kind of code often found in user programs so optimizing the system considering the operating system to be a typical program also provides optimization for user programs (although this hypothesis is only partially true). In general, everything that could be done to shrink the size of the operating system in memory was done. (Historical note: Actually UCSD's hands were tied after the introduction of the Western Digital p-Machine chip set. Due to an agreement with WD UCSD could not modify the p-machine, they had to remain compatible with the hardware version of the p-machine, Later, when Softech Microsystems took over the project, the p-machine was optimized even further for version IV.0.) The whole key to optimizing a user program is to make it "look" a lot like the Pascal operating system. This doesn't mean the program has to be an operating system, rather the program should generate approximately the same frequency as the various p-codes emitted for the operating system.

Tools Required for Optimization

If you are serious about shortening and speeding up your programs you will need a couple of tools. The most important tool is a p-code disassembler. Such a program is available from ABT in Saratoga, Ca. ABT's Pascal Tools II package contains five programs in addition to the p-code disassembler. For our purposes, however, the p-code disassembler is well worth the price of the package. More information on the Pascal Tools II package can be obtained directly from ABT. The p-code disassembler (called DUMP-CODE) is self prompting and extremely easy to use. All you provide is the name of an output .TEXT file and the name of an input .CODE file. DUMP-CODE reads the .CODE file, disassembles it, and outputs the disassembled listing to the specified TEXT file.

Also available is Datamost's PDQ (Pascal Disk Qtility Program), which offers a *symbolic* p-Code disassembler/assembler. With this package you can disassemble a Pascal program into p-code assembly language, modify it, and reassemble the program back into p-code machine code. For those individuals who want to make modifications to existing programs, this may be the only way to go.

The disassemblies listed in this manual were produced by Thomas Brennan's *DECODE* program. As this book goes to press I have no details on the commercial availability of this product.

Optimizing for Compactness

Apple Pascal's performance, much like that of Applesoft and Integer BASIC, is affected by the placement of variable names within a program. Not only does the placement of variable definitions affect the speed of an executing program, it also affects the amount of p-code generated for the program. In particular, the first 16 words reserved in a procedure or program are treated differently from the remainder. Furthermore, the first 16 words of variables defined in a program (the first 16 words of global variables) are treated specially. By taking advantage of this fact you can both reduce the amount of code generated for your program and speed it up.

To understand how the judicious placement of variables can affect the size and speed of a program look at pages 230 and 231 of the Apple Pascal Operating System's Manual. These two pages describe the p-codes used for loading and storing data. Loading and storing data (especially loading data) are the most frequently used instructions in any program. With this in mind the UCSD p-machine was designed with 32 one-byte instructions that allow immediate access to the first 16 words of data in the currently activated procedure. Access to the first 16 words of data in the main procedure is also provided. Loading such data is accomplished with the SLDL (short load local) and SLDO (short load global) instructions.

Since each scalar variable (i.e., INTEGER, CHAR, BOOLEAN, or enumerated) requires one word of storage you have room for exactly 16 scalar variables within a procedure in order to take advantage of these special load instructions. REAL type variables require two words of storage and array variables require even more. Therefore you should avoid declaring arrays and REAL variables at the beginning of a procedure. Variables declared within the same statement are allocated ***backwards***. That is, if you have a declaration of the form:

```
I,J,K:INTEGER;
```

space is first allocated for K, then J, then I (See Figure 2-1). When attempting to optimize a procedure by using the technique being described you should never declare more than one variable per statement. This can cause a few gotcha's to sneak up on you if you're not careful. Instead, declare each variable in a separate statement, e.g.:

```
I:INTEGER;
J:INTEGER;
K:INTEGER;
```

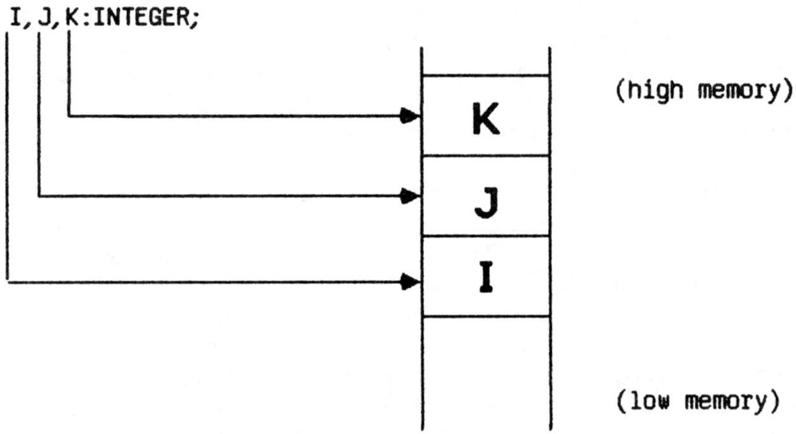

Note that space is first allocated for K, then J, and finally I.

Figure 2-1

In order to optimize a program to make it as compact as possible, you should declare the most-used scalar variables within a procedure as the first 16 scalar variables. This will allow the Apple Pascal compiler to generate one-byte opcodes to load these variables instead of the two or three-byte opcodes normally required. It's very easy to determine which variables are used the most. Simply run the CROSSREF program found on the Apple3: diskette and it will print out a table of all the variables used within a program and the frequency of their use. To use the CROSSREF program you should strip out all the comments (the CROSSREF program isn't smart enough to do this for you) and isolate the procedure or function you wish to optimize. Do not run CROSSREF on an entire program as it will print every occurrence of a variable found anywhere in a program. You don't want to print the occurrences of the variable I in the next procedure when optimizing the current procedure. Once you've isolated the procedure you wish to optimize and have stripped out the comments, use CROSSREF to list out the variables and their frequencies. With the exception of non-scalar variables (i.e., REALs, SETs, RECORDs, and ARRAYs) you should declare all (scalar) variables in order of decreasing frequency. At the top of the procedure the most-used variable should be declared first, the second most-used variable declared second, etc. . This will shorten the program up somewhat and even speed things up a little bit. If you have less than 16 scalar variables they should all be declared before any non-scalar variables are defined. REALS and other non-scalar variables cannot take advantage of the SLDL and SLDO instructions so declaring them ahead of a scalar variable won't buy you anything and, in fact, it may hurt you.

Before concluding the discussion on the importance of the first 16 scalar variables, it should be pointed out that the parameters to a function or procedure count as elements of the first 16 words of storage. So when optimizing for compactness you should avoid passing rarely used data in the parameter list (use a global variable instead) and avoid passing non-scalar variables. Furthermore, passing parameter data by reference causes a lot of code to be generated for each occurence of the pass by reference variable. If you must use the pass by reference technique, you should copy the data into a local variable (hopefully one that occupies one of the first 16 words of storage), use the data, and then store the data kept in local storage back into the pass by reference variable before exiting the procedure or function. It should also be pointed out that parameters on the stack are duplicated when a procedure is invoked. This means if you're running out of memory at run-time (i.e., you keep getting stack overflows) you should attempt to re-code the program using as few parameters as possible. This is especially true if you are using recursive procedures and functions.

Apple Pascal emits two-byte opcodes for loads and stores of data whose offset into the current procedure is in the range 0..127 words (with the exception of loading one of the first 16 words as described above). A three-byte opcode is required to access beyond the 127th word of storage. Since scalars, REALS, SETS, and RECORD variables can all take advantage of the two-byte opcodes, you should consult the cross-reference listing and place the most-often used variables next in the declarations. Just remember, ARRAY, RECORD, and SET variables eat up lots of memory and can severely limit the number of variables so defined. An array variable may be accessed twice as often as the nearest scalar or REAL variable, but if the array is very large it won't let you take advantage of the two-byte opcodes for any other variables. And the *SUM* of the occurrences of all the other variables may well be larger than the number of occurrences of the array variable in question. To maximize the code usage you should use the CROSSREF and DUMPPCODE programs considerably in order to "hone" your program.

Accessing only the variables in the current procedure and in the outermost procedure (i.e., the program) will produce the smallest possible code. Accessing intermediate variables (global variables which are not defined in the main program) is one of the most inefficient methods (both in terms of speed and compactness) for accessing data in the Apple Pascal system. Accessing intermediate variables always takes at least three bytes and may even take four. Accessing intermediate variables should be avoided whenever possible.

Optimizing REAL Variable Accesses

REAL variables represent a real problem (pardon the pun). When assigning a constant to a REAL variable there are three methods you can employ:

```
1: Standard assignment, R := 2.3;
2: Integer constant,    R := 4;
3: Variable assignment, R := RCONST;
```

(The last trick is probably employed by the seasoned Applesoft programmer who thinks he can speed things up by storing often-used constants in a variable and accessing the variable instead of the constant.) The first method uses up ten bytes of storage and probably executes the fastest of the three. The second method (using an integer constant) requires only six bytes, but is, by far, the slowest of the three methods. The last method requires only eight bytes and probably executes only a little slower than the first version. Note that if you use the last version, you really don't save any memory unless you make at least six assignments using the RCONST variable. Remember, you will have to use the first method to initialize the RCONST variable which takes ten bytes. Since you only save two bytes using the third method, it will take five accesses of RCONST in order to break even, six accesses before you are saving anything. Since you rarely use the same constant six times in any given procedure you should almost never use the third method. If you wish to reduce the amount of code generated (and you are storing an integer constant into a real varible) use the second method. If you are optimizing for speed (or need to store a real value with a fractional part) you should use the first method.

Optimizing String Accesses

The most important optimization you can make regarding a string is to make sure you do not declare the string to be any longer than it needs to be. The default length is 80 characters and this is almost always longer than necessary. By careful research you can probably discover the maximum string length required for a given variable. You're only wasting memory if you declare a string longer than it needs to be. On the other hand, do make sure that the string is long enough to handle any requirements. If it isn't, a run-time error will occur. In general, if you are reading a string from the console or some other device you should make sure that you have plenty of space reserved in case the input is crazy. But if the string is only used internally (which means you have control over the data stored in it) you needn't allocate any more space than is absolutely necessary.

One of the biggest string optimizations you can perform is to make sure you do not duplicate a string constant anywhere. This problem occurs quite frequently in WRITELN statements, e.g.:

```
WRITELN('The variable I has the value:',I);
WRITELN('The variable J has the value:',J);
```

These statements could be converted to:

```
THEVAR := 'The variable ';
HASVAL := 'Has the value:';
WRITELN(THEVAR,'I',HASVAL,I);
WRITELN(THEVAR,'J',HASVAL,J);
```

Using this technique will save you quite a bit of code. Note that THEVAR should be a string of maximum length 13 characters (since it will never be longer than 13 characters) and the string HASVAL should be defined to have a maximum length of 14 characters.

Optimizing Array and Subrange Accesses

One of the largest optimizations you can make to a large program is also the easiest. It is also the most dangerous. The Apple Pascal compiler generates a lot of code every time an array element is accessed. In addition to generating the code required to access the array element, Apple Pascal also emits a considerable amount of code that checks the array index (at runtime) to make sure it is within the range declared. The generation of this extra code can be turned off using the (*$R-*) compiler option. This simple statement can reduce a program's code by as much as 20% and will increase its speed noticably. This option, when placed at the front of a *debugged* program, can drastically improve the memory/speed situation. However, there's no such thing as a free lunch . . .

When you turn the RANGECHECK option off, you are promising the Pascal compiler that you will never access an array element that 'just aint there'. If you do, strange things will happen to the program, the best of 'em being the variables in your program start taking on mysterious values. At worst the system will hang, or may arbitrarily start writing data to the disk. If you turn off the RANGECHECK option, make *sure* that your program is fully debugged and that you don't get any "value range errors", because now the system won't be nice enough to report it.

One of the nice things about the RANGECHECK option is that it can be turned on and off selectively with the (*$R+*) and (*$R−*) options respectively. That means you can turn the range checking off for a section of code where you're absolutely sure that no bounds errors occur and turn it back on when you're not sure a bounds error won't occur. Incidently, the bounds checking is used in several places in addition to array bounds checking. For example, all string accesses use the RANGECHECK mechanism, as does any usage of a user-defined scalar variable (such as a subrange). The (*$R-*) option can speed these accesses up as well.

Optimizing I/O Instructions

After every call to an I/O routine the Apple Pascal compiler emits a call to the IO_ERROR routine that checks to see if an I/O error occurred (aborting if one did). While this is a fairly important function for input and peripheral I/O, it is an absolute waste for output directed to the console device, since an error will never be returned by such a device. Since the output statements WRITE and WRITELN make up a large percentage of statements in a Pascal program, eliminating the unnecessary calls to IO_ERROR can save an quite a bit of memory.

To turn the I/O checking off use the (*$I−*) compiler option. To turn the I/O checking back on use the (*$I+*) option. These options are messages to the compiler itself and no code is generated for them (the same is true for the RANGECHECK options). In general, it is a wise idea to leave the I/O checking on when performing input or output to a file as you have no control over the data being input and you can't be sure that when you output to some device an error won't be returned. Of course if you are sure, you can save a few bytes by leaving the I/O checking off; but an ounce of prevention . . .

Optimizing IF and CASE Statements

As is often pointed out in literature on the Pascal language, a CASE statement of the form:

```
CASE I OF

<VAL1>:STMT1;
<VAL2>:STMT2;
  .     .
  .     .
```

```
<VALn>:STMTn

END
```

performs the same function as the statments:

```
IF I=<VAL1> THEN STMT1
ELSE IF I=<VAL2> THEN STMT2
  •
  •
ELSE IF I=<VALn> THEN STMTn;
```

Despite the fact that the action performed by these two statements is the same, the code generated is completely different. As it turns out, if you wish to compare a variable against several constants, the CASE statement is usually the faster of the two. Also, less code is generated for the case statement *providing there are more than four cases.* Four cases is the break-even point and if there are fewer than four cases the IF..ELSE IF statement generates less code. The CASE statement executes faster than the IF..ELSE IF statement except for the trivial case where only one comparison is made. In general, if you want the code to run faster use the CASE statement. If you want to save space, use the IF statement if there are fewer than four cases, use the CASE statement if there are greater than (or equal to) four cases.

There is one problem associated with the use of the CASE statement. It is only optimal if the case values are contiguous. If you have two case values of one and 124, an enormous amount of code is generated. In fact, 124 bytes of table data is generated on top of the instructions required for the CASE statement itself. As a general rule of thumb, the Apple Pascal compiler takes the smallest case value and the largest case value and creates a table whose length is equal to the difference of these two values. Obviously if you have some entries that are spaced quite a bit apart you should use the IF..THEN statement if you wish to save code. The CASE statement doesn't execute slower if the case values are spaced far apart, so if speed is your primary goal you should still use the CASE statement.

Using FILLCHAR to Initilize Arrays

If you ever need to initialize an array to zero you shouldn't use the loop:

```
    FOR I := 0 TO <ARYSIZE> DO ARY [I] := 0;
```

This generates a lot of code and executes slowly. A much better approach is to use the built-in procedure FILLCHAR to initialize the array to zero. FILLCHAR was intended to be used with strings and packed arrays of characters, but it doesn't perform any type checking on its operands so it can be used to set any data type structure to zero.

To zero out an integer array you would use the statement:

```
FILLCHAR(ARY,SIZEOF(ARY),CHR(0));
```

Note the CHR(0) parameter. FILLCHAR works only with characters so you will need to convert the value zero to the null character (whose character code value is zero) in order to use this procedure.

In theory, the FILLCHAR procedure can be used with any data type declarable in Apple Pascal (including arrays, sets, records, scalars, and combinations of these extended types). However, FILLCHAR should only be used with arrays of integers since storing zeros into sets, and records may produce strange results. Zeroing out a user defined scalar variable sets that variable to the value of the first element declared in that type (e.g., if COLORS = (RED, GREEN, BLUE, YELLOW) then zeroing out a variable of type COLORS sets it to RED). Zeroing out a set variable produces the empty set. Zeroing out a REAL variable sets each REAL element to zero. Zeroing out a record variable sets each element of the record to zero.

As mentioned previously, FILLCHAR operates *much* faster and produces less code than the equivalent FOR loop.

Optimizing for Speed

If you've got lots of room but your program doesn't run fast enough, you're probably more interested in speeding up your program than in shrinking it. Speeding a program up is, in many ways, much more difficult than shrinking it. The techniques described in this section will help you improve the performance of your programs. There is, however, no substitute for a better algorithm. If you program is sorting data using the bubble sort don't expect the techniques presented here to noticeably improve the performance of your system. Improving the speed of a program requires a lot of careful thought and experimentation. The techniques presented here should be used only after you feel you have exhausted alternate algorithms as a source of performance improvement.

The techniques presented here for improving the performance of an Apple Pascal program are quite similar to those used to shrink a program. In general, the less p-code you have to interpret, the faster the program will run. Since loads and stores are executed much more often than anything else, you should concentrate on optimizing these first.

Dynamic vs. Static Optimization

When we optimized for compactness, a *static* frequency analysis was performed to determine the number of times a variable ocurred within a given procedure. A *static* frequency analysis is one in which the number of times a variable appears is counted. By declaring the variables that occurred most often early in the declaration list we were able to reduce the size of the code produced by the Apple Pascal compiler. Access to variables declared as one of the first 16 words of storage (and as one of the first 128 words of storage) not only requires less space, but executes faster as well. So one of the first things we can do to speed up a program is to make sure that the more frequently used variables are declared first.

A simple static frequency analysis, like that done with the code optimization, will not suffice for speed optimization. Consider the short code sequence:

```
X := 45;
Y := X+2;
Z := X+Y;
A := Z+X+(Y*X)+X*(Z-2*X);
```

```
B := X+Y+Z+ A DIV X;
X := X*B;

FOR I := 0 TO 2000 DO
FOR J := 0 TO 2000 DO M := 0;
```

Although X, Y, Z, A, and B occur in the program much more often than I, J, or M they are not accessed as many times. For example, X is accessed 11 times, Y is accessed four times, Z is accessed four times, and A and B are accessed twice. On the other hand, although they appear in the program only once, I is accessed 2001 times, and J and M are accessed a whopping 4,004,000 times, yet they are accessed only once! The amount of time you would save by making sure that I, J, and M were declared as one of the first 16 variables (as opposed to variables declared after the first 128 words of storage) would be measured in hours!

Analyzing variable usage, as opposed to variable occurence, is known as dynamic frequency analysis. Obviously, dynamic frequency analysis is very hard to perform. In addition to loops, you have to worry about CASE statements, IF..THEN..ELSE statements, parameter values passed to procedures and functions, REPEAT..UNTIL and WHILE loops, and a whole gamut of other statements that tend to obscure the number of times a variable is accessed. To perform a dynamic frequency analysis, start with a static frequency analysis. Chances are, if a variable is used quite often it is also accessed the most during the execution of the program. So check out the most-often used variables first.

Pay close attention to loops. In general, variable accesses that occur outside of loops aren't even worth worrying about. Improving the access time of such variables may not be noticeable. Don't forget, the FOR loop isn't the only loop construct available in Pascal—watch for REPEAT..UNTIL and WHILE loops as well. Nested loops, especially ones with a large range, are prime targets. Program segments buried deep within nested loops should be scruntinized to make sure that variables within them sure the short form of the load and store instructions. Other forms of optimization (such as using REAL constants instead of integer contants when initializing a REAL variable) should be performed inside a loop as well. Hopefully you are smart enough to realize that all one-time initialization should take place *outside* the range of a loop since initializing the variable each time the loop executes is a waste of time.

3
Using LST Files to Debug and Optimize Pascal Programs

The Apple Pascal compiler supports a special compile-time option that allows you to list a compiled program to a device along with other useful information. The "(*$L <fileid>*)" option accomplishes this. This compiler option sends a listing of the compiled program to the specified file. Although any arbitrary disk file or device may be used, I recommend you send all listings to the printer using the command:

```
(*$L PRINTER:*)
```

This option should only be used after all the syntax errors have been removed from your program.

The list option writes a listing of the program to the printer device along with five additional columns of information. The first column is the line number of the current line; the second column contains the segment number of the current procedure; the third column contains the procedure number; the fourth column contains the lex level; and the fifth column contains the current offset into the procedure. As it turns out this information is quite valuable, especially the segment, routine, and offset values.

Program listing 3.1 is a example of a program compilation using the {$L PRINTER:} option. The first column in the listing is the line number. This information can be useful when editing a program within the editor. For example, if you are at the beginning of the file, you need only type "n<rtn>" to position the cursor at line number n + 1. To jump to an arbitrary line from any point in the program type "JBn<rtn>" and the cursor will be positioned at the beginning of the desired line.

The second column of numbers in listing 3.1 is the segment number. The typical user program is assigned to segment number one. If you use any SEGMENT PROCEDUREs or FUNCTIONs within your Pascal program, each segment procedure will increase the segment number by one starting at segment number 7. Segment numbers 0, and 2-6 are reserved for use by the system. A maximum of seven segmented procedures (including the main program body, segment one) is available to the user. This means that segments one and 7 through 12 are available to the user.

The third column in the listing is the procedure number. The value varies from one to a maximum of 127 (assuming you have 127 procedures declared within the current segment) for each segment procedure defined. If you will look at listing 3.1, lines 24-43, you will notice that procedure A has a procedure number of one and its subordinate B has a procedure number of two. Note that the main program also has a procedure number of one and procedure D also has a procedure number of two. The difference is that A and B are in segment seven while the main program and D are in segment one. So the segment number and the procedure number are used to uniquely identify any given procedure.

The fourth column contains the lex level value. For the purposes of this discussion it is only important to realize that this column contains a "D" or a digit. If a "D" appears in this column then the offset value (in the fifth column) refers to a data offset. If a digit appears in this column then the value in the fifth column is a code offset.

The fifth column contains a code or data offset value. This magic number is the whole key to code optimization and debugging run-time errors in the Apple Pascal system. Whenever column four contains a "D", column five contains a data offset. This occurs in the variable declaration portion of the program. For example, if you look at lines 11 through 16 in listing 3.1 you can see an example of data offsets in the listing. These values correspond to words of data allocated by the Pascal compiler. For example, the "3" appearing before the "I:INTEGER;" declaration tells you that I occupies the third word of storage allocated in this block. Likewise the "5" before the "R:REAL;" declaration tells you that the variable R occupies the fifth word of storage allocated in this block. By looking at the next line you can tell how many words of storage were allocated. For example, at line 14 (the line after the R declaration) the offset is seven. So R required two words of storage. This data offset information is important because this is the easiest way to determine which variables lie in the first 16 words of storage, which lie in the first 128 words of storage, and which lie beyond. This, of course, is important information if you're trying to optimize your program via variable accesses as mentioned in the previous sections. Notice that two words of storage are used up by the main program before any variables are allocated at all. This is due to the fact that two words of parameter data is allocated for a main program (this corresponds to the INPUT,OUTPUT parameters in a standard Pascal program). This preallocation occurs only in the main program, normal procedures and functions begin allocating storage at word one.

Although listing 3.1 doesn't provide any examples, parameters declared in a procedure or function are allocated before the local variables. So if you have a procedure definition of the form:

```
PROCEDURE XXX(I,J:INTEGER);
VAR M,N:INTEGER;
BEGIN

   .
   .

END;
```

then I and J will be allocated storage before M and N are. For this reason, you should be careful when defining procedures with lots of parameters if you are attempting to optimize for code compactness. Another thing to consider is that parameters actually occupy twice the allocated storage on the stack. Parameter data is pushed onto the stack by the invoking routine and then this data is copied above the activation record once the program begins executing. Because of this duplication you should never pass an array by value unless you have lots of room and don't mind the delay associated with copying the array data. In general, it would be better to pass the array by reference and copy it into a local array using the MOVELEFT routine. That way only one copy of the array would be maintained and the array would only have to be copied once (when passed by value the array has to be copied twice, once by the invoking routine when the array is pushed onto the stack and once when the procedure being called copies the array into its local data area.

When the value in the lex level column is a digit (as opposed to a "D") then the value in the offset column is a code offset instead of a data offset. The code offset value is the number of bytes emitted for the current procedure up to, but not including, the current line. This information has two practical uses: it can be used to compare two different program constructs to see which requires the least amount of memory, and it is quite useful when debugging Pascal run-time errors.

To use the code offset when optimizing the object code produced is very easy. Simply compile a program using the old and new algorithms. To determine how much code a given line of Pascal generates simply subtract the offset on the next line from the offset on the line in question. This gives you the number of bytes generated by the line of Pascal source code. Obviously, the algorithm that produces the least amount of code is the most optimal in terms of code compactness.

Debugging Run-time Errors

Have you ever gotten one of those ugly run-time errors of the form:

```
<run-time message>
S#n P#n I#nn
(press space to continue)
```

If you're like most people you start inserting WRITELN statements in order to pinpoint the line where the problem exists. There is a much easier solution to the problem of discovering the line that contains the error. The S#n, P#n, and I#nn values give the the segment number, procedure number and code offset where the error occurred. By looking on the program listing you can easily pinpoint the location of the infracting line.

As an example, refer to listing 3.2. This program contains four lines, all of which have a run-time error on them. The first two lines have division by zero errors, the third line has a floating point run-time error, and the fourth line has a string overflow error. If you were to compile this program and run it you would get the error:

```
Divide by Zero
S#1 P#1 I#4
(press space to continue)
```

This tells you that the error took place in segment number one, procedure number one, at code offset four. By looking at the listing at segment one, procedure one, you find that the line which contains code offset four is line number 19 (actually it begins at code offset zero and continues through code offset six, therefore the desired location is contained on this line). By looking at the line ("I := I DIV 0") you will notice that the reason we get a division by zero error is because, sure enough, there is a division by zero. If we correct this problem by dividing by one instead of zero we obtain the program shown in listing 3.3. If this program was compiled and executed, you would get the run-time error:

```
Divide by Zero
S#1 P#1 I#20
Press space to continue
```

By looking at the program listing you can see that the statement:

```
R := R / 0.0;
```

is the one where the problem occurred. Obviously there is a division by zero here, fixing it yields the program shown in listing 3.4.

Upon compiling and executing the corrected program you get the run-time error message:

```
Floating Pt. Error
S#1 P#1 I#30
Press Reset
```

By consulting the program listings you will notice that this error is happening at line #21,

```
I := TRUNC(3.3E5);
```

The cause of this error is the fact that 330000 is too large to be converted to an integer. By fixing this problem we obtain the program shown in listing 3.5.

When you compile and execute the program shown in listing 3.5 you get the run-time error message:

```
String Overflow
S#1 P#1 I#63
Press space to Continue
```

The problem here is the fact that the string "HELLO THERE HOW ARE YOU" is much too large to fit in a string variable that may contain a maximum of ten characters. This is easily pinpointed by looking for code offset 63 which occurs at line 22.

Correcting this last problem by shortening the string yields the program shown in listing 3.6. This program compiles and runs correctly.

Listing 3-1

```
1   1:D    1 {$L PRINTER:}
1   1:D    1
1   1:D    1 (*****************************************************)
1   1:D    1 (*                                                   *)
1   1:D    1 (*  LST file example:                                *)
1   1:D    1 (*                                                   *)
1   1:D    1 (*****************************************************)
1   1:D    1
1   1:D    1 program SHOW_LST_FORMAT;
1   1:D    3
1   1:D    3 var     I:integer;
1   1:D    4         J:integer;
1   1:D    5         R:real;
1   1:D    7         X:array [0..15] of integer;
1   1:D   23         M:integer;
1   1:D   24         S:string;
1   1:D   65
1   1:D   65
1   1:D   65
1   1:D   65
1   1:D   65 (* Segmented procedures follow.....   *)
1   1:D   65
1   1:D   65
7   1:D    1         segment procedure A;
7   1:D    1
7   1:D    1                 var     I:integer;
7   1:D    2                         R:real;
7   1:D    4
7   1:D    4
7   2:D    1                 procedure B;
7   2:0    0                 begin
7   2:0    0
7   2:1    0                         I := 0;
7   2:1    4
7   2:0    4                 end; {B}
7   2:0   16
7   2:0   16
7   1:0    0         begin {A}
7   1:0    0
7   1:1    0                 B;
7   1:1    2                 R := 1.1;
7   1:1   12
7   1:0   12         end; {A}
7   1:0   24
7   1:0   24
7   1:0   24
8   1:D    1         segment procedure C;
8   1:0    0         begin
8   1:0    0
8   1:1    0                 A;
8   1:1    3
8   1:0    3         end; {C}
8   1:0   16
8   1:0   16
8   1:0   16
```

Listing 3-1 (continued)

```
8   1:0   16 (* Standard procedures follow......  *)
8   1:0   16
8   1:0   16
1   2:D    1        procedure D;
1   2:D    1
1   3:D    1               procedure E;
1   3:0    0               begin
1   3:0    0
1   3:1    0                      I := 25;
1   3:1    3
1   3:0    3               end; {E}
1   3:0   16
1   2:0    0        begin {D}
1   2:0    0
1   2:1    0               E;
1   2:1    2               R := 2.6;
1   2:1   12
1   2:0   12        end; {D}
1   2:0   24
1   2:0   24
1   2:0   24
1   1:0    0 begin {main}
1   1:0    0
1   1:1    0        A;
1   1:1    5        C;
1   1:1    8        D;
1   1:1   10
1   1:0   10 end.
```

Listing 3-2

```
1   1:D    1 {$L PRINTER:}
1   1:D    1
1   1:D    1 (****************************************************)
1   1:D    1 (*                                                  *)
1   1:D    1 (*  Listing 3.2: Division by zero error #1.         *)
1   1:D    1 (*                                                  *)
1   1:D    1 (****************************************************)
1   1:D    1
1   1:D    1 program BAD_PROGRAM;
1   1:D    3
1   1:D    3 var     I:integer;
1   1:D    4         R:real;
1   1:D    6         S:string [10];
1   1:D   12
1   1:D   12
1   1:D   12
1   1:0    0 begin
1   1:0    0
1   1:1    0         I := I div 0;
1   1:1    7         R := R / 0.0;
1   1:1   23         I := trunc (3.3E5);
1   1:1   34         S := 'Hello there how are you?';
1   1:1   65
1   1:0   65 end.
```

Listing 3-3

```
1    1:D     1 {$L PRINTER:}
1    1:D     1
1    1:D     1 (*****************************************************)
1    1:D     1 (*                                                   *)
1    1:D     1 (*  Listing 3.3: Division by zero error #2.          *)
1    1:D     1 (*                                                   *)
1    1:D     1 (*****************************************************)
1    1:D     1
1    1:D     1 program BAD_PROGRAM;
1    1:D     3
1    1:D     3 var     I:integer;
1    1:D     4         R:real;
1    1:D     6         S:string [10];
1    1:D    12
1    1:D    12
1    1:D    12
1    1:0     0 begin
1    1:0     0
1    1:1     0         I := I div 1;
1    1:1     7         R := R / 0.0;
1    1:1    23         I := trunc (3.3E5);
1    1:1    34         S := 'Hello there how are you?';
1    1:1    65
1    1:0    65 end.
```

Listing 3-4

```
1    1:D     1 {$L PRINTER:}
1    1:D     1
1    1:D     1 (*****************************************************)
1    1:D     1 (*                                                   *)
1    1:D     1 (*  Listing 3.4: Floating point error.               *)
1    1:D     1 (*                                                   *)
1    1:D     1 (*****************************************************)
1    1:D     1
1    1:D     1 program BAD_PROGRAM;
1    1:D     3
1    1:D     3 var     I:integer;
1    1:D     4         R:real;
1    1:D     6         S:string [10];
1    1:D    12
1    1:D    12
1    1:D    12
1    1:0     0 begin
1    1:0     0
1    1:1     0         I := I div 1;
1    1:1     7         R := R / 0.1;
1    1:1    23         I := trunc (3.3E5);
1    1:1    34         S := 'Hello there how are you?';
1    1:1    65
1    1:0    65 end.
```

Listing 3-5

```
 1   1:D    1 {$L PRINTER:}
 1   1:D    1
 1   1:D    1 (****************************************************)
 1   1:D    1 (*                                                  *)
 1   1:D    1 (*  Listing 3.5: String overflow.                   *)
 1   1:D    1 (*                                                  *)
 1   1:D    1 (****************************************************)
 1   1:D    1
 1   1:D    1 program BAD_PROGRAM;
 1   1:D    3
 1   1:D    3 var      I:integer;
 1   1:D    4          R:real;
 1   1:D    6          S:string [10];
 1   1:D   12
 1   1:D   12
 1   1:D   12
 1   1:0    0 begin
 1   1:0    0
 1   1:1    0          I := I div 1;
 1   1:1    7          R := R / 0.1;
 1   1:1   23          I := trunc (3.3);
 1   1:1   34          S := 'Hello there how are you?';
 1   1:1   65
 1   1:0   65 end.
```

Listing 3-6

```
 1   1:D    1 {$L PRINTER:}
 1   1:D    1
 1   1:D    1 (****************************************************)
 1   1:D    1 (*                                                  *)
 1   1:D    1 (*  Listing 3.6: Working program.                   *)
 1   1:D    1 (*                                                  *)
 1   1:D    1 (****************************************************)
 1   1:D    1
 1   1:D    1 program BAD_PROGRAM;
 1   1:D    3
 1   1:D    3 var      I:integer;
 1   1:D    4          R:real;
 1   1:D    6          S:string [10];
 1   1:D   12
 1   1:D   12
 1   1:D   12
 1   1:0    0 begin
 1   1:0    0
 1   1:1    0          I := I div 1;
 1   1:1    7          R := R / 0.1;
 1   1:1   23          I := trunc (3.3);
 1   1:1   34          S := 'Hello ';
 1   1:1   47
 1   1:0   47 end.
```

4

Examining Compiler-Generated Code

In the program listings that follow an attempt will be made to describe the code generated by the Pascal compiler for certain code segments. While the examples provided are certainly not all -inclusive (i.e., they do not list all possible code generation sequences) they are fairly representative and careful study may help you write better, shorter, and faster Pascal programs.

With the exception of listing 4.19, all of the disassembled listings were produced with the DECODE p-code disassembler written by T. Brennan. Listing 4.19 was produced by the DUMPPCODE utility found on ABT's Pascal Tools II diskette. Alas, DECODE contained a bug and couldn't be used for this particular listing.

Integer Variable Allocation

Listing 4.1 demonstrates the code generated for integer variable was declared as one of the first 16 words (I), 127 words (J), and beyond (K) within the Apple Pascal program. The two p-code instructions at locations 0002 and 0003 handle the assignment "I: = I". SLDO 3 (short load global) loads the value contained in I onto the top of the stack. Note that this instruction is only one byte long since I was declared as one of the first 16 words of storage in the system. The next instruction (SRO 3, store global) stores the TOS into I. Unfortunately there is no short store global so this instruction must be at least two bytes long. Since the address of I is less than 128, the address following the SRO instruction is only one byte long and the entire instruction is two bytes long.

The p-code instructions at addresses 0005 and 0007 handle the assignment "J: = J". Note that both instructions are two bytes long since J was purposely declared so that it was not one of the first 16 words of storage used. For this reason, the LDO (load global) instead of SLDO instruction had to be used to load J onto the TOS.

The p-code instructions at locations 0009 and 000C handle the assignment "K: = K". In this case K is declared beyond the first 127 words of storage so a three byte instruction must be used. For more information on how the "BIG" parameter operates on the LDO and SRO instructions consult the chapter on p-Code instructions. The RBP instruction returns control to the Pascal operating system.

Real Variable Accesses

Listing 4.2 demonstrates the various loading and storing techniques employed by Apple Pascal for real variables and constants. The instructions at addresses 0002, 0004, and 000A are used to implement the Pascal statement "R = 1.1;". The LAO instruction loads the address of R onto the stack. Later this address will be used to store the data on TOS into the variable. The next instruction (LDC) pushes the two-word constant 8C3FCDCC onto the evaluation stack. In case you haven't guessed, this is the floating point representtion for the value 1.1 The third instruction in this sequence (STM 2) stores the two words on the TOS into the variable pointed at by the address on NOS. The effect of these three instructions is to load the constant 1.1 into the real variable R.

The next four instructions (at addresses 000C, 000E,000F, and 0010) handle the assignment "S: = 4;". The address of S is pushed onto the stack, the integer constant "4" is pushed onto the stack and converted to a floating point number, and finally the floating point value on TOS is stored in the variable S.

The four instructions at addresses 0012, 0014, 0016, and 0018 load the addresses of R and S onto the stack (respectively) and then load the two-word datum contained within S and store the data in the real variable R. This handles the assignment "R: = S".

The next four instructions handle the "R: = −1.1" assignment. Note tht this sequence of instructions is identical to that for the statement "R: = 1.1" except for the addition of the NGR instruction that negates the value on TOS after 1.1 is loaded. The RBP instruction at location 0025 returns contol to the Pascal operating system.

Array Allocation

Listings 4.3 and 4.4 show the code generated for identical programs using array accesses. Listing 4.3 shows the code generated with the {$R+} option set (the default condition). Listing 4.4 shows the code generated with the {$R−} option set. Since listing three is the more general case it will be desdribed.

The instructions at locations 0002 and 0003 sstore "1" into the variable "J". The LAO instruction at address 0005 loads the address of the first member of the array "I" onto the stack. The SLDC instruction at address 0007 loads the index into array I onto the stack. The instructions at addresses 0008, 0009, and 000A check this index to make sure that it is in the range 0..10. The IXA instruction at address 000B adds TOS to NOS to compute the address of the desired element in the I array.

The instructions at addresses 000F..001E handle the assignment "R[0]: = 1.1". The address of the first element of R is pushed onto the stack followed by the desired index into the R array (zero). This index is checked to make sure it lies in the range 0..10 and then a pointer to the array element is computed by the execution of the IXA 2 instruction. The four-byte representation of "1.1" is pushed on the stack and then this data is stored into R[0] using the STM 2 instruction.

The instructions between 0020 and 0030 handle the assignment "R[J]: = 1.1;" except the value contained in J is loaded onto the stack instead of zero as the index into the array.

The instructions at addresses 0032 through 003D handle the assignment "I[J]: = J;". The LAO instruction loads the address of the first element of the I array onto the stack. LDO 36 loads the value contained within J onto the stack and the following three instructions check to make sure that this value is in the range 0..10. The IXA instruction adds TOS to NOS which creates a pointer to the array element in question. Finally, the value contained in J is loaded onto the stack and stored into the specified array element.

Listing four shows the same program with the {$R−} option set. Note that considerably less code was generated since the two SLDC instructions and CHK instructions were not emitted in the code stream after each array access.

> **Note:** The DECODE program uses PUSH instead of SLDC but SLDC is the correct p-code convention.

Set Operations

Listings 4.5 and 4.6 show the type of code generated by the Apple Pascal compiler whenever set operations are encountered. Listing 4.5 shows the code generated when the sets being operated on fit into one word of storage. Listing 4.6 shows the code generated when the sets need more than one word of storage allocated to them. Since the latter case is the more general, it will be described fully.

The set type SET OF LARGEI was declared so that it would exactly require three words of storage (i.e., 48 bits). This short program shows three set assignments, set union, set difference, set intersection, and set inclusion. The instructions at addresses 0002..0007 handle the assignment "S: = [ ];". The LAO instruction at address 0002 loads the address of S onto the stack. The SLDC instruction at address 0004 loads the value for the empty set onto the TOS. The ADJ instruction loads an additional two bytes of zero onto TOS thus adjusting the data on TOS so that it occupies the same amount of space as does the set variable S. The STM instruction at address 0007 stores the three words on TOS at the address previously pushed by the LAO instruction. This stores the empty set on TOS (three words) into the set variable S.

The instructions at addresses 0009..0011 handle the Pascal assignment "S: = [8,11];". The LAO instruction loads the address of S onto the stack, this address must be pushed for the STM instruction later on. The LDCI instruction pushes the data for the set [8,11] onto the stack. The SLDC instruction that follows pushes the number of words in the set of TOS (one) onto the stack. The ADJ instruction looks at the one on TOS and adjusts the set so that it occupies three words. This is accomplished by pushing two zeroes onto the TOS. Finally, the STM instruction at address 0011 stores the three-word set on TOS into the set variable S. In a similar manner, the instructions at addresses 0013..0019 store the set [0] into the set variable R.

The instructions in the range 001B..002A handle the Pascal assignment "Q: = R + S;". The LAO instruction at address 001B loads the address of Q onto the stack so that the value of the set expression on the right hand side of the assignment statement can be stored in Q. The LAO, LDM, and SLDC instructions at addresses 001D..0021 load the set variable R onto TOS along with a length byte denoting the length of the set R. The instructions of addresses 0022..0026 push the set variable S onto the stack. The UNI instruction at address 0027 takes the set union of the two sets just pushed onto the stack. Once the set union is taken, the ADJ instruction is executed to make sure that the set on TOS is exactly three words long and then the resulting set is stored into Q using the STM instruction at address 002A.

The instructions at 002C..003B perform exactly the same operation except that the set difference is taken instead of the set union. As before the address of Q is pushed onto the stack, R and S are pushed onto the stack, the set difference is taken, the set is adjusted to fit into three bytes, and the set on TOS is stored into the variable Q.

The instructions in the range 003D..004C handle the Pascal assignment "Q: = R*S;". The code generated is identical to that generated for set union and set difference except the INT instruction (set intersection) is emitted in place of the UNI or DIF instructions.

The p-code instructions at addresses 004E..0058 handle the two Pascal statements "I: = 2;" and "B: = I IN Q;". The SLDC 2 and SRO 13 instructions handle the assignment to I. Next I is pushed onto the stack with the SLDO instruction. The LAO, LDM, and SLDC instruction sequence that follows pushes the set Q onto the stack. The INN instruction at address 0057 checks to see if the scalar on NOS (I) is in the set on TOS (Q). The SRO instruction stores the Boolean result of this operation in the Boolean variable B.

Accessing Record Elements

Listings 4.7 and 4.8 show the code generated for record element accesses. Listing 4.7 shows the code generated with the {$R+} option set and listing 4.8 shows the code generated with the {$R−} option set. The only difference between the two listings is the addition of several SLDC and CHK instructions whenever an array element is accessed.

The instructions at addresses 0002..0019 handle the assignments to the elements of the M record. This code is identical to the code that would have been generated had each assignment been made to a separate variable.

The code at addresses 001A..001E handles the record assignment "N:=M;". The first LAO instruction loads the address of N onto the stack and the second LAO instruction loads the address of M onto the stack. the MOV instruction that follows moves eight words of data from the address on the TOS (M) to the data pointed at by the address on NOS (M). This transfers the data from the record M to the record N.

The p-code instructions in the range 0020..0027 handle the Pascal assignment "L[0]:=M;". This section of code begins with a LAO instruction that loads the address of L onto the stack. The next two instructions load the index (zero) onto the stack, scale it appropriately, and add this index to the base address on the TOS. The LAO instruction at address 0025 loads the address of M onto the TOS and the MOV instruction at address 0027 copies the data in M into the L[0] array element. The code from address 0029 to 0030 performs essentially the same operation except that L[1] is loaded instead of L[0].

Accessing String Variables

Listing 4.9 shows the code generated in response to some simple string operations. The instructions in the range 0002..0012 handle the assignment "S:='HELLO THERE';". The LAO instruction at address 0002 loads the address of S onto the stack. The NOP at address 0004 is used to align the string that follows on a word boundry. This is required by some 16-bit processors (including the LSI-II and 68000). The LSA instruction at address 0005 pushes a pointer to the string that follows the LSA instruction. Finally, the SAS instruction at address 0012 copies the string pointed at by the address on TOS into S (whose address is on NOS).

The three instructions at addresses 0014, 0016, and 0018 handle the assignment "T: = S". The first two instructions load the addresses of T and S onto the stack and the SAS instruction that follows copies the data from the S string to the T string.

The instructions at addresses 001A..001F handle the null string assignment at line 17. Once again the interleaving NOP is there so that the string address pushed on the stack by the LSA instruction is an even value. Other than the fact that the string being assigned is empty, the code is identical to that generated by the first string assignment in the code stream.

The instructions in the range 0021..0024 handle the character assignment "T: = 'A';". This code is quite a bit different from the assignments discussed so far, instead of issuing an LSA instruction, a SLDA instruction pushes 65 (the ASCII code for an 'A') onto the stack. The SAS instruction looks at the high order byte of the source string address on the TOS. If it is zero (pointers never have a high order byte of zero, character constants always do) then a single character assignment is made to the destination address. If the high order byte is not zero, then a normal string assignment is performed as in the previous example.

Pointer Variable Usage

Listing 4.10 shows some simple pointer variable manipulations. The three instructions at 0002..0004 handle the Pascal assignment "I: = P^;", the instructions at 0006..0008 handle the Pascal assignment "P^; = I;", and the instructions at 0009 and 000A handle the assignment "P: = Q;".

The SLDO instruction loads the contents of P onto the TOS. The SIND 0 instruction that follows loads the data pointed at by the value on TOS (i.e. P) onto TOS, and then the SRO instruction stores this data into the variable I. This effectively loads the data pointed at by P into the variable I.

The code for "P^: = I;" is equally simple. The SLDO instruction at address 0006 loads the value contained in P onto the stack, the SLDO instruction at address 0007 loads the value contained in I onto the stack, and the STO instruction at address 0008 stores the data on TOS (I) at the address specified on NOS (P). This stores the data contained in I at the address specified in the P variable.

The code for the Pascal statement "P: =Q;" is especially trivial. The value contained in Q is loaded into P using the SRO instruction. This copies the pointer value in Q to the P variable.

Code Generator for a FOR Loop

Listing 4.11 shows how the Apple Pascal compiler generates code for the Pascal FOR loop. You will note one interesting feature to the code generated in this simple program: the Apple Pascal compiler automatically reserves a "phantom" variable for use by the FOR loop. In this program example, word offset 132 is used to hold the phantom value. Apple Pascal reserves one word of storage for every FOR loop encountered within a program, if you're trying to minimize the space required by a program you should keep this in mind.

The code for the FOR loop begins at address 0002. First, the variable I is loaded with the value zero (the initial value for the loop) and the phantom variable at offset 132 is loaded wih 127 (the final value of the loop). At address 0009 the actual loop begins. I and the phantom variable are pushed onto the stack and compared with the LEQI instruction at address 000D. If I is less than or equal to the phantom variable then the FJP instruction at address 000E is ignored, otherwise the loop terminates by jumping to address 001E. If I is less than or equal to the phantom variable then control drops through to location 0010. The instructions at addresses0010..0016 handle the Pascal assignment statement "A[I]: =I;". The instructions at addresses 0017, 0018, 0019, and 001A push I onto the stack, add one to it, and stores the incremented value back into I. The UJP instruction at address 001C transfers control back to address 0009 so that the loop can be repeated.

While Loops

Listing 4.12 gives an example of the amount of code generated whenever the WHILE loop is encountered. Note that the code generated for the WHILE loop is shorter than that generated for a FOR loop performing the same function. Under certain circumstances it also executes a little faster (although under other circumstances it executes slower). Therefore you should never substitute a FOR loop for a WHILE loop if the WHILE loop is a more logical choice.

As with the FOR loop, the code for the WHILE loop begins with an initialization section. The difference here, of course, is that the initialization phase is handled by the explicit Pascal statement "I: = 0;". The code for this initialization section is at addresses 0002 and 0003. The loop proper begins at address 0005 where I is pushed onto the stack and compared wtih 127. If I is greater than 127 the LEQI instruction at address 0007 aborts the execution of the loop, otherwise control drops to the code at address 000A that handles the assignment "A[I]: = I;". I is incremented at addresses 0011..0014 and the UJP instruction at address 0016 returns control to the top of the loop at address 0005.

The REPEAT..UNTIL Loop

A Repeat..Until loop and the p-code generated for it is shown in listing 4.13. As is the case with the WHILE loop, the REPEAT..UNTIL loop generates less code and may execute faster than an equivalent FOR loop. So you should always use the REPEAT..UNTIL loop in a situation if it is more appropriate.

Addresses 0002 and 0003 handle the initialization code "I: = 0;". The loop begins at address 0005. Unlike the WHILE loop, the REPEAT..UNTIL loop checks for loop termination at the end of the loop. Therefore the code encountered at the beginning of the loop is the code for the assignment "A[I]: = I ;". At addresses 0011 through 0014 I is pushed onto the stack, compared with 127, and program control is transferred to address 0005 if I is less than or equal to 127.

The IF..THEN..ELSE Statement

Listing 4.14 presents the code that the Apple Pascal compiler generates for the IF THEN ELSE statement. There are six IF statements in this program, the first one's code occupies locations 0002..000E, the second uses 0010..0016, the third requires locations 0018..001F, the fourth's code resides at 0021.0027, the fifth is at 0029..002F, and the sixth IF statement's code is at 0031..003C. Since all of these differ only by the operation performed, only two forms will be discussed, a version with the optional ELSE clause and a version without.

The code beginning at address 0002 handles the Pascal statement:

```
IF I=0 THEN I:=-1
  ELSE I := 0;
```

The SLDO instruction at address 0002 pushes the variable I onto the stack, the SLDC instruction at address 0003 pushes zero onto the stack, and the EQUI instruction at address 0004 replaces these two items on the stack with TRUE if I is equal to zero and FALSE if I is not equal to zero. The FJP instruction at address 0005 jumps to location 000D if the value on TOS is FALSE (i.e., I did not equal zero). If TOS is TRUE (I equaled zero) then program control continues at address 0007 at which point the value one is pushed onto the stack and this is negated and stored in I. At address 000B an unconditional jump is taken to the first byte past the IF..THEN..ELSE at address 0010. If I did not equal zero then the former FJP instruction transfers control to the first instruction past the UJP instruction at address 000D. The two instructions that follow push zero onto the stack and then store the TOS into the variable I.

The instructions from 0010..0016 handle an IF statement without the ELSE clause. The only difference here is the fact that the FJP instruction jumps to the end of the code for the IF statement and there is no UJP instruction sandwiched in there.

The CASE Statement

Listings 4.15 and 4.16 show how the Apple Pascal compiler generates code for the CASE statement. The listings are identical except for an extra case element in listing 4.16. This single addition (case = 24) is solely responsible for the 46 additional bytes generated in listing 4.16. Since the listings are so similar, listing 4.16 will be discussed.

The code for the first CASE statement resides in the range 0002..0027. The code sequence begins by pushing the value contained in I onto the stack. Then an UJP to the case jump at location 0019 is taken. Apple Pascal generates code for the individual cases of a case statement *before* the actual case jump. So the code between 0005 and 0017 handles each of the cases in the first case statement. 0005..0008 handles the case "0:I: = 1;", 000A..000D handles the case "1:I: = 0;", 000F..0012 handles the case "2:I: = 3;", and 0014..0017 handles the case "3:I: = 2;".

The XJP instruction at address 0019 handles all the work. It expects a case value on the top of the stack which it compares to the minimum and maximum values which are contained within the case statement. If the value on TOS is outside this range then a jump to location 0028 is taken. IF the value on TOS is within this range, then a branch is taken to the address that is found at the appropriate entry in the table following the XJP instruction. In this case, if I=0 then control is transferred to location 0005, if I=1 control is transferred to location 000A, if I=2 then control is transferred to location 000F, and if I=3 then control is transferred to location 0014.

The second CASE statement which appears in listing 4.16 generated considerable more code because the case values are disjoint. This case statement demonstrates two things: the entries in the case table when two case values are present before one statement; and the type of code that is generated if the case values are widely separated (disjoint). Of interest here is the fact that the addresses between the values four and twenty-four all point at location 70. This points at a UJP instruction in the middle of the XJP instruction that jumps to location 007A. If one of these values appears on the TOS then control is transferred to the first statement past the CASE statement without executing any of the cases.

Expressions in Apple Pascal

Listings 4.17 and 4.18 show how Apple Pascal generates code for various arithmetic expressions. Listing 4.17 demonstrates the code generated for simple expressions. Listing 4.18 lists the code generated for a few somewhat complex expressions. While these listings are certainly not all-encompassing, they do demonstrate the code generated by the more popular functions and operators.

The code from 0002..0006 in lisitng 4.17 handles the two asssignments "I: = 0;" and "J: = I;". "J: = PRED(I);" is handled by the code at addresses 0008.000B. I is pushed onto the stack, one is subtracted from it, and the result is stored into I. Likewise, the code from 000D..0010 handles the assignment "J: = SUCC(I);" by pushing I, adding one to it, and storing the result into J.

The arithmetic operations; addition, subtraction, multiplication, division, and modulo; are shown between locations 0012..0029. In each example I is pushed onto the stack, J is pushed onto the stack, the specific operation is performed, and the result is stored into K. Arithmetic negation is handled at addresses 002B..002D. Here I is pushed onto the stack, negated, and stored into K.

The binary Boolean operators' code appears between locations 002F and 005B. As is the case with the arithmetic operators the two operands are pushed onto the stack the operation is performed, and the result is stored into B. The set inclusion operation (IN) is performed at addresses 004D..0051. It is a little different from the other binary operations in that three operands are pushed onto the stack. First I is pushed onto the stack (SLDO 3), then the value three is pushed onto the stack (the bit map corresponding to the set [0,1]), and finally the value one is pushed onto the stack (the number of words occupied by the set on TOS). The INN instruction performs the set inclusion operation which leaves true or false on the top of the stack. This value is stored into B by the SRO 6 instruction following the INN instruction. Logical negation (NOT) is demonstrated by the code generated for B: = NOT(C) at addresses 005D..005F.

ODD, ORD, and CHR are not true functions. This fact is demonstrated by the code generated for ODD and ORD at addresses 0061..0065. ODD,

ORD, and CHR are simply "compiler functions" that allows the compiler to treat integer values as Boolean or character values and vice versa. As you can see in the code generated, I is stored into B with no intervening p-codes when B: =ODD(I) is executed and likewise for I: =ORD(B).

Listing 4.18 shows the code generated for complex expressions. Anyone familiar with an HP calculator will feel right at home with this type of code (since it is all reverse polish notation). No attempt, however, will be made to explain this code because even for the TI buffs, this code is fairly easy to follow.

String Handling Functions

Listing 4.19 shows the p-code generated for some of the built-in string functions in Apple Pascal. Note that this disassembly was produced with ABT's DUMPCODE disassembler instead of DECODE. DECODE contained a small bug which prevented it from listing a few instructions at the end of the listing. The most peculiar thing you should notice about this listing is the fact that it does not begin with a pair of NOP instuctions. Instead there is a jump instruction that branches to the end of the program where 30 is pushed onto the stack, special procedure number twenty-one is called, and then the program jumps back to location 0002. This short piece of code at the end of the program is used to load an intrinsic unit off the disk. In this case, the LONGINT intrinsic unit must be accessed because of the call to the STR routine. Two bytes are reserved at the beginning of every program for this jump in case the initialization code is required. The jump is patched in (as in this case) if an intrinsic segment must be loaded from disk.

As with all the programs presented thus far the actual program code begins at address 0002. At location 0002 the address of S is pushed onto the stack. The NOP that follows is used to align the string that follows on a word boundry. The LSA instruction at address 0005 pushes the address of the string "HELLO" onto the stack. Finally, the SAS instruction at address 000C is used to store "HELLO" into the string variable S. This code handles the assignment S: ="HELLO";.

The code at address 000E..0012 handles the assignment I: = LENGTH(S);. The code begins by pushing the address of S onto the stack. This address points at the length byte of the string stored in S. Next an index into the string that points at the length byte is pushed onto the stack. Since the address of S is also the address of the length of the string, this value pushed is zero. The LDB instruction at address 0011 adds TOS and TOS-1 and pushes the byte pointed at by that sum. Since TOS contains zero and TOS-1 contains the address of the length byte of S, the length byte of S (with a higher order byte of zero) is pushed onto the stack. This length byte is stored into the variable I by the SRO instruction at address 0012.

The Pascal instruction I: = POS('HE',S); is handled by the p-code in the range 0014..0020. The NOP at address 0014 is used to align the string that follows on a word boundry. The LSA instruction at address 0015 pushes the address of the string 'HE' that follows the LSA instruction The LAO instruction at address 0019 pushes the address of S onto the stack. Two words of zero (parameters required by the POS routine) are pushed and then the POS routine is called with the CXP instruction at address 001D. Upon returning from the POS routine the position of the string 'HE' is left on the top of the stack. This value is stored into I with the SRO instruction at address 0020.

The assignment S: = CONCAT(S,'THERE'); is handled by the code in the range 0022..0040. The code begins by pushing the address of S onto the stack. This address will be used to store the concatenated string back into S. The next two instructions store the value zero into the variable with word offset 49. The astute reader will notice that there was no 49th variable defined in the VAR list. The variable at offset 49 is a "phantom" variable much like those used by the FOR loops in Apple Pascal. The variable at offset 49 is actually a string variable with a maximum length of 86 characters (long enough to hold the concatenation of S and "HELLO"). By storing zero into offset 49 the phantom stirng is initialized to the empty string.

The four instructions at addresses 0027..002C concatenate the phantom string (currently empty) with the string S. The CSP 0,23 is responsible for the concatenation. The concatenated string may have a maximum of 80 characters or an error will result. The five instructions at addresses 002F..003B concatenate the phantom string withg "THERE". The result is left in the phantom string. An error results if the concatenated string is longer than

86 characters. Finally, the phantom string is copied into S by the two instructions at addresses 003E..0040 (remember, the address of S was pushed onto the stack before all the concatenation operations were performed).

The assignment S:=COPY(S,1,5); is handled by the p-code at addresses 0042..004F. The address of S is pushed twice, once in order to provide a storage address, once because S appears as a parameter to COPY. Next the values one and five (also parameters to the COPY routine) are pushed and the COPY function in the Pascal O/S is called via the CXP 0,25 instruction. The string extracted from S was stored in the phantom string at offset 49. This string is copied into S by the two instructions at addresses 004D and 004F.

The instructions at addresses 0051..0055 handle the Pascal statement delete(S,1,2);. The address of S and the values one and two are pushed onto the stack and then the Pascal O/S routine DELETE is called via the CXP 0,26 instruction.

The insert command is handled by the code in ther ange 0058..0061. The address of the string 'HE' is pushed onto the stack, the address of S is pushed, a maximum length (80) is pushed, and the character position for insertion (one) is pushed. Then the Pascal O/S insert procedure is called via the CXP 0,24 instruction.

The code at addresses 0064..006E handle the procedure invocation STR(I,S);. I is pushed onto the stack and converted to a BCD value (i.e., a long integer) with the CXP 30,4 instruction. Then the address of S is pushed (along with some parameters to STR) and this BCD value is converted to a string with the CXP 30,4 instruction at address 006E. The 18 pushed onto TOS before executing CXP 30,4 instructs the LONG integer routines to perform the STR function.

The SLDC 30 and CSP Routine No.22 (misnamed TRUNC in the listing, this is actually a ULS [unload segment]) instructions undo what was done by the CSP Routine No.21 at address 0077 when the program first began running.

Procedure Definitions and Calls

Listings 4.20, 4.21, and 4.22 demonstrate procedure and function calls. Listing 4.20 demonstrates some non-segmented procedure calls including nested and recursive procedure invocations. The CLP (call local procedure) p-code is used to call a *local* procedure (i.e., a procedure contained within the currently executing procedure) and the OGP (call global procedure) p-Code is used to call a procedure at the same or lower lex level. Beyond these two comments, the code in listing 4.20 is fairly obvious.

Listing 4.21 demonstrates some segmented procedure calls. The only operational difference between the program in listing 4.20 and the program in listing 4.21 is the inclusion of SEGMENT PROCEDURE B. This routine gets called by the CXP (call external procedure) p-Code at address 0004. Note that the CXP instruction has two parameters. The first parameter (7) is the segment number and the second parameter (1) is the procedure number within the segment.

Listing 4.22 demonstrates an Apple Pascal FUNCTION call. The two SDLC (PUSH) instructions at addresses 0002 and 0003 push two words onto the stack. The function value will be returned in the first word pushed, the second word pushed is ignored unless the function happens to return a REAL value. The CLP instruction (call local procedure) calls the II function which stores zero into the first word pushed and pops the extra word off of the top of the stack (by virtue of the RNP 1 instruction). Finally, the value left on the top of stack after the function returns (in this case zero) is stsored in variable I by the instruction at address 0006.

And So On . . .

These examples of generated code area far from complete. If you're curious, or if you want to be able to optimize your Apple Pascal code segments, you should definitely purchase the PASCAL TOOLS II package from ABT or the PDQ package from DATAMOST. Comparisons of these two programs with the DECODE program are given in listings 4.23 through 4.26. All three programs provide certain advantages and disadvantages when used to disassemble Pascal programs. If you're interested in disecting Pascal programs, and your budget allows it, I would recommend that you obtain all of these packages. I found them all to be quite useful.

Listing 4-1

```
 1    1:D     1 {$l PRINTER:}
 1    1:D     1 (*****************************************************)
 1    1:D     1 (*                                                   *)
 1    1:D     1 (*  Listing 4.1: Variable allocation/access examples *)
 1    1:D     1 (*                                                   *)
 1    1:D     1 (*****************************************************)
 1    1:D     1
 1    1:D     1
 1    1:D     1 program ALLOCATION_EXAMPLES;
 1    1:D     3
 1    1:D     3 var     I:integer;
 1    1:D     4         A:array [0..15] of integer;
 1    1:D    20         J:integer;
 1    1:D    21         B:array [0..127] of integer;
 1    1:D   149         K:integer;
 1    1:D   150
 1    1:0     0 begin
 1    1:0     0
 1    1:1     0         I := I;    (* In these examples, note the     *)
 1    1:1     5         J := J;    (* number of bytes required for    *)
 1    1:1     9         K := K;    (* load and storing each variable.*)
 1    1:1    15
 1    1:0    15 end.
```

SEGMENT_NAME : ALLOCATI   SEG_NUM : 1

TOTAL PROCEDURES : 1   SEG_NUM_INDEX : 0

PROC #	ROOT_SEG	LEX	PARAMS	DATA	START	OFFSET	SIZE	$START	$EXIT
1	ALLOCATI	0	4	294	1	0	17	0200	020F

Offset ($):	Mnemonic	Par1	Par2	Hexcode	Opcode
0(0000):	NOP			D7	NOP
1(0001):	NOP			D7	NOP
2(0002):	SLDO	3		EA	Load Global Word
3(0003):	SRO	3		AB03	Store Global Word
5(0005):	LDO	20		A914	Load Global Word
7(0007):	SRO	20		AB14	Store Global Word
9(0009):	LDO	149		A98095	Load Global Word
12(000C):	SRO	149		AB8095	Store Global Word
15(000F):	RBP	0		C100	Return Base Procedure

Listing 4-2

```
 1    1:D     1 {$l PRINTER:}
 1    1:D     1 (****************************************************************)
 1    1:D     1 (*                                                              *)
 1    1:D     1 (*  Listing 4.2: Various forms of accessing REAL variables.     *)
 1    1:D     1 (*                                                              *)
 1    1:D     1 (****************************************************************)
 1    1:D     1
 1    1:D     1
 1    1:D     1 program ALLOCATION_EXAMPLES_REAL;
 1    1:D     3
 1    1:D     3 var     R:real;
 1    1:D     5         S:real;
 1    1:D     7
 1    1:0     0 begin
 1    1:0     0
 1    1:1     0         R := 1.1;  (* Assigning a REAL constant                 *)
 1    1:1    12         R := 4;    (* Assigning an INTEGER constant.            *)
 1    1:1    18         R := S;    (* Assigning a REAL variable.                *)
 1    1:1    26         R := -1.1; (* Assigning a negative REAL constant.       *)
 1    1:1    37
 1    1:0    37 end.
```

```
SEGMENT_NAME : ALLOCATI    SEG_NUM : 1

TOTAL PROCEDURES : 1      SEG_NUM_INDEX : 0
```

```
PROC #  ROOT_SEG   LEX  PARAMS  DATA  START  OFFSET  SIZE   $START  $EXIT

 1      ALLOCATI    0     4      8      1      0      39     0200    0225

 Offset ($):   Mnemonic   Par1  Par2   Hexcode    Opcode


    0(0000):   NOP                     D7         NOP
    1(0001):   NOP                     D7         NOP
    2(0002):   LAO          3          A503       Load Global Address
    4(0004):   LDC          2 16268    B3028C3F   Load Multiple Constant
                             -13107        CDCC
   10(000A):   STM          2          BD02       Store Multiple Word
   12(000C):   LAO          3          A503       Load Global Address
   14(000E):   PUSH         4          04         Load Constant
   15(000F):   FLT                     8A         Float (TOS-1) Integer -> Real
   16(0010):   STM          2          BD02       Store Multiple Word
   18(0012):   LAO          3          A503       Load Global Address
   20(0014):   LAO          5          A505       Load Global Address
   22(0016):   LDM          2          BC02       Load Multiple Word
   24(0018):   STM          2          BD02       Store Multiple Word
   26(001A):   LAO          3          A503       Load Global Address
   28(001C):   LDC          2 16268    B3028C3F   Load Multiple Constant
                             -13107        CDCC
   34(0022):   NGR                     92         Exponent Real
   35(0023):   STM          2          BD02       Store Multiple Word
   37(0025):   RBP          0          C100       Return Base Procedure
```

Listing 4-3

```
1   1:D    1 {$1 PRINTER:}
1   1:D    1 (*****************************************************************)
1   1:D    1 (*                                                               *)
1   1:D    1 (*  Listing 4.3: Array accesses.                                 *)
1   1:D    1 (*                                                               *)
1   1:D    1 (*****************************************************************)
1   1:D    1
1   1:D    1
1   1:D    1 program ALLOCATION_EXAMPLES_ARRAYS;
1   1:D    3
1   1:D    3 var      I:array [0..10] of integer;
1   1:D   14          R:array [0..10] of real;
1   1:D   36          J:integer;
1   1:D   37
1   1:0    0 begin
1   1:0    0
1   1:1    0          J := 1;
1   1:1    5          I [0] := 0;
1   1:1   15          R [0] := 1.1;
1   1:1   32          R [J] := 1.1;
1   1:1   50          I [J] := J;
1   1:1   62
1   1:0   62 end.
```

SEGMENT_NAME : ALLOCATI   SEG_NUM : 1

TOTAL PROCEDURES : 1   SEG_NUM_INDEX : 0

Listing 4-3 (continued)

```
PROC #  ROOT_SEG   LEX  PARAMS  DATA  START  OFFSET  SIZE  $START  $EXIT

 1      ALLOCATI   0     4      68     1       0     64    0200    023E

 Offset ($):     Mnemonic  Par1  Par2   Hexcode    Opcode

    0(0000):     NOP                    D7         NOP
    1(0001):     NOP                    D7         NOP
    2(0002):     PUSH       1           01         Load Constant
    3(0003):     SRO       36           AB24       Store Global Word
    5(0005):     LAO        3           A503       Load Global Address
    7(0007):     PUSH       0           00         Load Constant
    8(0008):     PUSH       0           00         Load Constant
    9(0009):     PUSH      10           0A         Load Constant
   10(000A):     CHK                    88         Range Check
   11(000B):     IXA        1           A401       Index Array
   13(000D):     PUSH       0           00         Load Constant
   14(000E):     STO                    9A         Store Indirect Word
   15(000F):     LAO       14           A50E       Load Global Address
   17(0011):     PUSH       0           00         Load Constant
   18(0012):     PUSH       0           00         Load Constant
   19(0013):     PUSH      10           0A         Load Constant
   20(0014):     CHK                    88         Range Check
   21(0015):     IXA        2           A402       Index Array
   23(0017):     LDC        2 16268     B3028C3F   Load Multiple Constant
                           -13107         CDCC
   30(001E):     STM        2           BD02       Store Multiple Word
   32(0020):     LAO       14           A50E       Load Global Address
   34(0022):     LDO       36           A924       Load Global Word
   36(0024):     PUSH       0           00         Load Constant
   37(0025):     PUSH      10           0A         Load Constant
   38(0026):     CHK                    88         Range Check
   39(0027):     IXA        2           A402       Index Array
   41(0029):     LDC        2 16268     B3028C3F   Load Multiple Constant
                           -13107         CDCC
   48(0030):     STM        2           BD02       Store Multiple Word
   50(0032):     LAO        3           A503       Load Global Address
   52(0034):     LDO       36           A924       Load Global Word
   54(0036):     PUSH       0           00         Load Constant
   55(0037):     PUSH      10           0A         Load Constant
   56(0038):     CHK                    88         Range Check
   57(0039):     IXA        1           A401       Index Array
   59(003B):     LDO       36           A924       Load Global Word
   61(003D):     STO                    9A         Store Indirect Word
   62(003E):     RBP        0           C100       Return Base Procedure
```

Listing 4-4

```
1    1:D     1 {$1 PRINTER:}
1    1:D     1 (*****************************************************************)
1    1:D     1 (*                                                               *)
1    1:D     1 (*  Listing 4.4: Array accesses with {$R-} option.               *)
1    1:D     1 (*                                                               *)
1    1:D     1 (*****************************************************************)
1    1:D     1
1    1:D     1 {$R-}
1    1:D     1 program ALLOCATION_EXAMPLES_ARRAYS;
1    1:D     3
1    1:D     3 var     I:array [0..10] of integer;
1    1:D    14         R:array [0..10] of real;
1    1:D    36         J:integer;
1    1:D    37
1    1:0     0 begin
1    1:0     0
1    1:1     0         J := 1;
1    1:1     5         I [0] := 0;
1    1:1    12         R [0] := 1.1;
1    1:1    26         R [J] := 1.1;
1    1:1    40         I [J] := J;
1    1:1    49
1    1:0    49 end.
```

```
SEGMENT_NAME : ALLOCATI     SEG_NUM : 1

TOTAL PROCEDURES : 1      SEG_NUM_INDEX : 0
```

Listing 4-4 (continued)

```
PROC #  ROOT_SEG   LEX  PARAMS  DATA  START  OFFSET  SIZE   $START  $EXIT

  1     ALLOCATI    0     4      68     1       0     51     0200   0231

 Offset ($):   Mnemonic   Par1  Par2   Hexcode     Opcode


    0(0000):   NOP                     D7          NOP
    1(0001):   NOP                     D7          NOP
    2(0002):   PUSH          1         01          Load Constant
    3(0003):   SRO          36         AB24        Store Global Word
    5(0005):   LAO           3         A503        Load Global Address
    7(0007):   PUSH          0         00          Load Constant
    8(0008):   IXA           1         A401        Index Array
   10(000A):   PUSH          0         00          Load Constant
   11(000B):   STO                     9A          Store Indirect Word
   12(000C):   LAO          14         A50E        Load Global Address
   14(000E):   PUSH          0         00          Load Constant
   15(000F):   IXA           2         A402        Index Array
   17(0011):   LDC           2 16268   B3028C3F    Load Multiple Constant
                              -13107       CDCC
   24(0018):   STM           2         BD02        Store Multiple Word
   26(001A):   LAO          14         A50E        Load Global Address
   28(001C):   LDO          36         A924        Load Global Word
   30(001E):   IXA           2         A402        Index Array
   32(0020):   LDC           2 16268   B3028C3F    Load Multiple Constant
                              -13107       CDCC
   38(0026):   STM           2         BD02        Store Multiple Word
   40(0028):   LAO           3         A503        Load Global Address
   42(002A):   LDO          36         A924        Load Global Word
   44(002C):   IXA           1         A401        Index Array
   46(002E):   LDO          36         A924        Load Global Word
   48(0030):   STO                     9A          Store Indirect Word
   49(0031):   RBP           0         C100        Return Base Procedure
```

Listing 4-5

```
 1    1:D     1 {$l PRINTER:}
 1    1:D     1 (*****************************************************************)
 1    1:D     1 (*                                                               *)
 1    1:D     1 (*  Listing 4.5: Small sets.                                     *)
 1    1:D     1 (*                                                               *)
 1    1:D     1 (*****************************************************************)
 1    1:D     1
 1    1:D     1 program ALLOCATION_EXAMPLES_SETS;
 1    1:D     3 type
 1    1:D     3         SMALLI = 0..11;
 1    1:D     3
 1    1:D     3 var     S: set of SMALLI;
 1    1:D     4         R: set of SMALLI;
 1    1:D     5         Q: set of SMALLI;
 1    1:D     6         B: boolean;
 1    1:D     7         I: integer;
 1    1:D     8
 1    1:0     0 begin
 1    1:0     0
 1    1:1     0         S := [];  (* Empty set *)
 1    1:1     7         S := [0];
 1    1:1    13         S := [0,1];
 1    1:1    19         S := [0,1,2];
 1    1:1    25         S := [0,1,2,3];
 1    1:1    31         S := [4,5,6,7];
 1    1:1    39         S := [8,9,10,11];
 1    1:1    47         R := [0];
 1    1:1    53         Q := R + S;
 1    1:1    62         Q := R - S;
 1    1:1    71         Q := R * S;
 1    1:1    80         I := 2;
 1    1:1    83         B := I in Q;
 1    1:1    89
 1    1:0    89 end.
```

SEGMENT_NAME : ALLOCATI   SEG_NUM : 1

TOTAL PROCEDURES : 1   SEG_NUM_INDEX : 0

PROC #	ROOT_SEG	LEX	PARAMS	DATA	START	OFFSET	SIZE	$START	$EXIT
1	ALLOCATI	0	4	10	1	0	91	0200	0259

Offset ($):	Mnemonic	Par1	Par2	Hexcode	Opcode
0(0000):	NOP			D7	NOP
1(0001):	NOP			D7	NOP
2(0002):	PUSH	0		00	Load Constant
3(0003):	ADJ	1		A001	Adjust Set
5(0005):	SRO	3		AB03	Store Global Word
7(0007):	PUSH	1		01	Load Constant
8(0008):	PUSH	1		01	Load Constant

Listing 4-5 (continued)

```
 9(0009):   ADJ      1     A001     Adjust Set
11(000B):   SRO      3     AB03     Store Global Word
13(000D):   PUSH     3     03       Load Constant
14(000E):   PUSH     1     01       Load Constant
15(000F):   ADJ      1     A001     Adjust Set
17(0011):   SRO      3     AB03     Store Global Word
19(0013):   PUSH     7     07       Load Constant
20(0014):   PUSH     1     01       Load Constant
21(0015):   ADJ      1     A001     Adjust Set
23(0017):   SRO      3     AB03     Store Global Word
25(0019):   PUSH    15     0F       Load Constant
26(001A):   PUSH     1     01       Load Constant
27(001B):   ADJ      1     A001     Adjust Set
29(001D):   SRO      3     AB03     Store Global Word
31(001F):   LDCI   240     C7F000   Load Constant
34(0022):   PUSH     1     01       Load Constant
35(0023):   ADJ      1     A001     Adjust Set
37(0025):   SRO      3     AB03     Store Global Word
39(0027):   LDCI  3840     C7000F   Load Constant
42(002A):   PUSH     1     01       Load Constant
43(002B):   ADJ      1     A001     Adjust Set
45(002D):   SRO      3     AB03     Store Global Word
47(002F):   PUSH     1     01       Load Constant
48(0030):   PUSH     1     01       Load Constant
49(0031):   ADJ      1     A001     Adjust Set
51(0033):   SRO      4     AB04     Store Global Word
53(0035):   SLDO     4     EB       Load Global Word
54(0036):   PUSH     1     01       Load Constant
55(0037):   SLDO     3     EA       Load Global Word
56(0038):   PUSH     1     01       Load Constant
57(0039):   UNI            9C       Compare Set Union  (Or)
58(003A):   ADJ      1     A001     Adjust Set
60(003C):   SRO      5     AB05     Store Global Word
62(003E):   SLDO     4     EB       Load Global Word
63(003F):   PUSH     1     01       Load Constant
64(0040):   SLDO     3     EA       Load Global Word
65(0041):   PUSH     1     01       Load Constant
66(0042):   DIF            85       Compare Set (And Not)
67(0043):   ADJ      1     A001     Adjust Set
69(0045):   SRO      5     AB05     Store Global Word
71(0047):   SLDO     4     EB       Load Global Word
72(0048):   PUSH     1     01       Load Constant
73(0049):   SLDO     3     EA       Load Global Word
74(004A):   PUSH     1     01       Load Constant
75(004B):   INT            8C       Compare Set Intersect (And)
76(004C):   ADJ      1     A001     Adjust Set
78(004E):   SRO      5     AB05     Store Global Word
80(0050):   PUSH     2     02       Load Constant
81(0051):   SRO      7     AB07     Store Global Word
83(0053):   SLDO     7     EE       Load Global Word
84(0054):   SLDO     5     EC       Load Global Word
85(0055):   PUSH     1     01       Load Constant
86(0056):   INN            8B       Compare Set Membership
87(0057):   SRO      6     AB06     Store Global Word
89(0059):   RBP      0     C100     Return Base Procedure
```

Listing 4-6

```
1    1:D     1 {$l PRINTER:}
1    1:D     1 (*****************************************************************)
1    1:D     1 (*                                                               *)
1    1:D     1 (*  Listing 4.6: Large sets.                                     *)
1    1:D     1 (*                                                               *)
1    1:D     1 (*****************************************************************)
1    1:D     1
1    1:D     1 program ALLOCATION_EXAMPLES_SETS;
1    1:D     3 type
1    1:D     3         LARGEI = 0..47;
1    1:D     3
1    1:D     3 var     S: set of LARGEI;
1    1:D     6         R: set of LARGEI;
1    1:D     9         Q: set of LARGEI;
1    1:D    12         B: boolean;
1    1:D    13         I: integer;
1    1:D    14
1    1:0     0 begin
1    1:0     0
1    1:1     0         S := [];
1    1:1     9         S := [8,11];
1    1:1    19         R := [0];
1    1:1    27         Q := R + S;
1    1:1    44         Q := R - S;
1    1:1    61         Q := R * S;
1    1:1    78         I := 2;
1    1:1    81         B := I in Q;
1    1:1    90
1    1:0    90 end.
```

```
SEGMENT_NAME : ALLOCATI      SEG_NUM : 1

TOTAL PROCEDURES : 1       SEG_NUM_INDEX : 0
```

```
PROC #  ROOT_SEG   LEX  PARAMS  DATA  START  OFFSET  SIZE   $START  $EXIT

  1     ALLOCATI    0      4     22      1       0     92    0200    025A

 Offset ($):    Mnemonic   Par1  Par2   Hexcode    Opcode


    0(0000):    NOP                     D7         NOP
    1(0001):    NOP                     D7         NOP
    2(0002):    LAO           3         A503       Load Global Address
    4(0004):    PUSH          0         00         Load Constant
    5(0005):    ADJ           3         A003       Adjust Set
    7(0007):    STM           3         BD03       Store Multiple Word
    9(0009):    LAO           3         A503       Load Global Address
   11(000B):    LDCI       2304         C70009     Load Constant
   14(000E):    PUSH          1         01         Load Constant
   15(000F):    ADJ           3         A003       Adjust Set
   17(0011):    STM           3         BD03       Store Multiple Word
   19(0013):    LAO           6         A506       Load Global Address
```

Listing 4-6 (continued)

```
21(0015):   PUSH   1    01     Load Constant
22(0016):   PUSH   1    01     Load Constant
23(0017):   ADJ    3    A003   Adjust Set
25(0019):   STM    3    BD03   Store Multiple Word
27(001B):   LAO    9    A509   Load Global Address
29(001D):   LAO    6    A506   Load Global Address
31(001F):   LDM    3    BC03   Load Multiple Word
33(0021):   PUSH   3    03     Load Constant
34(0022):   LAO    3    A503   Load Global Address
36(0024):   LDM    3    BC03   Load Multiple Word
38(0026):   PUSH   3    03     Load Constant
39(0027):   UNI         9C     Compare Set Union  (Or)
40(0028):   ADJ    3    A003   Adjust Set
42(002A):   STM    3    BD03   Store Multiple Word
44(002C):   LAO    9    A509   Load Global Address
46(002E):   LAO    6    A506   Load Global Address
48(0030):   LDM    3    BC03   Load Multiple Word
50(0032):   PUSH   3    03     Load Constant
51(0033):   LAO    3    A503   Load Global Address
53(0035):   LDM    3    BC03   Load Multiple Word
55(0037):   PUSH   3    03     Load Constant
56(0038):   DIF         85     Compare Set (And Not)
57(0039):   ADJ    3    A003   Adjust Set
59(003B):   STM    3    BD03   Store Multiple Word
61(003D):   LAO    9    A509   Load Global Address
63(003F):   LAO    6    A506   Load Global Address
65(0041):   LDM    3    BC03   Load Multiple Word
67(0043):   PUSH   3    03     Load Constant
68(0044):   LAO    3    A503   Load Global Address
70(0046):   LDM    3    BC03   Load Multiple Word
72(0048):   PUSH   3    03     Load Constant
73(0049):   INT         8C     Compare Set Intersect (And)
74(004A):   ADJ    3    A003   Adjust Set
76(004C):   STM    3    BD03   Store Multiple Word
78(004E):   PUSH   2    02     Load Constant
79(004F):   SRO    13   AB0D   Store Global Word
81(0051):   SLDO   13   F4     Load Global Word
82(0052):   LAO    9    A509   Load Global Address
84(0054):   LDM    3    BC03   Load Multiple Word
86(0056):   PUSH   3    03     Load Constant
87(0057):   INN         8B     Compare Set Membership
88(0058):   SRO    12   AB0C   Store Global Word
90(005A):   RBP    0    C100   Return Base Procedure
```

Listing 4-7

```
1   1:D    1 {$1 PRINTER:}
1   1:D    1 (*****************************************************************)
1   1:D    1 (*                                                               *)
1   1:D    1 (*  Listing 4.7: Records with {$R+} option.                       *)
1   1:D    1 (*                                                               *)
1   1:D    1 (*****************************************************************)
1   1:D    1
1   1:D    1 program ALLOCATION_EXAMPLES_RECORDS;
1   1:D    3 type
1   1:D    3         MYTYPE = record
1   1:D    3
1   1:D    3                         I:integer;
1   1:D    3                         R:real;
1   1:D    3                         B:boolean;
1   1:D    3                         A:array [0..3] of char;
1   1:D    3
1   1:D    3                 end;
1   1:D    3
1   1:D    3 var     M: MYTYPE;
1   1:D   11         N: MYTYPE;
1   1:D   19         L: array [0..1] of MYTYPE;
1   1:D   35
1   1:D   35
1   1:0    0 begin
1   1:0    0
1   1:1    0         M.I := 0;
1   1:1    5         M.R := 1.1;
1   1:1   16         M.B := TRUE;
1   1:1   19         M.A [0] := 'A';
1   1:1   29
1   1:1   29         N := M;
1   1:1   35
1   1:1   35         L [0] := M;
1   1:1   47         L [1] := N;
1   1:1   59
1   1:0   59 end.
```

```
SEGMENT_NAME : ALLOCATI     SEG_NUM : 1

TOTAL PROCEDURES : 1      SEG_NUM_INDEX : 0
```

Listing 4-7 (continued)

```
PROC #  ROOT_SEG  LEX  PARAMS  DATA  START  OFFSET  SIZE   $START  $EXIT

 1      ALLOCATI   0     4      64     1       0     61     0200    023B

 Offset ($):   Mnemonic   Par1   Par2   Hexcode    Opcode


     0(0000):  NOP                        D7         NOP
     1(0001):  NOP                        D7         NOP
     2(0002):  PUSH        0              00         Load Constant
     3(0003):  SRO         3              AB03       Store Global Word
     5(0005):  LAO         4              A504       Load Global Address
     7(0007):  LDC         2 16268        B3028C3F   Load Multiple Constant
                           -13107            CDCC
    14(000E):  STM         2              BD02       Store Multiple Word
    16(0010):  PUSH        1              01         Load Constant
    17(0011):  SRO         6              AB06       Store Global Word
    19(0013):  LAO         7              A507       Load Global Address
    21(0015):  PUSH        0              00         Load Constant
    22(0016):  PUSH        0              00         Load Constant
    23(0017):  PUSH        3              03         Load Constant
    24(0018):  CHK                        88         Range Check
    25(0019):  IXA         1              A401       Index Array
    27(001B):  PUSH       65              41         Load Constant
    28(001C):  STO                        9A         Store Indirect Word
    29(001D):  LAO        11              A50B       Load Global Address
    31(001F):  LAO         3              A503       Load Global Address
    33(0021):  MOV         8              A808       Move Word Block
    35(0023):  LAO        19              A513       Load Global Address
    37(0025):  PUSH        0              00         Load Constant
    38(0026):  PUSH        0              00         Load Constant
    39(0027):  PUSH        1              01         Load Constant
    40(0028):  CHK                        88         Range Check
    41(0029):  IXA         8              A408       Index Array
    43(002B):  LAO         3              A503       Load Global Address
    45(002D):  MOV         8              A808       Move Word Block
    47(002F):  LAO        19              A513       Load Global Address
    49(0031):  PUSH        1              01         Load Constant
    50(0032):  PUSH        0              00         Load Constant
    51(0033):  PUSH        1              01         Load Constant
    52(0034):  CHK                        88         Range Check
    53(0035):  IXA         8              A408       Index Array
    55(0037):  LAO        11              A50B       Load Global Address
    57(0039):  MOV         8              A808       Move Word Block
    59(003B):  RBP         0              C100       Return Base Procedure
```

Listing 4-8

```
1   1:D    1 {$l PRINTER:}
1   1:D    1 (****************************************************************)
1   1:D    1 (*                                                              *)
1   1:D    1 (*  Listing 4.8: Records with {$R-} option.                      *)
1   1:D    1 (*                                                              *)
1   1:D    1 (****************************************************************)
1   1:D    1
1   1:D    1 {$R-}
1   1:D    1 program ALLOCATION_EXAMPLES_RECORDS;
1   1:D    3 type
1   1:D    3         MYTYPE = record
1   1:D    3
1   1:D    3                          I:integer;
1   1:D    3                          R:real;
1   1:D    3                          B:boolean;
1   1:D    3                          A:array [0..3] of char;
1   1:D    3
1   1:D    3                  end;
1   1:D    3
1   1:D    3 var     M: MYTYPE;
1   1:D   11         N: MYTYPE;
1   1:D   19         L: array [0..1] of MYTYPE;
1   1:D   35
1   1:D   35
1   1:0    0 begin
1   1:0    0
1   1:1    0         M.I := 0;
1   1:1    5         M.R := 1.1;
1   1:1   16         M.B := TRUE;
1   1:1   19         M.A [0] := 'A';
1   1:1   26
1   1:1   26         N := M;
1   1:1   32
1   1:1   32         L [0] := M;
1   1:1   41         L [1] := N;
1   1:1   50
1   1:0   50 end.
```

```
SEGMENT_NAME : ALLOCATI     SEG_NUM : 1

TOTAL PROCEDURES : 1      SEG_NUM_INDEX : 0
```

Listing 4-8 (continued)

PROC #	ROOT_SEG	LEX	PARAMS	DATA	START	OFFSET	SIZE	$START	$EXIT
1	ALLOCATI	0	4	64	1	0	52	0200	0232

Offset ($):	Mnemonic	Par1	Par2	Hexcode	Opcode
0(0000):	NOP			D7	NOP
1(0001):	NOP			D7	NOP
2(0002):	PUSH	0		00	Load Constant
3(0003):	SRO	3		AB03	Store Global Word
5(0005):	LAO	4		A504	Load Global Address
7(0007):	LDC	2	16268 -13107	B3028C3F CDCC	Load Multiple Constant
14(000E):	STM	2		BD02	Store Multiple Word
16(0010):	PUSH	1		01	Load Constant
17(0011):	SRO	6		AB06	Store Global Word
19(0013):	LAO	7		A507	Load Global Address
21(0015):	PUSH	0		00	Load Constant
22(0016):	IXA	1		A401	Index Array
24(0018):	PUSH	65		41	Load Constant
25(0019):	STO			9A	Store Indirect Word
26(001A):	LAO	11		A50B	Load Global Address
28(001C):	LAO	3		A503	Load Global Address
30(001E):	MOV	8		A808	Move Word Block
32(0020):	LAO	19		A513	Load Global Address
34(0022):	PUSH	0		00	Load Constant
35(0023):	IXA	8		A408	Index Array
37(0025):	LAO	3		A503	Load Global Address
39(0027):	MOV	8		A808	Move Word Block
41(0029):	LAO	19		A513	Load Global Address
43(002B):	PUSH	1		01	Load Constant
44(002C):	IXA	8		A408	Index Array
46(002E):	LAO	11		A50B	Load Global Address
48(0030):	MOV	8		A808	Move Word Block
50(0032):	RBP	0		C100	Return Base Procedure

Listing 4-9

```
    1   1:D     1 {$1 PRINTER:}
    1   1:D     1 (******************************************************************)
    1   1:D     1 (*                                                                *)
    1   1:D     1 (*  Listing 4.9: String accesses with the {$R+} option.          *)
    1   1:D     1 (*                                                                *)
    1   1:D     1 (******************************************************************)
    1   1:D     1
    1   1:D     1 program ALLOCATION_EXAMPLES_STRINGS;
    1   1:D     3
    1   1:D     3 var     S:string;
    1   1:D    44         T:string;
    1   1:D    85
    1   1:0     0 begin
    1   1:0     0
    1   1:1     0         S := 'Hello there';
    1   1:1    20         T := S;
    1   1:1    26         T := '';
    1   1:1    33         T := 'A';
    1   1:1    38
    1   1:0    38 end.
```

```
________________________________________________

SEGMENT_NAME : ALLOCATI     SEG_NUM : 1

TOTAL PROCEDURES : 1      SEG_NUM_INDEX : 0
________________________________________________


________________________________________________

PROC #  ROOT_SEG   LEX  PARAMS  DATA  START  OFFSET  SIZE   $START  $EXIT

  1     ALLOCATI    0      4     164     1      0      40     0200    0226

 Offset ($):   Mnemonic   Par1  Par2   Hexcode    Opcode


    0(0000):   NOP                     D7         NOP
    1(0001):   NOP                     D7         NOP
    2(0002):   LAO          3          A503       Load Global Address
    4(0004):   NOP                     D7         NOP
    5(0005):   LSA         11          A60B       Load String Constant
                          Hello        48656C6C6F
                           ther        2074686572
                          e            65
   18(0012):   SAS         80          AA50       Assign String
   20(0014):   LAO         44          A52C       Load Global Address
   22(0016):   LAO          3          A503       Load Global Address
   24(0018):   SAS         80          AA50       Assign String
   26(001A):   LAO         44          A52C       Load Global Address
   28(001C):   NOP                     D7         NOP
   29(001D):   LSA          0          A600       Load String Constant
   31(001F):   SAS         80          AA50       Assign String
   33(0021):   LAO         44          A52C       Load Global Address
   35(0023):   PUSH        65          41         Load Constant
   36(0024):   SAS         80          AA50       Assign String
   38(0026):   RBP          0          C100       Return Base Procedure
```

Listing 4-10

```
1    1:D     1 {$l PRINTER:}
1    1:D     1 (**************************************************************)
1    1:D     1 (*                                                            *)
1    1:D     1 (*  Listing 4.10: Pointer usage.                              *)
1    1:D     1 (*                                                            *)
1    1:D     1 (**************************************************************)
1    1:D     1
1    1:D     1 program ALLOCATION_EXAMPLES_POINTERS;
1    1:D     3
1    1:D     3 var      P: ^integer;
1    1:D     4          Q: ^integer;
1    1:D     5          I: integer;
1    1:D     6
1    1:0     0 begin
1    1:0     0
1    1:1     0          I := P^;
1    1:1     6          P^ := I;
1    1:1     9          P := Q;
1    1:1    12
1    1:0    12 end.
```

```
SEGMENT_NAME : ALLOCATI     SEG_NUM : 1

TOTAL PROCEDURES : 1       SEG_NUM_INDEX : 0
```

PROC #	ROOT_SEG	LEX	PARAMS	DATA	START	OFFSET	SIZE	$START	$EXIT
1	ALLOCATI	0	4	6	1	0	14	0200	020C

```
 Offset ($):    Mnemonic   Par1  Par2   Hexcode    Opcode

    0(0000):    NOP                     D7         NOP
    1(0001):    NOP                     D7         NOP
    2(0002):    SLDO        3           EA         Load Global Word
    3(0003):    SIND        0           F8         Load Indexed Indirect Word
    4(0004):    SRO         5           AB05       Store Global Word
    6(0006):    SLDO        3           EA         Load Global Word
    7(0007):    SLDO        5           EC         Load Global Word
    8(0008):    STO                     9A         Store Indirect Word
    9(0009):    SLDO        4           EB         Load Global Word
   10(000A):    SRO         3           AB03       Store Global Word
   12(000C):    RBP         0           C100       Return Base Procedure
```

Listing 4-11

```
1   1:D     1 {$l PRINTER:}
1   1:D     1 (******************************************************************)
1   1:D     1 (*                                                                *)
1   1:D     1 (*  Listing 4.11: For loops.                                      *)
1   1:D     1 (*                                                                *)
1   1:D     1 (******************************************************************)
1   1:D     1
1   1:D     1 {$R-}
1   1:D     1 program FOR_LOOP_EXAMPLE;
1   1:D     3
1   1:D     3 var      I: integer;
1   1:D     4          A: array [0..127] of integer;
1   1:D   132
1   1:D   132
1   1:0     0 begin
1   1:0     0
1   1:1     0          for I := 0 to 127 do A [I] := I;
1   1:1    30
1   1:0    30 end.
```

SEGMENT_NAME : FORLOOPE   SEG_NUM : 1

TOTAL PROCEDURES : 1   SEG_NUM_INDEX : 0

PROC #	ROOT_SEG	LEX	PARAMS	DATA	START	OFFSET	SIZE	$START	$EXIT
1	FORLOOPE	0	4	260	1	0	32	0200	021E

Offset ($):	Mnemonic	Par1	Par2	Hexcode	Opcode
0(0000):	NOP			D7	NOP
1(0001):	NOP			D7	NOP
2(0002):	PUSH	0		00	Load Constant
3(0003):	SRO	3		AB03	Store Global Word
5(0005):	PUSH	127		7F	Load Constant
6(0006):	SRO	132		AB8084	Store Global Word
9(0009):	SLDO	3		EA	Load Global Word
10(000A):	LDO	132		A98084	Load Global Word
13(000D):	LEQI			C8	Compare
14(000E):	FJP	30		A10E	Jump If False
16(0010):	LAO	4		A504	Load Global Address
18(0012):	SLDO	3		EA	Load Global Word
19(0013):	IXA	1		A401	Index Array
21(0015):	SLDO	3		EA	Load Global Word
22(0016):	STO			9A	Store Indirect Word
23(0017):	SLDO	3		EA	Load Global Word
24(0018):	PUSH	1		01	Load Constant
25(0019):	ADI			82	Add
26(001A):	SRO	3		AB03	Store Global Word
28(001C):	UJP	9		B9F6	Unconditional Jump
30(001E):	RBP	0		C100	Return Base Procedure

Listing 4-12

```
1   1:D    1 {$1 PRINTER:}
1   1:D    1 (*****************************************************************)
1   1:D    1 (*                                                               *)
1   1:D    1 (*  Listing 4.12: While loops.                                   *)
1   1:D    1 (*                                                               *)
1   1:D    1 (*****************************************************************)
1   1:D    1
1   1:D    1 {$R-}
1   1:D    1 program WHILE_LOOP_EXAMPLE;
1   1:D    3
1   1:D    3 var    I: integer;
1   1:D    4        A: array [0..127] of integer;
1   1:D  132
1   1:D  132
1   1:0    0 begin
1   1:0    0
1   1:1    0        I := 0;
1   1:1    5        while (I <= 127) do begin
1   1:1   10
1   1:3   10              A [I] := I;
1   1:3   17              I := I + 1;
1   1:3   22
1   1:2   22        end;
1   1:2   24
1   1:0   24 end.
```

```
SEGMENT_NAME : WHILELOO     SEG_NUM : 1

TOTAL PROCEDURES : 1      SEG_NUM_INDEX : 0
```

PROC #	ROOT_SEG	LEX	PARAMS	DATA	START	OFFSET	SIZE	$START	$EXIT
1	WHILELOO	0	4	258	1	0	26	0200	0218

```
Offset ($):   Mnemonic   Par1  Par2   Hexcode    Opcode

  0(0000):    NOP                     D7         NOP
  1(0001):    NOP                     D7         NOP
  2(0002):    PUSH         0          00         Load Constant
  3(0003):    SRO          3          AB03       Store Global Word
  5(0005):    SLDO         3          EA         Load Global Word
  6(0006):    PUSH       127          7F         Load Constant
  7(0007):    LEQI                    C8         Compare
  8(0008):    FJP         24          A10E       Jump If False
 10(000A):    LAO          4          A504       Load Global Address
 12(000C):    SLDO         3          EA         Load Global Word
 13(000D):    IXA          1          A401       Index Array
 15(000F):    SLDO         3          EA         Load Global Word
 16(0010):    STO                     9A         Store Indirect Word
 17(0011):    SLDO         3          EA         Load Global Word
 18(0012):    PUSH         1          01         Load Constant
 19(0013):    ADI                     82         Add
 20(0014):    SRO          3          AB03       Store Global Word
 22(0016):    UJP          5          B9F6       Unconditional Jump
 24(0018):    RBP          0          C100       Return Base Procedure
```

Listing 4-13

```
1   1:D     1 {$1 PRINTER:}
1   1:D     1 (*****************************************************************)
1   1:D     1 (*                                                               *)
1   1:D     1 (*  Listing 4.13: Repeat Until loops.                            *)
1   1:D     1 (*                                                               *)
1   1:D     1 (*****************************************************************)
1   1:D     1
1   1:D     1 {$R-}
1   1:D     1 program REPEAT_LOOP_EXAMPLE;
1   1:D     3
1   1:D     3 var     I: integer;
1   1:D     4         A: array [0..127] of integer;
1   1:D   132
1   1:D   132
1   1:0     0 begin
1   1:0     0
1   1:1     0         I := 0;
1   1:1     5         repeat
1   1:1     5
1   1:2     5               A [I] := I;
1   1:2    12               I := I + 1;
1   1:2    17
1   1:1    17         until (I > 127);
1   1:1    22
1   1:0    22 end.
```

SEGMENT_NAME : REPEATLO   SEG_NUM : 1

TOTAL PROCEDURES : 1   SEG_NUM_INDEX : 0

PROC #	ROOT_SEG	LEX	PARAMS	DATA	START	OFFSET	SIZE	$START	$EXIT
1	REPEATLO	0	4	258	1	0	24	0200	0216

Offset ($):	Mnemonic	Par1	Par2	Hexcode	Opcode
0(0000):	NOP			D7	NOP
1(0001):	NOP			D7	NOP
2(0002):	PUSH	0		00	Load Constant
3(0003):	SRO	3		AB03	Store Global Word
5(0005):	LAO	4		A504	Load Global Address
7(0007):	SLDO	3		EA	Load Global Word
8(0008):	IXA	1		A401	Index Array
10(000A):	SLDO	3		EA	Load Global Word
11(000B):	STO			9A	Store Indirect Word
12(000C):	SLDO	3		EA	Load Global Word
13(000D):	PUSH	1		01	Load Constant
14(000E):	ADI			82	Add
15(000F):	SRO	3		AB03	Store Global Word
17(0011):	SLDO	3		EA	Load Global Word
18(0012):	PUSH	127		7F	Load Constant
19(0013):	GTRI			C5	Compare
20(0014):	FJP	5		A1F6	Jump If False
22(0016):	RBP	0		C100	Return Base Procedure

Listing 4-14

```
 1   1:D    1 {$1 PRINTER:}
 1   1:D    1 (*********************************************************************)
 1   1:D    1 (*                                                                   *)
 1   1:D    1 (*  Listing 4.14: If..then..else statements.                         *)
 1   1:D    1 (*                                                                   *)
 1   1:D    1 (*********************************************************************)
 1   1:D    1
 1   1:D    1 {$R-}
 1   1:D    1 program IF_STATEMENT;
 1   1:D    3
 1   1:D    3 var     I: integer;
 1   1:D    4
 1   1:0    0 begin
 1   1:0    0
 1   1:1    0         if I = 0 then I := -1
 1   1:1    7         else I := 0;
 1   1:1   16
 1   1:1   16         if (I <> 0) then I := 0;
 1   1:1   24
 1   1:1   24         if (I >= 0) then I := -1;
 1   1:1   33
 1   1:1   33         if (I > 0) then I := 0;
 1   1:1   41
 1   1:1   41         if (I <= 0) then I := 1;
 1   1:1   49
 1   1:1   49         if (I < 0 ) then I := 0
 1   1:1   54         else I := 1;
 1   1:1   62
 1   1:0   62 end.
```

```
SEGMENT_NAME : IFSTATEM     SEG_NUM : 1

TOTAL PROCEDURES : 1      SEG_NUM_INDEX : 0
```

Listing 4-14 (continued)

PROC #	ROOT_SEG	LEX	PARAMS	DATA	START	OFFSET	SIZE	$START	$EXIT
1	IFSTATEM	0	4	2	1	0	64	0200	023E

Offset ($):	Mnemonic	Par1	Par2	Hexcode	Opcode
0(0000):	NOP			D7	NOP
1(0001):	NOP			D7	NOP
2(0002):	SLDO	3		EA	Load Global Word
3(0003):	PUSH	0		00	Load Constant
4(0004):	EQUI			C3	Compare
5(0005):	FJP	13		A106	Jump If False
7(0007):	PUSH	1		01	Load Constant
8(0008):	NGI			91	2-s Complement
9(0009):	SRO	3		AB03	Store Global Word
11(000B):	UJP	16		B903	Unconditional Jump
13(000D):	PUSH	0		00	Load Constant
14(000E):	SRO	3		AB03	Store Global Word
16(0010):	SLDO	3		EA	Load Global Word
17(0011):	PUSH	0		00	Load Constant
18(0012):	NEQI			CB	Compare
19(0013):	FJP	24		A103	Jump If False
21(0015):	PUSH	0		00	Load Constant
22(0016):	SRO	3		AB03	Store Global Word
24(0018):	SLDO	3		EA	Load Global Word
25(0019):	PUSH	0		00	Load Constant
26(001A):	GEQI			C4	Compare
27(001B):	FJP	33		A104	Jump If False
29(001D):	PUSH	1		01	Load Constant
30(001E):	NGI			91	2-s Complement
31(001F):	SRO	3		AB03	Store Global Word
33(0021):	SLDO	3		EA	Load Global Word
34(0022):	PUSH	0		00	Load Constant
35(0023):	GTRI			C5	Compare
36(0024):	FJP	41		A103	Jump If False
38(0026):	PUSH	0		00	Load Constant
39(0027):	SRO	3		AB03	Store Global Word
41(0029):	SLDO	3		EA	Load Global Word
42(002A):	PUSH	0		00	Load Constant
43(002B):	LEQI			C8	Compare
44(002C):	FJP	49		A103	Jump If False
46(002E):	PUSH	1		01	Load Constant
47(002F):	SRO	3		AB03	Store Global Word
49(0031):	SLDO	3		EA	Load Global Word
50(0032):	PUSH	0		00	Load Constant
51(0033):	LESI			C9	Compare
52(0034):	FJP	59		A105	Jump If False
54(0036):	PUSH	0		00	Load Constant
55(0037):	SRO	3		AB03	Store Global Word
57(0039):	UJP	62		B903	Unconditional Jump
59(003B):	PUSH	1		01	Load Constant
60(003C):	SRO	3		AB03	Store Global Word
62(003E):	RBP	0		C100	Return Base Procedure

Listing 4-15

```
 1    1:D    1 {$l PRINTER:}
 1    1:D    1 (*******************************************************************)
 1    1:D    1 (*                                                                 *)
 1    1:D    1 (*  Listing 4.15: Case statement w/contiguous cases.               *)
 1    1:D    1 (*                                                                 *)
 1    1:D    1 (*******************************************************************)
 1    1:D    1
 1    1:D    1 {$R-}
 1    1:D    1 program CASE_STATEMENT;
 1    1:D    3
 1    1:D    3 var     I: integer;
 1    1:D    4
 1    1:0    0 begin
 1    1:0    0
 1    1:1    0         case I of
 1    1:1    5
 1    1:1    5                 0: I := 1;
 1    1:1   10                 1: I := 0;
 1    1:1   15                 2: I := 3;
 1    1:1   20                 3: I := 2;
 1    1:1   25
 1    1:1   25         end;
 1    1:1   40
 1    1:1   40         case I of
 1    1:1   43
 1    1:1   43                 0,1: I := 2;
 1    1:1   48                 2,3: I := 3;
 1    1:1   53                 4:   I := 0;
 1    1:1   58
 1    1:1   58         end;
 1    1:1   76
 1    1:0   76 end.
```

SEGMENT_NAME : CASESTAT   SEG_NUM : 1

TOTAL PROCEDURES : 1   SEG_NUM_INDEX : 0

Listing 4-15 (continued)

```
PROC #  ROOT_SEG   LEX  PARAMS  DATA  START  OFFSET  SIZE   $START  $EXIT

  1     CASESTAT    0     4       2     1       0     78     0200    024C

 Offset ($):    Mnemonic   Par1   Par2   Hexcode      Opcode

     0(0000):   NOP                      D7           NOP
     1(0001):   NOP                      D7           NOP
     2(0002):   SLDO          3          EA           Load Global Word
     3(0003):   UJP          25          B914         Unconditional Jump
     5(0005):   PUSH          1          01           Load Constant
     6(0006):   SRO           3          AB03         Store Global Word
     8(0008):   UJP          40          B91E         Unconditional Jump
    10(000A):   PUSH          0          00           Load Constant
    11(000B):   SRO           3          AB03         Store Global Word
    13(000D):   UJP          40          B919         Unconditional Jump
    15(000F):   PUSH          3          03           Load Constant
    16(0010):   SRO           3          AB03         Store Global Word
    18(0012):   UJP          40          B914         Unconditional Jump
    20(0014):   PUSH          2          02           Load Constant
    21(0015):   SRO           3          AB03         Store Global Word
    23(0017):   UJP          40          B90F         Unconditional Jump
    25(0019):   XJP           0      3   AC00000300   Case Jump
                      UJP        40        B908
                              5     10     1B001800
                             15     20     15001200
    40(0028):   SLDO          3          EA           Load Global Word
    41(0029):   UJP          58          B90F         Unconditional Jump
    43(002B):   PUSH          2          02           Load Constant
    44(002C):   SRO           3          AB03         Store Global Word
    46(002E):   UJP          76          B91C         Unconditional Jump
    48(0030):   PUSH          3          03           Load Constant
    49(0031):   SRO           3          AB03         Store Global Word
    51(0033):   UJP          76          B917         Unconditional Jump
    53(0035):   PUSH          0          00           Load Constant
    54(0036):   SRO           3          AB03         Store Global Word
    56(0038):   UJP          76          B912         Unconditional Jump
    58(003A):   XJP           0      4   AC00000400   Case Jump
                      UJP        76        B90A
                             43     43     17001900
                             48     48     16001800
                             53            1500
    76(004C):   RBP           0          C100         Return Base Procedure
```

Listing 4-16

```
 1   1:D     1 {$1 PRINTER:}
 1   1:D     1 (*******************************************************************)
 1   1:D     1 (*                                                                 *)
 1   1:D     1 (*  Listing 4.16: Case statement w/non-contiguous cases.           *)
 1   1:D     1 (*                                                                 *)
 1   1:D     1 (*******************************************************************)
 1   1:D     1
 1   1:D     1 {$R-}
 1   1:D     1 program CASE_STATEMENT;
 1   1:D     3
 1   1:D     3 var     I: integer;
 1   1:D     4
 1   1:0     0 begin
 1   1:0     0
 1   1:1     0         case I of
 1   1:1     5
 1   1:1     5                 0: I := 1;
 1   1:1    10                 1: I := 0;
 1   1:1    15                 2: I := 3;
 1   1:1    20                 3: I := 2;
 1   1:1    25
 1   1:1    25         end;
 1   1:1    40
 1   1:1    40         case I of
 1   1:1    43
 1   1:1    43                 0,1: I := 2;
 1   1:1    48                 2,3: I := 3;
 1   1:1    53                 4:   I := 0;
 1   1:1    58                 24:  I := -2;
 1   1:1    64
 1   1:1    64         end;
 1   1:1   122
 1   1:0   122 end.
```

SEGMENT_NAME : CASESTAT   SEG_NUM : 1

TOTAL PROCEDURES : 1   SEG_NUM_INDEX : 0

Listing 4-16 (continued)

```
PROC #  ROOT_SEG   LEX  PARAMS  DATA  START  OFFSET  SIZE   $START  $EXIT

  1     CASESTAT    0     4       2     1       0     124    0200    027A

 Offset ($):   Mnemonic   Parl  Par2   Hexcode    Opcode


    0(0000):   NOP                     D7         NOP
    1(0001):   NOP                     D7         NOP
    2(0002):   SLDO          3         EA         Load Global Word
    3(0003):   UJP          25         B914       Unconditional Jump
    5(0005):   PUSH          1         01         Load Constant
    6(0006):   SRO           3         AB03       Store Global Word
    8(0008):   UJP          40         B91E       Unconditional Jump
   10(000A):   PUSH          0         00         Load Constant
   11(000B):   SRO           3         AB03       Store Global Word
   13(000D):   UJP          40         B919       Unconditional Jump
   15(000F):   PUSH          3         03         Load Constant
   16(0010):   SRO           3         AB03       Store Global Word
   18(0012):   UJP          40         B914       Unconditional Jump
   20(0014):   PUSH          2         02         Load Constant
   21(0015):   SRO           3         AB03       Store Global Word
   23(0017):   UJP          40         B90F       Unconditional Jump
   25(0019):   XJP           0     3   AC00000300 Case Jump
                      UJP   40           B908
                             5    10     1B001800
                            15    20     15001200
   40(0028):   SLDO          3         EA         Load Global Word
   41(0029):   UJP          64         B915       Unconditional Jump
   43(002B):   PUSH          2         02         Load Constant
   44(002C):   SRO           3         AB03       Store Global Word
   46(002E):   UJP         122         B94A       Unconditional Jump
   48(0030):   PUSH          3         03         Load Constant
   49(0031):   SRO           3         AB03       Store Global Word
   51(0033):   UJP         122         B945       Unconditional Jump
   53(0035):   PUSH          0         00         Load Constant
   54(0036):   SRO           3         AB03       Store Global Word
   56(0038):   UJP         122         B940       Unconditional Jump
   58(003A):   PUSH          2         02         Load Constant
   59(003B):   NGI                     91         2-s Complement
   60(003C):   SRO           3         AB03       Store Global Word
   62(003E):   UJP         122         B93A       Unconditional Jump
   64(0040):   XJP           0    24   AC00001800 Case Jump
                      UJP  122           B932
                            43    43     1D001F00
                            48    48     1C001E00
                            53    70     1B000C00
                            70    70     0E001000
                            70    70     12001400
                            70    70     16001800
                            70    70     1A001C00
                            70    70     1E002000
                            70    70     22002400
                            70    70     26002800
                            70    70     2A002C00
                            70    70     2E003000
                            58           3E00
  122(007A):   RBP           0         C100       Return Base Procedure
```

Listing 4-17

```
 1    1:D     1 {$l PRINTER:}
 1    1:D     1 (*******************************************************************)
 1    1:D     1 (*                                                                 *)
 1    1:D     1 (*  Listing 4.17: Some simple aritmetic expressions.               *)
 1    1:D     1 (*                                                                 *)
 1    1:D     1 (*******************************************************************)
 1    1:D     1
 1    1:D     1 {$R-}
 1    1:D     1 program EXPRESSIONS;
 1    1:D     3
 1    1:D     3 var      I: integer;
 1    1:D     4          J: integer;
 1    1:D     5          K: integer;
 1    1:D     6          B: boolean;
 1    1:D     7          C: boolean;
 1    1:D     8          D: boolean;
 1    1:D     9
 1    1:0     0 begin
 1    1:0     0
 1    1:1     0          I := 0;
 1    1:1     5          J := I;
 1    1:1     8          J := pred (I);
 1    1:1    13          J := succ (I);
 1    1:1    18          K := I + J;
 1    1:1    23          K := I - J;
 1    1:1    28          K := I * J;
 1    1:1    33          K := I div J;
 1    1:1    38          K := I mod J;
 1    1:1    43          K := -I;
 1    1:1    47          B := I = J;
 1    1:1    52          B := I <> J;
 1    1:1    57          B := I >= J;
 1    1:1    62          B := I <= J;
 1    1:1    67          B := I > J;
 1    1:1    72          B := I < J;
 1    1:1    77          B := I IN [0,1];
 1    1:1    83          B := C and D;
 1    1:1    88          B := C or D;
 1    1:1    93          B := not C;
 1    1:1    97          B := odd (I);
 1    1:1   100          I := ord (B);
 1    1:1   103
 1    1:0   103 end.

-------------------------------------------------

SEGMENT_NAME : EXPRESSI    SEG_NUM : 1

TOTAL PROCEDURES : 1      SEG_NUM_INDEX : 0

-------------------------------------------------
```

Listing 4-17 (continued)

PROC #	ROOT_SEG	LEX	PARAMS	DATA	START	OFFSET	SIZE	$START	$EXIT
1	EXPRESSI	0	4	12	1	0	105	0200	0267

Offset ($):	Mnemonic	Par1	Par2	Hexcode	Opcode
0(0000):	NOP			D7	NOP
1(0001):	NOP			D7	NOP
2(0002):	PUSH	0		00	Load Constant
3(0003):	SRO	3		AB03	Store Global Word
5(0005):	SLDO	3		EA	Load Global Word
6(0006):	SRO	4		AB04	Store Global Word
8(0008):	SLDO	3		EA	Load Global Word
9(0009):	PUSH	1		01	Load Constant
10(000A):	SBI			95	Subtract
11(000B):	SRO	4		AB04	Store Global Word
13(000D):	SLDO	3		EA	Load Global Word
14(000E):	PUSH	1		01	Load Constant
15(000F):	ADI			82	Add
16(0010):	SRO	4		AB04	Store Global Word
18(0012):	SLDO	3		EA	Load Global Word
19(0013):	SLDO	4		EB	Load Global Word
20(0014):	ADI			82	Add
21(0015):	SRO	5		AB05	Store Global Word
23(0017):	SLDO	3		EA	Load Global Word
24(0018):	SLDO	4		EB	Load Global Word
25(0019):	SBI			95	Subtract
26(001A):	SRO	5		AB05	Store Global Word
28(001C):	SLDO	3		EA	Load Global Word
29(001D):	SLDO	4		EB	Load Global Word
30(001E):	MPI			8F	Multiply
31(001F):	SRO	5		AB05	Store Global Word
33(0021):	SLDO	3		EA	Load Global Word
34(0022):	SLDO	4		EB	Load Global Word
35(0023):	DVI			86	Divide
36(0024):	SRO	5		AB05	Store Global Word
38(0026):	SLDO	3		EA	Load Global Word
39(0027):	SLDO	4		EB	Load Global Word
40(0028):	MODI			8E	Mod
41(0029):	SRO	5		AB05	Store Global Word
43(002B):	SLDO	3		EA	Load Global Word
44(002C):	NGI			91	2-s Complement
45(002D):	SRO	5		AB05	Store Global Word
47(002F):	SLDO	3		EA	Load Global Word
48(0030):	SLDO	4		EB	Load Global Word
49(0031):	EQUI			C3	Compare
50(0032):	SRO	6		AB06	Store Global Word
52(0034):	SLDO	3		EA	Load Global Word
53(0035):	SLDO	4		EB	Load Global Word
54(0036):	NEQI			CB	Compare
55(0037):	SRO	6		AB06	Store Global Word
57(0039):	SLDO	3		EA	Load Global Word
58(003A):	SLDO	4		EB	Load Global Word
59(003B):	GEQI			C4	Compare
60(003C):	SRO	6		AB06	Store Global Word
62(003E):	SLDO	3		EA	Load Global Word
63(003F):	SLDO	4		EB	Load Global Word
64(0040):	LEQI			C8	Compare

Listing 4-17 (continued)

```
 65(0041):   SRO    6   AB06   Store Global Word
 67(0043):   SLDO   3   EA     Load Global Word
 68(0044):   SLDO   4   EB     Load Global Word
 69(0045):   GTRI       C5     Compare
 70(0046):   SRO    6   AB06   Store Global Word
 72(0048):   SLDO   3   EA     Load Global Word
 73(0049):   SLDO   4   EB     Load Global Word
 74(004A):   LESI       C9     Compare
 75(004B):   SRO    6   AB06   Store Global Word
 77(004D):   SLDO   3   EA     Load Global Word
 78(004E):   PUSH   3   03     Load Constant
 79(004F):   PUSH   1   01     Load Constant
 80(0050):   INN        8B     Compare Set Membership
 81(0051):   SRO    6   AB06   Store Global Word
 83(0053):   SLDO   7   EE     Load Global Word
 84(0054):   SLDO   8   EF     Load Global Word
 85(0055):   LAND       84     Compare
 86(0056):   SRO    6   AB06   Store Global Word
 88(0058):   SLDO   7   EE     Load Global Word
 89(0059):   SLDO   8   EF     Load Global Word
 90(005A):   LOR        8D     Compare (Or)
 91(005B):   SRO    6   AB06   Store Global Word
 93(005D):   SLDO   7   EE     Load Global Word
 94(005E):   LNOT       93     Compare (Not)
 95(005F):   SRO    6   AB06   Store Global Word
 97(0061):   SLDO   3   EA     Load Global Word
 98(0062):   SRO    6   AB06   Store Global Word
100(0064):   SLDO   6   ED     Load Global Word
101(0065):   SRO    3   AB03   Store Global Word
103(0067):   RBP    0   C100   Return Base Procedure
```

Listing 4-18

```
 1    1:D     1 {$1 PRINTER:}
 1    1:D     1 (*****************************************************************)
 1    1:D     1 (*                                                               *)
 1    1:D     1 (*  Listing 4.18: Some complex aritmetic expressions.            *)
 1    1:D     1 (*                                                               *)
 1    1:D     1 (*****************************************************************)
 1    1:D     1
 1    1:D     1 {$R-}
 1    1:D     1 program EXPRESSIONS;
 1    1:D     3
 1    1:D     3 var     I: integer;
 1    1:D     4         J: integer;
 1    1:D     5         K: integer;
 1    1:D     6         R: real;
 1    1:D     8         B: boolean;
 1    1:D     9
 1    1:0     0 begin
 1    1:0     0
 1    1:1     0         I := 1;
 1    1:1     5         J := 2;
 1    1:1     8         K := (I+J) * (J-I) + J div I;
 1    1:1    21         R := (I+J) / (I - R) + J / I;
 1    1:1    43         B := (I=0) and (J=1) or (K >= 0);
 1    1:1    56
 1    1:0    56 end.
```

```
SEGMENT_NAME : EXPRESSI     SEG_NUM : 1

TOTAL PROCEDURES : 1       SEG_NUM_INDEX : 0
```

Listing 4-18 (continued)

PROC #	ROOT_SEG	LEX	PARAMS	DATA	START	OFFSET	SIZE	$START	$EXIT
1	EXPRESSI	0	4	12	1	0	58	0200	0238

Offset ($):	Mnemonic	Par1	Par2	Hexcode	Opcode
0(0000):	NOP			D7	NOP
1(0001):	NOP			D7	NOP
2(0002):	PUSH	1		01	Load Constant
3(0003):	SRO	3		AB03	Store Global Word
5(0005):	PUSH	2		02	Load Constant
6(0006):	SRO	4		AB04	Store Global Word
8(0008):	SLDO	3		EA	Load Global Word
9(0009):	SLDO	4		EB	Load Global Word
10(000A):	ADI			82	Add
11(000B):	SLDO	4		EB	Load Global Word
12(000C):	SLDO	3		EA	Load Global Word
13(000D):	SBI			95	Subtract
14(000E):	MPI			8F	Multiply
15(000F):	SLDO	4		EB	Load Global Word
16(0010):	SLDO	3		EA	Load Global Word
17(0011):	DVI			86	Divide
18(0012):	ADI			82	Add
19(0013):	SRO	5		AB05	Store Global Word
21(0015):	LAO	6		A506	Load Global Address
23(0017):	SLDO	3		EA	Load Global Word
24(0018):	SLDO	4		EB	Load Global Word
25(0019):	ADI			82	Add
26(001A):	SLDO	3		EA	Load Global Word
27(001B):	LAO	6		A506	Load Global Address
29(001D):	LDM	2		BC02	Load Multiple Word
31(001F):	FLO			89	Float (TOS) Integer -> Real
32(0020):	SBR			96	Subtract Real
33(0021):	FLO			89	Float (TOS) Integer -> Real
34(0022):	DVR			87	Divide Real
35(0023):	SLDO	4		EB	Load Global Word
36(0024):	SLDO	3		EA	Load Global Word
37(0025):	FLT			8A	Float (TOS-1) Integer -> Real
38(0026):	FLO			89	Float (TOS) Integer -> Real
39(0027):	DVR			87	Divide Real
40(0028):	ADR			83	Add Real
41(0029):	STM	2		BD02	Store Multiple Word
43(002B):	SLDO	3		EA	Load Global Word
44(002C):	PUSH	0		00	Load Constant
45(002D):	EQUI			C3	Compare
46(002E):	SLDO	4		EB	Load Global Word
47(002F):	PUSH	1		01	Load Constant
48(0030):	EQUI			C3	Compare
49(0031):	LAND			84	Compare
50(0032):	SLDO	5		EC	Load Global Word
51(0033):	PUSH	0		00	Load Constant
52(0034):	GEQI			C4	Compare
53(0035):	LOR			8D	Compare (Or)
54(0036):	SRO	8		AB08	Store Global Word
56(0038):	RBP	0		C100	Return Base Procedure

Listing 4-19

```
 1  1:D     1 {$L PRINTER:}
 1  1:D     1 {$R-}
 1  1:D     1 PROGRAM BUILTINS;
 1  1:D     3 VAR B:PACKED ARRAY [0..7] OF CHAR;
 1  1:D     7     S:STRING;
 1  1:D    48     I:INTEGER;
 1  1:D    49
 1  1:0     0 BEGIN
 1  1:0     0
 1  1:1     0   S:= 'HELLO';
 1  1:1    14   I:= LENGTH(S);
 1  1:1    20   I:= POS('HE',S);
 1  1:1    34   S:= CONCAT(S,' THERE');
 1  1:1    66   S:= COPY(S,1,5);
 1  1:1    81   DELETE(S,1,2);
 1  1:1    88   INSERT('HE',S,1);
 1  1:1   100   STR(I,S);
 1  1:1   113
 1  1:0   113 END.

DUMPCODE of file SYSTEM.WRK.CODE

Segment: No: Size: Addr: SegKind: Text:

BUILTINS  0  008E  0001  LINKED

Dump of Segment Tale for segment 0
  SegNo = 1   Num Procs = 1
    1:  0088

Listing of disassembled code for segment 0
Begin Proc:
0000:  B9 74         UJP    0076
0002:  A5 07         LAO    7
0004:  D7            NOP
0005:  A6 05         LSA    5,'HELLO'
000C:  AA 50         SAS    80
000E:  A5 07         LAO    7
0010:  00            SLDC   0
0011:  BE            LDB
0012:  AB 30         SRO    48
0014:  D7            NOP
0015:  A6 02         LSA    2,'HE'
0019:  A5 07         LAO    7
001B:  00            SLDC   0
001C:  00            SLDC   0
001D:  CD 00 1B      CXP    0,27
0020:  AB 30         SRO    48
0022:  A5 07         LAO    7
0024:  00            SLDC   0
0025:  AB 31         SRO    49
0027:  A5 31         LAO    49
0029:  A5 07         LAO    7
002B:  50            SLDC   80
002C:  CD 00 17      CXP    0,23
002F:  A5 31         LAO    49
0031:  A6 06         LSA    6,' THERE'
0039:  D7            NOP
003A:  56            SLDC   86
003B:  CD 00 17      CXP    0,23
003E:  A5 31         LAO    49
```

Listing 4-19 (continued)

```
0040:  AA 50          SAS    80
0042:  A5 07          LAO    7
0044:  A5 07          LAO    7
0046:  A5 31          LAO    49
0048:  01             SLDC   1
0049:  05             SLDC   5
004A:  CD 00 19       CXP    0,25
004D:  A5 31          LAO    49
004F:  AA 50          SAS    80
0051:  A5 07          LAO    7
0053:  01             SLDC   1
0054:  02             SLDC   2
0055:  CD 00 1A       CXP    0,26
0058:  D7             NOP
0059:  A6 02          LSA    2,'HE'
005D:  A5 07          LAO    7
005F:  50             SLDC   80
0060:  01             SLDC   1
0061:  CD 00 18       CXP    0,24
0064:  A9 30          LDO    48
0066:  12             SLDC   18
0067:  CD 1E 04       CXP    30,4
006A:  A5 07          LAO    7
006C:  50             SLDC   80
006D:  0C             SLDC   12
006E:  CD 1E 04       CXP    30,4
0071:  1E             SLDC   30
0072:  9E 16          CSP    TRUNC
0074:  B9 05          UJP    007B
0076:  1E             SLDC   30
0077:  9E 15          CSP    Routine No.21
0079:  B9 F6          UJP    -10
007B:  C1 00          RBP    0
                 JTAB[-10] = 0002
                 Data Segment Size: 00B4
                 Parameter Size:    0004
                 Exit IC:           0071
                 Entry IC:          0000
                 Lex Level: 0, Procedure No.: 1
```

Listing 4-20

```
 1    1:D    1 {$1 PRINTER:}
 1    1:D    1 (*****************************************************************)
 1    1:D    1 (*                                                               *)
 1    1:D    1 (*  Listing 4.20: Procedure definitions and calls.               *)
 1    1:D    1 (*                                                               *)
 1    1:D    1 (*****************************************************************)
 1    1:D    1
 1    1:D    1 {$R-}
 1    1:D    1 program CALLS_AND_PROCS;
 1    1:D    3
 1    2:D    1         procedure A;
 1    2:0    0         begin end;
 1    2:0   12
 1    3:D    1         procedure B;
 1    3:D    1
 1    4:D    1                 procedure C;
 1    4:0    0                 begin end;
 1    4:0   12
 1    3:0    0         begin {B}
 1    3:0    0
 1    3:1    0                 B; { Recursive call }
 1    3:1    2                 C; { Call child procedure }
 1    3:1    4                 A; { Call procedure at same level }
 1    3:1    6
 1    3:0    6         end;
 1    3:0   18
 1    3:0   18
 1    3:0   18
 1    1:0    0 begin
 1    1:0    0
 1    1:1    0         A;
 1    1:1    4         B;
 1    1:1    6
 1    1:0    6 end.
```

SEGMENT_NAME : CALLSAND   SEG_NUM : 1

TOTAL PROCEDURES : 4   SEG_NUM_INDEX : 0

Listing 4-20 (continued)

```
___________________________________________________

PROC #  ROOT_SEG   LEX  PARAMS  DATA  START  OFFSET  SIZE   $START  $EXIT

  1     CALLSAND    0     4      0      1      42      8     022A    0230

 Offset ($):   Mnemonic    Par1  Par2   Hexcode     Opcode

    0(0000):   NOP                      D7          NOP
    1(0001):   NOP                      D7          NOP
    2(0002):   CLP          2           CE02        Call Local Procedure
    4(0004):   CLP          3           CE03        Call Local Procedure
    6(0006):   RBP          0           C100        Return Base Procedure
___________________________________________________

PROC #  ROOT_SEG   LEX  PARAMS  DATA  START  OFFSET  SIZE   $START  $EXIT

  2     CALLSAND    1     0      0      1      0       2     0200    0200

 Offset ($):   Mnemonic    Par1  Par2   Hexcode     Opcode

    0(0000):   RNP          0           AD00        Return Non-Base Procedure
___________________________________________________

PROC #  ROOT_SEG   LEX  PARAMS  DATA  START  OFFSET  SIZE   $START  $EXIT

  3     CALLSAND    1     0      0      1      24      8     0218    021E

 Offset ($):   Mnemonic    Par1  Par2   Hexcode     Opcode

    0(0000):   CGP          3           CF03        Call Global Procedure
    2(0002):   CLP          4           CE04        Call Local Procedure
    4(0004):   CGP          2           CF02        Call Global Procedure
    6(0006):   RNP          0           AD00        Return Non-Base Procedure
___________________________________________________

PROC #  ROOT_SEG   LEX  PARAMS  DATA  START  OFFSET  SIZE   $START  $EXIT

  4     CALLSAND    2     0      0      1      12      2     020C    020C

 Offset ($):   Mnemonic    Par1  Par2   Hexcode     Opcode

    0(0000):   RNP          0           AD00        Return Non-Base Procedure
```

Listing 4-21

```
1   1:D    1 {$l PRINTER:}
1   1:D    1 (*******************************************************************)
1   1:D    1 (*                                                                 *)
1   1:D    1 (*  Listing 4.21: Segment procedure calls.                         *)
1   1:D    1 (*                                                                 *)
1   1:D    1 (*******************************************************************)
1   1:D    1
1   1:D    1 {$R-}
1   1:D    1 program CALLS_AND_PROCS;
1   1:D    3
7   1:D    1         segment procedure B;
7   1:D    1
7   1:D    1
7   2:D    1                 procedure C;
7   2:0    0                 begin end;
7   2:0   12
7   1:0    0         begin end; {B}
7   1:0   12
1   2:D    1         procedure A;
1   2:0    0         begin end;
1   2:0   12
1   3:D    1         procedure D;
1   3:D    1
1   4:D    1                 procedure E;
1   4:0    0                 begin end;
1   4:0   12
1   3:0    0         begin {D}
1   3:0    0
1   3:1    0                 E;
1   3:1    2                 D;
1   3:1    4                 A;
1   3:1    6
1   3:0    6         end;
1   3:0   18
1   3:0   18
1   1:0    0 begin
1   1:0    0
1   1:1    0         A;
1   1:1    4         B;
1   1:1    7
1   1:0    7 end.
```

```
SEGMENT_NAME : CALLSAND     SEG_NUM : 1

TOTAL PROCEDURES : 4      SEG_NUM_INDEX : 0
```

Listing 4-21 (continued)

```
-----------------------------------------------------

PROC #  ROOT_SEG   LEX  PARAMS  DATA  START  OFFSET  SIZE   $START  $EXIT

  1     CALLSAND    0     4      0      2      42      9     042A    0431

 Offset ($):    Mnemonic    Par1  Par2   Hexcode     Opcode


    0(0000):    NOP                      D7          NOP
    1(0001):    NOP                      D7          NOP
    2(0002):    CLP          2           CE02        Call Local Procedure
    4(0004):    CXP          7     1     CD0701      Call External Procedure
    7(0007):    RBP          0           C100        Return Base Procedure
-----------------------------------------------------

PROC #  ROOT_SEG   LEX  PARAMS  DATA  START  OFFSET  SIZE   $START  $EXIT

  2     CALLSAND    1     0      0      2       0      2     0400    0400

 Offset ($):    Mnemonic    Par1  Par2   Hexcode     Opcode


    0(0000):    RNP          0           AD00        Return Non-Base Procedure

-----------------------------------------------------

PROC #  ROOT_SEG   LEX  PARAMS  DATA  START  OFFSET  SIZE   $START  $EXIT

  3     CALLSAND    1     0      0      2      24      8     0418    041E

 Offset ($):    Mnemonic    Par1  Par2   Hexcode     Opcode


    0(0000):    CLP          4           CE04        Call Local Procedure
    2(0002):    CGP          3           CF03        Call Global Procedure
    4(0004):    CGP          2           CF02        Call Global Procedure
    6(0006):    RNP          0           AD00        Return Non-Base Procedure

-----------------------------------------------------

PROC #  ROOT_SEG   LEX  PARAMS  DATA  START  OFFSET  SIZE   $START  $EXIT

  4     CALLSAND    2     0      0      2      12      2     040C    040C

 Offset ($):    Mnemonic    Par1  Par2   Hexcode     Opcode


    0(0000):    RNP          0           AD00        Return Non-Base Procedure
-----------------------------------------------------

SEGMENT_NAME : B          SEG_NUM : 7

TOTAL PROCEDURES : 2     SEG_NUM_INDEX : 1

-----------------------------------------------------
```

Listing 4-21 (continued)

```
PROC #  ROOT_SEG   LEX  PARAMS  DATA  START  OFFSET  SIZE   $START  $EXIT
  1       B          1     0       0     1      12      2     020C    020C
 Offset ($):   Mnemonic   Par1  Par2   Hexcode    Opcode

    0(0000):   RNP          0           AD00       Return Non-Base Procedure
```

```
PROC #  ROOT_SEG   LEX  PARAMS  DATA  START  OFFSET  SIZE   $START  $EXIT
  2       B          2     0       0     1       0      2     0200    0200
 Offset ($):   Mnemonic   Par1  Par2   Hexcode    Opcode

    0(0000):   RNP          0           AD00       Return Non-Base Procedure
```

Listing 4-22

```
1   1:D    1 {$l PRINTER:}
1   1:D    1 (*****************************************************************)
1   1:D    1 (*                                                               *)
1   1:D    1 (*  Listing 4.22: Function calls.                                *)
1   1:D    1 (*                                                               *)
1   1:D    1 (*****************************************************************)
1   1:D    1
1   1:D    1 {$R-}
1   1:D    1 program INVOKING_FUNCTIONS;
1   1:D    3
1   1:D    3 var I : integer;
1   1:D    4
1   2:D    3         function II:integer;
1   2:0    0         begin
1   2:0    0
1   2:1    0                 II := 0;
1   2:1    3
1   2:0    3         end;
1   2:0   16
1   2:0   16
1   1:0    0 begin
1   1:0    0
1   1:1    0         I := II;
1   1:1    8
1   1:0    8 end.
```

SEGMENT_NAME : INVOKING   SEG_NUM : 1

TOTAL PROCEDURES : 2   SEG_NUM_INDEX : 0

Listing 4-22 (continued)

```
PROC #  ROOT_SEG  LEX  PARAMS  DATA  START  OFFSET  SIZE  $START  $EXIT

  1     INVOKING   0     4      2      1      16     10    0210    0218

 Offset ($):   Mnemonic   Parl  Par2   Hexcode    Opcode


    0(0000):   NOP                     D7         NOP
    1(0001):   NOP                     D7         NOP
    2(0002):   PUSH        0           00         Load Constant
    3(0003):   PUSH        0           00         Load Constant
    4(0004):   CLP         2           CE02       Call Local Procedure
    6(0006):   SRO         3           AB03       Store Global Word
    8(0008):   RBP         0           C100       Return Base Procedure
```

```
PROC #  ROOT_SEG  LEX  PARAMS  DATA  START  OFFSET  SIZE  $START  $EXIT

  2     INVOKING   1     4      0      1       0      5    0200    0203

 Offset ($):   Mnemonic   Parl  Par2   Hexcode    Opcode


    0(0000):   PUSH        0           00         Load Constant
    1(0001):   STL         1           CC01       Store Local Word
    3(0003):   RNP         1           AD01       Return Non-Base Procedure
```

Listing 4-23 Pascal Program

```
PROGRAM TEST_DISASSEMBLERS;
VAR I,J:INTEGER;
    B:BOOLEAN;
    C:CHAR;
    R:REAL;
    S:SET OF 1..15;
    P:PACKED ARRAY [0..15] OF BOOLEAN;
   RS:PACKED RECORD

         I:INTEGER;
         B:BOOLEAN;
         C:CHAR;
         A:PACKED ARRAY [0..5] OF CHAR;
        C2:CHAR;
         R:REAL;

       END;


PROCEDURE TSTPROC; BEGIN END;
FUNCTION TSTFUNCT:INTEGER;
BEGIN TSTFUNCT := 0; END;


BEGIN

    I:=0;
    J:=I;
    B:=FALSE;
    C:= 'A';
    R:=1.1;
    S:= [1,2,3,15];
    R:= I + J * 5.5 - (6.6 / I);
    IF (R<=I) THEN J := TRUNC(R);
    WHILE (I < 10) DO I := I+1;
    FOR J := 0 TO 100 DO R := R + 0.01;
    REPEAT

       I := I - 1;

    UNTIL I <= 0;

    FOR I := 0 TO 15 DO P [I] := FALSE;
    RS.I := 0;
    RS.B := TRUE;
    RS.C := 'A';
    RS.A [3] := RS.C;
    RS.R := 1.1;
    RS.C2 := RS.A [3];
    TSTPROC;
    I := TSTFUNCT;

END.
```

Listing 4-24 Dump p-Code

```
DUMPCODE of file TEST.DIS.CODE

Segment: No: Size: Addr: SegKind: Text:

TESTDISA  0  0114  0001  LINKED

Dump of Segment Tale for segment 0
  SegNo = 1    Num Procs = 3
    1:  010A    2:  000A    3:  001A

Listing of disassembled code for segment 0
Begin Proc:
0000:  AD 00              RNP    0
               Data Segment Size: 0000
               Parameter Size:    0000
               Exit IC:           0000
               Entry IC:          0000
               Lex Level: 1, Procedure No.: 2
Begin Proc:
000C:  00                 SLDC   0
000D:  CC 01              STL    1
000F:  AD 01              RNP    1
               Data Segment Size: 0000
               Parameter Size:    0004
               Exit IC:           000F
               Entry IC:          000C
               Lex Level: 1, Procedure No.: 3
Begin Proc:
001C:  D7                 NOP
001D:  D7                 NOP
001E:  00                 SLDC   0
001F:  AB 04              SRO    4
0021:  EB                 SLDO   4
0022:  AB 03              SRO    3
0024:  00                 SLDC   0
0025:  AB 05              SRO    5
0027:  41                 SLDC   65
0028:  AB 06              SRO    6
002A:  A5 07              LAO    7
002C:  B3 02              LDC    2,8C3FCDCC
0032:  BD 02              STM    2
0034:  C7 F2 7F           LDCI   32754
0037:  91                 NGI
0038:  01                 SLDC   1
0039:  A0 01              ADJ    1
003B:  AB 09              SRO    9
003D:  A5 07              LAO    7
003F:  EB                 SLDO   4
0040:  EA                 SLDO   3
0041:  B3 02 00           LDC    2,B0400000
0048:  89                 FLO
0049:  90                 MPR
004A:  89                 FLO
004B:  83                 ADR
004C:  B3 02              LDC    2,D3403333
0052:  EB                 SLDO   4
0053:  8A                 FLT
0054:  87                 DVR
0055:  96                 SBR
0056:  BD 02              STM    2
0058:  A5 07              LAO    7
```

Listing 4-24 (continued)

```
005A:  BC 02            LDM   2
005C:  EB               SLDO  4
005D:  8A               FLT
005E:  B4 02            LEQ-  2
0060:  A1 08            FJP   006A
0062:  A5 07            LAO   7
0064:  BC 02            LDM   2
0066:  9E 17            CSP   ROUND
0068:  AB 03            SRO   3
006A:  EB               SLDO  4
006B:  0A               SLDC  10
006C:  C9               LESI
006D:  A1 07            FJP   0076
006F:  EB               SLDO  4
0070:  01               SLDC  1
0071:  82               ADI
0072:  AB 04            SRO   4
0074:  B9 F6            UJP   -10
0076:  00               SLDC  0
0077:  AB 03            SRO   3
0079:  64               SLDC  100
007A:  AB 13            SRO   19
007C:  EA               SLDO  3
007D:  A9 13            LDO   19
007F:  C8               LEQI
0080:  A1 16            FJP   0098
0082:  A5 07            LAO   7
0084:  A5 07            LAO   7
0086:  BC 02            LDM   2
0088:  B3 02            LDC   2,233C0AD7
008E:  83               ADR
008F:  BD 02            STM   2
0091:  EA               SLDO  3
0092:  01               SLDC  1
0093:  82               ADI
0094:  AB 03            SRO   3
0096:  B9 F4            UJP   -12
0098:  EB               SLDO  4
0099:  01               SLDC  1
009A:  95               SBI
009B:  AB 04            SRO   4
009D:  EB               SLDO  4
009E:  00               SLDC  0
009F:  C8               LEQI
00A0:  A1 F2            FJP   -14
00A2:  00               SLDC  0
00A3:  AB 04            SRO   4
00A5:  0F               SLDC  15
00A6:  AB 13            SRO   19
00A8:  EB               SLDO  4
00A9:  A9 13            LDO   19
00AB:  C8               LEQI
00AC:  A1 12            FJP   00C0
00AE:  A5 0A            LAO   10
00B0:  EB               SLDO  4
00B1:  00               SLDC  0
00B2:  0F               SLDC  15
00B3:  88               CHK
00B4:  C0 10 01         IXP   16, 1
00B7:  00               SLDC  0
00B8:  BB               STP
```

Listing 4-24 (continued)

```
00B9:  EB               SLDO   4
00BA:  01               SLDC   1
00BB:  82               ADI
00BC:  AB 04            SRO    4
00BE:  B9 F0            UJP    -16
00C0:  00               SLDC   0
00C1:  AB 0B            SRO    11
00C3:  A5 0C            LAO    12
00C5:  01               SLDC   1
00C6:  00               SLDC   0
00C7:  01               SLDC   1
00C8:  BB               STP
00C9:  A5 0C            LAO    12
00CB:  08               SLDC   8
00CC:  08               SLDC   8
00CD:  41               SLDC   65
00CE:  BB               STP
00CF:  A5 0D            LAO    13
00D1:  03               SLDC   3
00D2:  00               SLDC   0
00D3:  05               SLDC   5
00D4:  88               CHK
00D5:  A5 0C            LAO    12
00D7:  08               SLDC   8
00D8:  08               SLDC   8
00D9:  BA               LDP
00DA:  BF               STB
00DB:  A5 11            LAO    17
00DD:  B3 02 00         LDC    2,8C3FCDCC
00E4:  BD 02            STM    2
00E6:  A5 0D            LAO    13
00E8:  03               SLDC   3
00E9:  00               SLDC   0
00EA:  05               SLDC   5
00EB:  88               CHK
00EC:  BE               LDB
00ED:  AB 10            SRO    16
00EF:  CE 02            CLP    2
00F1:  00               SLDC   0
00F2:  00               SLDC   0
00F3:  CE 03            CLP    3
00F5:  AB 04            SRO    4
00F7:  C1 00            RBP    0
          JTAB[-16] = 00A8
          JTAB[-14] = 0098
          JTAB[-12] = 007C
          JTAB[-10] = 006A
          Data Segment Size: 0022
          Parameter Size:    0004
          Exit IC:           00F7
          Entry IC:          001C
          Lex Level: 0, Procedure No.: 1
```

Listing 4-25 DECODE

```
SEGMENT_NAME : TESTDISA     SEG_NUM : 1

TOTAL PROCEDURES : 3      SEG_NUM_INDEX : 0


PROC #  ROOT_SEG    LEX  PARAMS  DATA  START  OFFSET  SIZE   $START  $EXIT

  1     TESTDISA     0      4     34     1      28     221    021C    02F7

 Offset ($):   Mnemonic   Par1  Par2   Hexcode    Opcode

    0(0000):   NOP                     D7         NOP
    1(0001):   NOP                     D7         NOP
    2(0002):   PUSH          0         00         Load Constant
    3(0003):   SRO           4         AB04       Store Global Word
    5(0005):   SLDO          4         EB         Load Global Word
    6(0006):   SRO           3         AB03       Store Global Word
    8(0008):   PUSH          0         00         Load Constant
    9(0009):   SRO           5         AB05       Store Global Word
   11(000B):   PUSH         65         41         Load Constant
   12(000C):   SRO           6         AB06       Store Global Word
   14(000E):   LAO           7         A507       Load Global Address
   16(0010):   LDC           2 16268   B3028C3F   Load Multiple Constant
                            -13107         CDCC
   22(0016):   STM           2         BD02       Store Multiple Word
   24(0018):   LDCI      32754         C7F27F     Load Constant
   27(001B):   NGI                     91         2-s Complement
   28(001C):   PUSH          1         01         Load Constant
   29(001D):   ADJ           1         A001       Adjust Set
   31(001F):   SRO           9         AB09       Store Global Word
   33(0021):   LAO           7         A507       Load Global Address
   35(0023):   SLDO          4         EB         Load Global Word
   36(0024):   SLDO          3         EA         Load Global Word
   37(0025):   LDC           2 16560   B302B040   Load Multiple Constant
                                 0         0000
   44(002C):   FLO                     89         Float (TOS) Integer -> Real
   45(002D):   MPR                     90         Multiply Real
   46(002E):   FLO                     89         Float (TOS) Integer -> Real
   47(002F):   ADR                     83         Add Real
   48(0030):   LDC           2 16595   B302D340   Load Multiple Constant
                             13107         3333
   54(0036):   SLDO          4         EB         Load Global Word
   55(0037):   FLT                     8A         Float (TOS-1) Integer -> Real
   56(0038):   DVR                     87         Divide Real
   57(0039):   SBR                     96         Subtract Real
   58(003A):   STM           2         BD02       Store Multiple Word
   60(003C):   LAO           7         A507       Load Global Address
   62(003E):   LDM           2         BC02       Load Multiple Word
   64(0040):   SLDO          4         EB         Load Global Word
   65(0041):   FLT                     8A         Float (TOS-1) Integer -> Real
   66(0042):   LEQREAL       2         B402       Compare
   68(0044):   FJP          78         A108       Jump If False
   70(0046):   LAO           7         A507       Load Global Address
   72(0048):   LDM           2         BC02       Load Multiple Word
```

Listing 4-25 (continued)

```
 74(004A):   RND       23          9E17        Call Standard Procedure
 76(004C):   SRO        3          AB03        Store Global Word
 78(004E):   SLDO       4          EB          Load Global Word
 79(004F):   PUSH      10          0A          Load Constant
 80(0050):   LESI                  C9          Compare
 81(0051):   FJP       90          A107        Jump If False
 83(0053):   SLDO       4          EB          Load Global Word
 84(0054):   PUSH       1          01          Load Constant
 85(0055):   ADI                   82          Add
 86(0056):   SRO        4          AB04        Store Global Word
 88(0058):   UJP       78          B9F6        Unconditional Jump
 90(005A):   PUSH       0          00          Load Constant
 91(005B):   SRO        3          AB03        Store Global Word
 93(005D):   PUSH     100          64          Load Constant
 94(005E):   SRO       19          AB13        Store Global Word
 96(0060):   SLDO       3          EA          Load Global Word
 97(0061):   LDO       19          A913        Load Global Word
 99(0063):   LEQI                  C8          Compare
100(0064):   FJP      124          A116        Jump If False
102(0066):   LAO        7          A507        Load Global Address
104(0068):   LAO        7          A507        Load Global Address
106(006A):   LDM        2          BC02        Load Multiple Word
108(006C):   LDC        2 15395    B302233C    Load Multiple Constant
                       -10486         0AD7
114(0072):   ADR                   83          Add Real
115(0073):   STM        2          BD02        Store Multiple Word
117(0075):   SLDO       3          EA          Load Global Word
118(0076):   PUSH       1          01          Load Constant
119(0077):   ADI                   82          Add
120(0078):   SRO        3          AB03        Store Global Word
122(007A):   UJP       96          B9F4        Unconditional Jump
124(007C):   SLDO       4          EB          Load Global Word
125(007D):   PUSH       1          01          Load Constant
126(007E):   SBI                   95          Subtract
127(007F):   SRO        4          AB04        Store Global Word
129(0081):   SLDO       4          EB          Load Global Word
130(0082):   PUSH       0          00          Load Constant
131(0083):   LEQI                  C8          Compare
132(0084):   FJP      124          A1F2        Jump If False
134(0086):   PUSH       0          00          Load Constant
135(0087):   SRO        4          AB04        Store Global Word
137(0089):   PUSH      15          0F          Load Constant
138(008A):   SRO       19          AB13        Store Global Word
140(008C):   SLDO       4          EB          Load Global Word
141(008D):   LDO       19          A913        Load Global Word
143(008F):   LEQI                  C8          Compare
144(0090):   FJP      164          A112        Jump If False
146(0092):   LAO       10          A50A        Load Global Address
148(0094):   SLDO       4          EB          Load Global Word
149(0095):   PUSH       0          00          Load Constant
150(0096):   PUSH      15          0F          Load Constant
151(0097):   CHK                   88          Range Check
152(0098):   IXP       16      1   C01001      Index Packed Array
155(009B):   PUSH       0          00          Load Constant
156(009C):   STP                   BB          Store Packed Field
157(009D):   SLDO       4          EB          Load Global Word
158(009E):   PUSH       1          01          Load Constant
159(009F):   ADI                   82          Add
160(00A0):   SRO        4          AB04        Store Global Word
162(00A2):   UJP      140          B9F0        Unconditional Jump
164(00A4):   PUSH       0          00          Load Constant
```

Listing 4-25 (continued)

```
  165(00A5):  SRO        11          AB0B       Store Global Word
  167(00A7):  LAO        12          A50C       Load Global Address
  169(00A9):  PUSH        1          01         Load Constant
  170(00AA):  PUSH        0          00         Load Constant
  171(00AB):  PUSH        1          01         Load Constant
  172(00AC):  STP                    BB         Store Packed Field
  173(00AD):  LAO        12          A50C       Load Global Address
  175(00AF):  PUSH        8          08         Load Constant
  176(00B0):  PUSH        8          08         Load Constant
  177(00B1):  PUSH       65          41         Load Constant
  178(00B2):  STP                    BB         Store Packed Field
  179(00B3):  LAO        13          A50D       Load Global Address
  181(00B5):  PUSH        3          03         Load Constant
  182(00B6):  PUSH        0          00         Load Constant
  183(00B7):  PUSH        5          05         Load Constant
  184(00B8):  CHK                    88         Range Check
  185(00B9):  LAO        12          A50C       Load Global Address
  187(00BB):  PUSH        8          08         Load Constant
  188(00BC):  PUSH        8          08         Load Constant
  189(00BD):  LDP                    BA         Load Packed Field
  190(00BE):  STB                    BF         Store Byte
  191(00BF):  LAO        17          A511       Load Global Address
  193(00C1):  LDC         2 16268    B3028C3F   Load Multiple Constant
                            -13107       CDCC
  200(00C8):  STM         2          BD02       Store Multiple Word
  202(00CA):  LAO        13          A50D       Load Global Address
  204(00CC):  PUSH        3          03         Load Constant
  205(00CD):  PUSH        0          00         Load Constant
  206(00CE):  PUSH        5          05         Load Constant
  207(00CF):  CHK                    88         Range Check
  208(00D0):  LDB                    BE         Load Byte
  209(00D1):  SRO        16          AB10       Store Global Word
  211(00D3):  CLP         2          CE02       Call Local Procedure
  213(00D5):  PUSH        0          00         Load Constant
  214(00D6):  PUSH        0          00         Load Constant
  215(00D7):  CLP         3          CE03       Call Local Procedure
  217(00D9):  SRO         4          AB04       Store Global Word
  219(00DB):  RBP         0          C100       Return Base Procedure
```

```
PROC #  ROOT_SEG   LEX  PARAMS  DATA  START  OFFSET  SIZE   $START  $EXIT

  2     TESTDISA    1      0      0     1       0      2     0200    0200

 Offset ($):  Mnemonic   Par1  Par2   Hexcode    Opcode

    0(0000):  RNP         0           AD00       Return Non-Base Procedure
```

```
PROC #  ROOT_SEG   LEX  PARAMS  DATA  START  OFFSET  SIZE   $START  $EXIT

  3     TESTDISA    1      4      0     1      12      5     020C    020F

 Offset ($):  Mnemonic   Par1  Par2   Hexcode    Opcode

    0(0000):  PUSH        0           00         Load Constant
    1(0001):  STL         1           CC01       Store Local Word
    3(0003):  RNP         1           AD01       Return Non-Base Procedure
```

Listing 4-26 Pascal Disk Utility (PDQ)

```
MM P-CODE ASSEMBLER [1.1]

                              .LEX    0
                              .PARAM  4
                              .DATA   34
                              .PROC   1
00:D7                              NOP
01:D7                              NOP
02:00                              SLDC    0
03:AB 04                           SRO     4
05:EB                              SLDO    4
06:AB 03                           SRO     3
08:00                              SLDC    0
09:AB 05                           SRO     5
0B:41                              SLDC    65
0C:AB 06                           SRO     6
0E:A5 07                           LAO     7
10:B3 02                           LDC     2,
12:  8C 3F                                  16268
14:  CD CC                                  -13107
16:BD 02                           STM     2
18:C7 F2 7F                        LDCI    32754
1B:91                              NGI
1C:01                              SLDC    1
1D:A0 01                           ADJ     1
1F:AB 09                           SRO     9
21:A5 07                           LAO     7
23:EB                              SLDO    4
24:EA                              SLDO    3
25:B3 02                           LDC     2,
28:  B0 40                                  16560
2A:  00 00                                  0
2C:89                              FLO
2D:90                              MPR
2E:89                              FLO
2F:83                              ADR
30:B3 02                           LDC     2,
32:  D3 40                                  16595
34:  33 33                                  13107
36:EB                              SLDO    4
37:8A                              FLT
38:87                              DVR
39:96                              SBR
3A:BD 02                           STM     2
3C:A5 07                           LAO     7
3E:BC 02                           LDM     2
40:EB                              SLDO    4
41:8A                              FLT
42:B4 02                           LEQREAL
44:A1 **                           FJP     P106
46:A5 07                           LAO     7
48:BC 02                           LDM     2
4A:9E 17                           TNC(P)
4C:AB 03                           SRO     3
4E:EB                       P106   SLDO    4
4F:0A                              SLDC    10
50:C9                              LESI
51:A1 **                           FJP     P118
53:EB                              SLDO    4
54:01                              SLDC    1
55:82                              ADI
```

Listing 4-26 (continued)

```
56:AB 04                    SRO     4
58:B9 F6                    UJP     P106
5A:00              P118     SLDC    0
5B:AB 03                    SRO     3
5D:64                       SLDC    100
5E:AB 13                    SRO     19
60:EA              P124     SLDO    3
61:A9 13                    LDO     19
63:C8                       LEQI
64:A1 **                    FJP     P152
66:A5 07                    LAO     7
68:A5 07                    LAO     7
6A:BC 02                    LDM     2
6C:B3 02                    LDC     2,
6E:  23 3C                           15395
70:  0A D7                           -10486
72:83                       ADR
73:BD 02                    STM     2
75:EA                       SLDO    3
76:01                       SLDC    1
77:82                       ADI
78:AB 03                    SRO     3
7A:B9 F4                    UJP     P124
7C:EB              P152     SLDO    4
7D:01                       SLDC    1
7E:95                       SBI
7F:AB 04                    SRO     4
81:EB                       SLDO    4
82:00                       SLDC    0
83:C8                       LEQI
84:A1 F2                    FJP     P152
86:00                       SLDC    0
87:AB 04                    SRO     4
89:0F                       SLDC    15
8A:AB 13                    SRO     19
8C:EB              P168     SLDO    4
8D:A9 13                    LDO     19
8F:C8                       LEQI
90:A1 **                    FJP     P192
92:A5 0A                    LAO     10
94:EB                       SLDO    4
95:00                       SLDC    0
96:0F                       SLDC    15
97:88                       CHK
98:C0 10 01                 IXP     16,1
9B:00                       SLDC    0
9C:BB                       STP
9D:EB                       SLDO    4
9E:01                       SLDC    1
9F:82                       ADI
A0:AB 04                    SRO     4
A2:B9 F0                    UJP     P168
A4:00              P192     SLDC    0
A5:AB 0B                    SRO     11
A7:A5 0C                    LAO     12
A9:01                       SLDC    1
AA:00                       SLDC    0
AB:01                       SLDC    1
AC:BB                       STP
AD:A5 0C                    LAO     12
AF:08                       SLDC    8
```

Listing 4-26 (continued)

```
B0:08                    SLDC    8
B1:41                    SLDC    65
B2:BB                    STP
B3:A5 0D                 LAO     13
B5:03                    SLDC    3
B6:00                    SLDC    0
B7:05                    SLDC    5
B8:88                    CHK
B9:A5 0C                 LAO     12
BB:08                    SLDC    8
BC:08                    SLDC    8
BD:BA                    LDP
BE:BF                    STB
BF:A5 11                 LAO     17
C1:B3 02                 LDC     2,
C4:  8C 3F                        16268
C6:  CD CC                        -13107
C8:BD 02                 STM     2
CA:A5 0D                 LAO     13
CC:03                    SLDC    3
CD:00                    SLDC    0
CE:05                    SLDC    5
CF:88                    CHK
D0:BE                    LDB
D1:AB 10                 SRO     16
D3:CE 02                 CLP     2
D5:00                    SLDC    0
D6:00                    SLDC    0
D7:CE 03                 CLP     3
D9:AB 04                 SRO     4
DB:C1 00           EXIT  RBP     0


                    .LEX   1
                    .PARAM 0
                    .DATA  0
                    .PROC  2
F0:AD 00           EXIT  RNP     0


                    .LEX   1
                    .PARAM 4
                    .DATA  0
                    .PROC  3
FC:00                    SLDC    0
FD:CC 01                 STL     1
00:AD 01           EXIT  RNP     1


                         .END
0 ERRORS FLAGGED ON THIS ASSEMBLY
```

Section Two

Internal Operation of the p-Machine

5
An Explanation of the P-code Instructions

In this section the various p-codes will be described. Each p-code will be discussed separately in a fashion not unlike that used by various manuals on assembly language programming.

The Apple Pascal "p-Machine" (the hardware that the p-code interpreter emulates) contains eight registers. These registers are:

SP: Stack pointer. This is a pointer to the top of the evaluation stack. It is used to pass parameters, return function values and as an operand source for several of the p-Machine instructions. Data is pushed onto the stack with the load instructions and popped off of the stack with the store instructions. On the 6502 (and the Apple in particular) the 6502 stack pointer and the p-Machine stack pointer are one and the same.

IPC: Interpreter program counter. This register points at the address of the next p-Code instruction to be fetched. In the 6502, the IPC register is maintained as a pair of zero page memory locations so that p-codes and any data following the instructions is easily obtained by using the indirect, post-indexed by Y addressing mode.

SEG: A pointer to the procedure dictionary of the segment to which the currently executing procedure belongs. On the 6502 SEG is maintained as a pair of zero page memory locations.

JTAB: A pointer to the jump table for the currently executing procedure. This pointer is maintained as two zero page memory locations on 6502 versions of the p-Machine.

KP: Program stack pointer. This is a pointer to the top of the program stack. Storage for variables, as well as space for any SEGMENT PROCEDURES are allocated on the program stack. The program stack starts in high memory and grows downward. On 6502 versions of the p-Machine, KP is maintained as a pair of zero page memory locations.

MP: Markstack pointer. This is a pointer to the base of the activation record for the currently executing procedure. Its value is always greater than KP and the space between KP and MP is the number of bytes allocated for local variables. On the 6502, MP is maintained as a pair of zero page memory locations.

NP: New pointer. This is a pointer to the p-Machine heap. The p-Machine heap starts in low memory and grows upward. The heap is where all dynamic variables are maintained. Dynamic variables are allocated with the NEW procedure and de-allocated with the RELEASE procedure. The heap is also used to allocate storage for user hardware drivers using the ATTACH.BIOS routines. On the Apple II, NP is maintained as a pair of zero page memory locations.

BASE: This is a pointer to the activation record of the most recently invoked base procedure. A base procedure is a main procedure such as the main program in a program listing or the latest invokation of a UNIT. Global variables are accessed by indexing off of the BASE register. BASE is maintained as a pair of zero page memory locations on the Apple II.

For a complete description of how these registers are used and how the p-Machine operates you should consult Appendix B of the Apple Pascal Operating System Reference Manual. Be ye forewarned, this material is not easy reading for someone who isn't well-versed in compiler theory and in fact it probably won't make sense at all. An understanding of how the p-Machine actually operates (in terms of variable allocation, procedure calls, et al.) is not required to understand how the individual p-codes function, so a "human-engineered" description of the operation of the p-Machine will not be presented here. That, alas, will be delegated to a future manual.

Instruction Formats

All of the p-code instructions consist of a one-byte opcode followed by zero, one, two, or more bytes. In general, parameters to an instruction take one of five forms. They are:

UB: Unsigned byte. This type of parameter is a single byte that contains a value in the range 0..255.

SB: Signed byte. This type of parameter is a single byte that is used to represent values in the range −128..127. The value is stored in the standard two's complement format with bit #7 being used as the sign bit.

DB: Identical to UB except the value is always in the range 0..127.

B: Big parameter. This is a variable length parameter that is one byte long if it is being used to represent values in the range 0..127 and two bytes long if it is being used to represent values in the range 128..32767. If an instruction uses a parameter of this type the length of the B parameter is determined by looking at the first byte. If bit #7 is clear, then this parameter is a single byte representing a value in the range 0..127. If the high order bit (bit #7) is set, then the parameter is two bytes long. The high order bit of the first byte is cleared and this byte is used as the high order byte of the resulting parameter. The second byte of the parameter is used as the low order byte of the parameter value.

Examples:

$01 — treated as the value $01
$7F — treated as the value $7F
$8100 — treated as the value $100
$FFFF — treated as the value $7FFF

Exceptions to these parameter types will be noted where applicable.

It will be assumed (as previously mentioned) that the reader is somewhat familiar with the operation of a stack-architecture machine. In particular it is assumed that the reader understands such terms as stack frames; activation records; static and dynamic links; and local, global, and intermediate variables. The author apologizes for not attempting to describe these concepts, but such a discussion would require more space than the rest of the manual takes up!

Constant (Immediate) Loads

Syntax: **SLDC UB (UB is a constant in the range 0..127)**
Opcode: **00-127 ($00-$7F)**
Operation: **Push opcode onto stack**

The SLDC instruction (Short LoaD Constant) is used to load values in the range 0..127 onto the evaluation stack. The SLDC instruction is exactly one byte long. The high order bit of the instruction is zero and the low order seven bits contain the data to be pushed onto the p-Machine evaluation stack. Since only 16-bit words may be pushed onto the evaluation stack, this instruction pushes two bytes; the low order byte being pushed is the opcode itself, the high order byte pushed is a zero.

The purpose of the SLDC instruction is to help reduce the size of the Pascal operating system. By performing a static analysis of the system the folks at UCSD determined that the constants used most often were in the range 0..127 (this also corresponds, strangely enough, to the ASCII character set). Normal load immediate instructions require three bytes—one for the opcode and two for the data to be pushed. By using this special form of the load constant instruction, the Apple Pascal compiler is able to save two bytes every time a constant in the range 0..127 is used. (Historical note: As it turns out, the SLDC opcode has been severely restricted in the version IV.0 of the UCSD Pascal system. The folks at Softech Microsystems have completely redone the p-code interpreter and the new SLDC instruction only loads the values in the range 0..31. The 96 opcodes freed up were used to optimize other operations in the UCSD p-machine. This information, however, only applies to the version IV.0 of the UCSD Pascal system, it does not apply to the Apple Pascal system).

SLDC UB OPERATION:

1. BEFORE

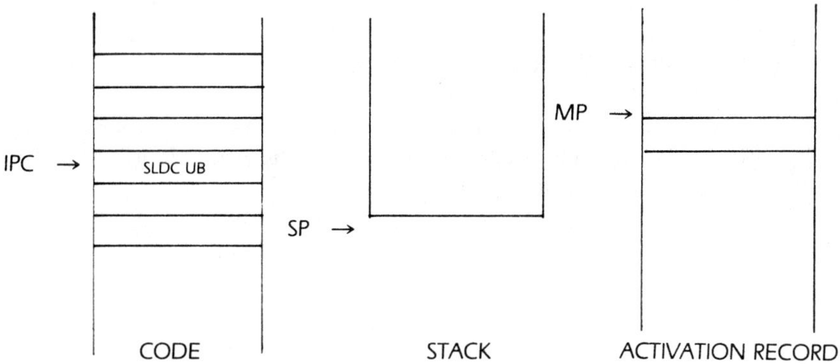

2. ACTION

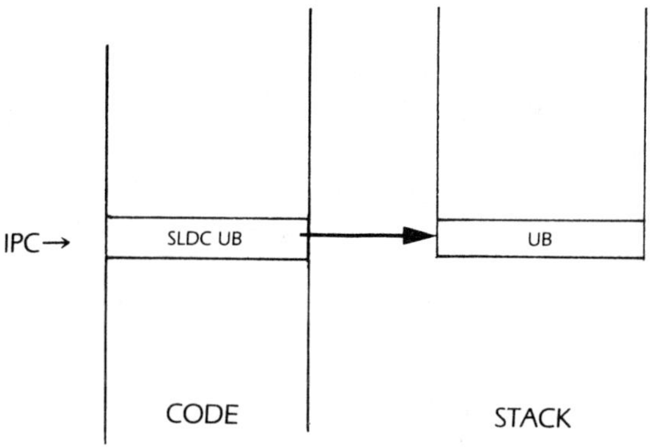

COPY OPCODE ONTO
TOP OF STACK

3. AFTER

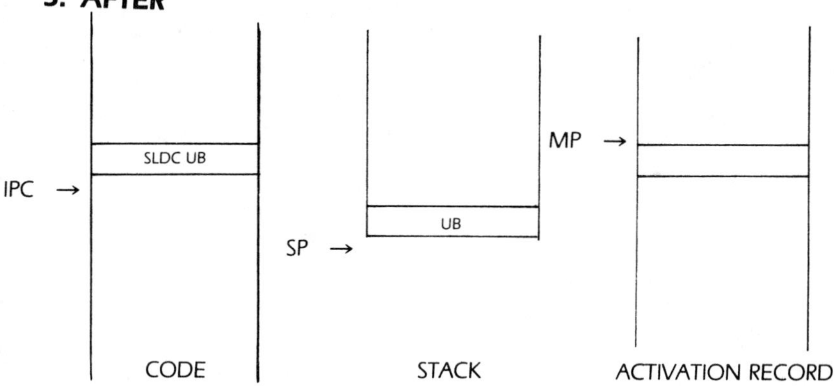

Syntax: LDCN
Opcode: 159 ($9F)
Operation: Push NIL (zero) onto the stack

LDCN (load constant nil) is a single byte instruction that pushes zero onto the 6502 stack. This instruction is emitted by the Apple Pascal compiler whenever you set a pointer to NIL.

LDCN OPERATION:

1. BEFORE

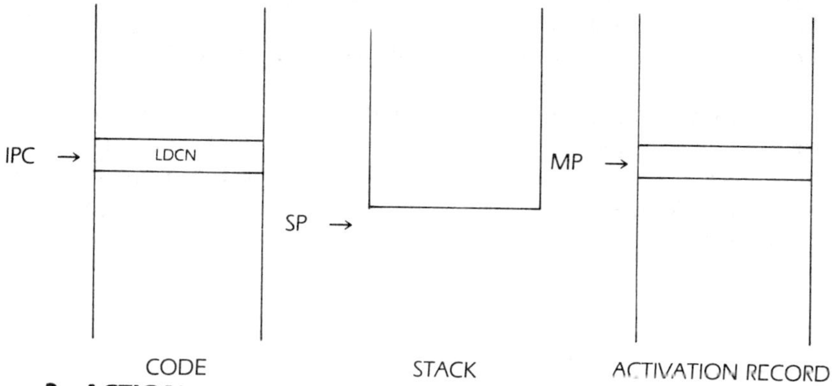

2. ACTION

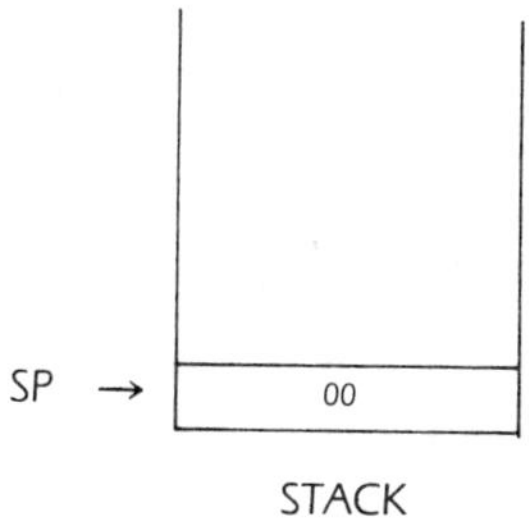

PUSH A ZERO WORD ONTO THE STACK

3. AFTER

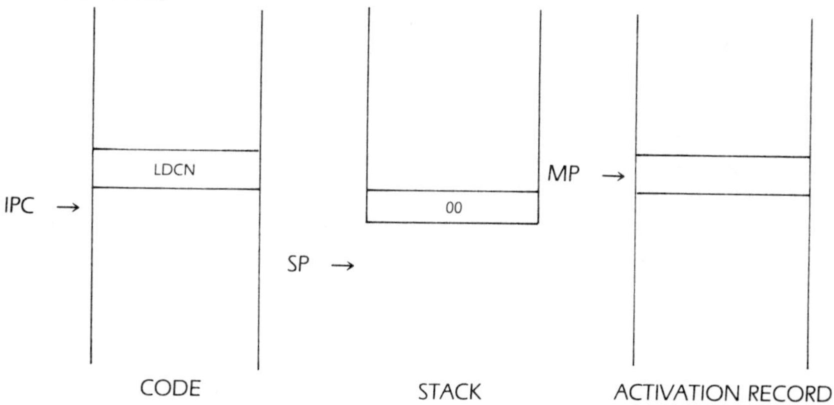

Syntax: **LDCI W (W is a value in the range −32768..32767)**
Opcode: **199 ($C7)**
Operation: **Pushes the one-word value W onto the stack**

LDCI (load constant immediate) pushes the one-word constant that follows the opcode onto the stack. This instruction is used to load constants that are greater than 127 onto the evaluation stack. The LDCI instruction is three bytes long — one byte for the opcode followed by two bytes of immediate data.

LDCI W OPERATION:

1. BEFORE

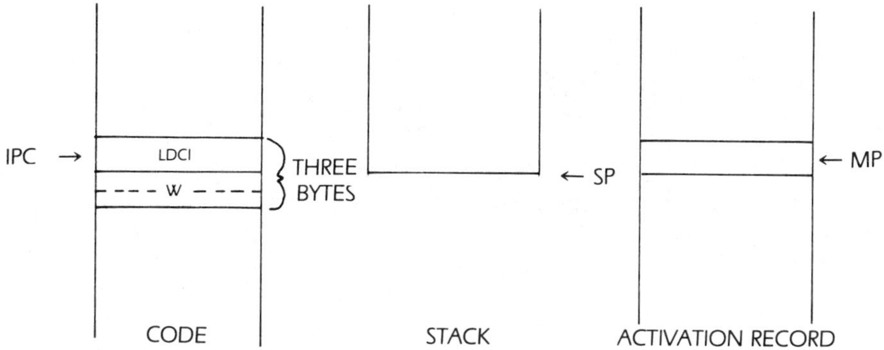

2. ACTION

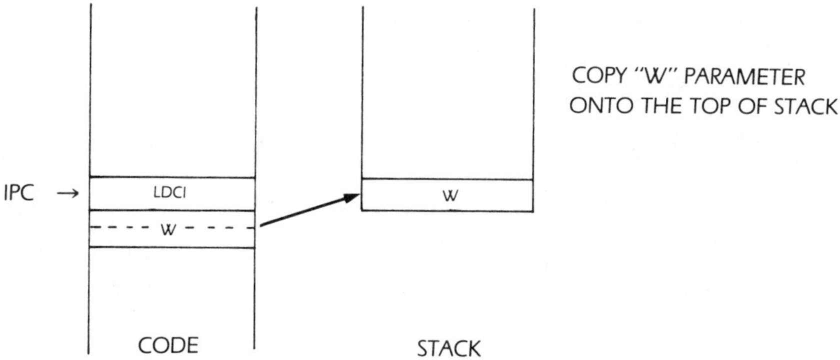

3. AFTER

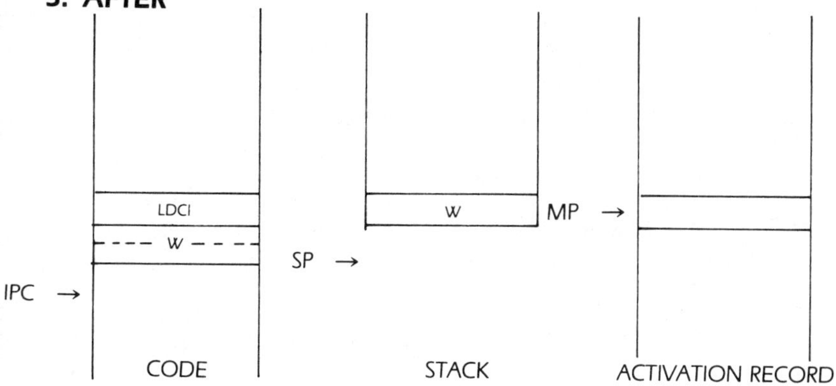

Local Loads and Stores

Syntax: SLDL n (n is in the range 1..16)
Opcode: 216..231 ($D8..$E7)
Operation: Loads a local variable onto the evaluation stack

The SLDL (Short LoaD Local) instruction is used to load a local variable onto the stack. The SLDL 1 instruction loads the first word of local storage onto the stack, the SLDL 2 instruction loads the second word of local storage onto the stack, etc. The SLDL instruction is one byte long with sixteen different opcodes being used for each local load instruction. The SLDL instruction was designed to help reduce the amount of code generated by the Apple Pascal compiler. The first 16 (or so) variables in a procedure or function will be loaded from memory using this instruction, so scalar variables you use often should be declared as one of the first 16 defined variables.

How the SLDL Instruction Works

Whenever an SLDL instruction is executed the variable number (in the range (1..16) is doubled and this value is subtracted from the MP register to obtain the address of the variable to be loaded. The two bytes pointed at by this address calculation are pushed onto the evaluation stack.

SLDL n OPERATION:

1. BEFORE

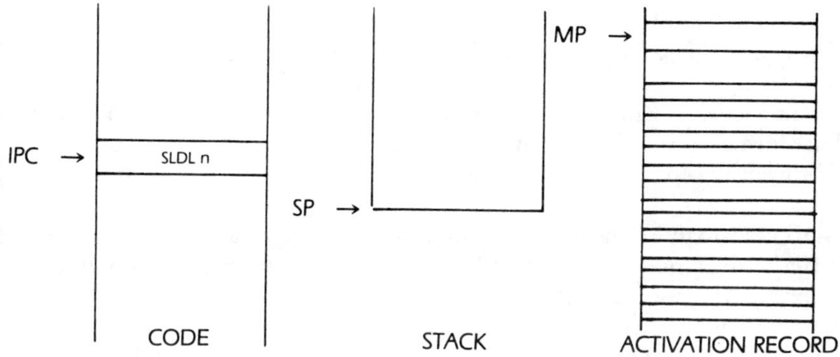

2. ACTION

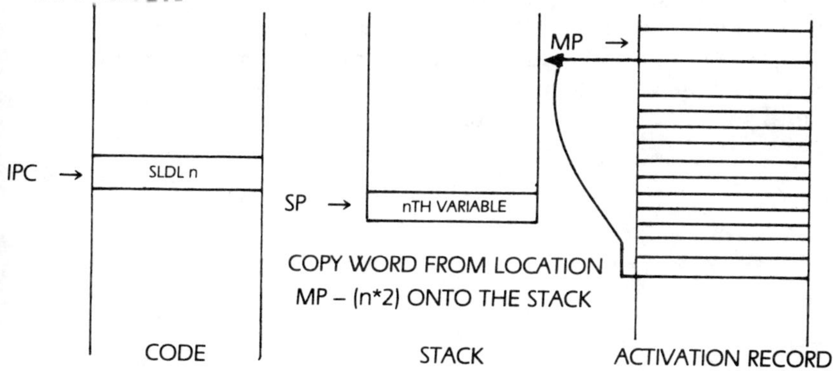

3. AFTER

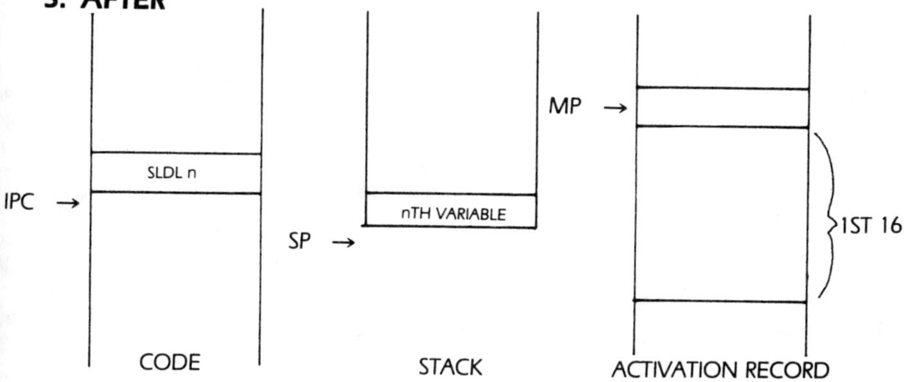

Syntax: **LDL B**
Opcode: **202 ($CA)**
Operation: **Load a local variable onto the evaluation stack**

Loads a local variable onto the evaluation stack. The LDL instruction is the long form of the SLDL instruction. It pushes scalar variables onto the stack that have an offset of 17..32767 words from the current activation record.

LDL is a variable-length instruction. If it is pushing a variable with a word offset in the range 17..127 the LDL instruction is two bytes long with the second byte containing the word offset. If the LDL instruction is being used to push a variable with an offset in the range 128..32767 then the instruction is three bytes long with the word offset occupying the second two bytes (see the description of the "B" type parameter). Once the B parameter is fetched, it is multiplied by two and this value is then subtracted from the value in the MP register. The resulting difference is the address in memory of the variable in question. The two bytes pointed at by this address are pushed onto the evaluation stack.

LDL B OPERATION:

1. BEFORE

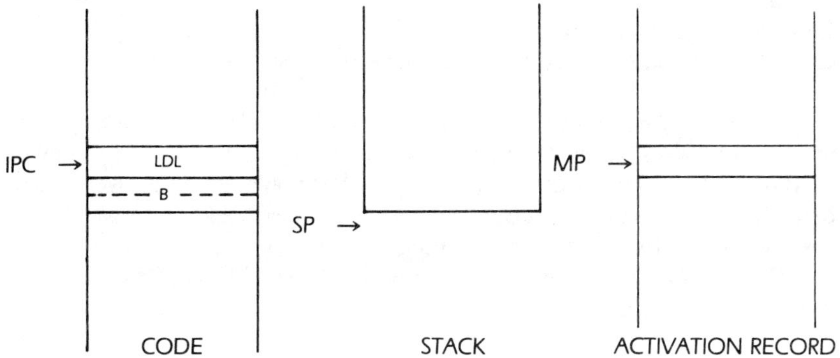

2. ACTION

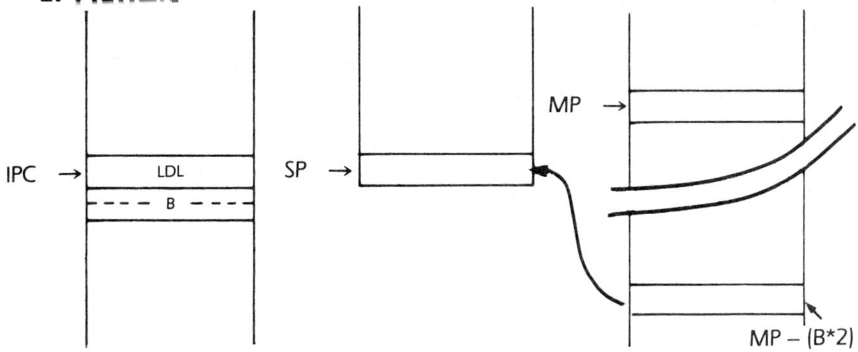

COPY WORD AT ADDRESS MP – (B*2) ONTO TOP OF STACK

3. AFTER

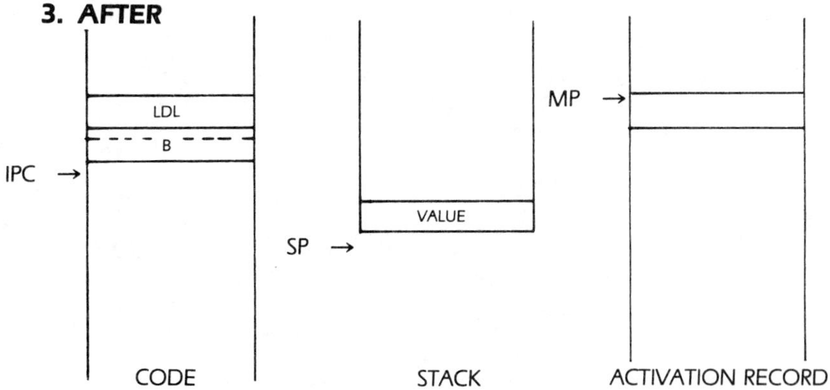

Syntax: **LLA B**
Opcode: **198 ($C6)**
Operation: **Loads the address of a local variable onto stack**

LLA (Load Local Address) loads the address of a local variable (as opposed to the actual data stored at that address) onto the evaluation stack. LLA is used when assigning pointer variables and when you are passing parameters by reference. Like the LDL instruction, LLA is a variable length instruction. It is two bytes long if you are pushing the address of a scalar with offset 0..127 and three bytes long if you are pushing the address of a scalar with word offset 128..32767.

The operation of the LLA instruction is similar to that of LDL—only simpler. After fetching the instruction operand (one or two bytes, see the description of "B" type parameters) the LLA instruction subtracts the operand value from the value contained in the MP register and pushes the difference. This difference is the address of the desired local variable.

LLA B OPERATION:

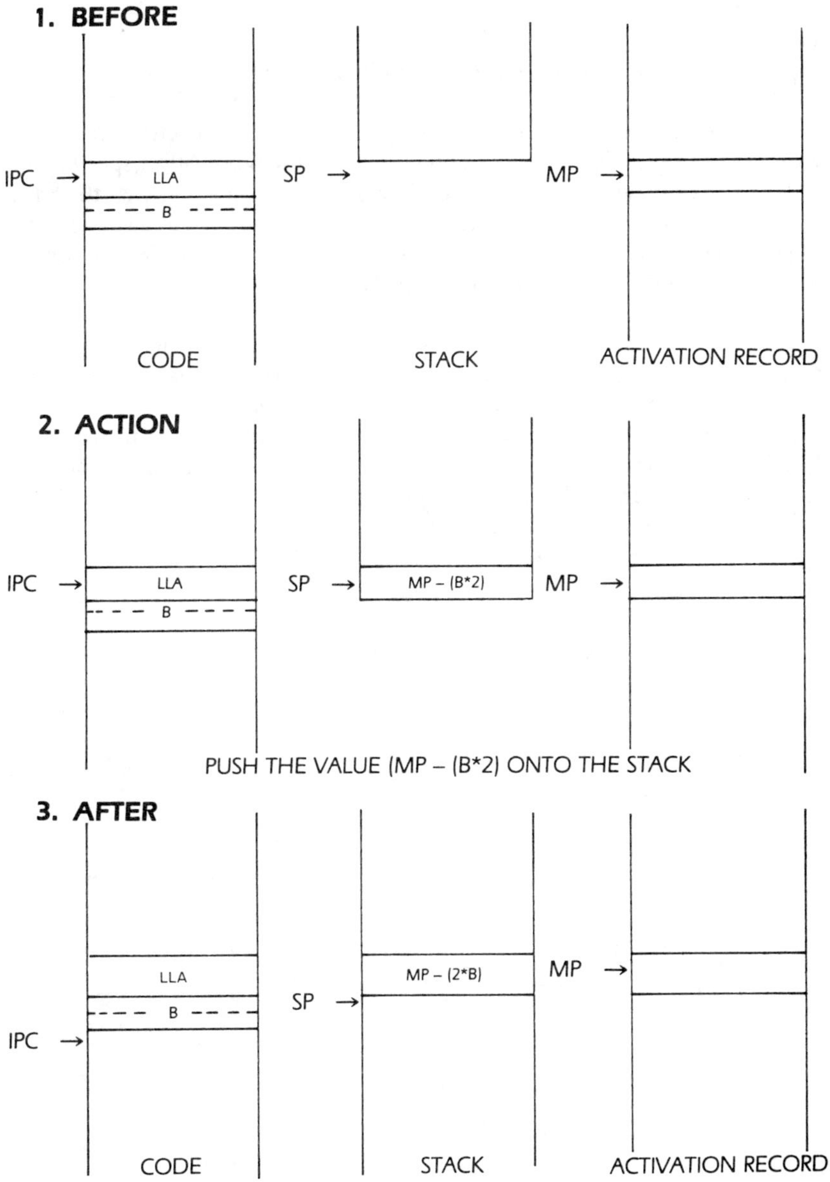

Syntax: **STL B**
Opcode: **204 ($CC)**
Operation: **Store top-of-stack (TOS) into a local variable**

This instruction is the inverse operation to the LDL instruction. It pops a word off of the evaluation stack and stores it at the word offset specified in the operand. As with any instruction having a "B" type parameter, the STL instruction is a variable length instruction requiring two bytes when storing into a variable with an offset of 0..127 and requiring two bytes when storing in a variable with an offset in the range 128..32767.

The operand (which is a word-offset) is converted to a byte offset (by multiplying it by two), this value is subtracted from the value in the MP register and then the value on the top of the evaluation stack is stored at the resultant address. Note that there is no "Short Store Local" instruction. Loading data occurs much more frequently than does storing data so a special case was made for the load local instruction. No such special case was created for the store instruction.

STL B OPERATION:

1. BEFORE

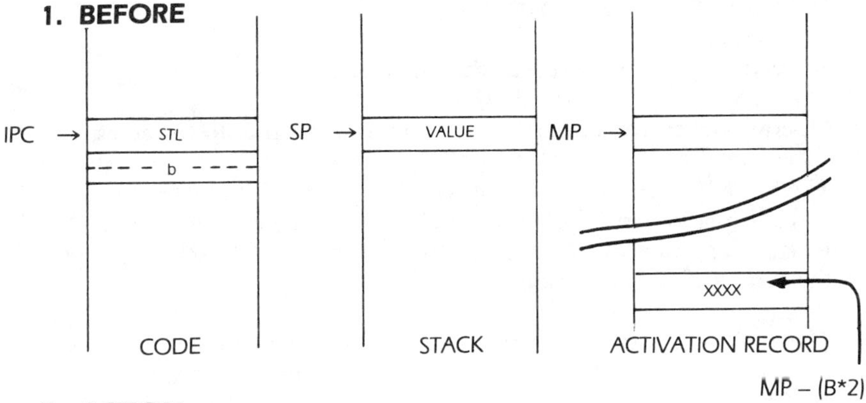

2. ACTION

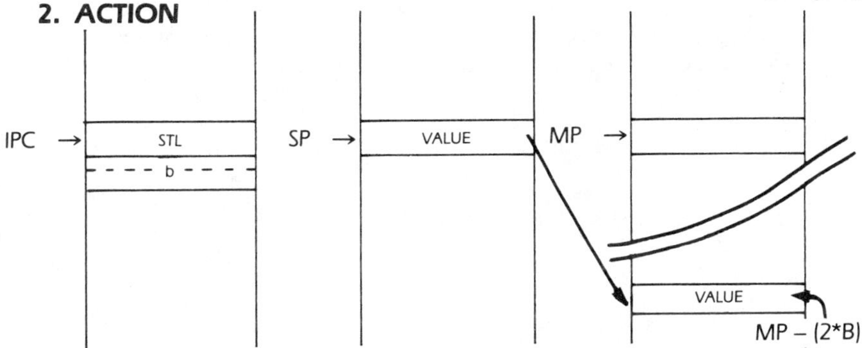

POP TOP OF STACK AND STORE INTO LOCATION MP – (2*B)

3. AFTER

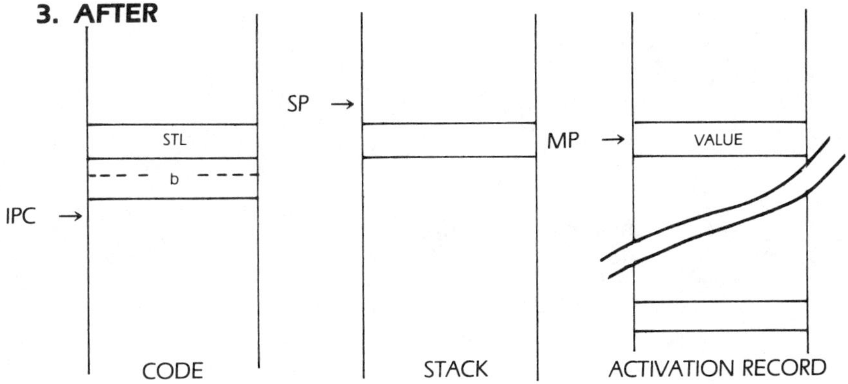

Global Loads and Stores

Syntax: **SLDO n (n is in the range 1..16)**
Opcode: **232..247 ($E8..$F7)**
Operation: **Loads a global variable with offset n onto the stack**

The SLDO instruction is similar to SLDL instruction except that it loads global variables instead of local variables onto the evaluation stack. Global variables are those which were declared in the main program (or unit) of the currently executing program.

The SLDO instruction extracts the offset n from the opcode, multiplies this value by two, and subtracts the doubled offset from the BASE register to obtain the address of the desired variable. The SLDO instruction is one byte long. Hence there are 16 different SLDO instructions required to provide access to the first 16 words of global storage.

SLDO n OPERATION:

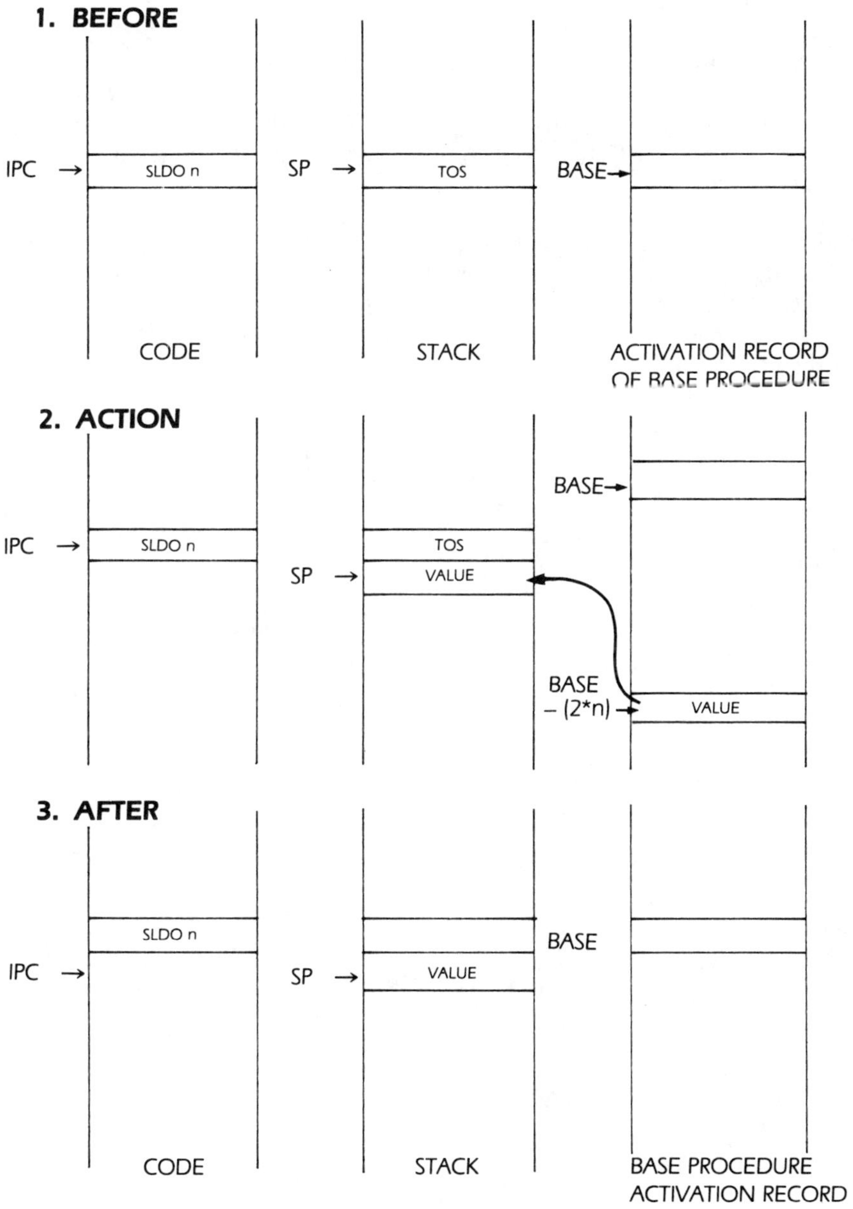

Syntax: **LDO B**
Opcode: **169 ($A9)**
Operation: **Load a global word**

LDO (Load global word) is the long version of the SLDO instruction. It loads the word with the specified offset from the BASE register and pushes it onto the stack.

The LDO instruction is two bytes long when loading one of the first 128 words of global storage; it is three bytes long if a variable located beyond the 128th word of storage is loaded. As with any word offset, the "B" parameter is multiplied by two to obtain a byte offset. This byte offset is then subtracted from the BASE register to obtain the address of the word to be loaded.

LDO B OPERATION:

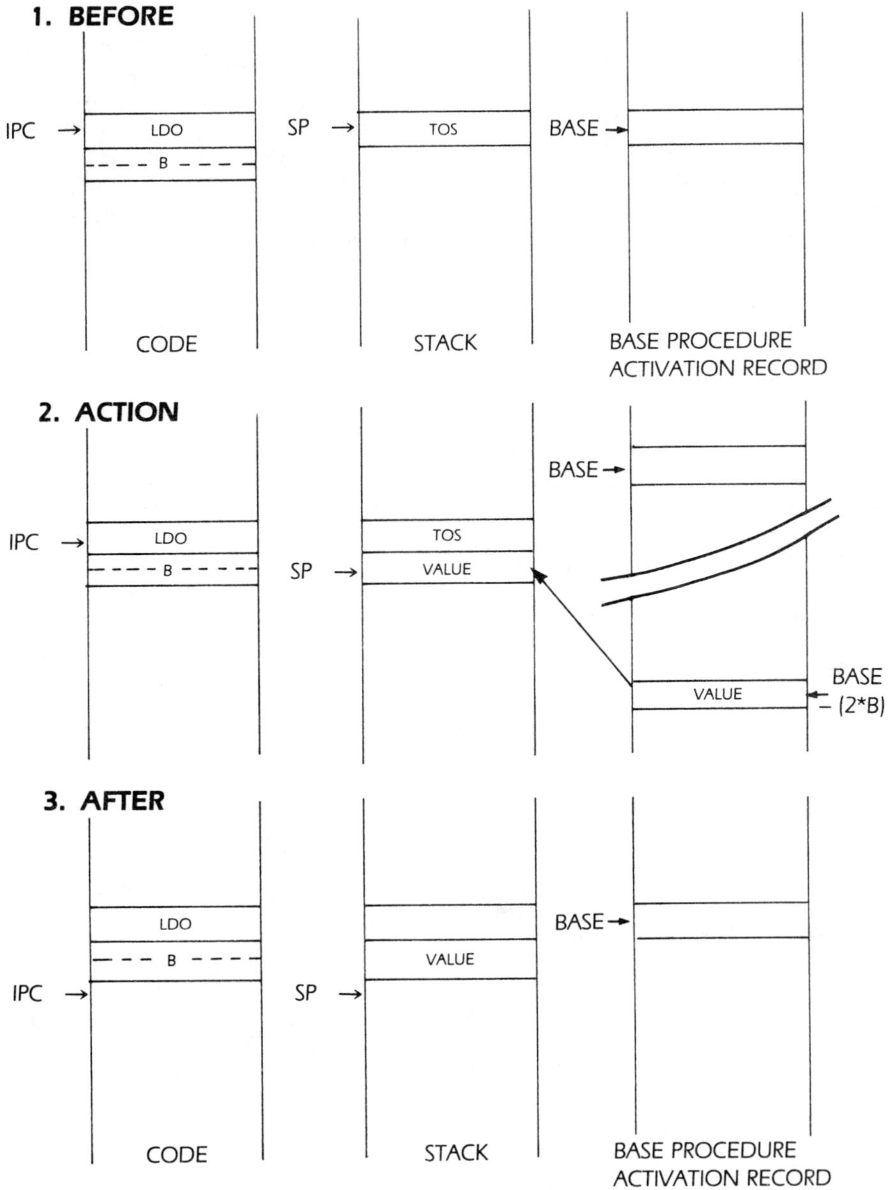

Syntax: LAO B
Opcode: 165 ($A5)
Operation: Load Global address of variable specified

The LAO instruction pushes the address (as opposed to the data stored at an address) of the global variable specified. Its operation is similar to the LLA instruction except that the offset is subtracted from the BASE register instead of the MP register. The LAO instruction is used when passing global variables by reference to a procedure or function.

LAO B OPERATION:

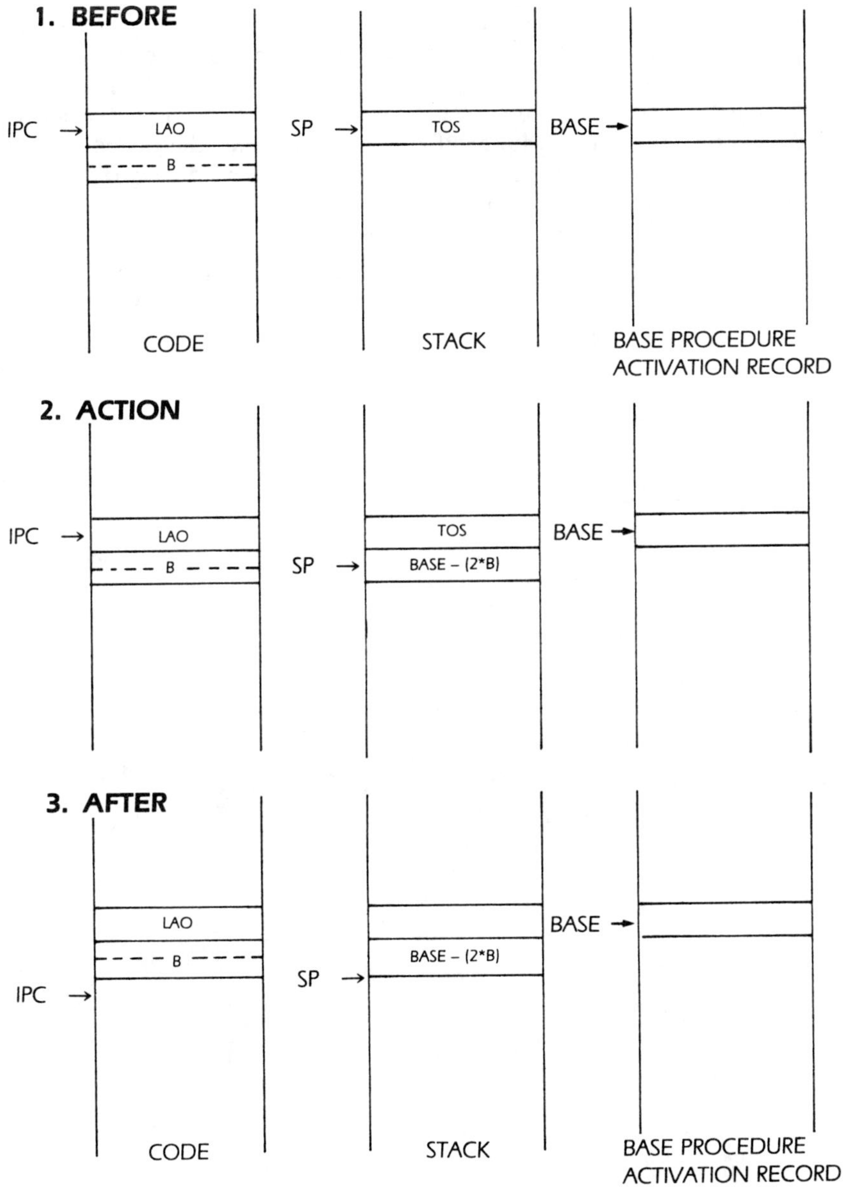

Syntax: **SRO B**
Opcode: **171 ($AB)**
Operation: **Stores TOS (top-of-stack at specified global offset)**

SRO (store global word) stores the data on the top of the evaluation stack into the global variable whose offset is specified after the opcode. This instruction is two bytes long if used to store data into a scalar variable with an offset of 127 or less. It is three bytes long if it is used to store data into a global variable with a word offset greater than 127.

SRO B OPERATION:

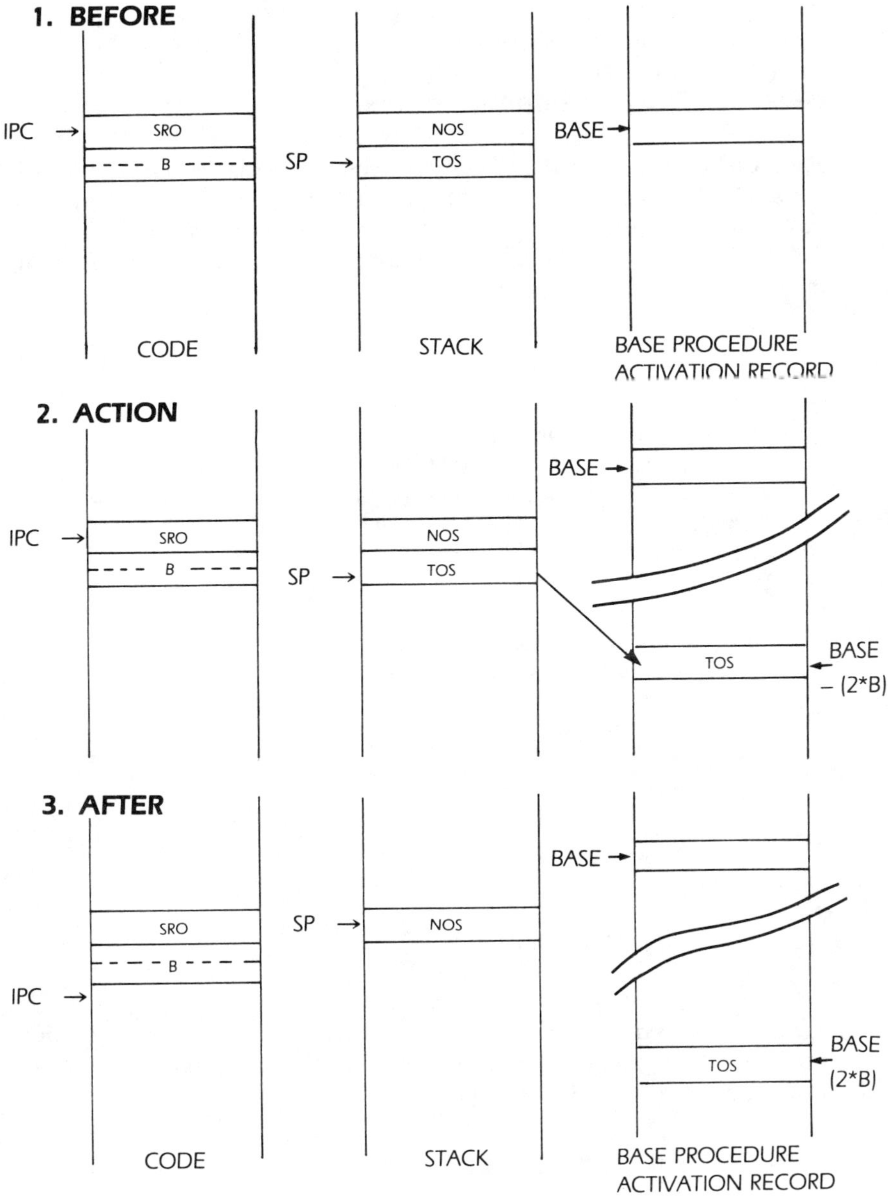

Intermediate Loads and Stores

Syntax: LOD DB,B
Opcode: 182 ($B6)
Operation: Load intermediate variable

The LOD instruction is used to load intermediate variables onto the top of the stack. An intermediate variable is one that is global to the currently executing procedure, but is not a global variable in the sense that it was defined in the main program. For example, consider the Pascal program segment:

```
PROGRAM MAIN;
VAR I:INTEGER;

  PROCEDURE INTERMED;
  VAR J:INTEGER;

     PROCEDURE LOCAL;
     VAR K:INTEGER
     BEGIN
        .
        .
        .

     WRITELN(I,' ',J,' ',K);

     END;

  BEGIN
     .
     .
     .
  END;

BEGIN
  .
  .
  .
END.
```

Within the procedure LOCAL variable I would be accessed using the LDO instruction, K would be accessed using the LDL instruction, and J would be accessed using the LOD instruction.

LOD is a little different from the local and global loads in that it requires two parameters instead of just one. The DB operand is used to tell the p-machine how many static links you must traverse in order to find the address from which you apply the B offset. A static link is a pointer to the activation record of the parent of the currently executing procedure. In the example above the procedure LOCAL has a static link that points to the procedure INTERMED and INTERMED has a static link that points to the activation record for MAIN.

The LOD instruction can be used to access variables in as many as 128 nested procedures. The MP register points at the activation record of the parent of the currently executing procedure. The address of this location is used as the temporary MP value. DB is decremented by one. If the new value of DB is zero, then the B operand is multiplied by two and subtracted from the temporary MP value in order to obtain the address of the variable in question. If DB is not zero, this process is repeated except the temporary MP value is used instead of the value in the MP register to find the next link.

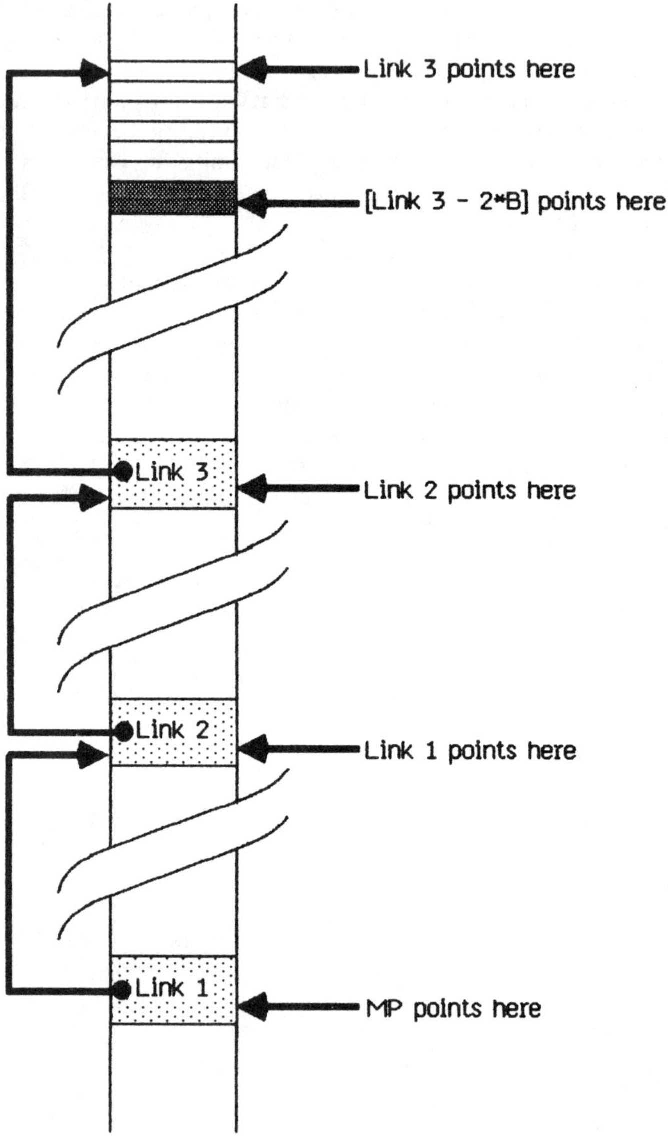
Link 3 points here
[Link 3 - 2*B] points here
Link 3
Link 2 points here
Link 2
Link 1 points here
Link 1
MP points here

Figure 5-1

This is an example of how a LOD 3,2 instruction would be handled. Three times a link is obtained and used to point at the activation record of the parent procedure (the first time the link address is obtained from the MP register). LINK3 points to the activation record of the procedure in which we wish to access the second variable. B (in this case, 2) is multiplied by two to obtain a byte offset which is then subtracted from LINK3 to obtain the address of the low-order byte of the variable to be loaded onto the evaluation stack. The high order byte of the variable (the next sequential memory location after the low-order byte) is pushed onto the evaluation stack and then the low-order byte is pushed onto the evaluation stack.

Syntax: **LDA DB,B**
Opcode: **178 ($B2)**
Operation: **Loads the address of an intermediate variable**

LDA (load intermediate address) is intermediate version of LLA and LAO. It pushes the address of the intermediate variable, as opposed to the value at that address, onto the evaluation stack. The address is calculated traversing DB static links and subtracting 2*B from the address of the target activation record.

LDA DB,B OPERATION:

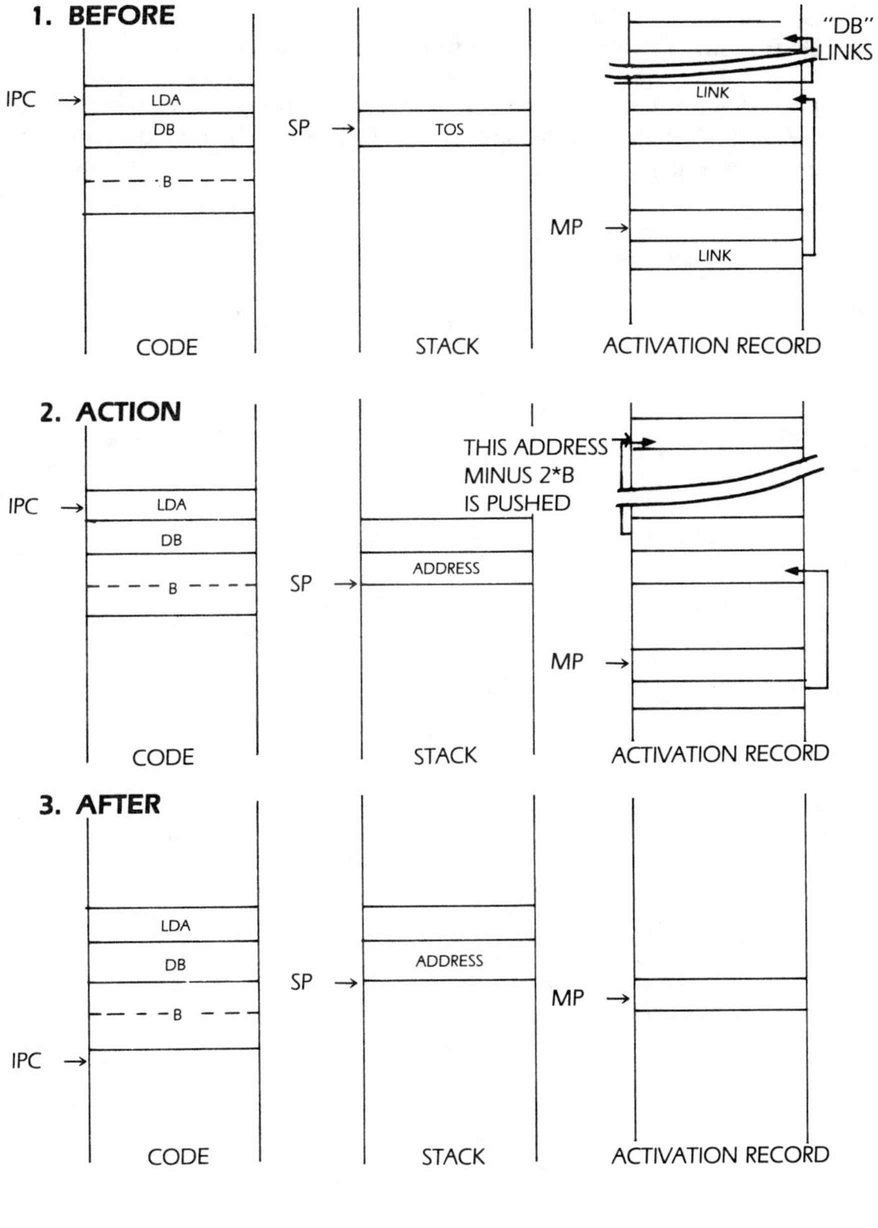

Syntax: **STR DB,B**
Opcode: **184 ($B8)**
Operation: **Store data into an intermediate variable**

The value on the top of the evaluation stack is popped and stored at the specified offset after traversing DB static links (see LOD for a discussion of static traversals).

STR DB,B OPERATION:

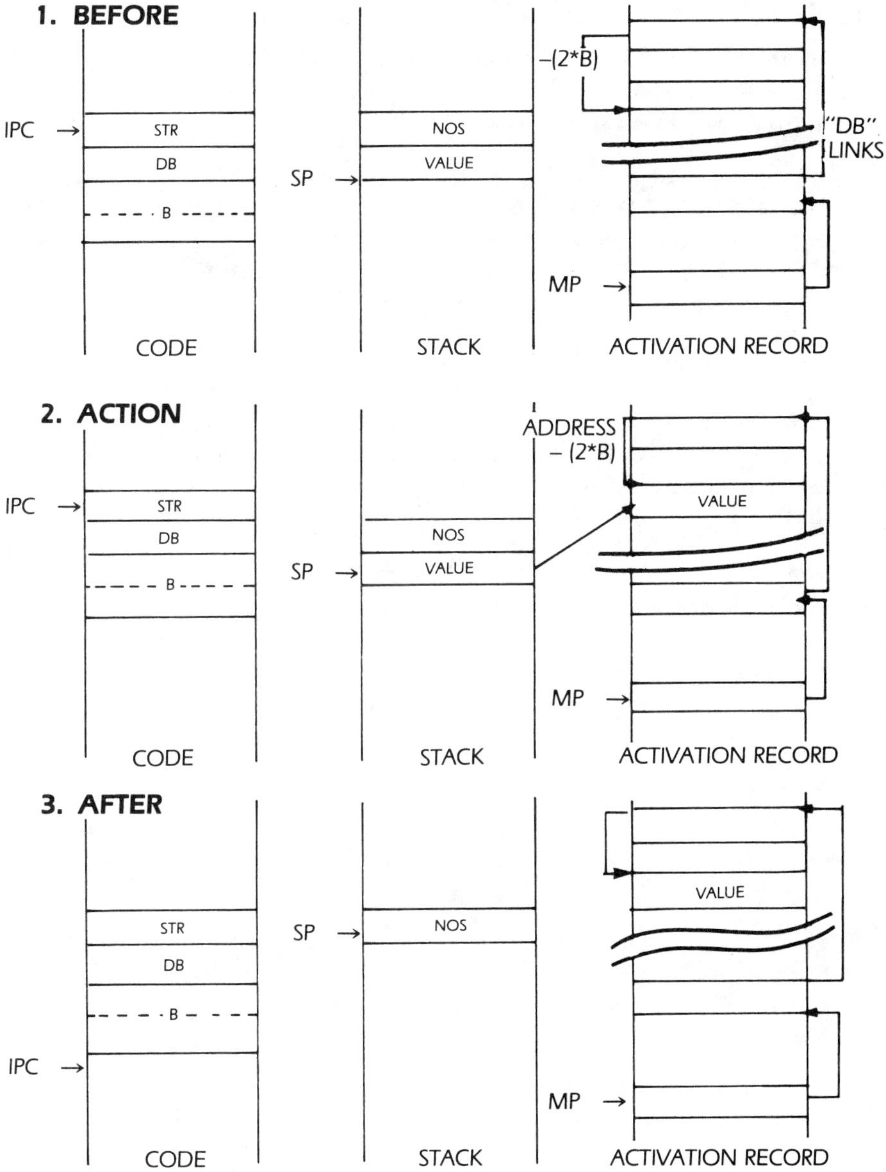

Indirect Loads and Stores

Syntax: **SIND n (n must be in the range 0..7)**
Opcode: **248+n ($F8+n)**
Operation: **Load word indirect, indexed**

The SIND instructions assume that the top of stack (TOS) points to some data structure. SIND0 replaces TOS with the word pointed at by TOS. SIND1 replaces TOS with the word pointed at by (TOS+2). SIND2 replaces TOS with the word pointed at by (TOS+4). Similarly, SINDn replaces TOS with the word pointed at by (TOS+ 2*n).

The SINDn instruction is used to access elements of a multi-word structure such as a record. SIND is the short form of the IND instruction to be described next. By defining often-accessed fields of a record as one of the first eight words of the record you can optimize record accesses since the SINDn instruction will be used in place of the longer and slower IND instruction.

SIND0 is a special case of the SINDn instruction. It is used to load a word indirectly and finds many uses beyond that of the record element access.

SIND n OPERATION:

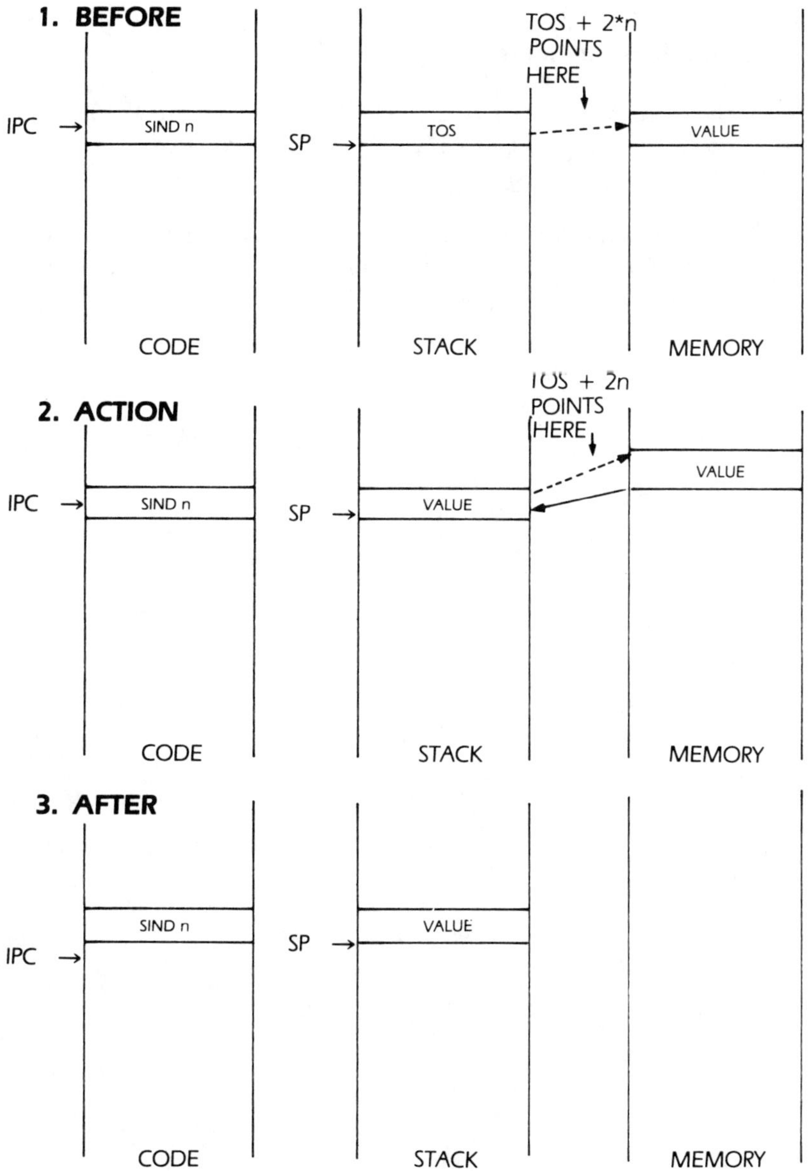

Syntax: **IND B**
Opcode: **163 ($A3)**
Operation: **Indirect indexed load**

IND is the more general form of the SINDn instruction. The B operand is multiplied by two and added to TOS. TOS is then replaced by the word pointed at by TOS.

IND is used to access elements of a record beyond the seventh word of data in the record. Note that B is a static index. That is, it cannot be changed during the execution of a program.

IND B OPERATION:

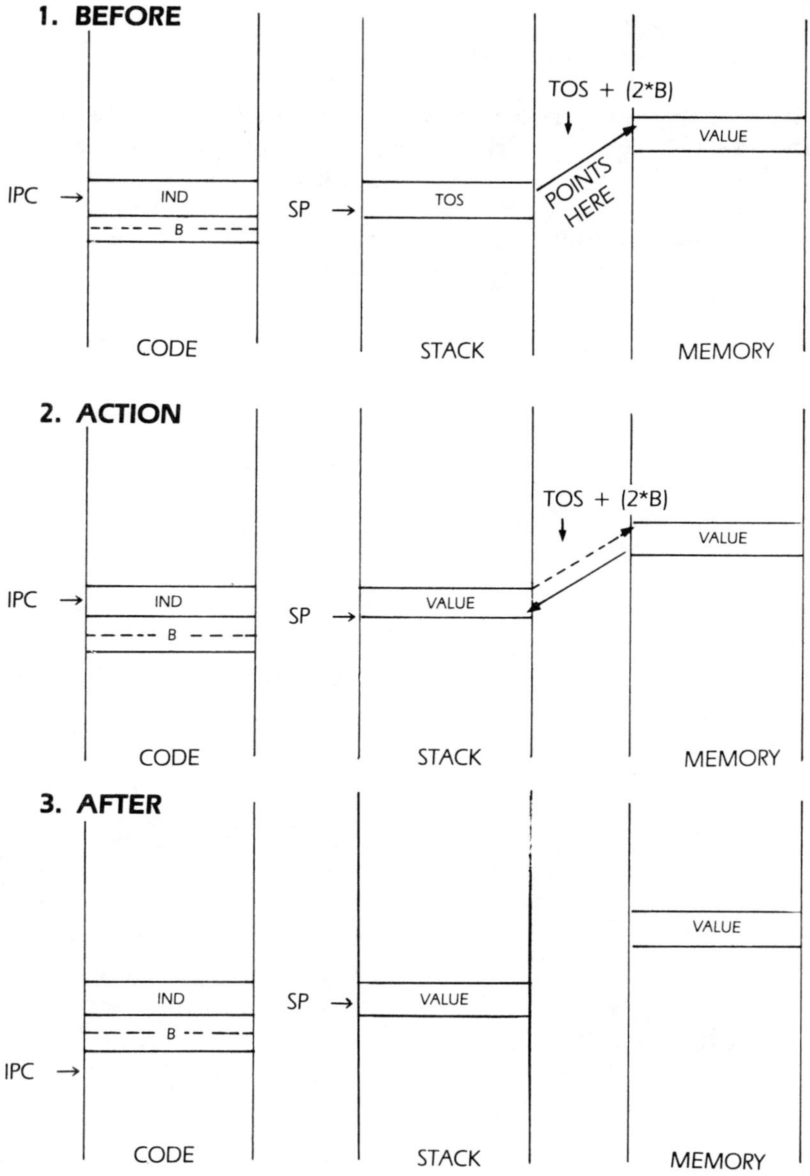

Syntax: **STO**
Opcode: **154 ($9A)**
Operation: **Store data indirect**

STO stores the data on TOS at the location specified by the word at NOS (next-on-stack). TOS is popped and saved at the address pointed at by the new TOS. Two words are popped off of the stack during the execution of the STO instruction. STO is used for storing data into arrays, records, parameters that were passed by reference, pointers, and other variables where the actual location isn't known at compile-time.

STO OPERATION:

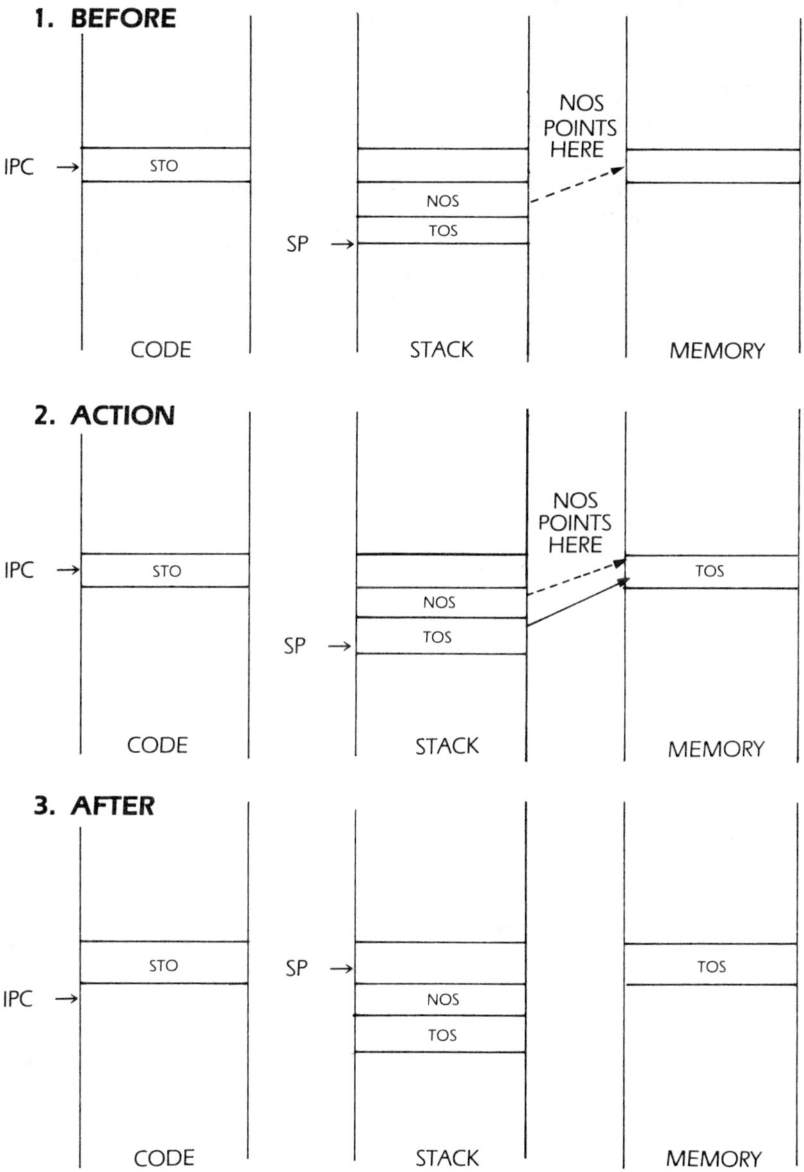

Extended Loads and Stores

Syntax: LDE UB,B
Opcode: 157 ($9D)
Operation: Load an extended word from intrinsic unit

LDE is used to load data from the global data segment of a segment procedure. UB is the data segment from which the data is to be loaded and B is the offset into that data segment where the word to be loaded can be found. The LDE instruction allows short, fast access to variables defined in the outer shell of intrinsic units.

LDE UB,B OPERATION:

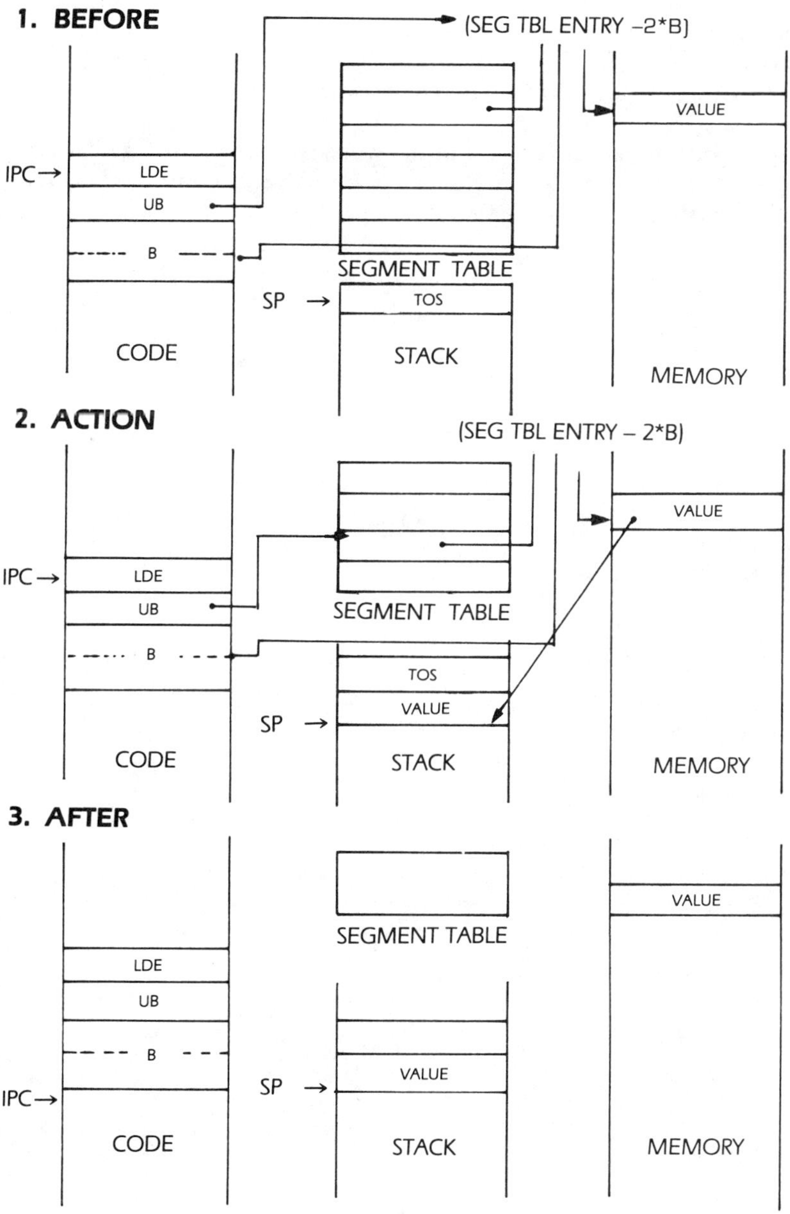

Syntax: LAE UB,B
Opcode: 167 ($A7)
Operation: Pushes address of extended word onto stack

LAE is used to load the address of the word with offset B in global data segment UB. As with the LDE instruction, LAE is used to access global variables within an intrinsic unit.

LAE UB,B OPERATION:

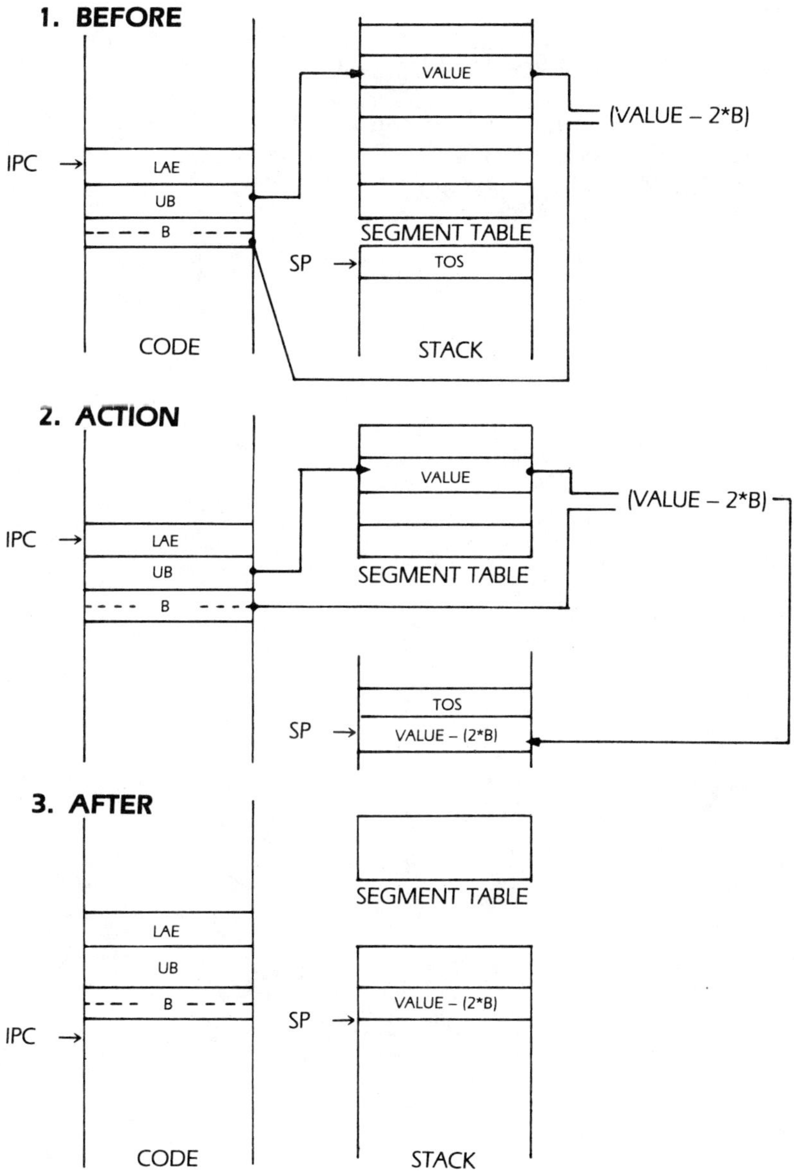

Syntax: **STE UB,B**
Opcode: **209 ($D1)**
Operation: **Store extended word**

STE is used to store data into a word in an intrisic unit's global variable area. UB is the data segment number, B is the word offset into the data segment where the word is to be stored.

STE UB,B OPERATION:

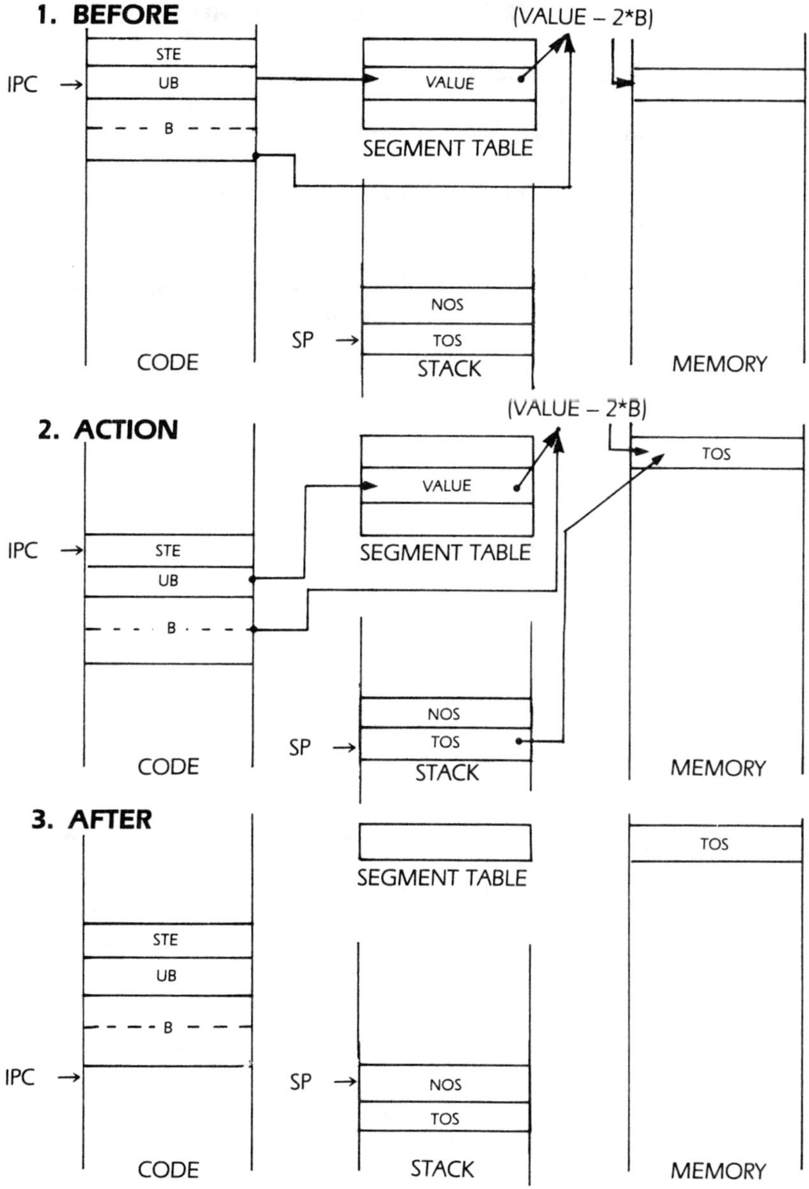

Multiple-Word Loads and Stores (Reals and Sets)

Syntax: LDC UB,<block>
Opcode: 179 ($B3)
Operation: Push <block> of words onto the stack

LDC is used to push a block of words (i.e., more than two) onto the evaluation stack. It is used primarily to load real constants and set constants onto the stack. UB is the number of words to push on the evaluation stack, <block> is a block of UB words that follows the opcode. After the <block> is pushed onto the stack the IPC is incremented past <block>.

LDC UB,<BLOCK> OPERATION:

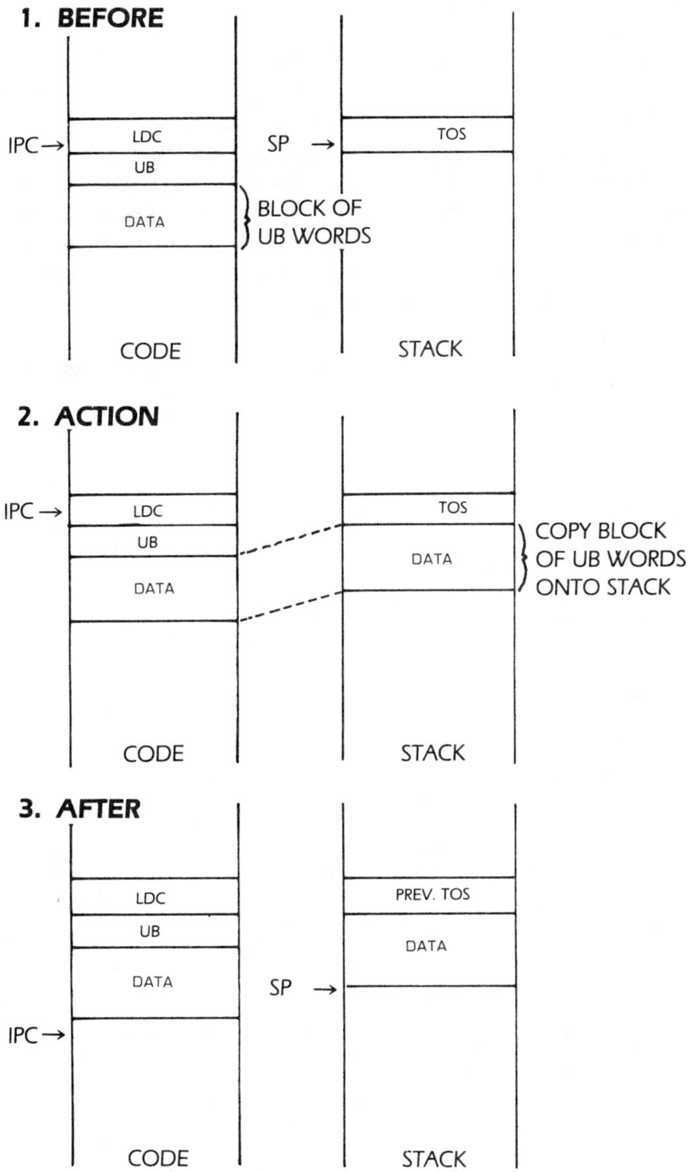

Syntax: **LDM UB**
Opcode: **188 ($BC)**
Operation: **Load multiple words**

LDM pushes a block of UB words where the address of the block is stored on TOS. LDM is used to load real and set variables onto the evaluation stack. Since the address of the variable must be on TOS, some calculations must be performed in order to place the address of the variable on the TOS. At the bare minimum, an LLA instruction (at least two bytes) must be executed before LDM can be executed. So to load a real or set variable at least four bytes are required. For this reason you should never declare a real or set variable as one of the first 16 variables declared. The first 16 words of storage should be reserved specifically for scalar variables since they can take advantage of the shorter SLDO and SLDL load instructions.

LDM UB OPERATION:

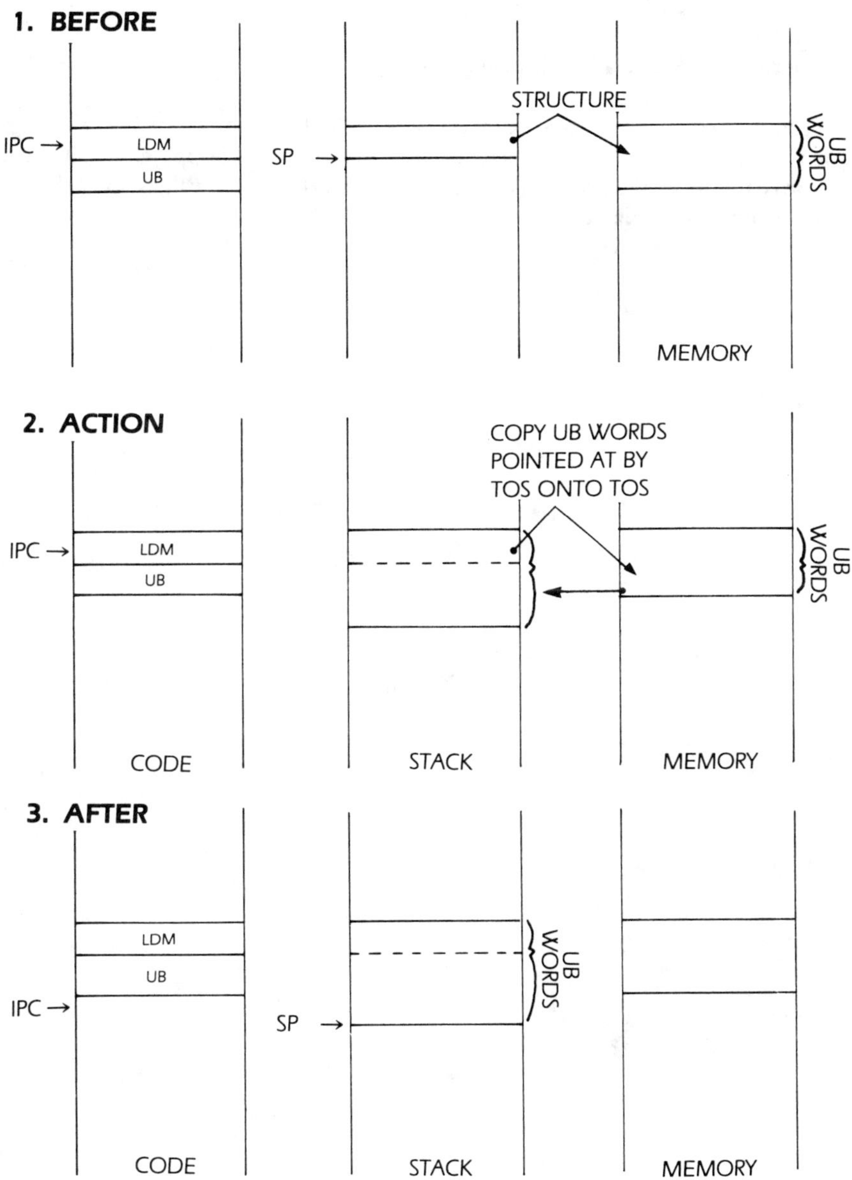

Syntax: STM UB
Opcode: 189 ($BD)
Operation: Store a block of words

STM is used to store a block of UB words. TOS is a block of UB words, it is stored at the location specified on the stack after popping off all the words to be stored. STM is used to store real and set values into their corresponding variables.

STM UB OPERATION:

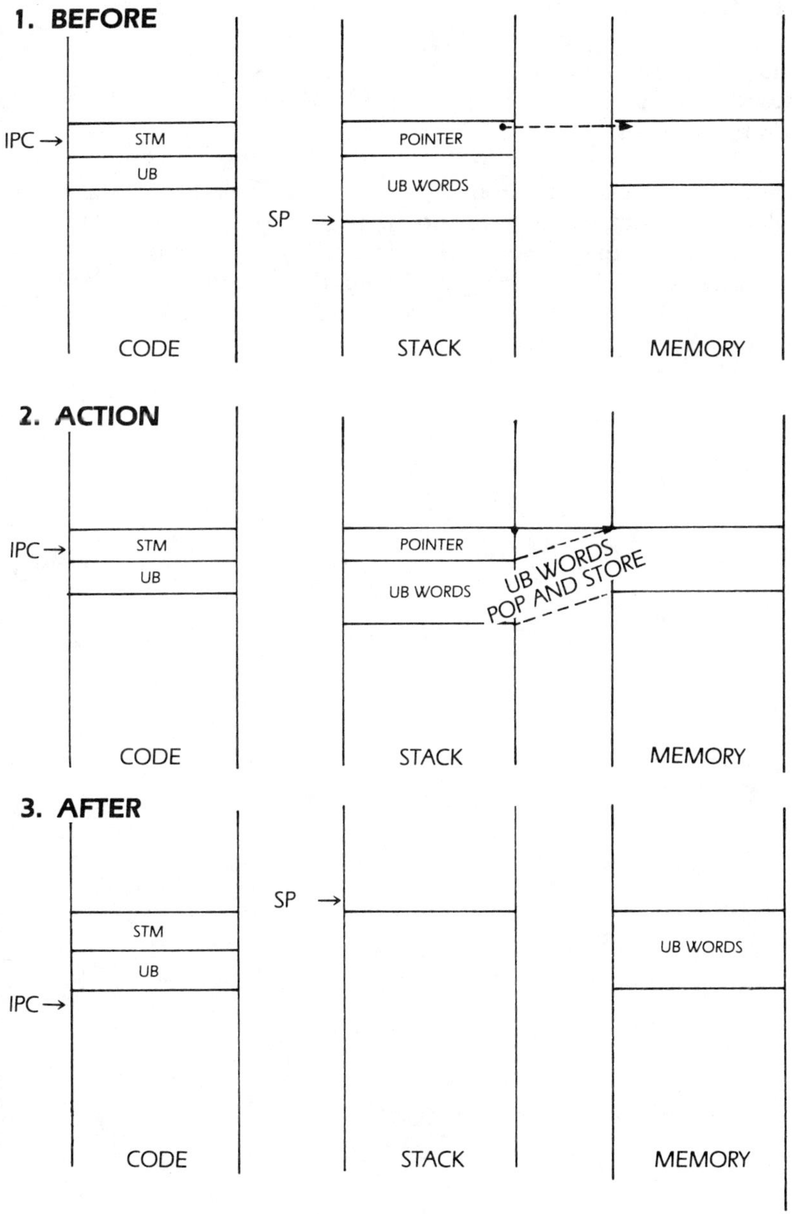

Byte Array Handling

Syntax: LDB
Opcode: 190 ($BE)
Operation: Load byte

LDB is used to load data from a byte array (such as a packed array of CHAR). TOS contains an index into the array (a byte index) and TOS – 1 contains a pointer to the base address of the byte array. TOS is popped and added to TOS – 1. The byte pointed at by this new pointer replaces TOS – 1. Since data pushed onto the stack must be 16 bits wide, the byte pushed is zero extended to 16 bits before being pushed.

LDB OPERATION:

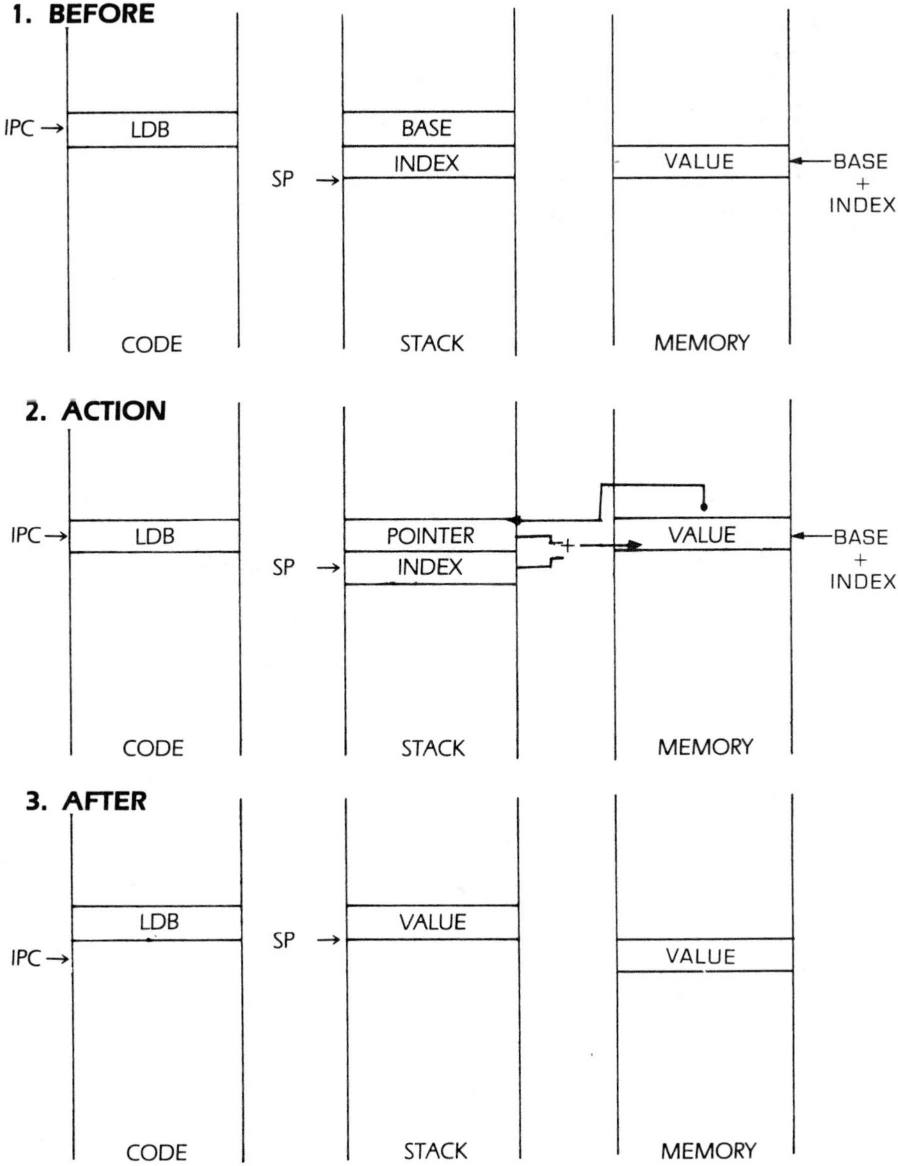

Syntax: **STB**
Opcode: **191 ($BF)**
Operation: **Store TOS into a byte array**

STB is used to store a byte into a byte array. STB stores the low-order byte of TOS into the array pointed at by TOS – 2 after adding the index at TOS – 1. The high-order byte of TOS is ignored (although it is usually zero). After the completion of this instruction the SP register is cut back by six (for three words).

STB OPERATION:

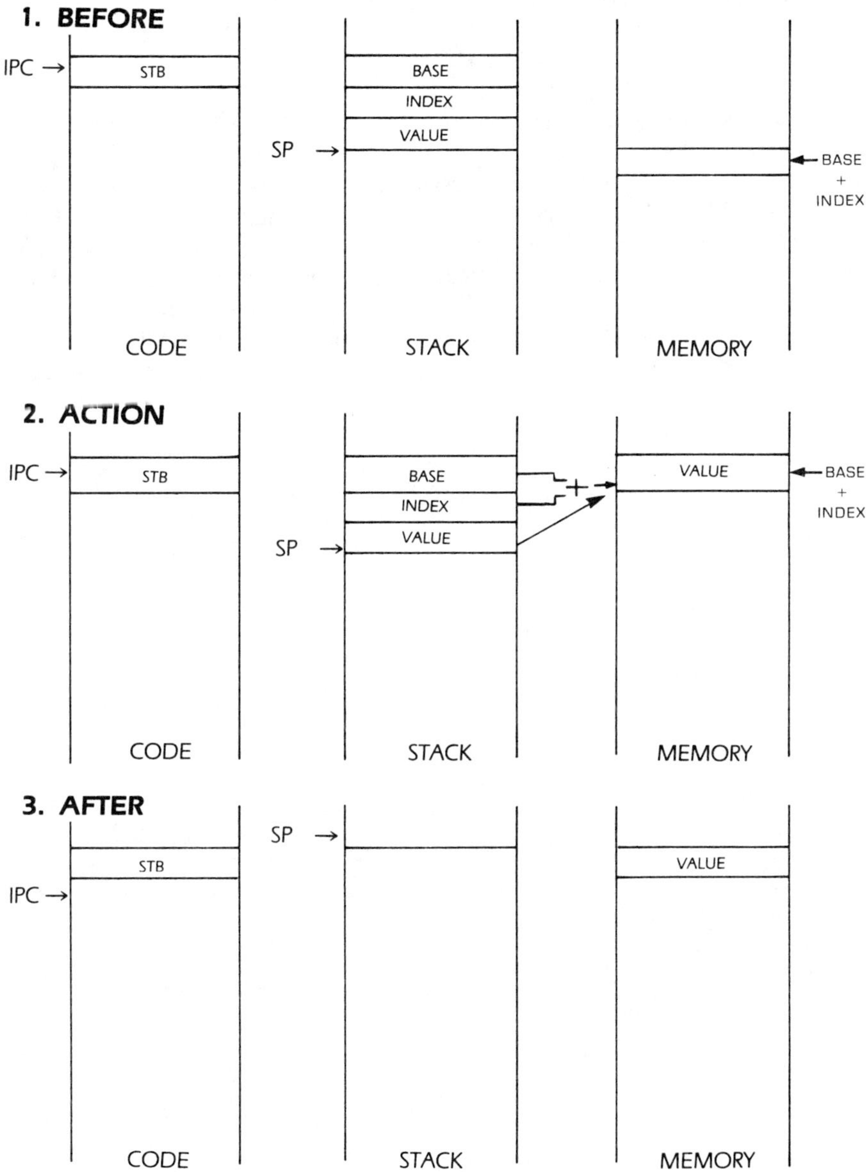

String Handling Instructions

Syntax: LSA UB,'Chars'
Opcode: 166 ($A6)
Operation: Load string address

LSA is used to push the address of a string constant onto the evaluation stack. UB is the number of characters in the string, it is followed by a block of UB bytes. The LSA instruction pushes a pointer to the byte in memory containing the UB. Since strings in Pascal consist of a length byte followed by a group of characters, the data following the UB opcode is a valid Pascal string. Once the pointer to the string is pushed, the value (UB + 2) is added to the IPC register so that execution continues with the next opcode after the last character in the string.

LSA UB, 'CHARS' OPERATION:

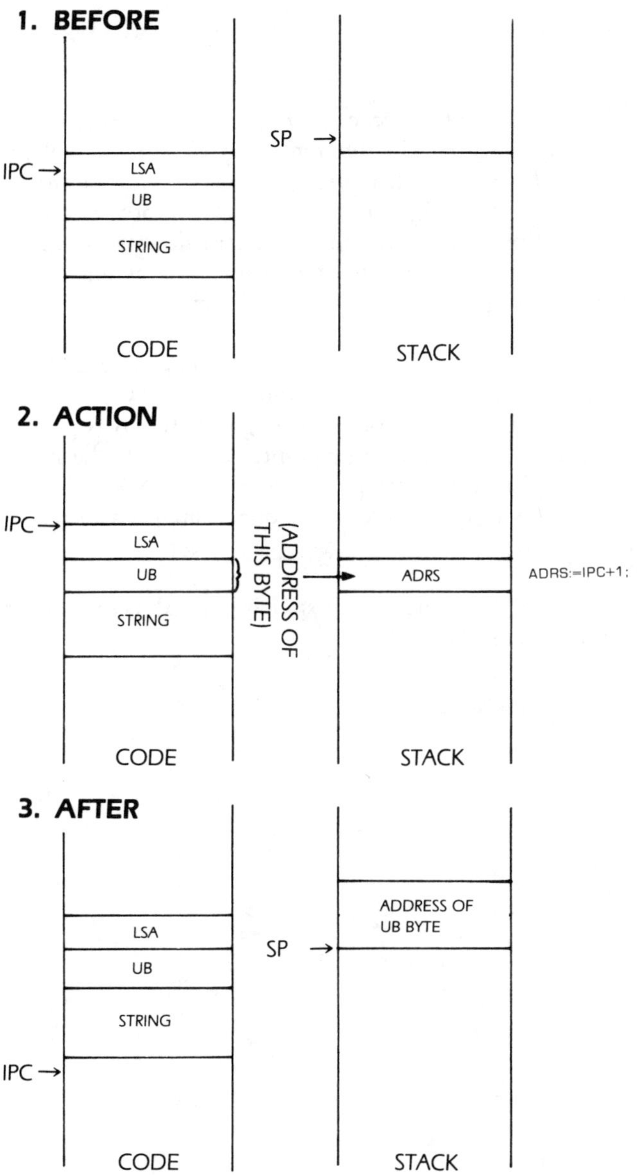

Syntax: **SAS UB**
Opcode: **170 ($AA)**
Operation: **String assignment**

SAS is used to assign one string to another. TOS is either a pointer to the source string or a single character. The differentiation is made by looking at the high order byte. If it is zero, then a single character is to be stored into the destination string. If the high-order byte of TOS is not zero, then TOS is a pointer to the string to be copied into the destination string. String pointers can never have a high order byte of zero since that would imply that the string is stored in page zero; and that never happens on the Apple.

TOS – 1 is a pointer to the destination string. UB is the maximum declared length of the destination string. If the string pointed at by TOS is larger than UB characters a run-time execution error is given. If UB is greater than or equal to the current size of the string pointed at by TOS, the string pointed at by TOS is copied to the string pointed at by TOS – 1. Since a string cannot be declared with a length less than one, a single character on TOS never generates an error.

After the execution of the SAS instruction the stack is popped by two words removing the two pointers on the TOS.

SAS UB OPERATION:

1. BEFORE

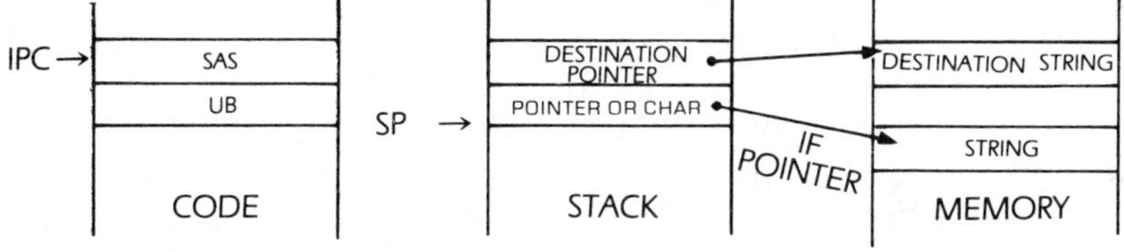

2a. ACTION IF A SINGLE CHARACTER

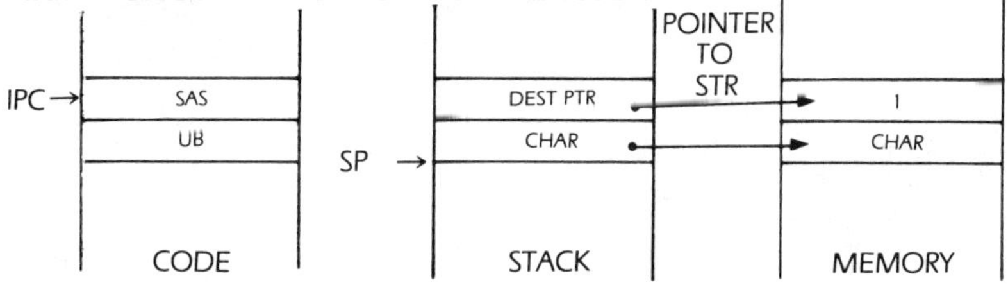

2b. ACTION IF A STRING POINTER

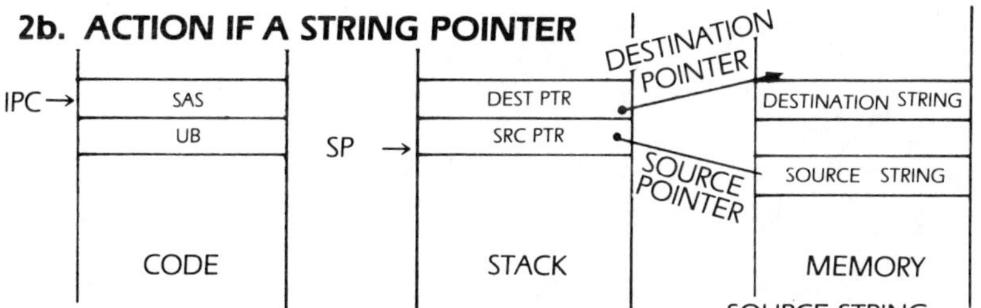

SOURCE STRING
IS COPIED TO
DESTINATION STRING

3. AFTER

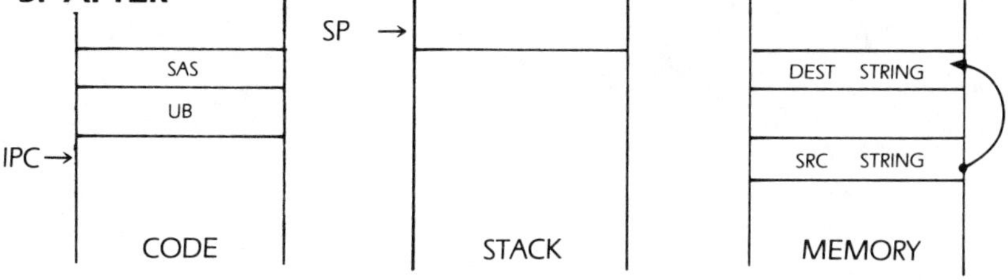

Syntax: **IXS**
Opcode: **155 ($9B)**
Operation: **Index string array**

IXS is used to create a pointer to a byte within a string. TOS contains an index into a string that is pointed at by TOS – 1. TOS is compared to the byte pointed at by TOS – 1. If TOS is greater than the byte pointed at by TOS (which is the current length of the string pointed at by TOS) then an execution error is given. If TOS is less than or equal to the byte pointed at by TOS—1 then IXS simply leaves everything on the stack.

IXS OPERATION:

1. BEFORE

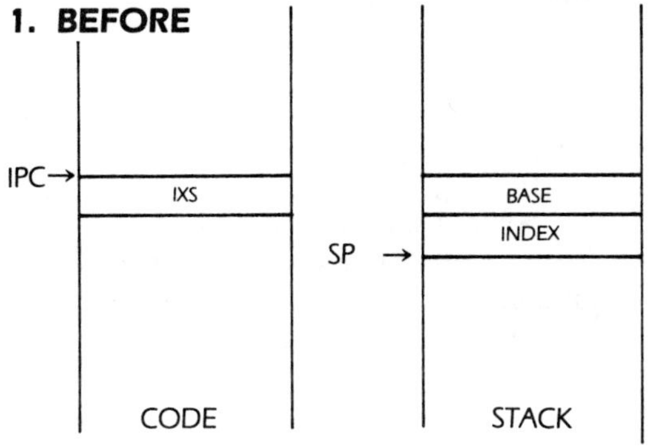

2. ACTION

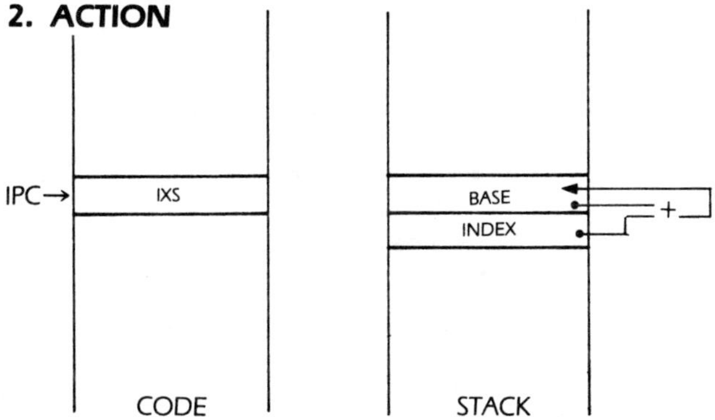

3. AFTER

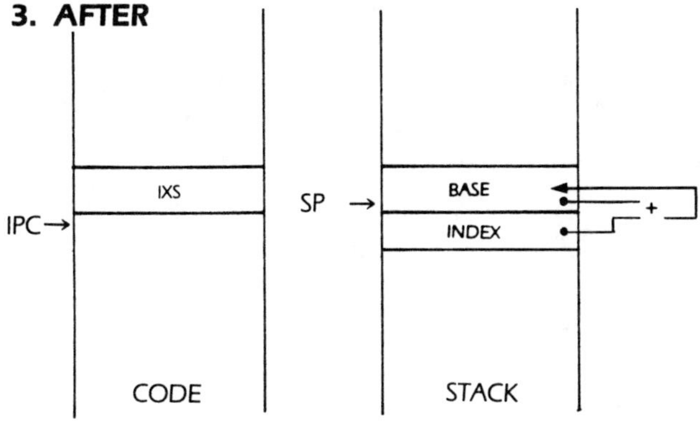

Record and Array Handling Instructions

Syntax: **MOV B**
Opcode: **168 ($A8)**
Operation: **Move a block of words**

MOV transfers a block of B words pointed at by TOS to a similar block of words pointed at by TOS – 1. MOV is used whenever a whole record or array is assigned to a similar variable. After the execution of the MOV instruction TOS and TOS – 1 are popped off of the stack.

MOV B OPERATION:

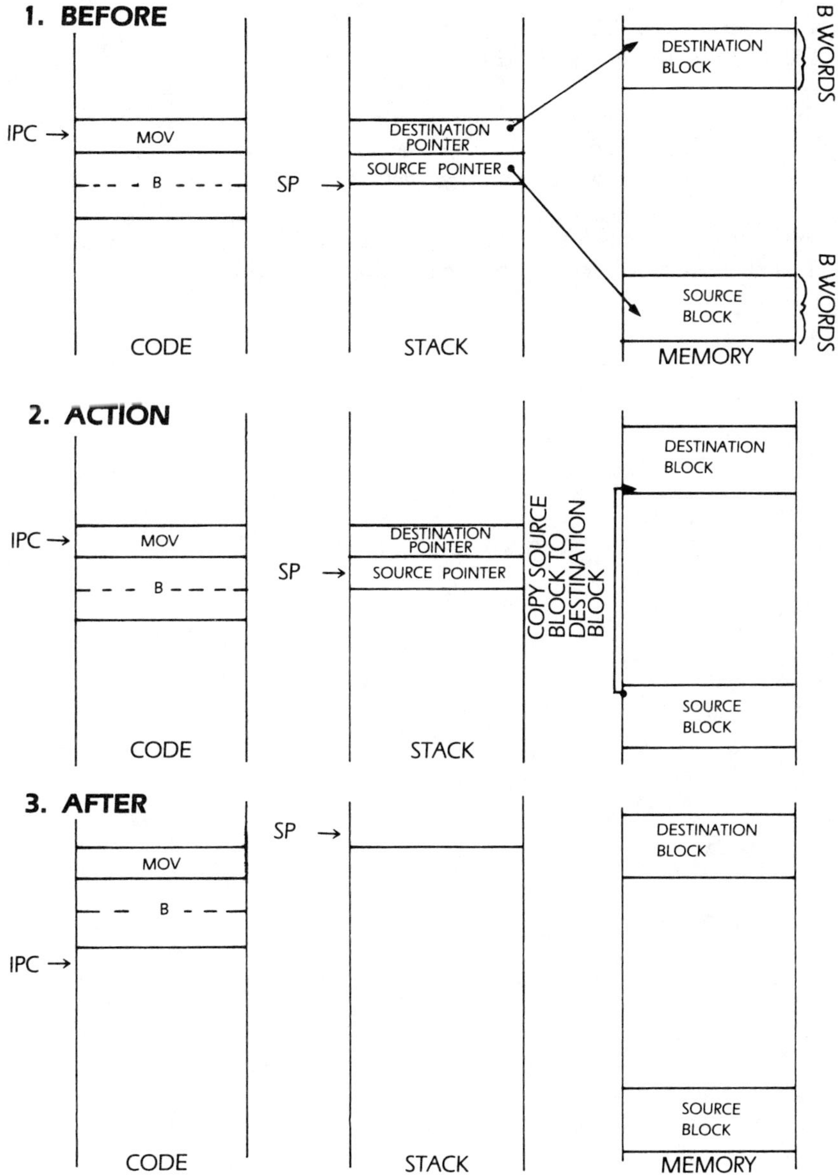

Syntax: **INC B**
Opcode: **162 ($A2)**
Operation: **Increment field pointer**

INC is used to form an index into a record. It is very similar to the IND instruction described earlier except the address of the word is left on the stack instead of the word at the specified address.

INC adds two times B to TOS and replaces TOS with this new value. INC is used create a pointer to some field within a record variable.

INC B OPERATION:

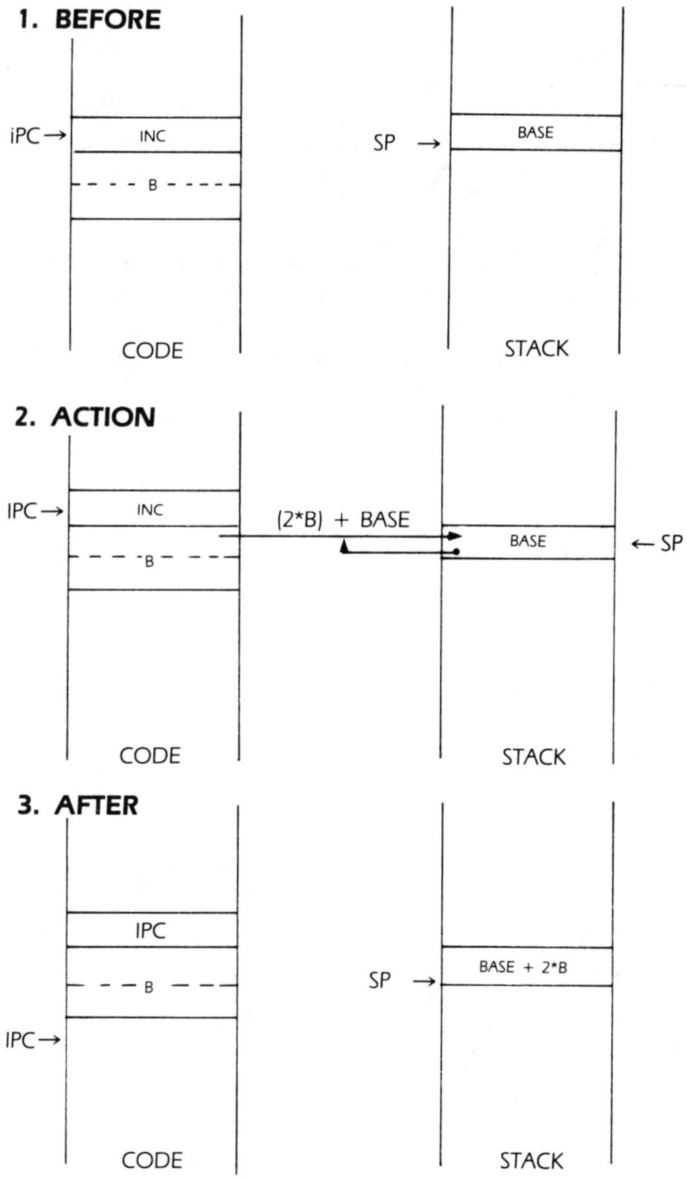

Syntax: IXA B
Opcode: 164 ($A4)
Operation: Index array

TOS is an index into the array whose base element is pointed at by TOS – 1. Each element of the array is of size B (the operand to IXA). TOS is popped and multiplied by B then added to TOS – 1 to obtain a pointer to the desired element.

IXA is used for loading the address of an array element where the array's elements are two words or larger apiece (INC is used for one-word arrays). For example, to obtain the address of the element of a REAL array, the B operand is equal to two (since there are two words per array element). In addition to arrays of REAL data, IXA is also used for obtaining the address of an element of an array of RECORD, STRING, SET, and other multi-element type.

IXA B OPERATION:

1. BEFORE

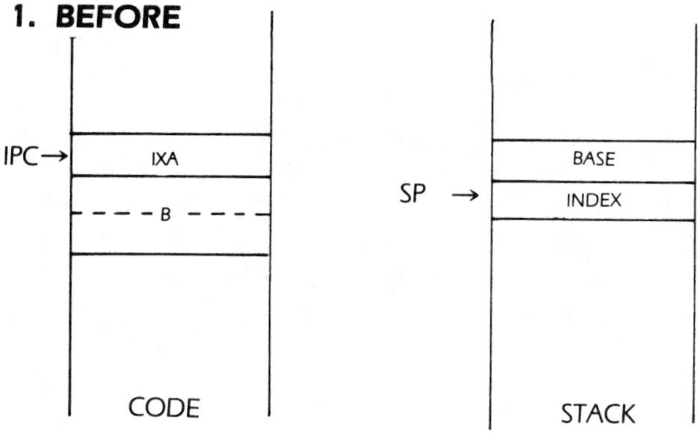

2. ACTION

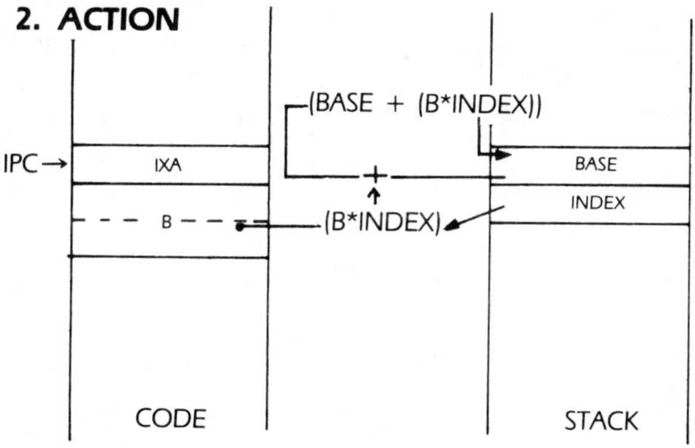

3. AFTER

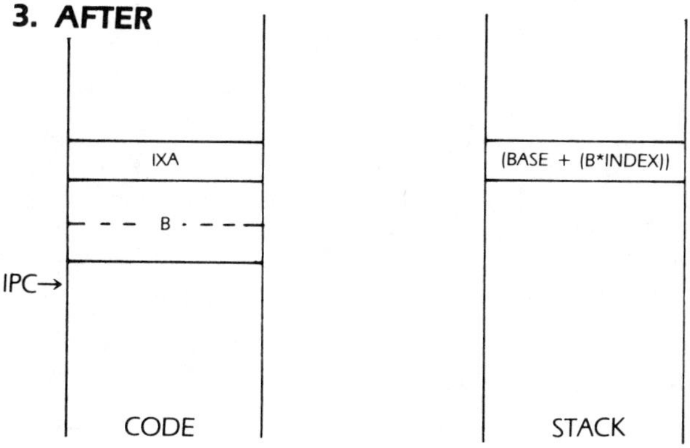

Syntax: **IXP UB1,UB2**
Opcode: **192 ($C0)**
Operation: **Index Packed Array**

IXP is used to push the address of an element of a packed array onto the stack. TOS is the index into the array. TOS – 1 is the base address of the array. UB1 is the number of elements per word (this must be greater than one, if it is less than or equal to one you would use IXA or INC instead). UB2 is the field width (in bits). A "packed field pointer" to the desired data is computed and pushed onto TOS (after index and base address are popped, of course).

A packed field pointer is three words long. The first word pushed (TOS – 2) is a word pointer to the word the field is in. The second word pushed (TOS – 1) is the field width, in bits. The last word pushed (TOS) is the right bit number of the field. This type of pointer is used by the LDP and STP instructions (to be described).

IXP UB1,UB2 OPERATION:

1. BEFORE

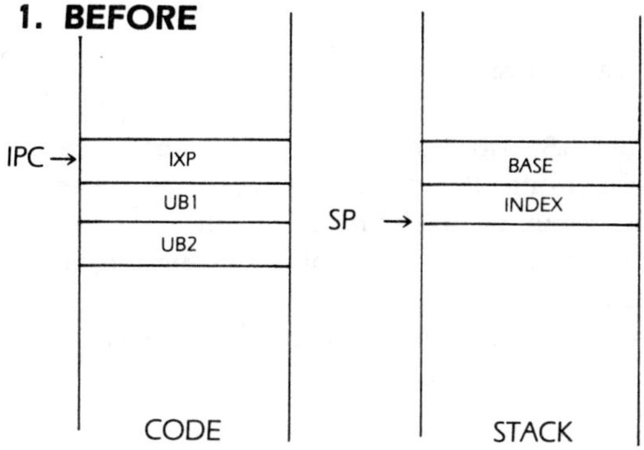

2. ACTION

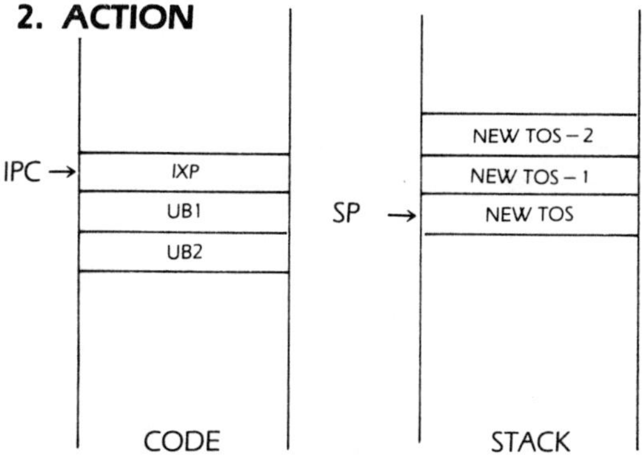

CALCULATION:
NEW TOS-2: = (INDEX DIV UB1)
+ BASE:
NEW TOS-1: = UB2;
NEW TOS 0: = (INDEX MOD UB1);

3. AFTER

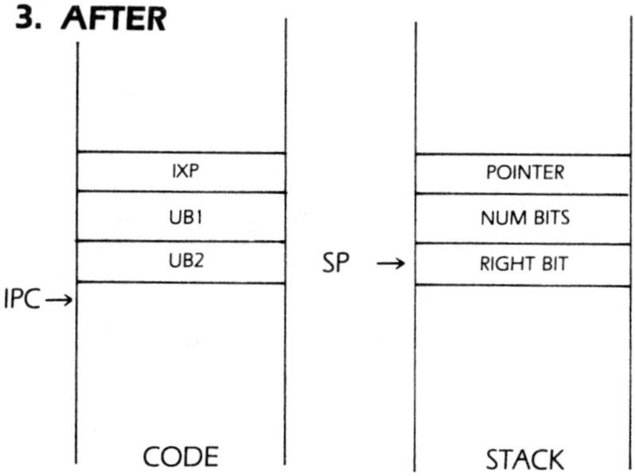

Syntax: **LPA UB,<bytes>**
Opcode: **208 ($D0)**
Operation: **Load packed array address**

LPA is almost identical to the LSA instruction described earlier. The difference is that the pointer pushed onto the evaluation stack isn't a pointer to the UB operand, but rather a pointer to the byte immediately past the UB parameter (the first byte of the block of bytes following the UB operand). LPA is used to load the address of a packed array of characters onto the stack. After LPA is executed the STM instruction might be executed in order to copy the immediate string into a packed array.

LPA UB,<BYTES> OPERATION:

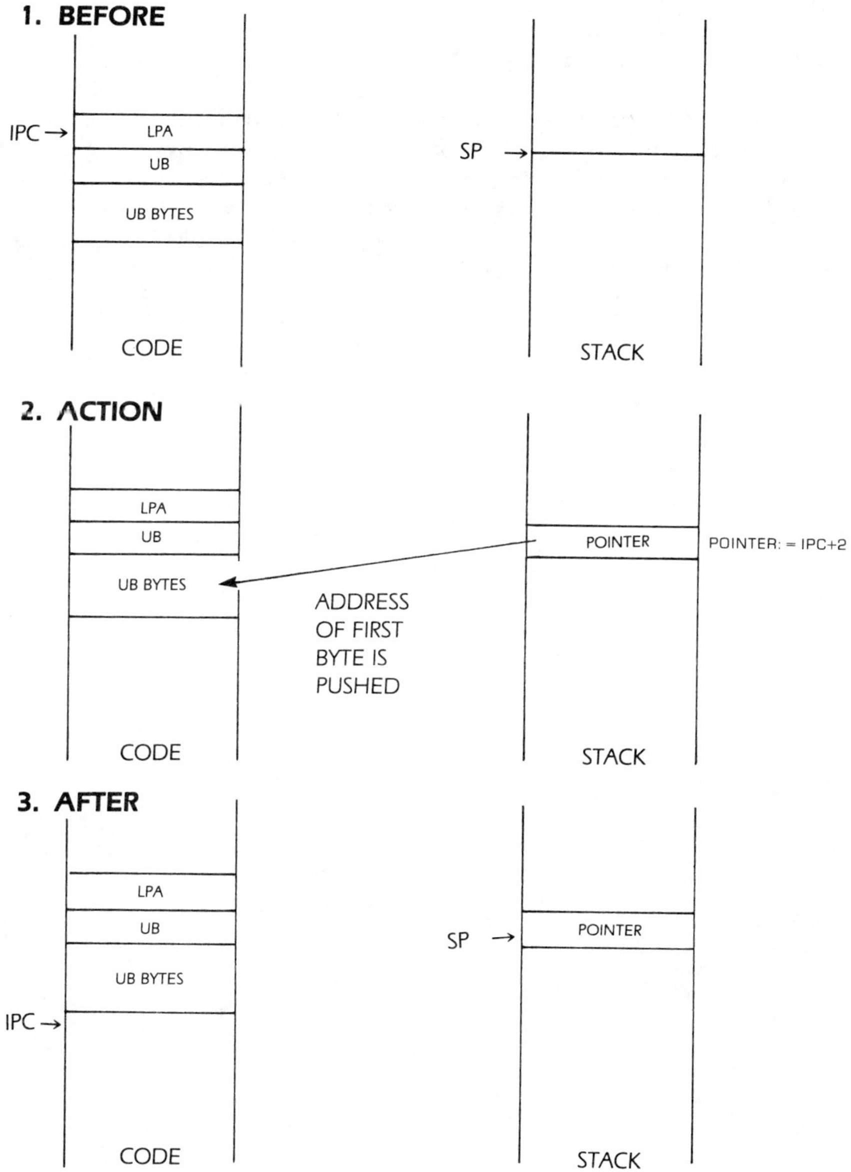

Syntax: **LDP**
Opcode: **186 ($BA)**
Operation: **Load a packed field**

LDP is used to load an element from a packed field. TOS, TOS – 1, and TOS – 2 contain a "packed field pointer" (see IXP for details). Load the field pointed at by this field pointer onto the TOS. Zero-fill any unused high-order bits when loading the packed data. After the execution of the LDP instruction TOS and TOS – 1 are popped and the packed data replaces TOS – 2 which becomes the new TOS.

LDP OPERATION:

1. BEFORE

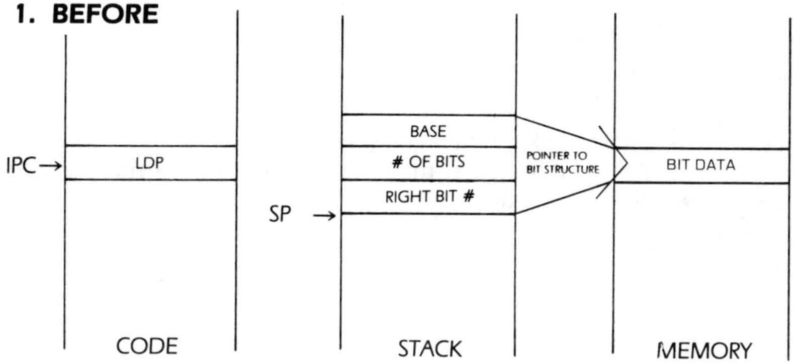

2. ACTION

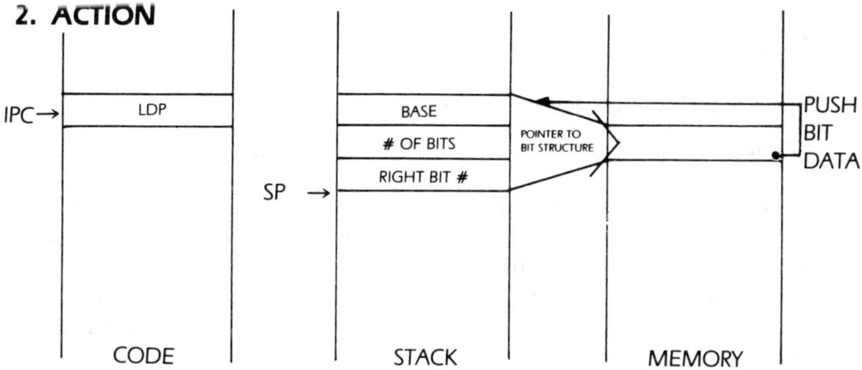

3. AFTER

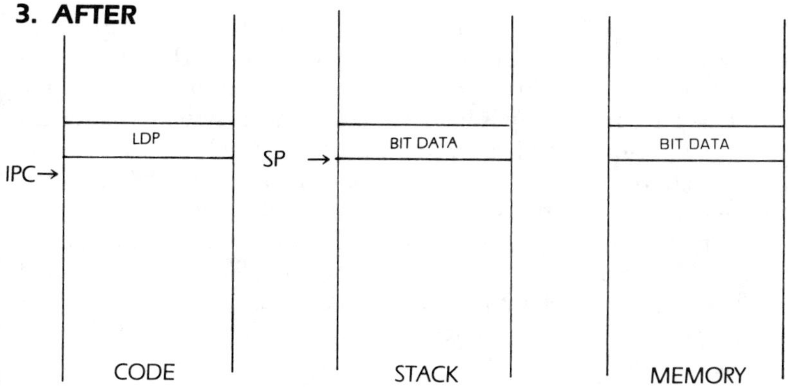

Syntax: **STP**
Opcode: **187 ($BB)**
Operation: **Store TOS into a packed field**

TOS is a field of some packed array or record. Store it into the packed field specified by the packed field pointer comprised of TOS – 1, TOS – 2, and TOS – 3 (see IXP for details). After the exection of the STP instruction the stack is cut back by four words.

Dynamic Variable Allocation
General

Dynamic variables (pointer variables) are allocated on the Apple Pascal "Heap". The heap is a stack that starts at low memory and grows upwards towards the program stack. Unlike the program and data stack, variables allocated on the heap are not automatically de-allocated when a procedure terminates. Variables allocated on the heap must be explicitly de-allocated using the Pascal RELEASE command.

The Apple Pascal operating system uses the memory just above the heap to store a copy of the current disk directory. The variable GDIRP in the SYSCOM memory area contains a pointer to the 2K block used to store the directory. As long as the heap is undisturbed the Pascal system will use this copy of the directory. The instant you allocate or de-allocate data on the stack, the GDIRP pointer is set to NIL and the next time the operating system attempts to access the directory a new copy of the directory will have to be read in off of the disk. In general, this process is completely transparent to the user. However, if you are opening and closing files often you should avoid allocating (or de-allocating) dynamic variables as this tends to hurt the performance of the system since the directory will have to be unnecessarily read in several times.

STP OPERATION:

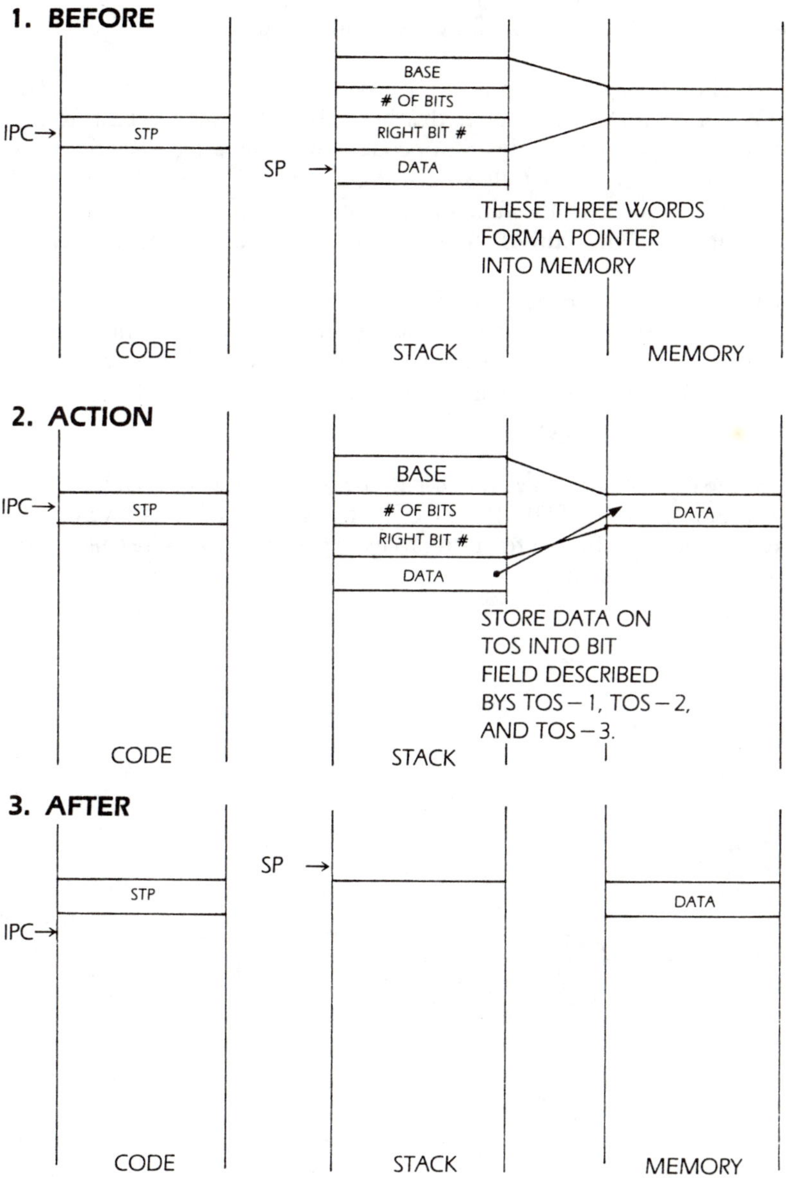

Syntax: **NEW**
Opcode: **158,1 ($9E,$1)**
Operation: **Allocate space for a dynamic variable**

NEW is used to allocate space for a dynamic variable whenever the Pascal NEW command is issued. Note that NEW is quite a bit different from the instructions seen so far in that the opcode is two bytes long. The 158 opcode is actually the CSP (for Call Special Procedure) which is followed by the procedure number of the function you wish to execute. There are several different special procedures, NEW happens to be the first such procedure.

NEW expects two words on TOS. TOS is the number of words to allocate to the dynamic variable and TOS – 1 is the address of the pointer variable. A copy of the NP register is stored in the pointer variable whose address is at TOS – 1 then TOS is multiplied by two and added to NP. TOS and TOS – 1 are both popped off of the evaluation stack.

After the dynamic variable is allocated, the p-machine checks GDIRP to see if it is non-NIL. If GDIRP isn't NIL it is set to NIL to prevent future directory accesses from attempting to use the memory area just allocated as a copy of the directory.

NEW OPERATION:

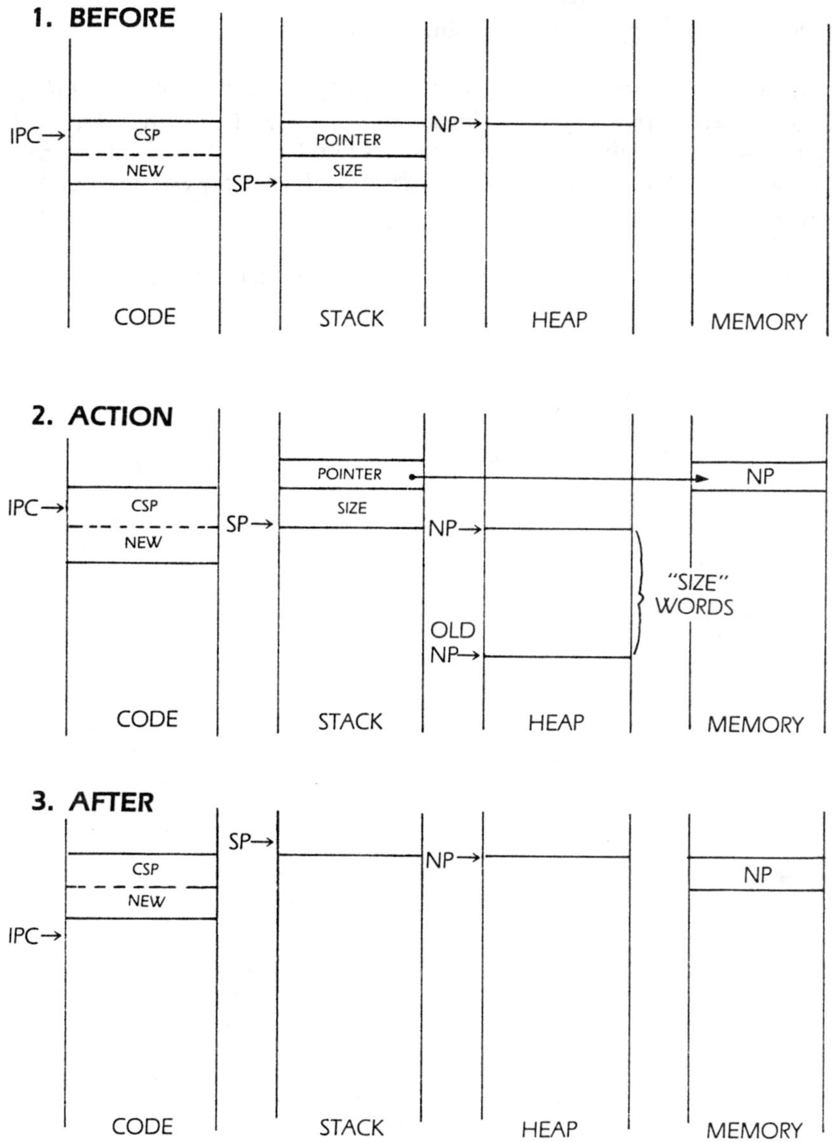

Syntax: **MRK**
Opcode: **158,31 ($9E,$1F)**
Operation: **Copy NP into a pointer variable**

The MRK instruction is emitted whenever the Pascal MARK procedure is encountered. MRK expects a single word on TOS. This is the address of some pointer variable (by convention, ^INTEGER). NP is copied into this variable. If GDIRP is non-NIL, it is set to NIL after the execution of this program.

MRK and RLS (described next) allow the user to dynamically allocate and de-allocate memory as necessary.

MRK OPERATION:

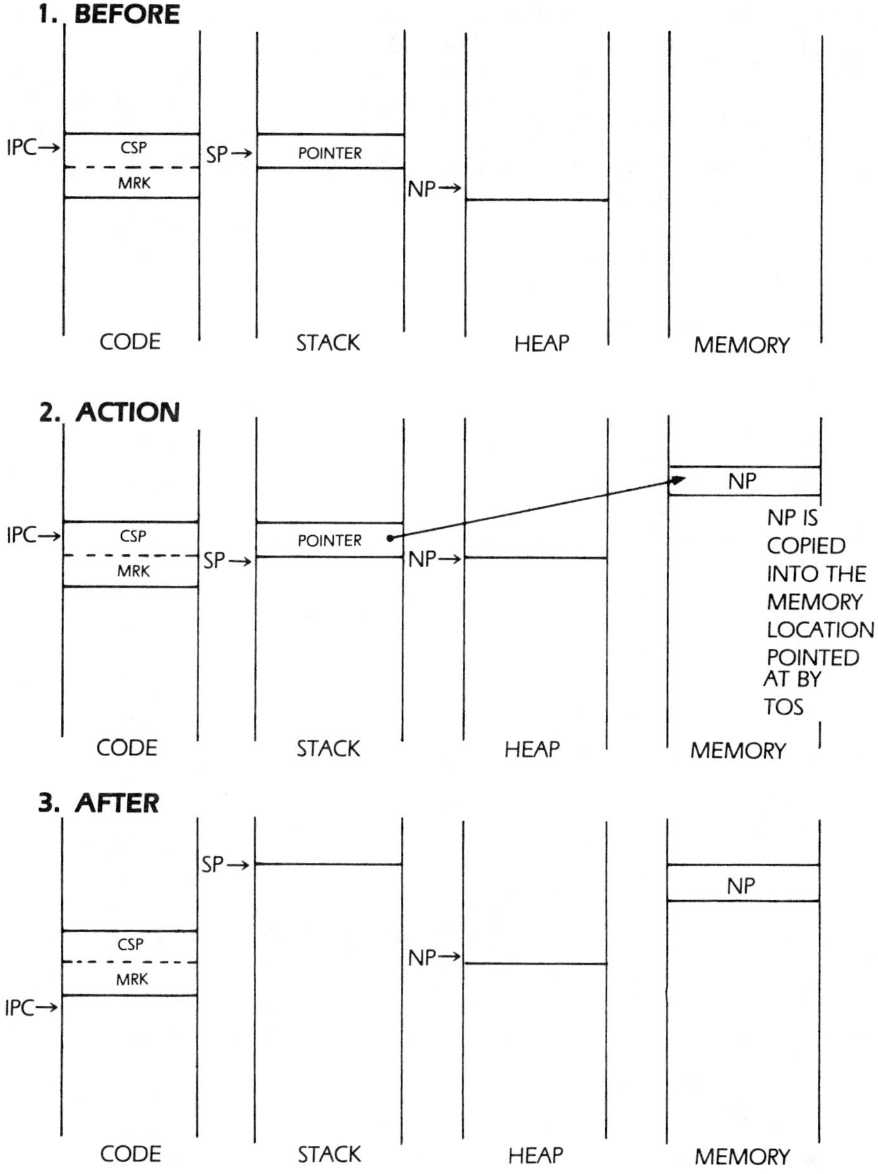

Syntax: **RLS**
Opcode: **158,32 ($9E,$20)**
Operation: **Release storage allocated by MRK**

RLS is the opposite of MRK. It is used to reset the value of NP to some previous value. TOS contains the value which is to be loaded into NP. It is popped and transferred to the NP register. After the execution of the RLS instruction, GDIRP is set to NIL.

RLS OPERATION:

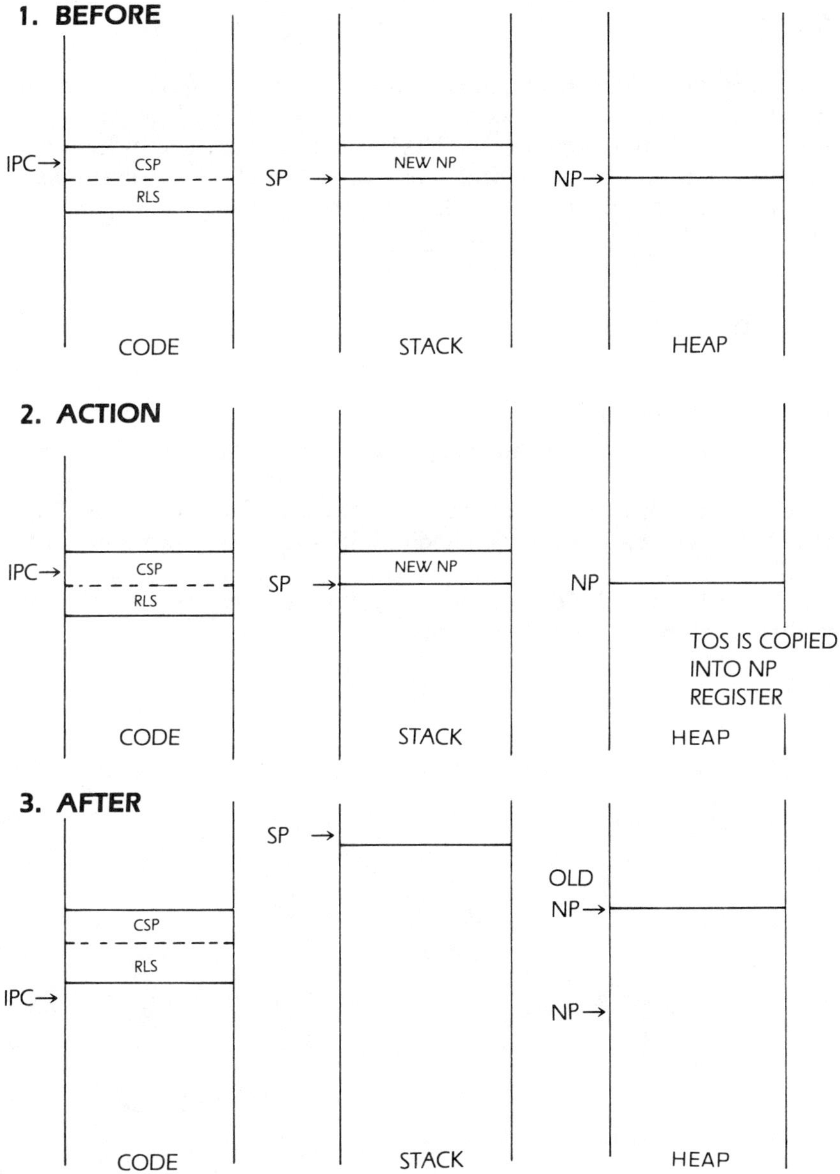

Top of Stack Arithmetic
General

The p-machine arithmetic and logical instructions take their operands from the stack and leave any results on the stack. For example, the ADI (add integers) instruction pops TOS and TOS – 1, adds them, and then pushes the result back onto the stack. Unary operators (like ABI – Absolute value) pop a single operand off of the stack, operate on it, and push the result back onto the stack.

Integer Operations

Syntax: **ABI**
Opcode: **128 ($80)**
Operation: **Take the absolute value of the integer on TOS**

ABI is a unary operator. It takes the absolute value of the integer on TOS. If TOS is positive, TOS is left unmodified, if TOS is negative it is negated, yielding the positive version of the number on TOS. Note that taking the absolute value of –32768 returns –32768 since there is no +32768 in the two's complement number system.

ABI OPERATION:

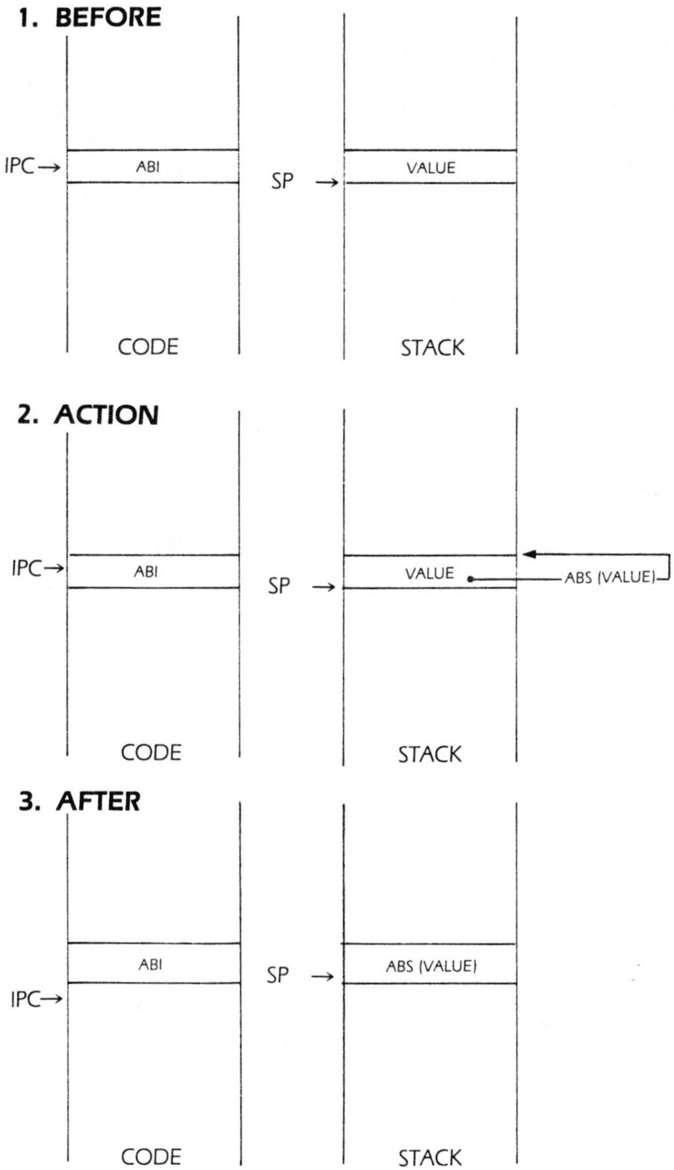

Syntax: **ADI**
Opcode: **130 ($82)**
Operation: **Add integer TOS to TOS – 1**

ADI is a binary operator that expects two words on TOS. TOS is popped and added to TOS – 1. The resulting sum replaces TOS – 1 as the new TOS. Note that the p-Machine does not report an error if arithmetic overflow occurs.

ADI OPERATION:

1. BEFORE

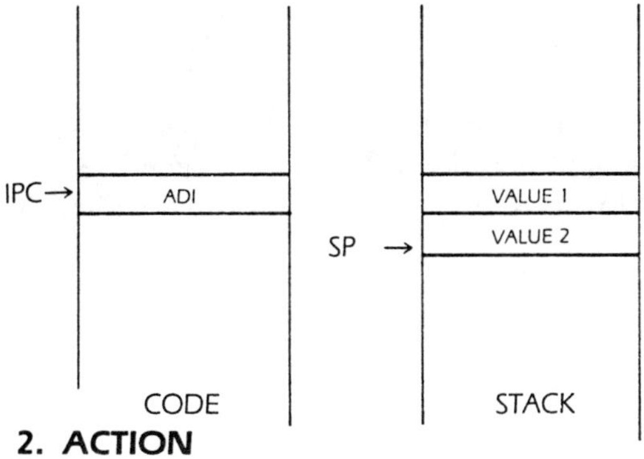

2. ACTION

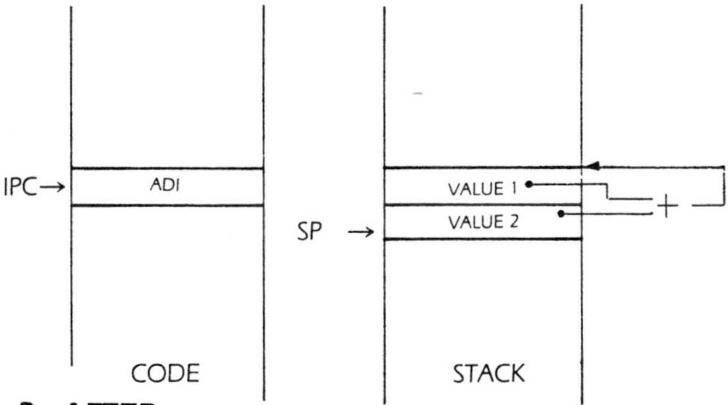

3. AFTER

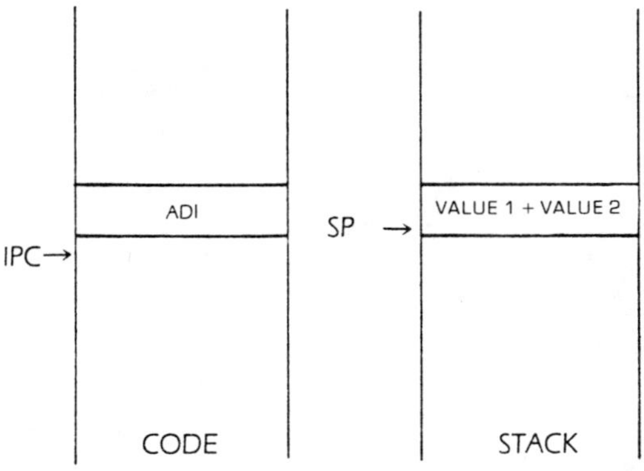

Syntax: **NGI**
Opcode: **145 ($91)**
Operation: **Negate integer TOS**

NGI is used to take the two's complement of TOS. TOS is popped, negated, and then pushed back onto the evaluation stack. Note that negating −32768 returns −32768 since, in the two's complement system, there is no +32768.

NGI OPERATION:

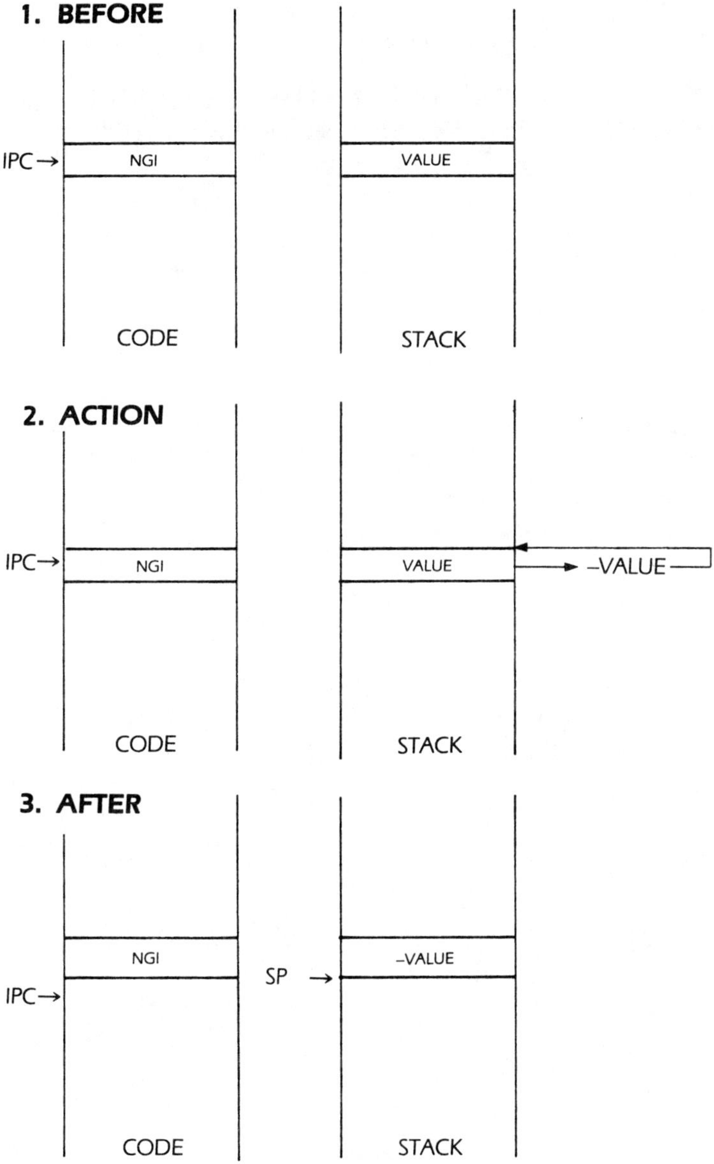

Syntax: **SBI**
Opcode: **149 ($95)**
Operation: **Subtract TOS from TOS – 1**

SBI pops TOS, subtracts it from TOS – 1, and replaces TOS – 1 with the difference obtained. The difference pushed becomes the new TOS.

SBI OPERATION:

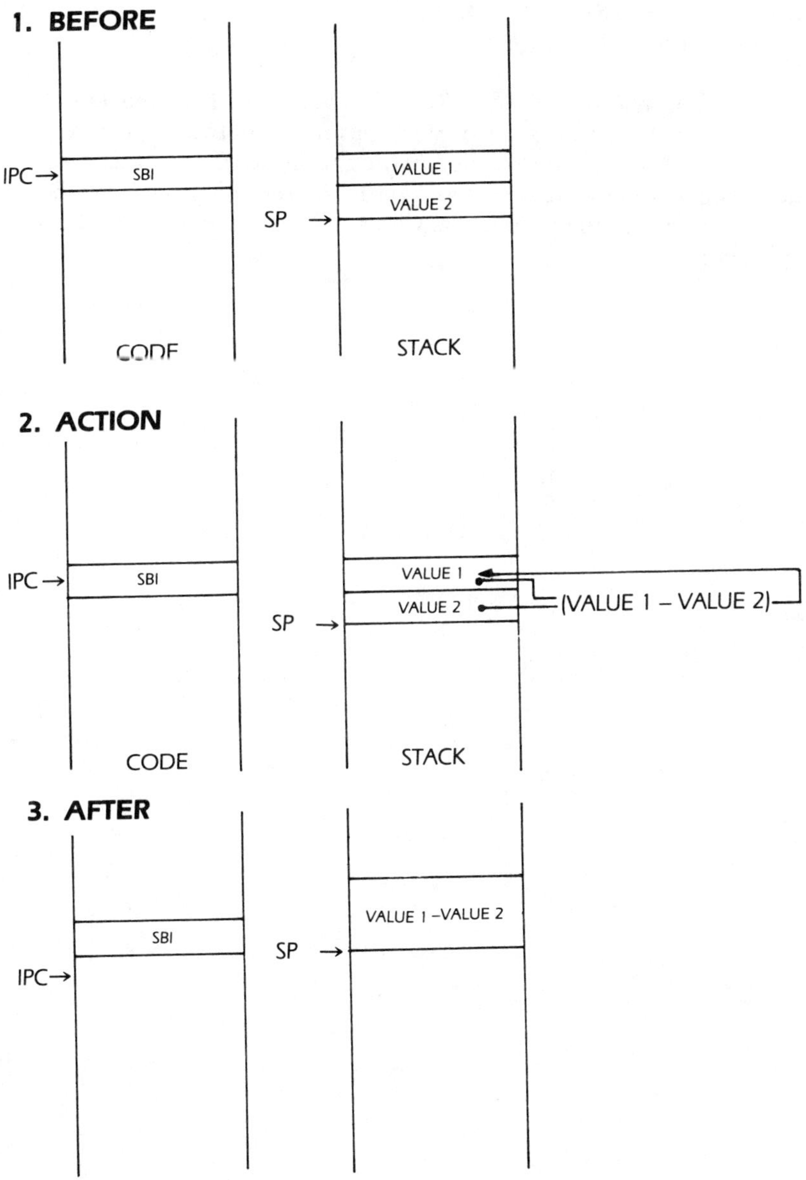

Syntax: **MPI**
Opcode: **143 ($8F)**
Operation: **Multiply integers**

MPI is used to multiply TOS by TOS – 1. The integer TOS and TOS – 1 are popped, the product is pushed. Since the product of two 16-bit integers may require 32 bits, this instruction may cause an overflow to occur if the values being multiplied are too large. No run-time error is given if overflow occurs; making sure the product fits within 16 bits is the responsibility of the programmer.

MPI OPERATION:

1. BEFORE

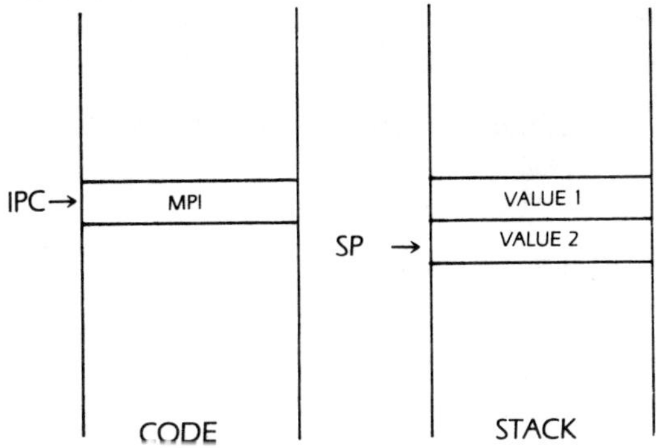

2. ACTION

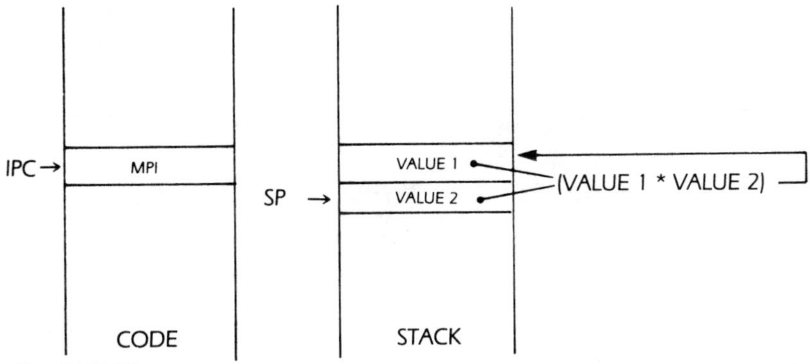

3. AFTER

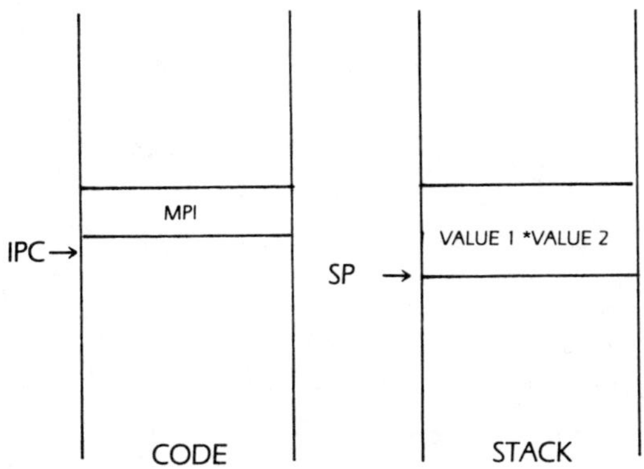

Syntax: **SQI**
Opcode: **152 ($98)**
Operation: **Square integer**

SQI replaces TOS with the square of the value on TOS. If overflow occurs, no error is given.

SQI OPERATION:

1. BEFORE

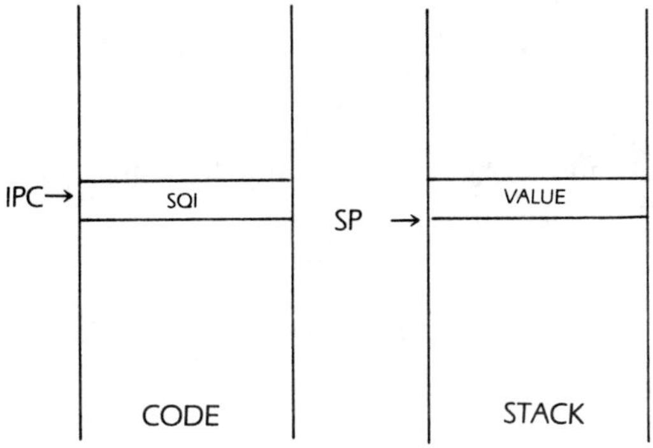

2. ACTION

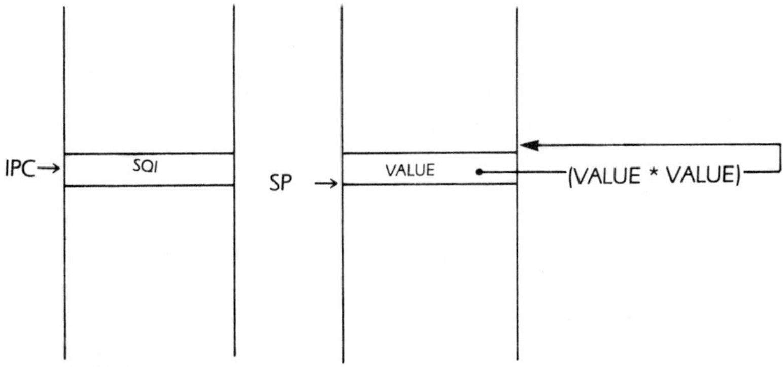

3. AFTER

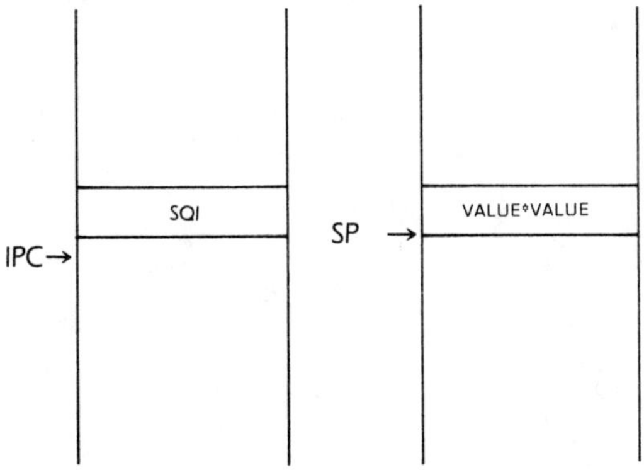

Syntax: **DVI**
Opcode: **134 ($86)**
Operation: **Divide integers**

DVI divides TOS – 1 by TOS and pushes the result. If a division by zero occurs, a run-time error is given.

DVI OPERATION:

1. BEFORE

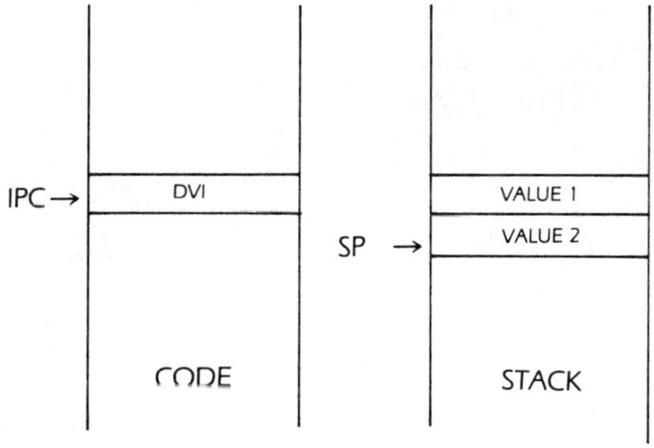

2. ACTION

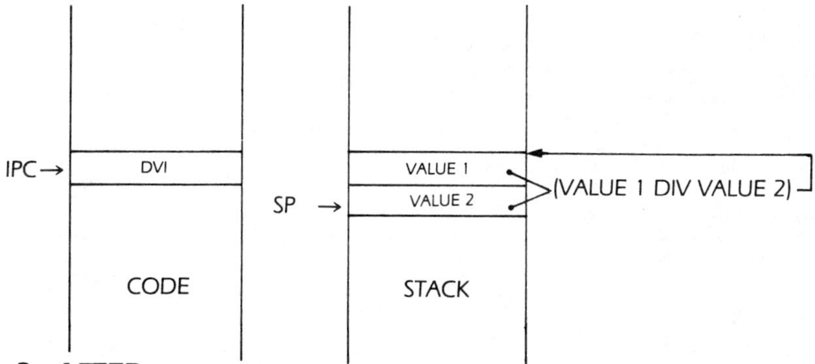

3. AFTER

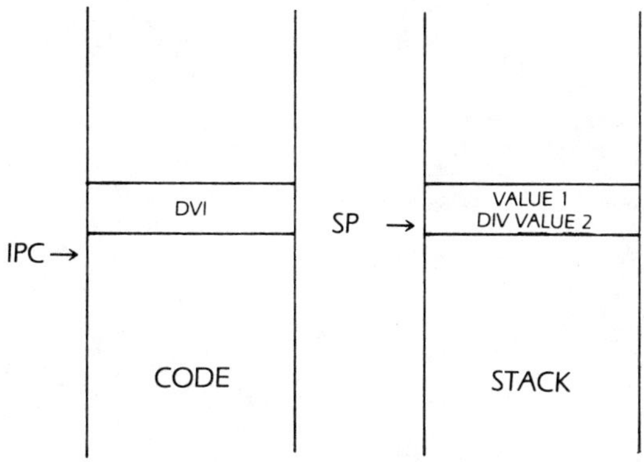

Syntax: MODI
Opcode: 142 ($BE)
Operation: Compute the modulo of two integers

MODI divides TOS – 1 by TOS and pushes the remainder. A division by zero run-time error is given if TOS – 1 is zero.

MODI OPERATION:

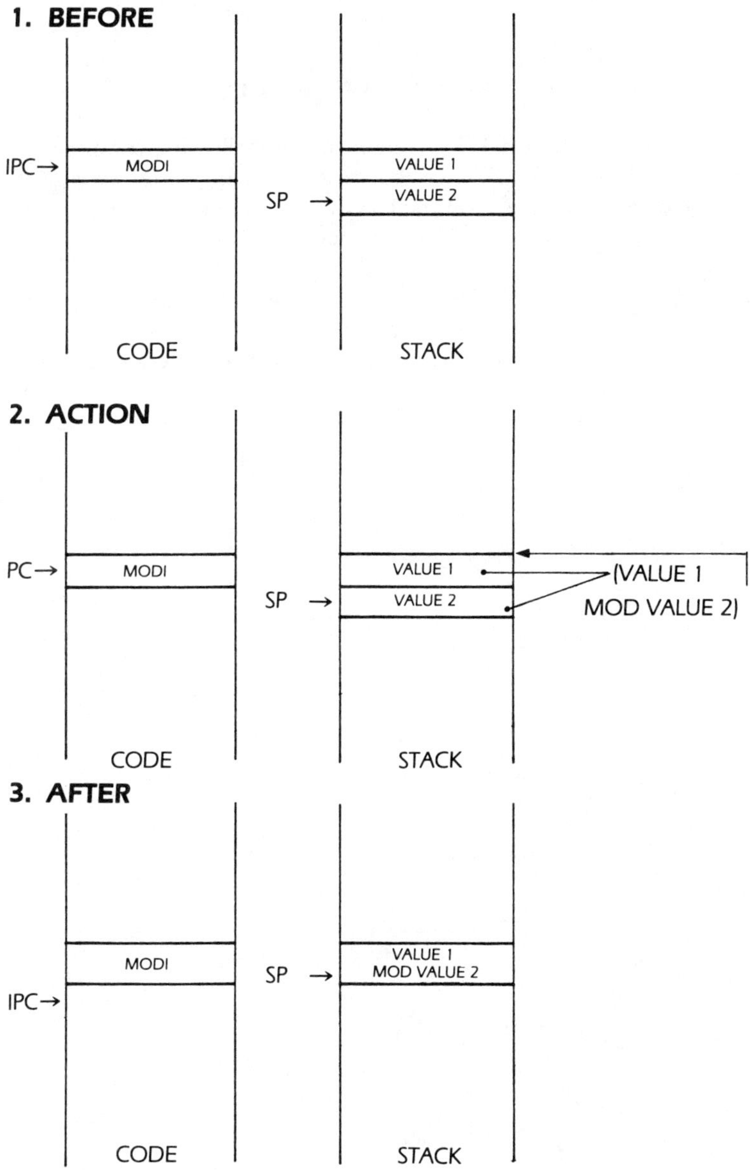

Syntax: CHK
Opcode: 136 ($88)
Operation: Check value to see if it is within a range

CHK expects three words on TOS. It performs the following comparison: TOS – 1 <= TOS – 2 <= TOS. If this relation is true, CHK pops TOS and TOS – 1 (leaving TOS – 2 on the top of the stack) and returns to the caller. If this relation does not hold a run-time error is given.

CHK is used to check to see if an array index is within bounds. It is also used to make sure that a value being stored into a subrange is within that subrange. You can prevent the emission of the CHK instruction by using the (*$R – *) compiler option.

CHK OPERATION:

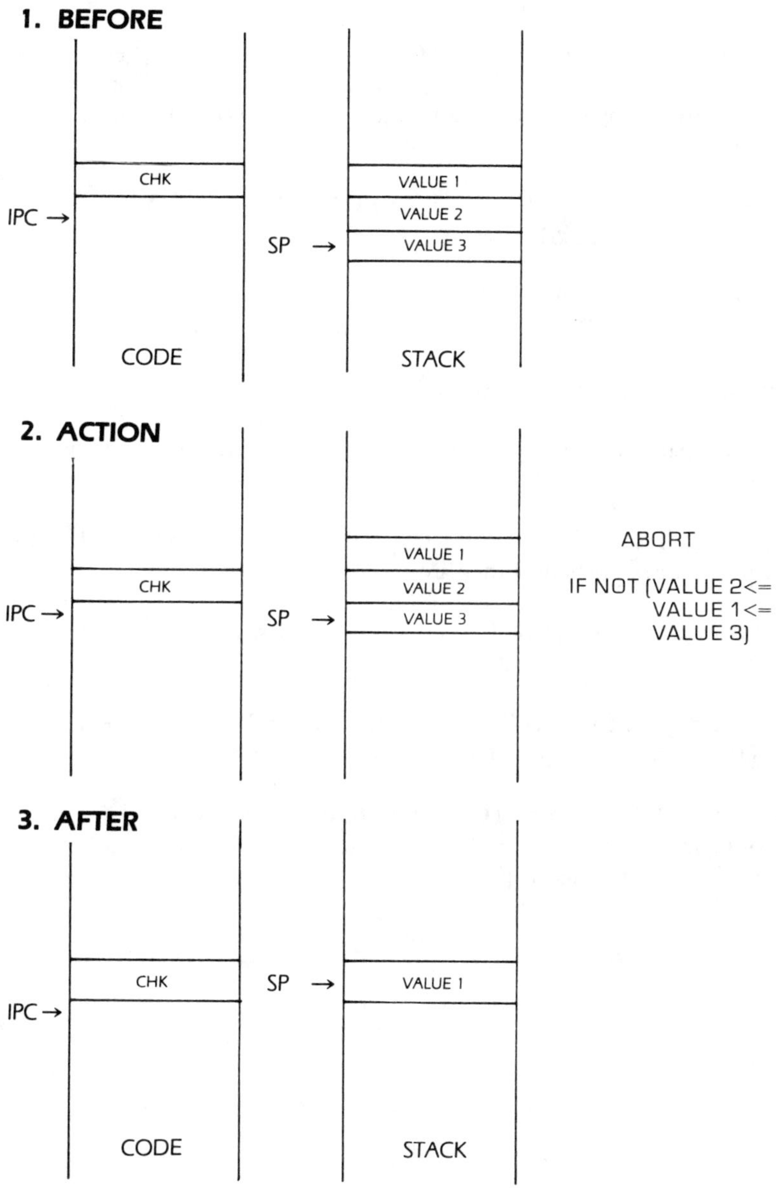

Integer Comparisons. General

The integer comparisons compare TOS – 1 with TOS. If the specified comparison is true the value $0001 (true) is pushed onto the evaluation stack. If the specified comparison does not hold, then $0000 (false) is pushed onto the evaluation stack.

Syntax:	**EQUI**	**NEQI**	**LEQI**
	LESI	**GEQI**	**GTRI**
Opcode:	**195 ($C3)**	**203 ($CB)**	**200 ($C8)**
	201 ($C9)	**196 ($C4)**	**197 ($C5)**

Operation: Compare two integers

EQUI compares TOS to TOS – 1. If they are equal, true is pushed; if they are not equal, false is pushed.

NEQI compares TOS to TOS – 1 to see if they are not equal. If they are not equal, true is pushed; if they are equal, false is pushed.

LEQI compares TOS – 1 to TOS. If TOS – 1 is less than or equal to TOS then true is pushed, otherwise false is pushed.

LESI compares the integer TOS – 1 to the integer TOS. If TOS – 1 is less than TOS then true is pushed, otherwise false is pushed.

GEQI and GTRI compare TOS – 1 to TOS to see if TOS – 1 is greater than or equal, or greater than TOS (respectively). If the relation holds, true is pushed otherwise false is pushed.

Non-Integer Comparisons

Syntax:	OPCODE:	OPERATION:
EQU UB	175	Compare TOS to NOS and push true if equal
NEQ UB	183	Push true if TOS <> NOS
LEQ UB	180	Push true if NOS <= TOS
LES UB	181	Push true if NOS < TOS
GEQ UB	176	Push true if NOS >= TOS
GTR UB	177	Push true if NOS > TOS

Where UB is:

2 if TOS, NOS are REAL.
4 if TOS, NOS are STRINGs.
6 if TOS, NOS are BOOLEAN.
8 if TOS, NOS are SETs.
10 if TOS, NOS are byte arrays.
12 if TOS, NOS are blocks of words.

Actual examples of these comparisons will be presented in the following sections.

REAL Operations

Syntax: FLT
Opcode: 138 ($8A)
Operation: Convert integer on TOS to a floating point number

FLT is a unary operator. It pops the two-byte integer value off of the stack, converts it to the equivalent floating point number, and pushes the floating point number back onto the stack. This opcode is emitted whenever an expression contains both integers and floating point values such as:

```
F*I
```

where F is a floating point value and I is an integer value. Note that this opcode is emitted whenever the compiler encounters an integer and has already determined that the expression is a floating point expression.

FLT OPERATION:

1. BEFORE

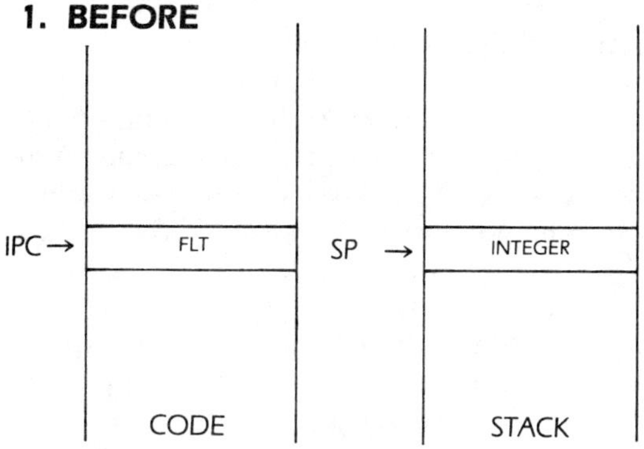

2. ACTION

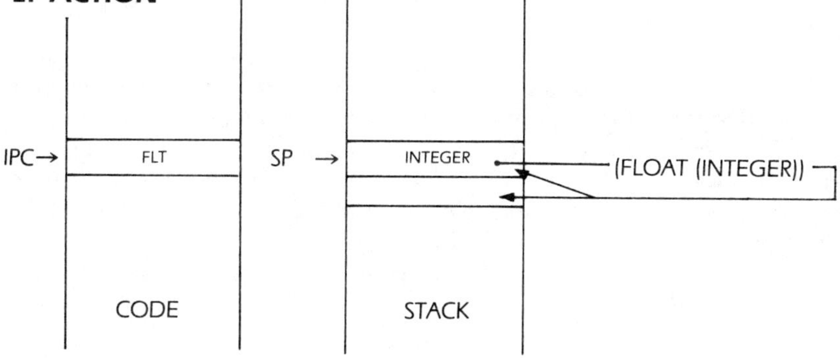

3. AFTER

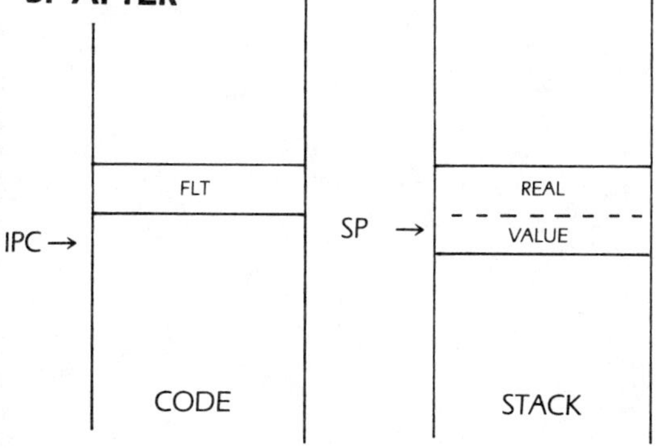

Syntax: **FLO**
Opcode: **137 ($89)**
Operation: **Convert NOS to a floating point value**

FLO is a unary operator that converts the integer NOS to a floating point value. TOS is assumed to be a floating point value, it is popped and saved in a temporary location while NOS is converted to a floating point value. After NOS is converted to a floating point value, the saved TOS is pushed back onto the stack.

FLO is used in situations where the compiler has determined that an expression is of type REAL but some integer values have already been pushed onto the evaluation stack. For example, a statement of the form:

```
F := I + F;
```

will cause the emission of the FLO opcode. If you can rearrange your expression so that the compiler realizes that the expression type is of type REAL early in the evaluation you can avoid the emission of the FLO opcode. This is highly desired as the FLO opcode executes a little slower than the FLT opcode. The previous example is easily modified by swapping I and F in the expression on the right hand side.

FLO OPERATION:

1. BEFORE

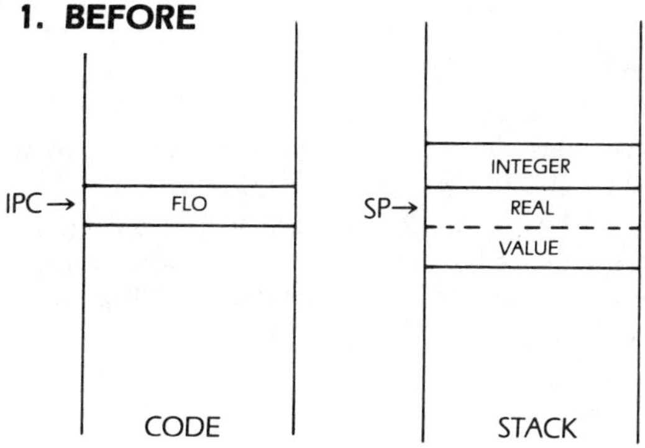

2. ACTION

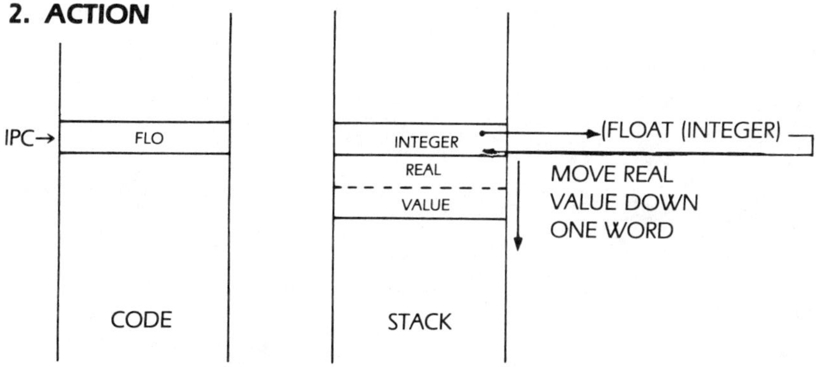

3. AFTER

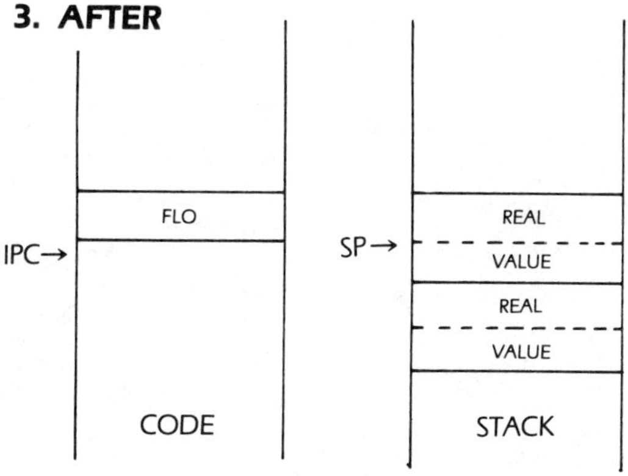

Syntax: TNC
Opcode: 158,22
Operation: Truncate REAL

TNC is a unary operator that takes the REAL on TOS, converts it to an integer by truncating it, and pushes the integer result. Note that TNC has a two-byte opcode. Opcode 158 is really the CSP (call special procedure) opcode with 22 being the special procedure number for the truncate routine. The TNC opcode is emitted anytime the Pascal TRUNC(–) function is encountered within an expression.

TNC OPERATION:

1. BEFORE

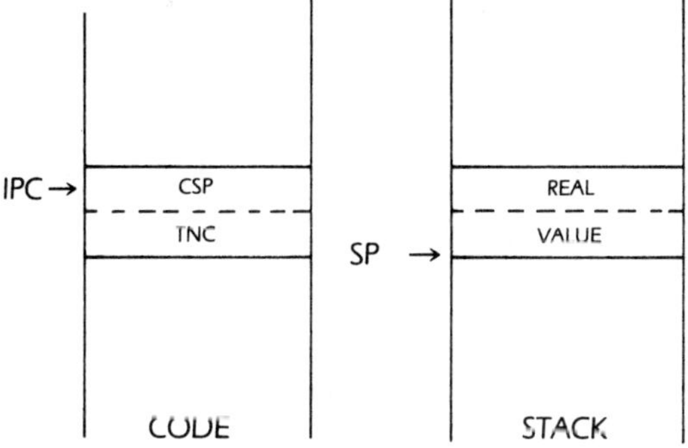

2. ACTION

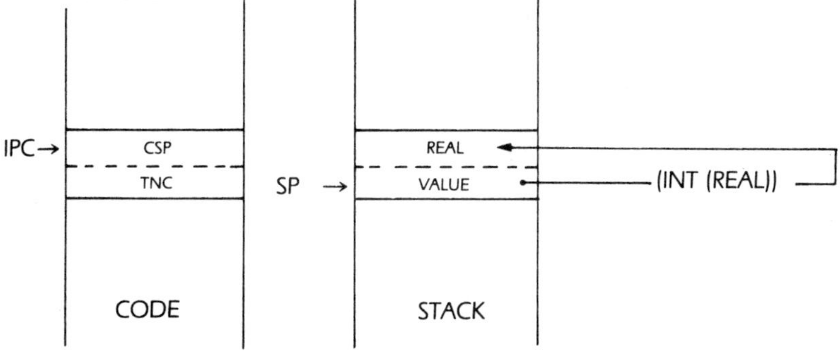

3. AFTER

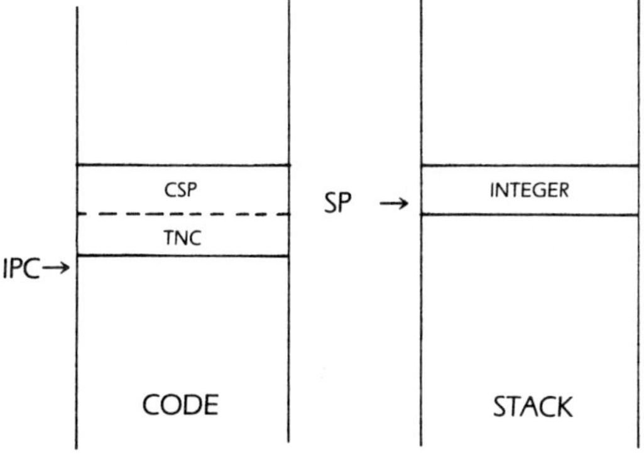

Syntax: **RND**
Opcode: **158,23**
Operation: **Round REAL on TOS and truncate**

RND is a unary operator that takes the REAL value on TOS, rounds it using the formulae:

```
IF X>=0 THEN ROUND := TRUNC(X+0.5)
ELSE ROUND := TRUNC(X-0.5);
```

Note that, like TNC, RND is a two-byte CSP instruction.

RND OPERATION:

1. BEFORE

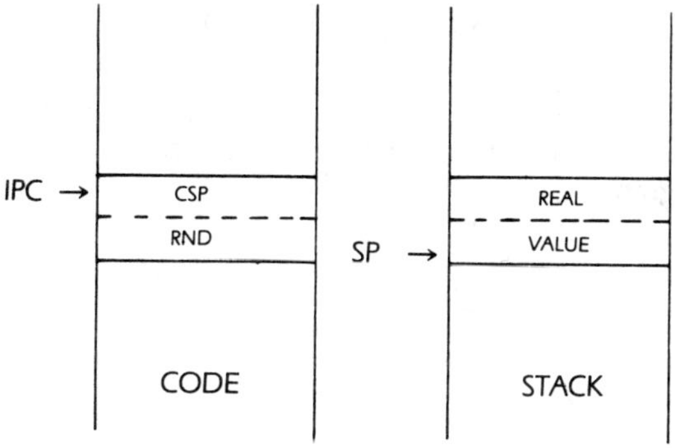

2. ACTION

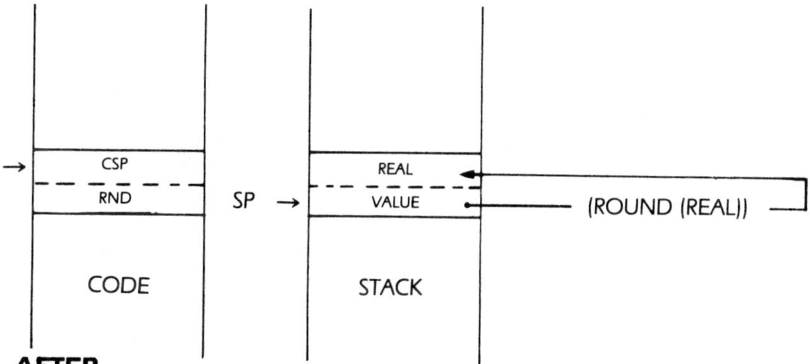

3. AFTER

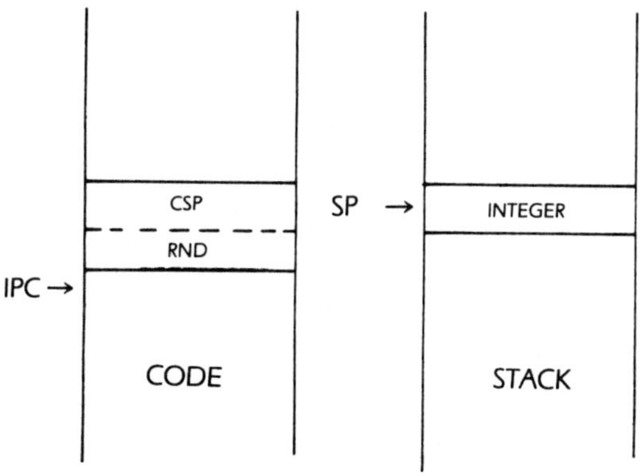

Syntax: **ABR**
Opcode: **129 ($81)**
Operation: **Take absolute value of REAL TOS**

ABR is a unary operator that takes the REAL value on TOS and pushes its absolute value. This opcode is emitted whenever the ABS function is encountered within the program.

ABR OPERATION:

1. BEFORE

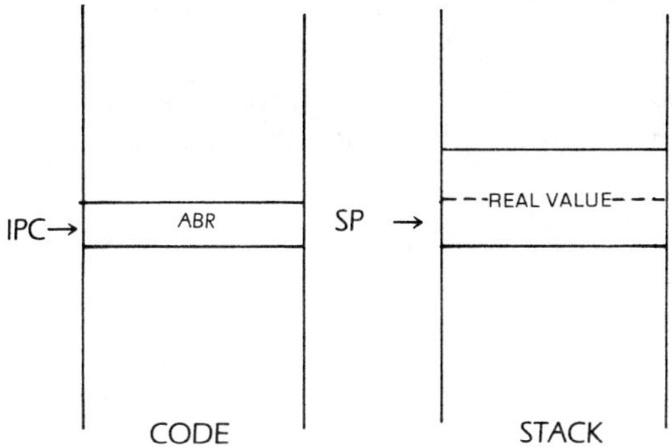

2. ACTION

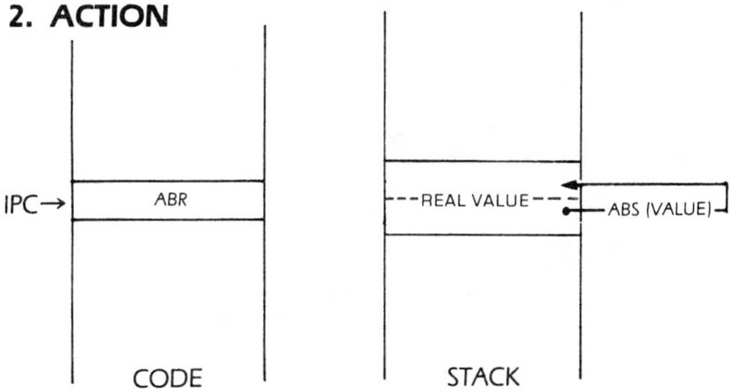

3. AFTER

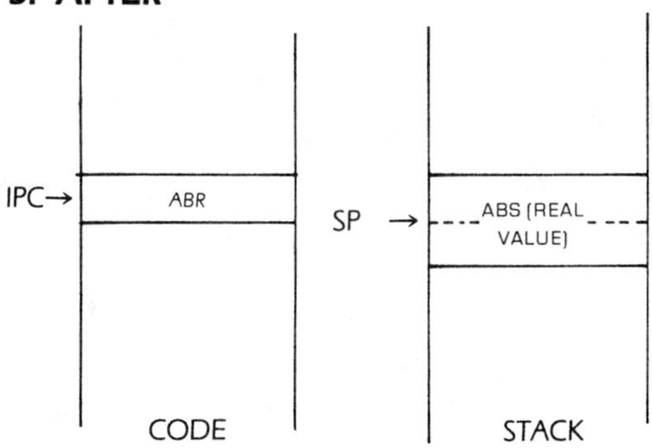

Syntax: ADR
Opcode: 131 ($83)
Operation: Add reals

ADR adds the REAL TOS to the REAL NOS and leaves the resulting sum on the TOS. If an overflow occurs, then an execution error results.

ADR OPERATION:

1. BEFORE

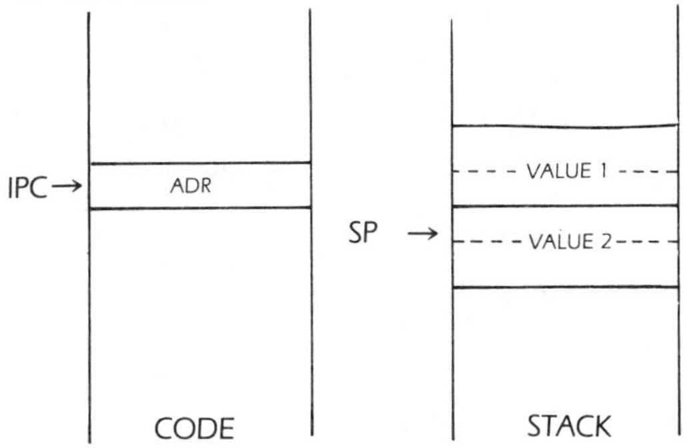

2. ACTION

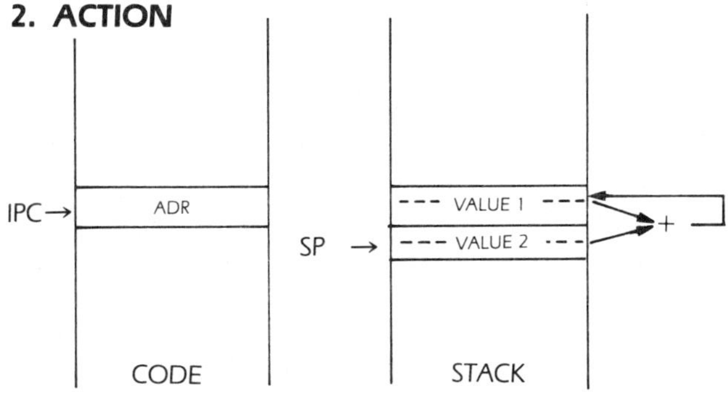

3. AFTER

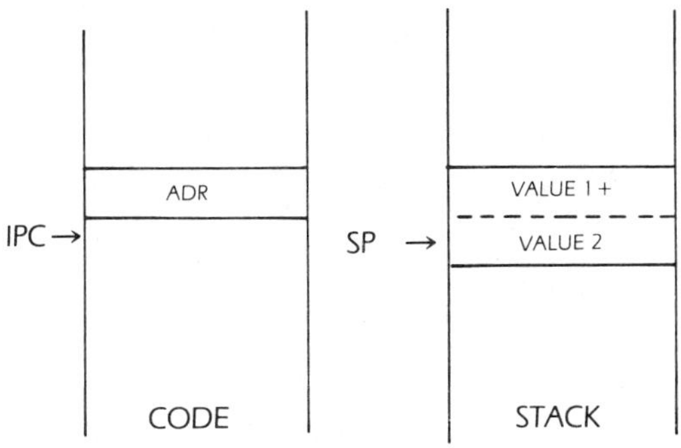

Syntax: **NGR**
Opcode: **146 ($92)**
Operation: **Negate REAL**

NGR is a unary operation that negates the REAL value on TOS. If TOS is negative, it becomes positive; if TOS is positive, it becomes negative.

NGR OPERATION:

1. BEFORE

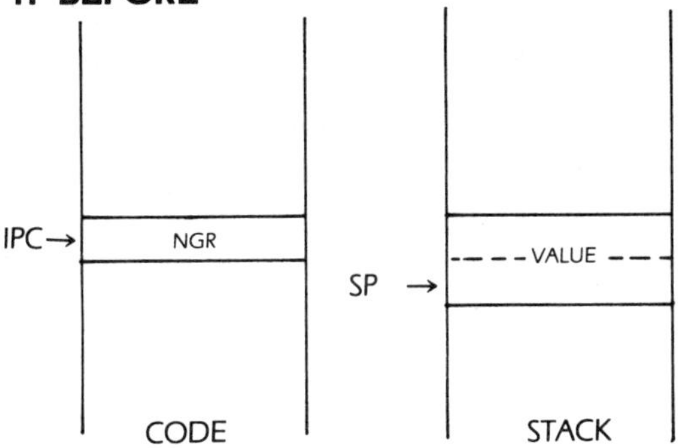

2. ACTION

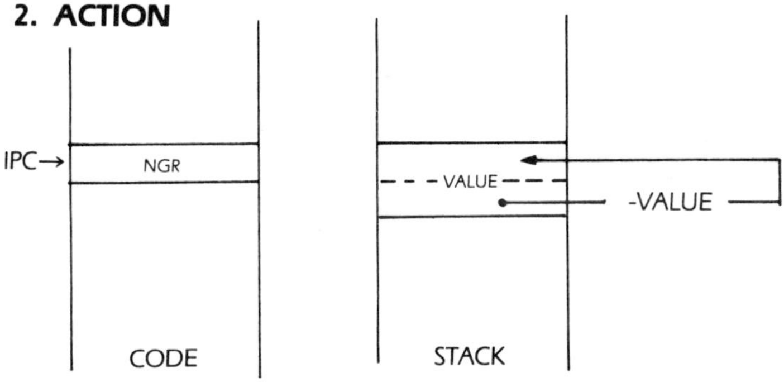

3. AFTER

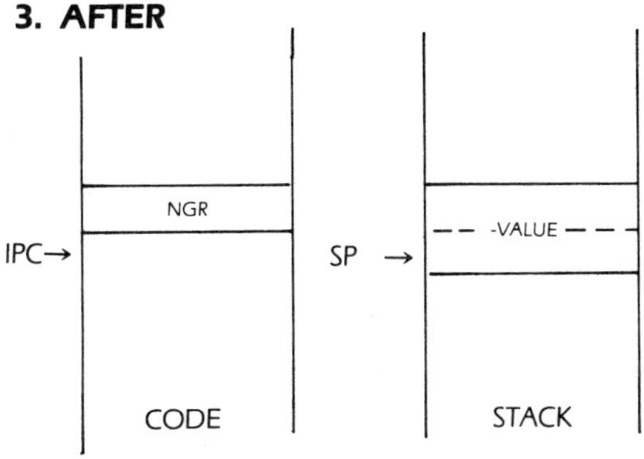

Syntax: **SBR**
Opcode: **150 ($96)**
Operation: **Subtract REALs**

SBR subtracts TOS from NOS and pushes the difference. If an underflow occurs a run-time error is given.

SBR OPERATION:

1. BEFORE

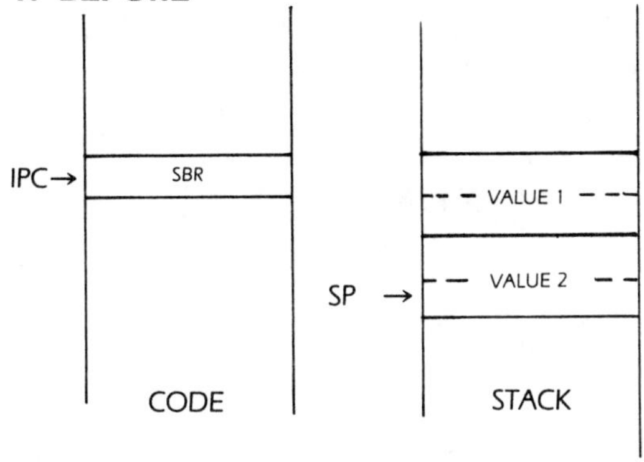

2. ACTION

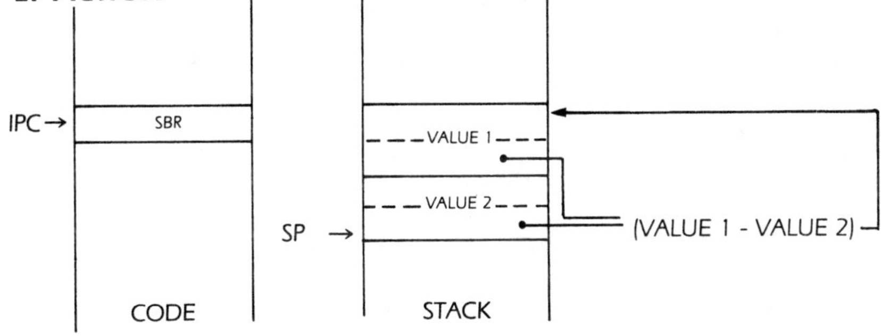

3. AFTER

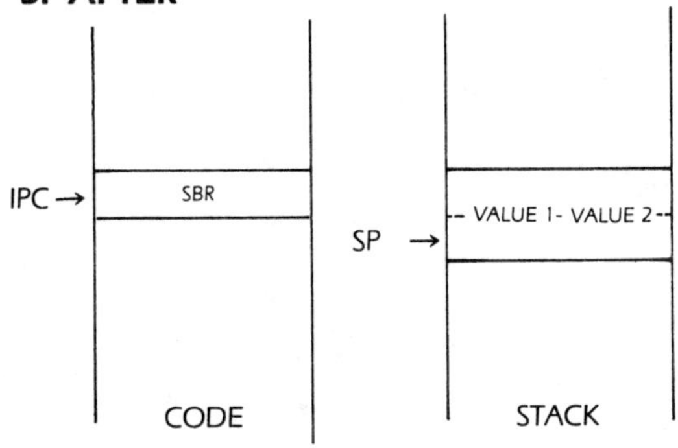

Syntax: **MPR**
Opcode: **144 ($90)**
Operation: **Multiply REALs**

TOS is multiplied by NOS and the resulting product is pushed. If an overflow occurs then a run-time error is reported.

MPR OPERATION:

1. BEFORE

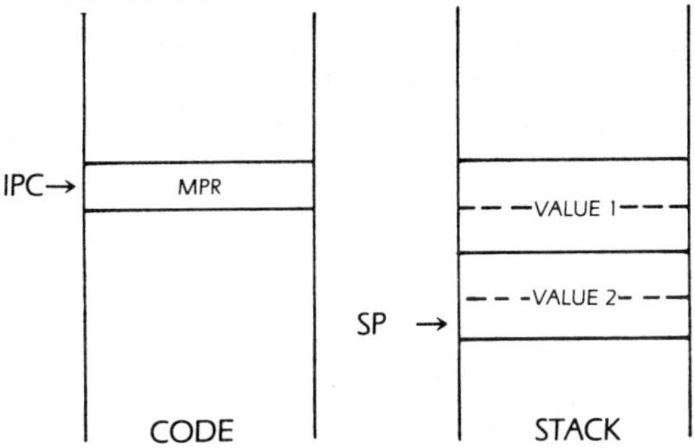

2. ACTION

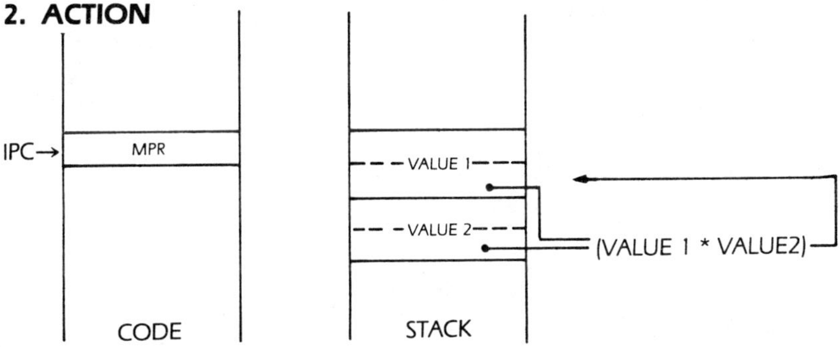

3. AFTER

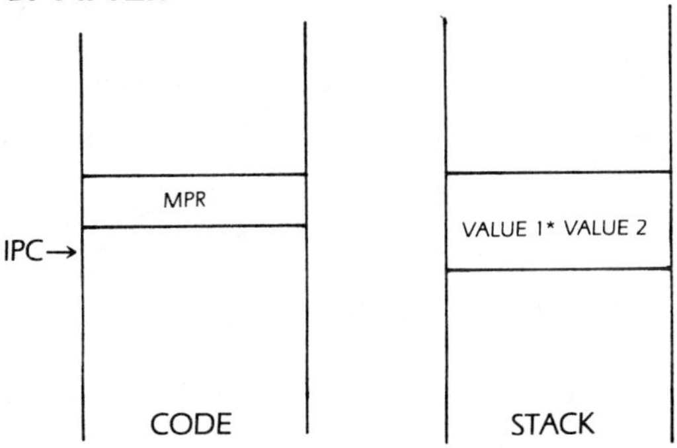

Syntax: **SQR**
Opcode: **153 ($99)**
Operation: **Square REAL TOS**

TOS is multiplied by itself and the resulting product is pushed. This opcode is emitted whenever the SQR function is encountered within a program. If an overflow occurs during the execution of this program a run-time error is given.

SQR OPERATION:

1. BEFORE

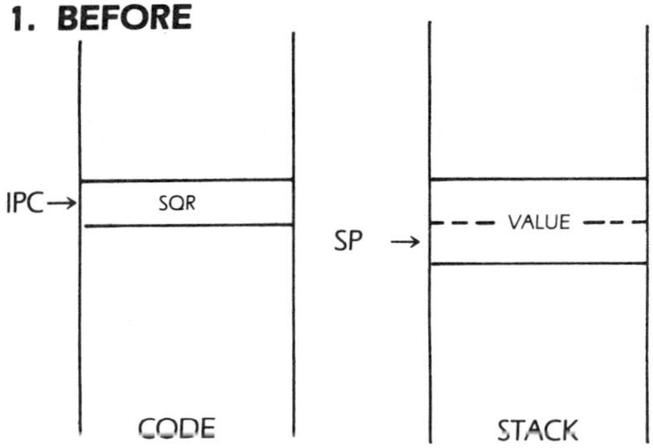

2. ACTION

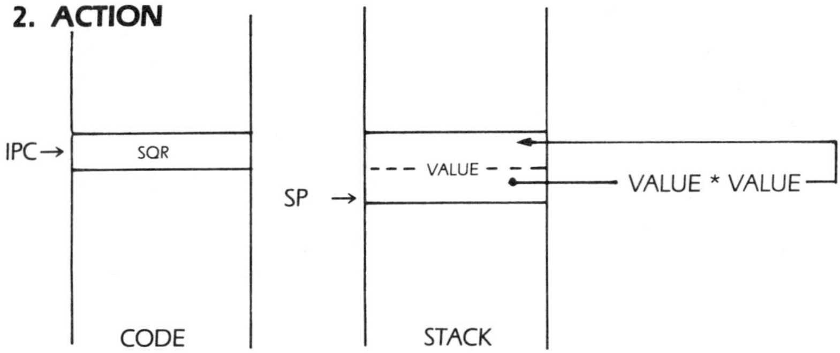

3. AFTER

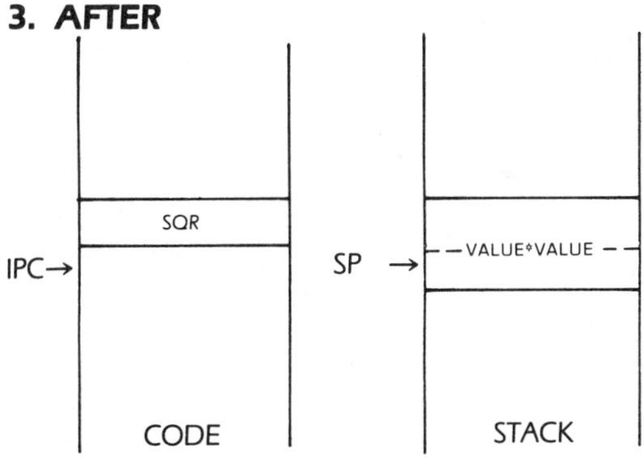

Syntax: **DVR**
Opcode: **135 ($87)**
Operation: **Divide REALs**

DVR divides the real NOS by the REAL TOS. The resulting quotient is pushed. A run-time error is given if division by zero is attempted.

DVR OPERATION:

1. BEFORE

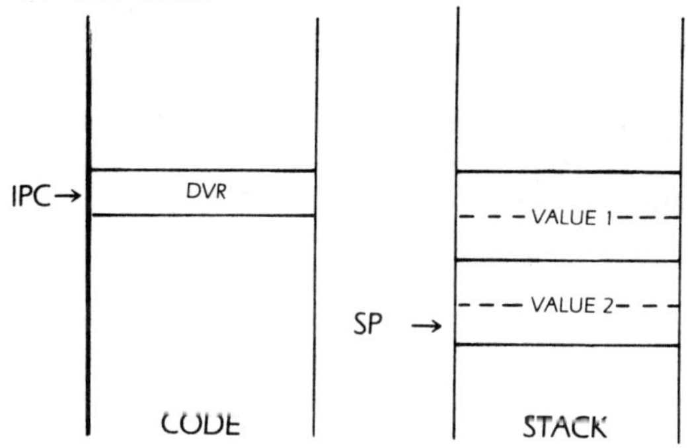

2. ACTION

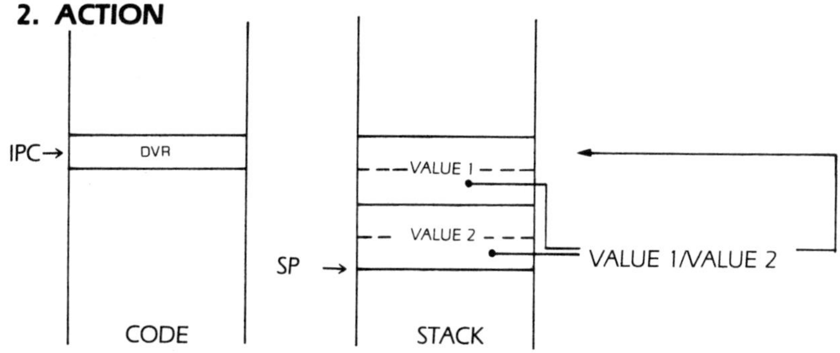

3. AFTER

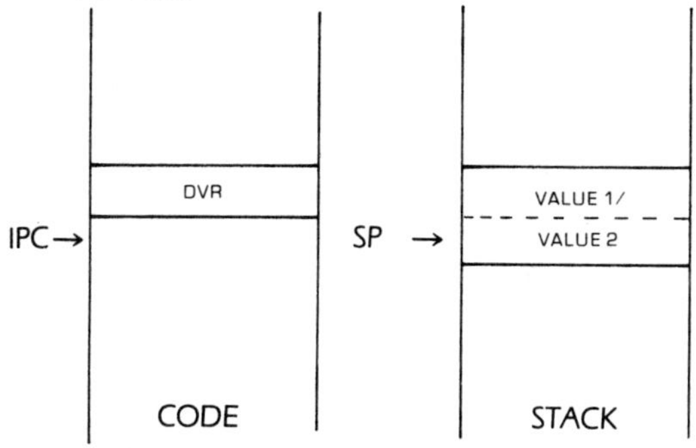

Syntax: **POT**
Opcode: **158,35**
Operation: **Compute power of ten**

POT expects an integer in the range 0..38 on the TOS. POT pushes the value of 10 raised to the TOS power onto the stack. If TOS is not in the range 0..38 an execution error is given. POT allows the rest of the system to operate in an implementation independent fashion as well as speed up certain floating point I/O processes.

POT OPERATION:

1. BEFORE

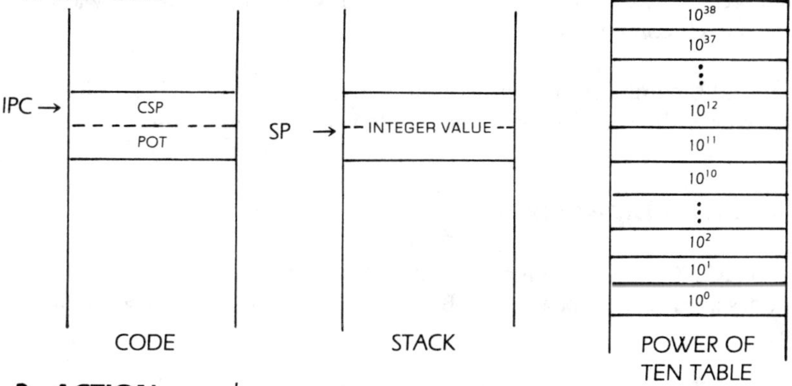

2. ACTION

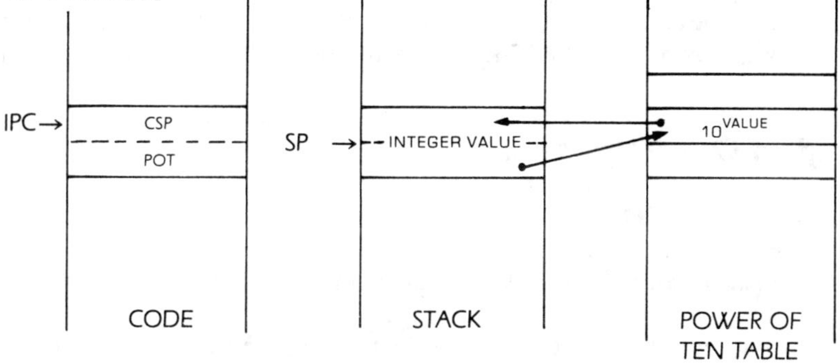

3. AFTER

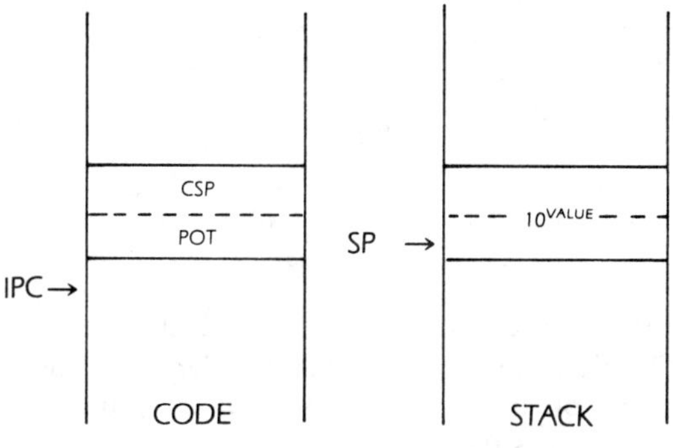

REAL Comparisons

The REAL comparisons are handled by the non-integer comparison operators previously described. The UB byte following the opcode is always two for a REAL comparison.

The REAL comparisons compare the REAL TOS to the REAL NOS and push true if the comparison is met. False is pushed otherwise.

STRING Comparisons

The STRING comparisons are also handled by the non-integer comparison opcodes already described. The UB byte for a STRING comparison is always four.

When comparing two strings TOS and NOS contain pointers to the strings which are to be compared. These strings are compared and TRUE is pushed if the comparison holds, FALSE is pushed otherwise.

Logical Operations

Syntax: LAND
Opcode: 132 ($84)
Operation: Peform logical AND operation

LAND logically ANDs TOS with NOS pushing the result back onto the stack. Note that a complete 16-bit bit-by-bit AND is performed even though only the low order bit is used in boolean operations. This knowledge lets you write code that performs a bit-by-bit AND operation on two integers using the ORD and ODD functions. For example, to AND the integer I with $0F you would use the statement:

```
ANDED := ORD(ODD(I) AND ODD(15));
```

which ANDs I with 15 ($0F) and places the result in ANDED. Note that the functions ORD and ODD do not generate any code. They are simply type transfer functions that let you treat integers as Boolean values and Boolean values (or any other scalar) as integers.

LAND OEPRATION:

1. BEFORE

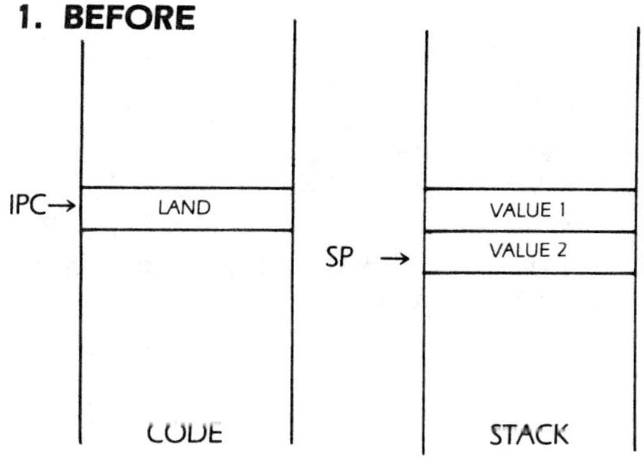

2. ACTION

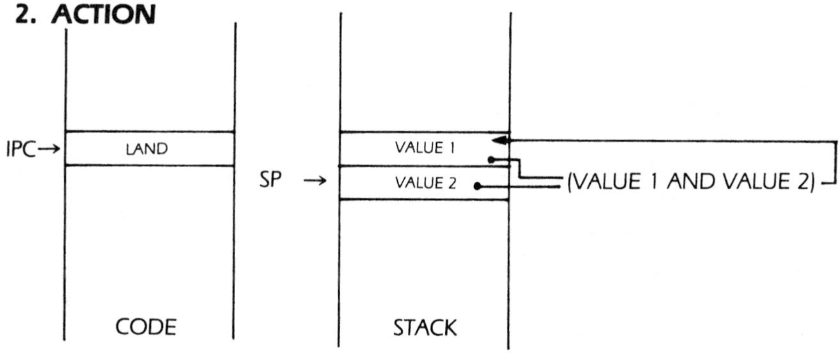

3. AFTER

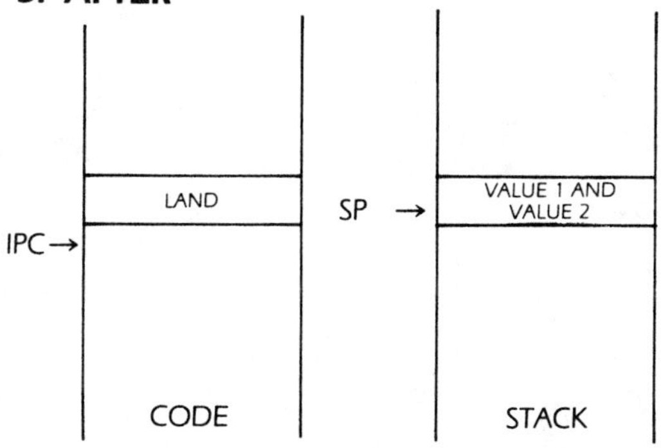

Syntax: **LOR**
Opcode: **141 ($8D)**
Operation: **Logical OR**

LOR logically ORs the value on TOS with NOS. The resulting value is pushed back onto the stack. This opcode is emitted whenever the OR operator is encountered within a logical expression. Although only bit zero is used in a Boolean operation, all 16-bits of the two words on TOS are OR'd together so this operation can be used to OR two integers together in the same manner as described for the AND opcode.

LOR OPERATION:

1. BEFORE

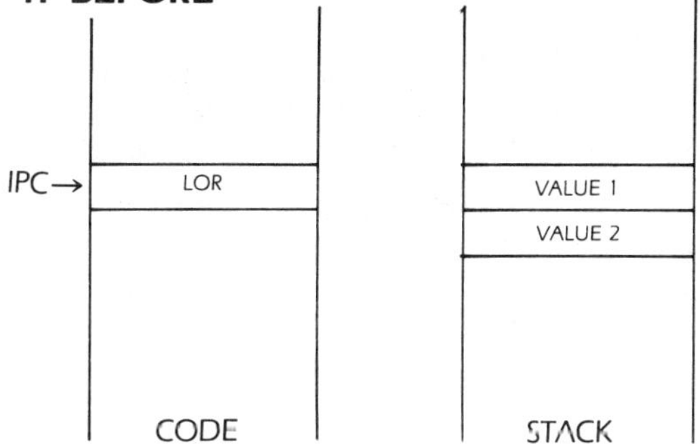

2. ACTION

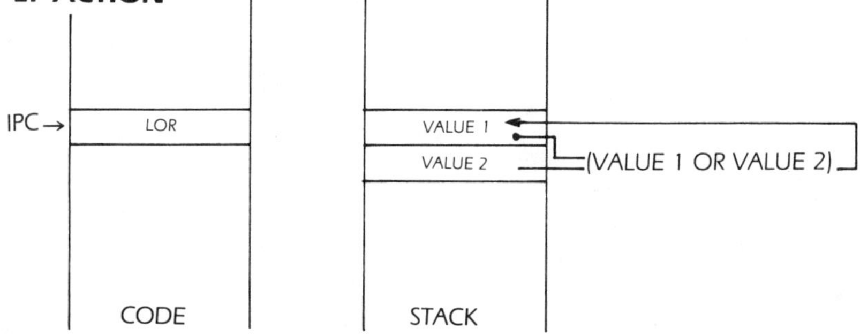

3. AFTER

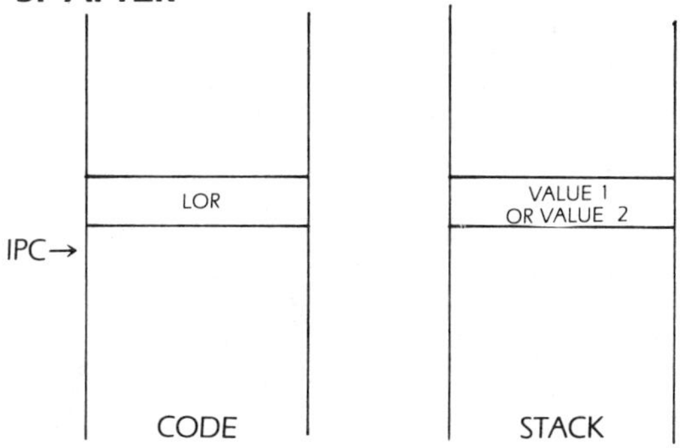

Syntax: LNOT
Opcode: 147 ($93)
Operation: Logical NOT

LNOT takes the one's complement, or logical negation, of the value on TOS. To rephrase the last statement, LNOT inverts all the bits of the word on TOS. LNOT is a unary operator affecting only the value on TOS. As with LAND and LOR, LNOT can be used to logically negate an integer by using the ODD and ORD procedures as follows:

```
NEGATED := ORD(NOT ODD(I));
```

LNOT OPERATION:

1. BEFORE

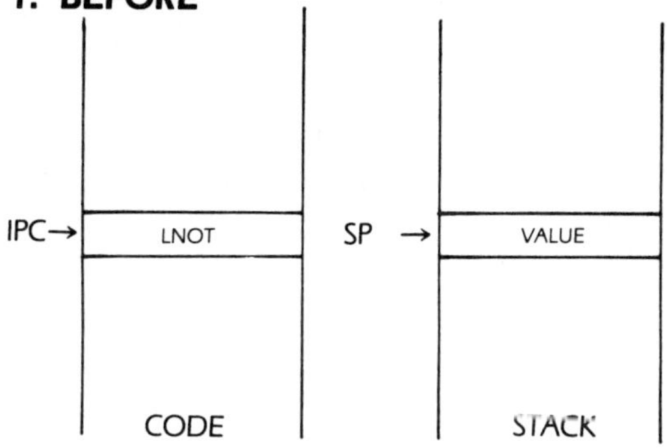

2. ACTION

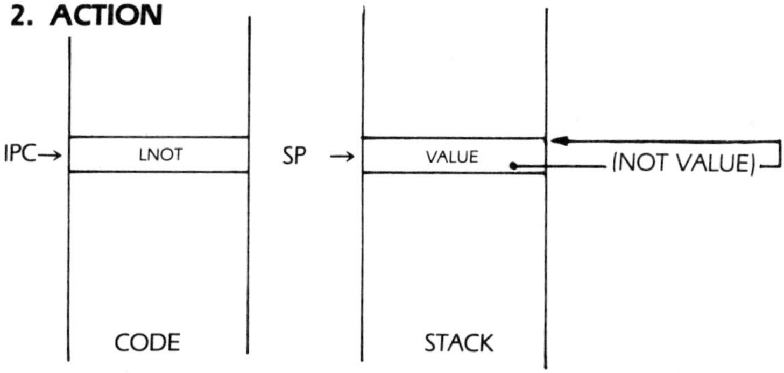

3. AFTER

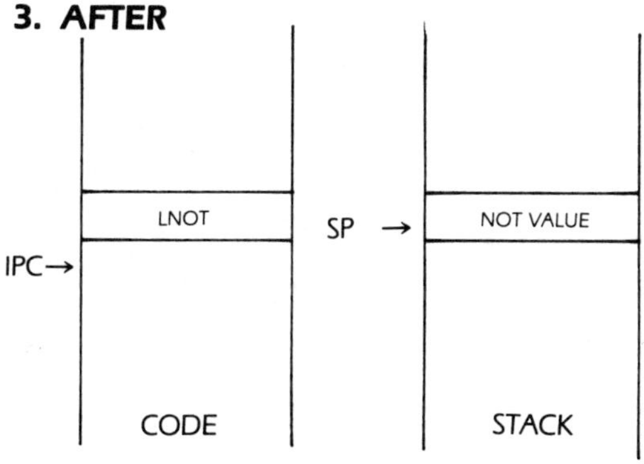

Logical Comparisons

The logical comparisons use the non-integer comparison opcodes previously described. For logical comparisons the UB byte is always set to six. A logical comparison always compares bit zero of NOS with bit zero of TOS (i.e., NOS and TOS are AND'd with one before the comparisons are made). TRUE is pushed if the comparison holds, FALSE is pushed otherwise.

Set Operations

Syntax: ADJ UB
Opcode: 160 ($A0)
Operation: Set adjust

Whenever set operations are performed on the evaluation stack the size of the set data is often modified. For example, if you have a set variable COLOR which is of type SET OF [RED,BLUE,...,GREEN] and you make the assignment COLOR := [BLUE]; the size of the set pushed onto the stack is not necessarily the size of the destination variable. The ADJ instruction is used to adjust the set on TOS so that its size matches the size of the variable that the set on TOS is to be stored into. This is accomplished by adding zeroes to the high order bits of the set on TOS or by truncating the high order bits of the set on TOS. UB is the number of words that the final set on TOS must occupy.

ADJ OPERATION:

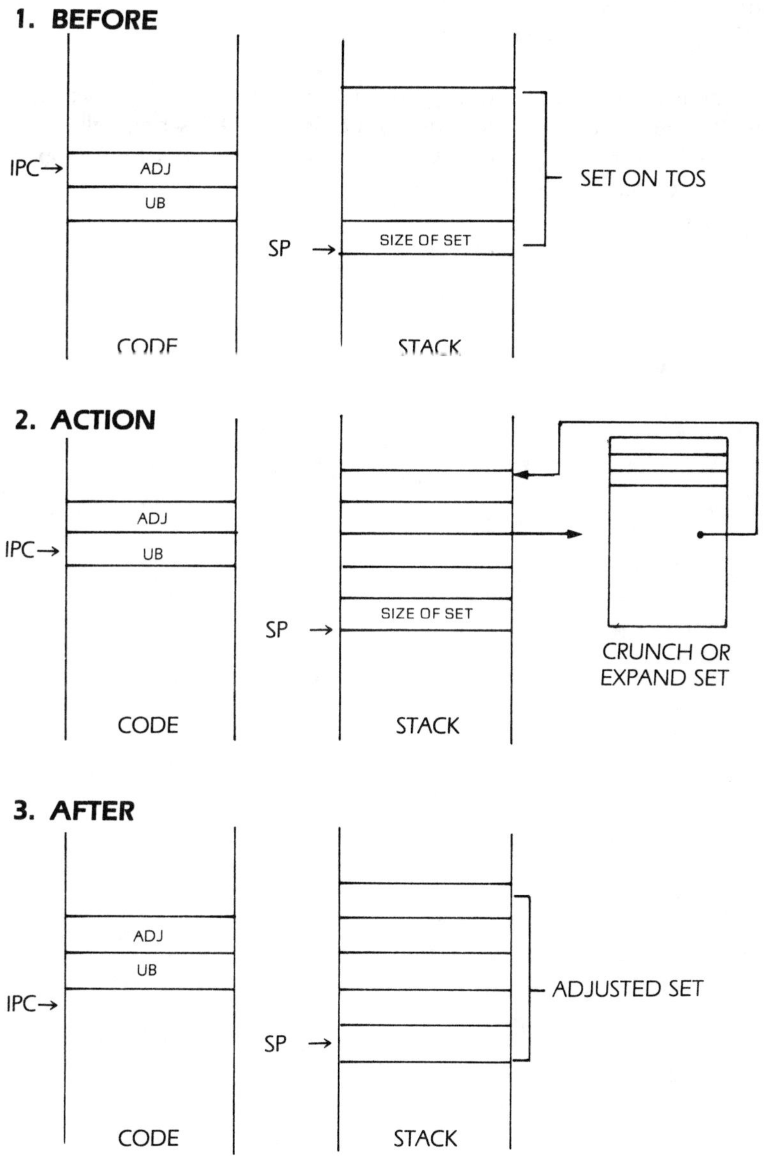

Syntax: SGS
Opcode: 151 ($97)
Operation: Build a singleton set

TOS contains an integer in the range 0..511. A set is created with a single element (the element whose element number is on TOS) set and all other bits set to zero. If the integer on TOS is not in the range 0..511 then give an execution error.

SGS OPERATION:

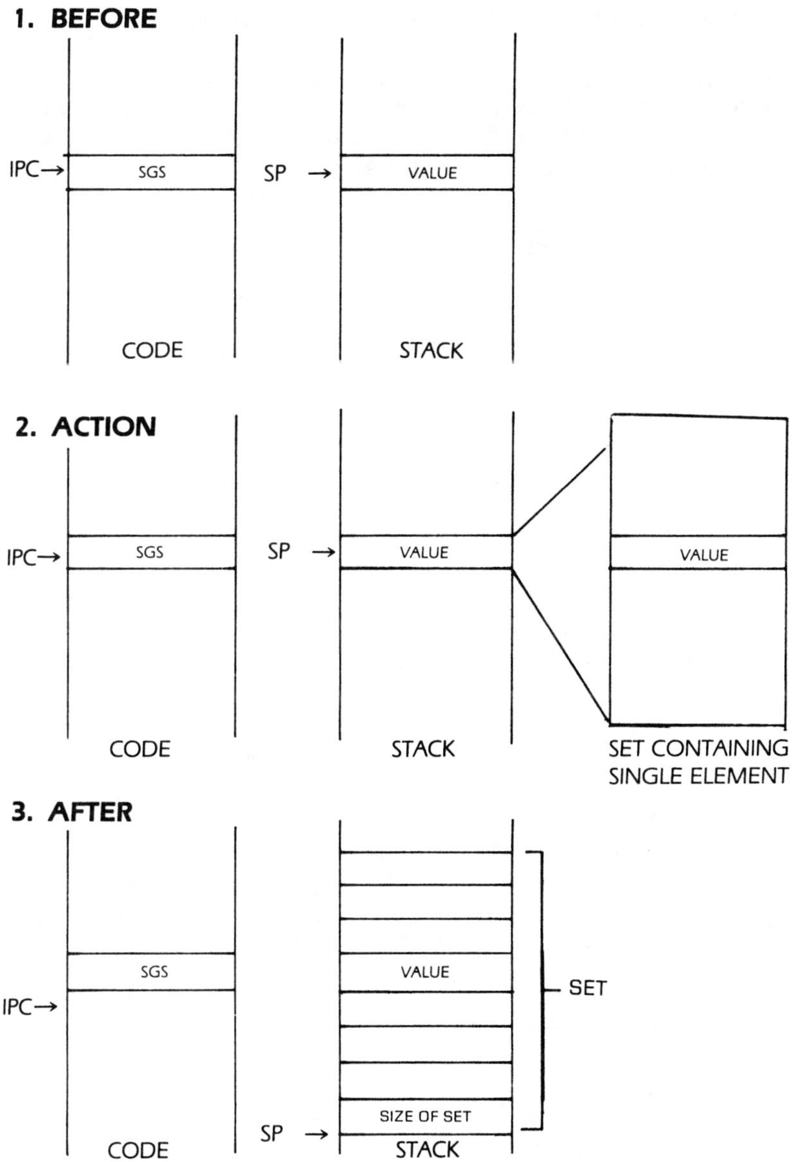

Syntax: **SRS**
Opcode: **148 ($94)**
Operation: **Build a subrange set**

The two integers on TOS and NOS are checked to make sure they are in the range 0..511. If either is out of this range then a run-time error results. Otherwise the set [TOS – 1..TOS] is pushed onto the evaluation stack. If TOS – 1 > TOS then the empty set ([]) is pushed.

SRS OPERATION:

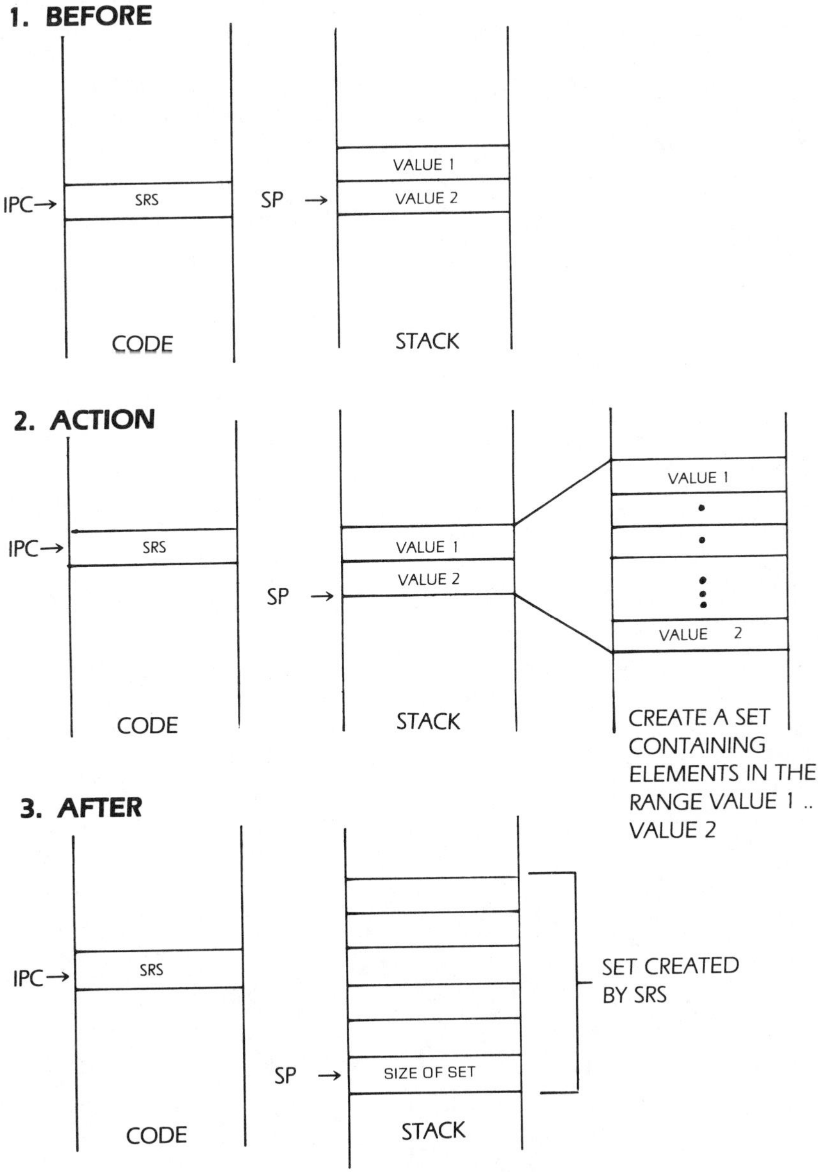

Syntax: **INN**
Opcode: **139 ($8B)**
Operation: **Set membership**

If the set on TOS contains the member whose bit number is specified by NOS, then push true, otherwise push false. This instruction can be used to see if a particular bit in a byte string is set.

INN OPERATION:

1. BEFORE

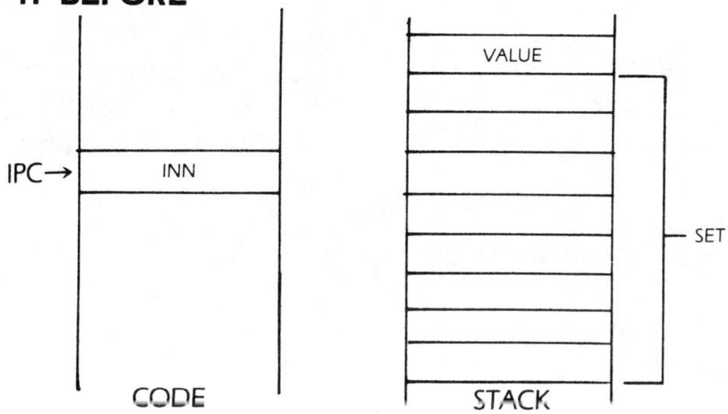

2. ACTION

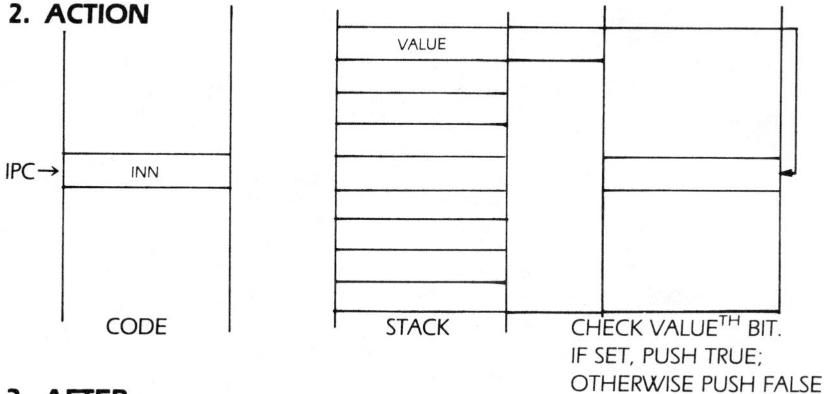

3. AFTER

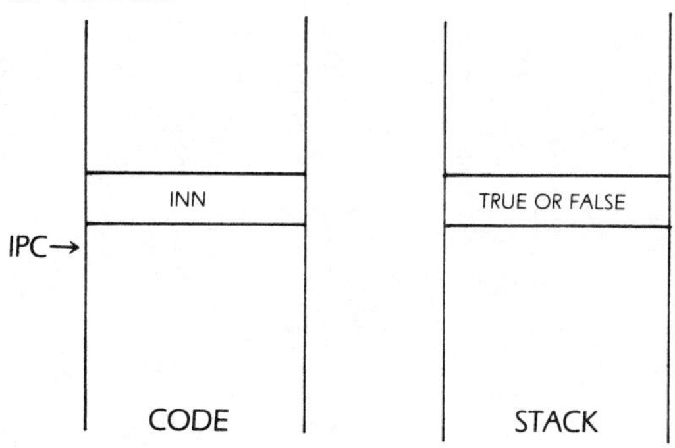

Syntax: **UNI**
Opcode: **156 ($9C)**
Operation: **Set union**

The union of the set on TOS and NOS is pushed onto the evaluation stack. The set union is obtained by ORing the set on TOS with the set on NOS. This instruction can be used to logically OR a byte string on TOS with a byte string on NOS.

The size of the resulting set is the size of the larger of the two sets.

UNI OPERATION:

1. BEFORE

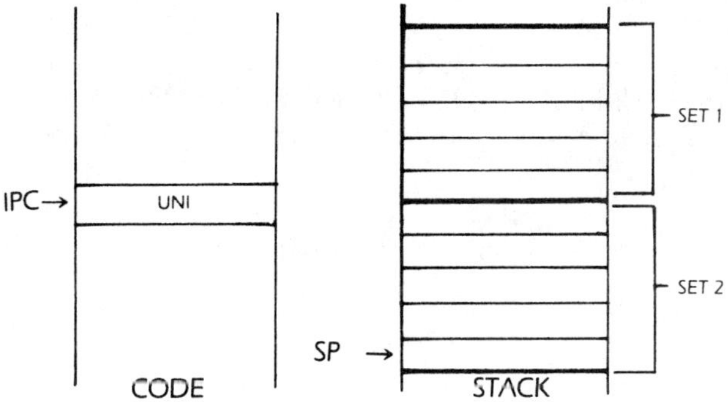

2. ACTION

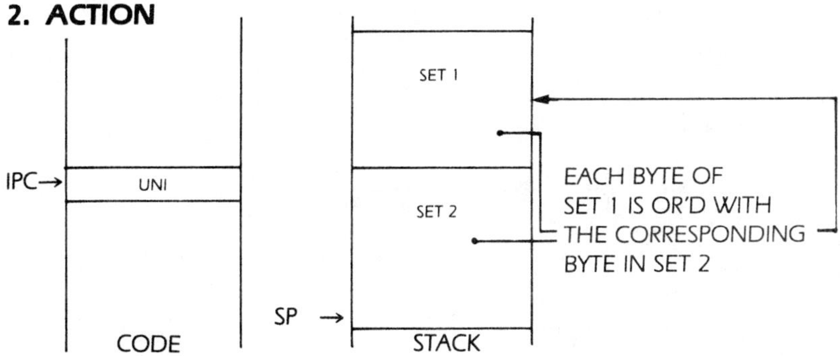

3. AFTER

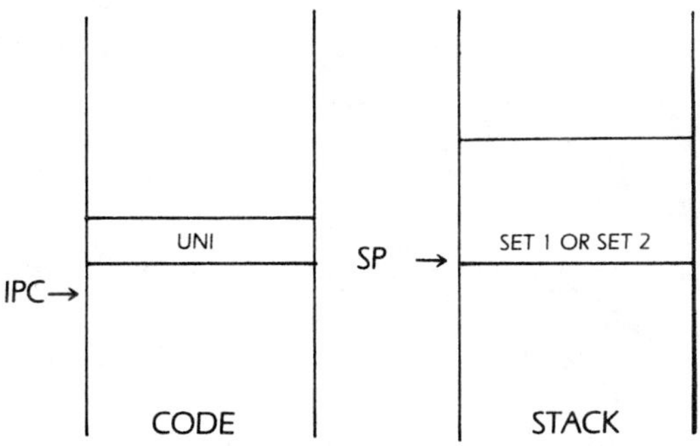

Syntax: INT
Opcode: 140 ($8C)
Operation: Set intersection

The INT instruction performs the intersection of the set on TOS with the set on NOS. This is accomplished by ANDing TOS with NOS. This instruction can be used to logically AND the byte string on TOS with the byte string on NOS.

The size of the resulting set is the larger of the links of the two sets.

INT OPERATION:

1. BEFORE

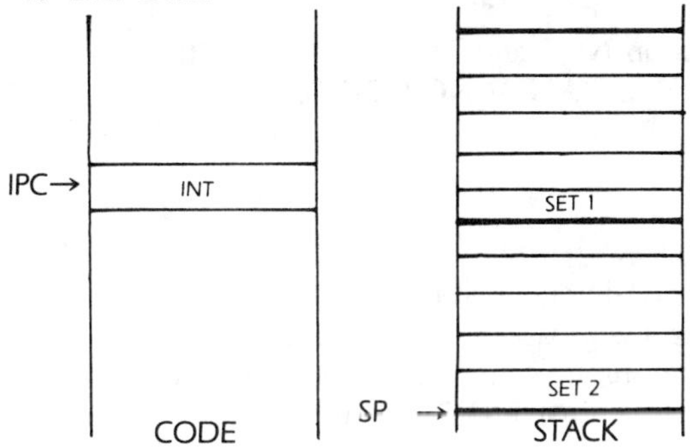

2. ACTION

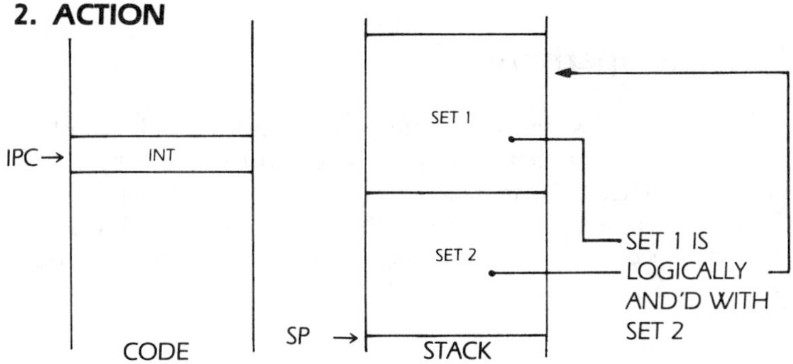

3. AFTER

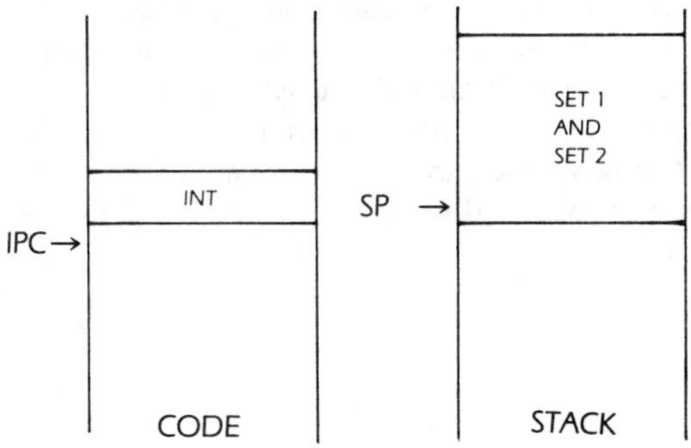

Syntax: **DIF**
Opcode: **133 ($85)**
Operation: **Set difference.**

The set difference of the sets on NOS and TOS is pushed onto the stack. The set difference consists of NOS AND (NOT TOS).

Set Comparisons

The set comparisons use the non-integer comparisons previously described. The UB byte of the non-integer comparison is always eight. Only the EQU, NEQ, LEQ, and GEQ operations are supported. LEQ checks for a subset, GEQ checks for a superset. TRUE or FALSE is pushed depending upon the comparison.

Byte Array Comparisons

The byte array comparisons use the non-integer comparisons already described. The UB byte is always set to ten for a byte array comparison. The byte array comparisons have a second parameter (in addition to the UB byte) that specifies the number of bytes that are to be compared. The LES, LEQ, GTR, and GEQ opcodes perform a lexicographical comparison and should be used with PACKED ARRAYs OF CHAR only.

Record and Word Arrays

Apple Pascal supports two instructions for comparing arrays and records: EQUWORD and NEQWORD. These comparisons use the non-integer comparison operators described earlier with the UB byte always set to twelve. As with the byte array comparisons, a second parameter follows the UB byte denoting the number of words which are to be compared. The word structure on TOS is compared to the word structure on NOS and TRUE or FALSE is pushed accordingly.

DIF OPERATION:

1. BEFORE

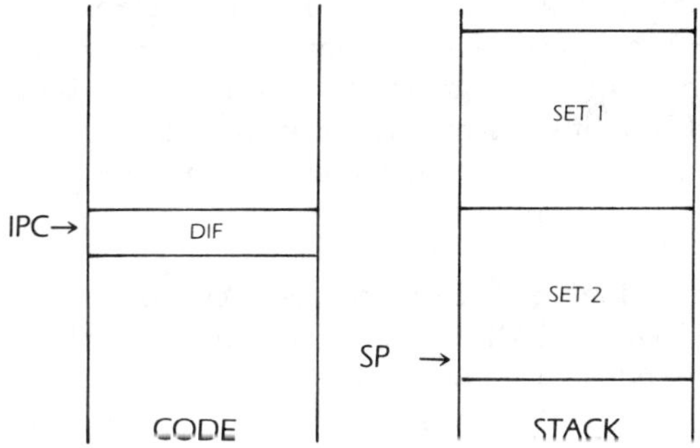

2. ACTION

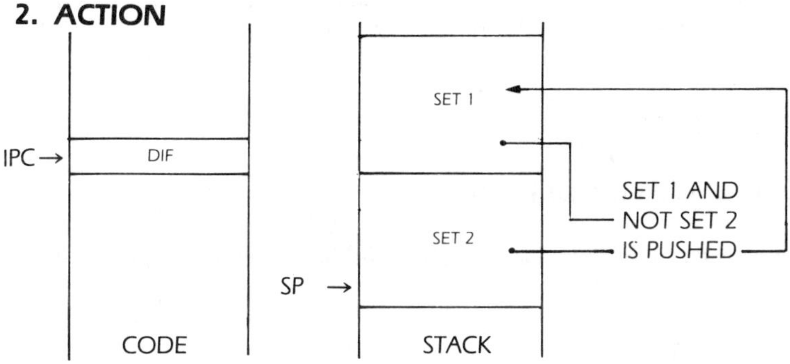

3. AFTER

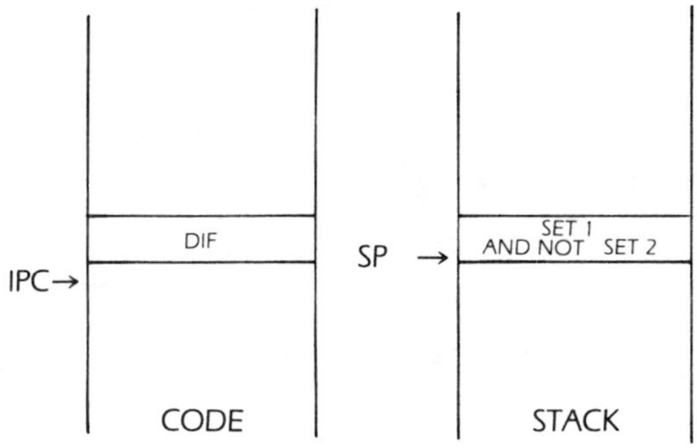

JUMPS

All jumps except the case jump are two bytes long. The first byte is the opcode and the second byte is a signed byte containing an offset. If the offset is positive (in the range 0..127) then this value is added to the IPC (program counter) register. If the offset is negative, it is used as an index into a "jump table" to determine the destination address to which the program must be directed.

The jump table is a word-aligned table of self-relative pointers whose last byte is pointed at by the p-Machine JTAB register. If the offset described above is negative it is sign-extended to 16 bits and added with the JTAB register to form an index into the jump table. The two bytes pointed at by this addition form a self-relative pointer to the destination address which is to be loaded into the IPC register. A self-relative pointer is a pointer whose value must be added to the address of the pointer in order to obtain the true effective address.

Syntax: UJP SB
Opcode: 185 ($B9)
Operation: Unconditional Jump

Control is transferred to the address specified in the SB parameter as described above.

UJP OPERATION:

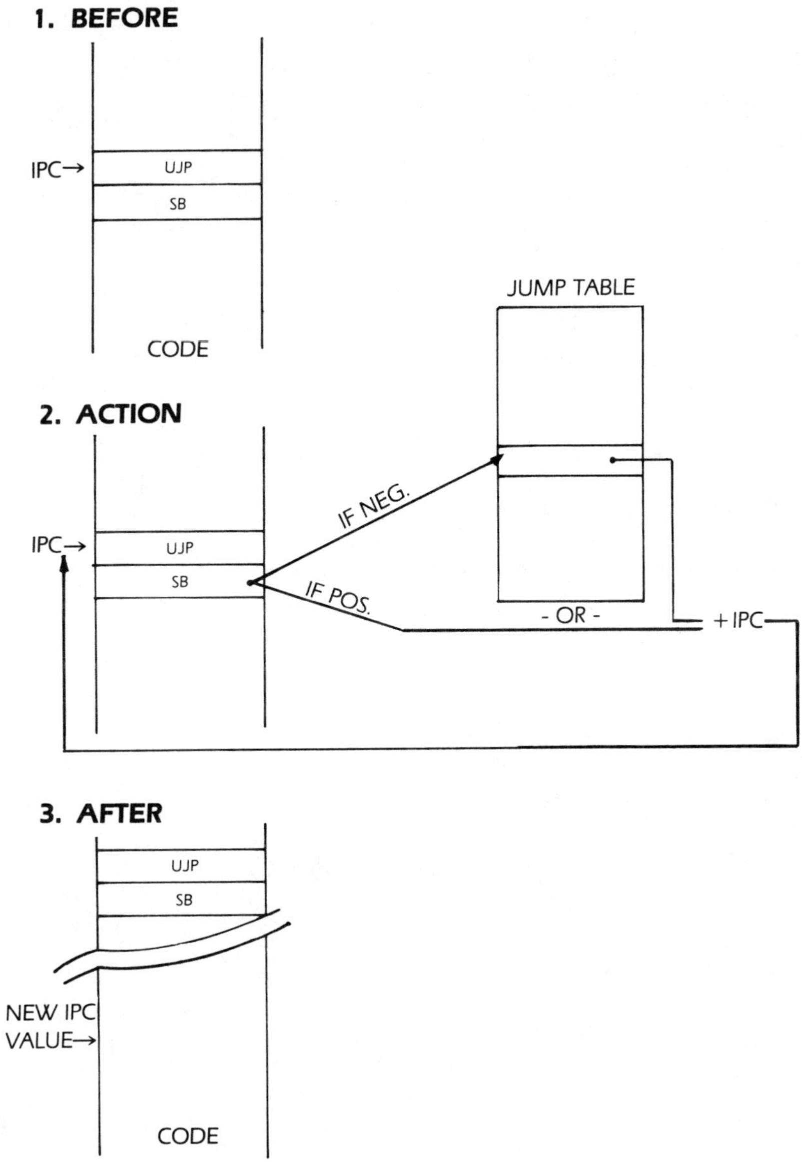

Syntax: **FJP SB**
Opcode: **161 ($A1)**
Operation: **False Jump**

The TOS is popped. If it is false, control is transferred to the address specified in the SB parameter as per the discussion

FJP OPERATION:

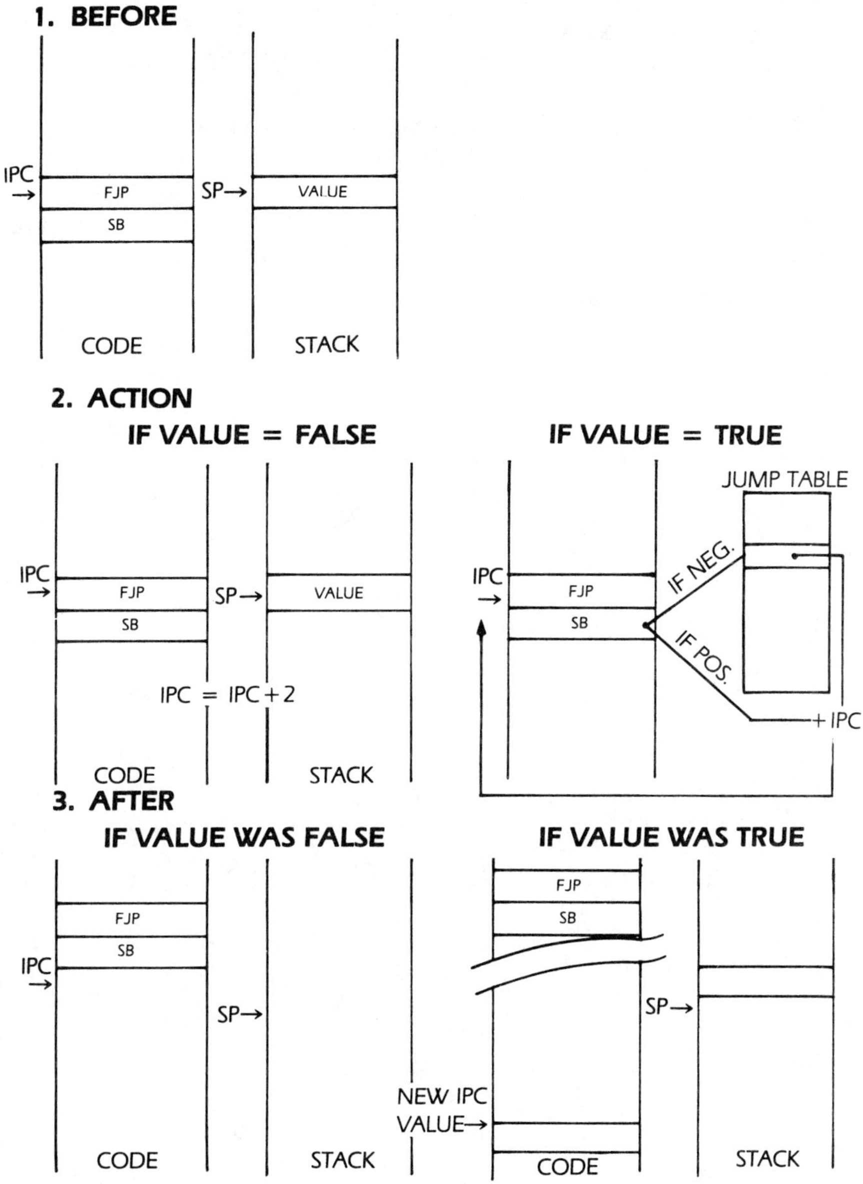

Syntax: EFJ SB
Opcode: 211 ($D3)
Operation: Equal False Jump

TOS is compared to NOS. If they are not equal then control is transferred to the address specified by the SB parameter.

See discussion on jumps on page 296.

EFJ OPERATION:

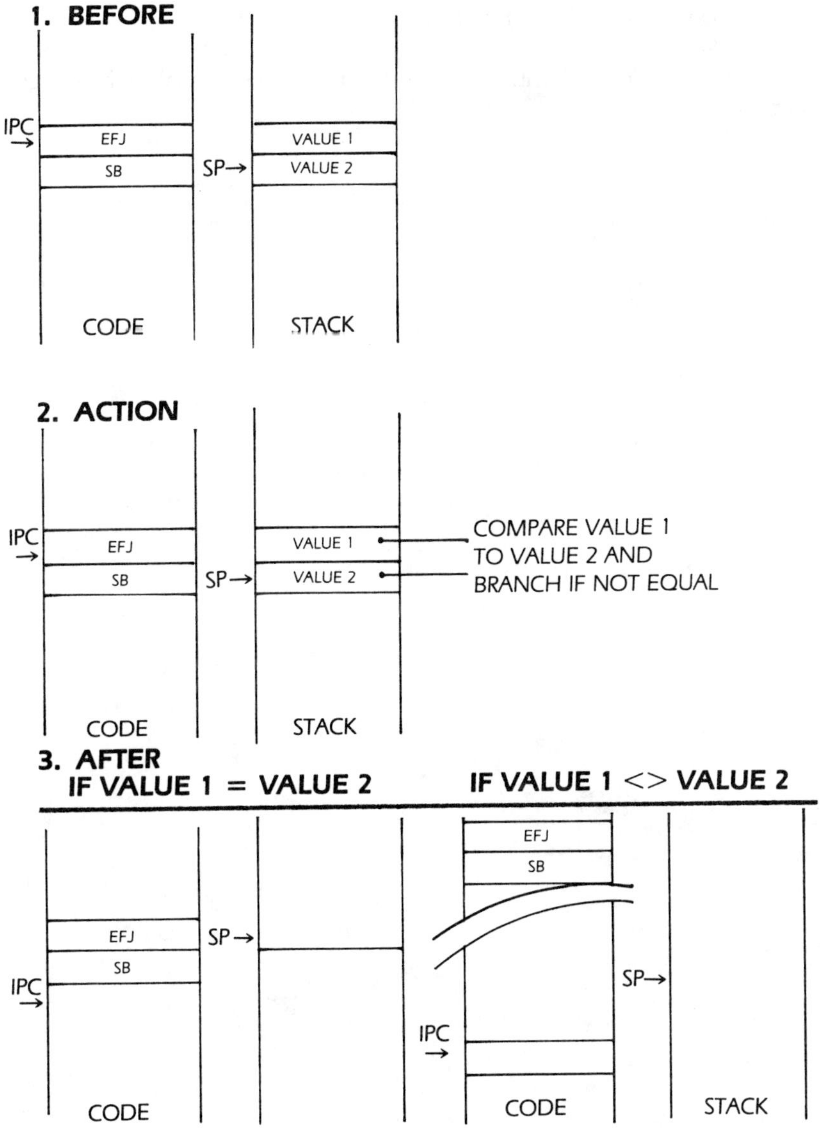

Syntax: **NFJ SB**
Opcode: **212 ($D4)**
Operation: **Not Equal False Jump**

Jumps to the specified location if the integer on TOS is equal to the integer on NOS.

NFJ OPERATION:

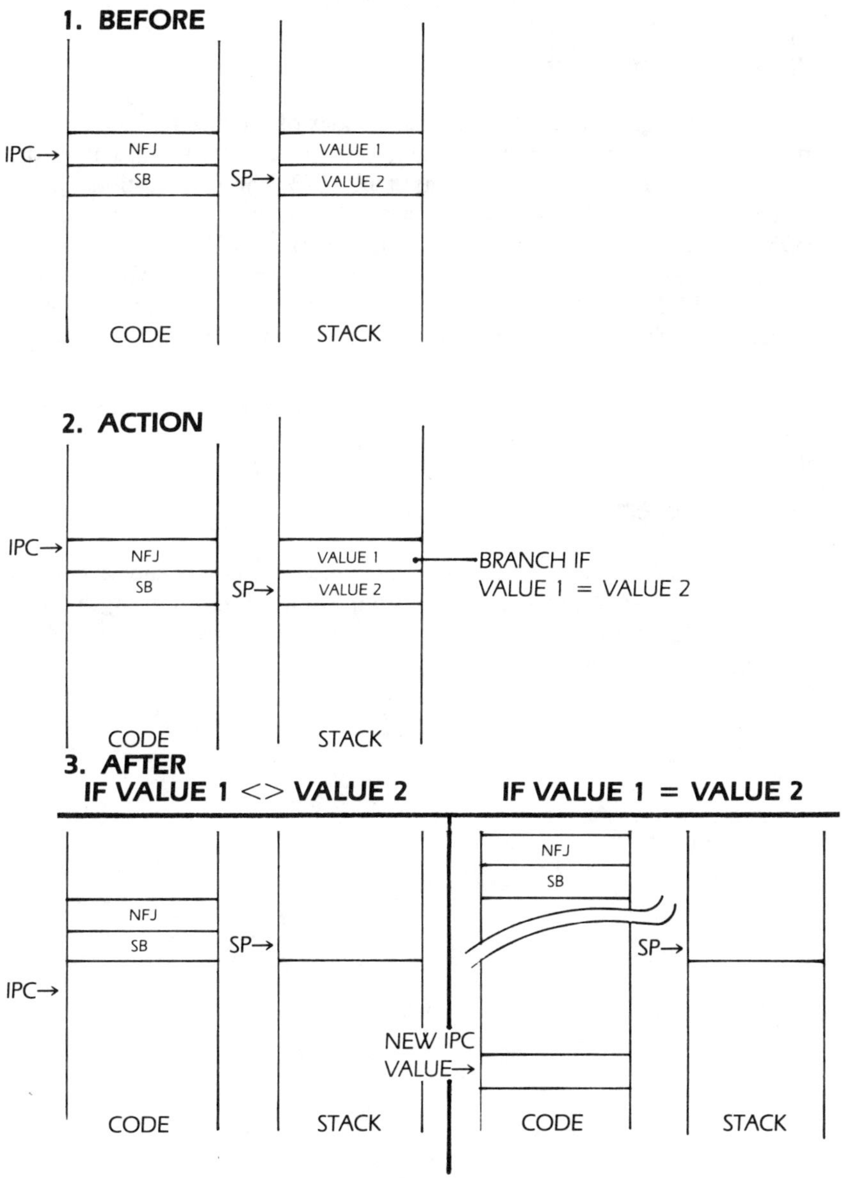

Syntax: XJP W1,W2,W3,<Case Table>
Opcode: 172 ($AC)
Operation: Case Jump

W1 is word aligned and is the minimum index of the case table (a NOP is inserted in the code stream, if necessary, to insure that W1 is word-aligned). W2 is the maximum index of the case table. W3 is an unconditional jump instruction (UJP) to the location just past the case table. If the value on TOS, which is the current index, is outside the range W1..W2 then execute the jump instruction "W3". If TOS is within the range W1..W2 then use the value (TOS – W1) as an index into the case table and use the two bytes pointed at by this index as a self-relative pointer to the destination location.

A self-relative pointer is a pointer whose value must be added to the address of the pointer in order to obtain the true effective address.

Procedure and Function Calls

A description of how the procedure and function calls actually operate is beyond the scope of this text. For more information concerning the procedure and function calls consult the Apple Pascal Operating System Manual, Pages 240 through 264.

XJP OPERATION:

1. BEFORE

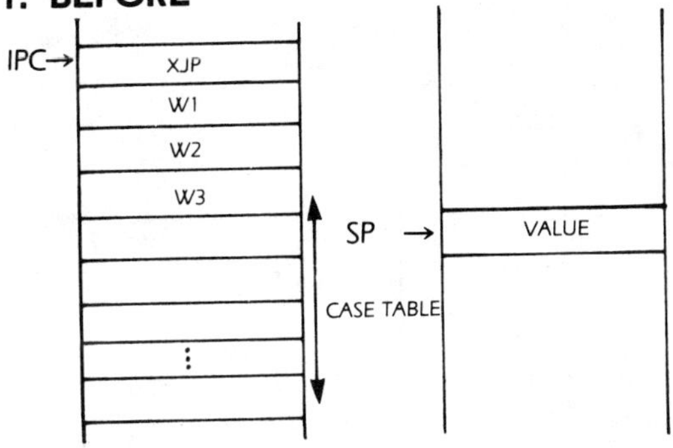

2a. ACTION IF (VALUE <W1) OR (VALUE >W2)

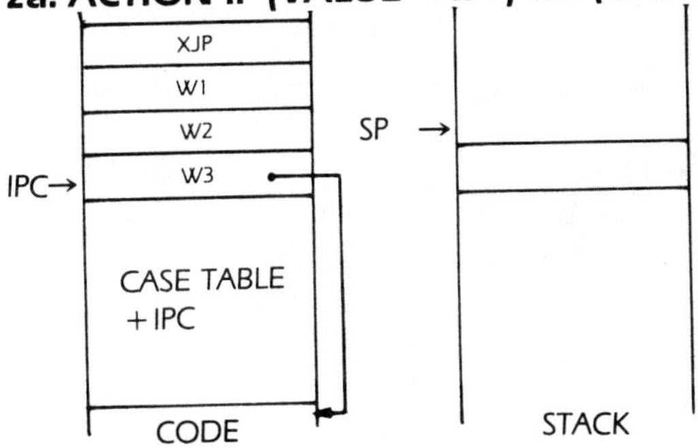

2b. ACTION OF (VALUE >=W1) OR (VALUE <=W2)

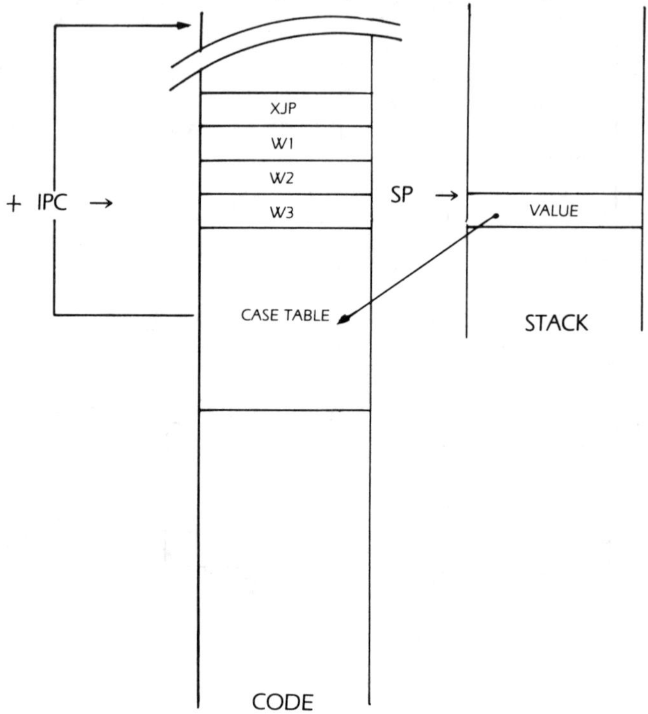

3. AFTER

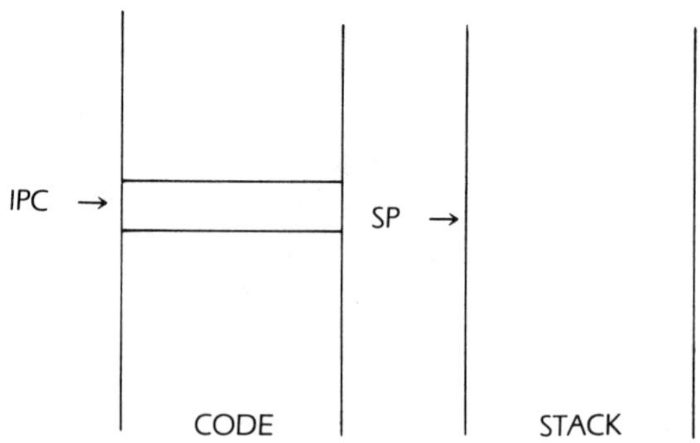

6

Inside the P-code Interpreter

The following section is intended for machine language programmers who would like some insight into the operation of the Apple Pascal P-code interpreter. This section provides a "road-map" to the p-code interpreter explaining how verious sections work. With this information an assembly language programmer can optimize the p-code interpreter, add new features, and take advantage of existing code. The Apple Pascal p-code interpreter is actually divided into three major sections: the p-code interpreter (proper), the Run-time support package (RSP) and the Basic Input/Output System (BIOS).

The p-code interpreter resides in bank #1 of the $D000..$DFFF range and in the $E000..$FFFF range. The RSP resides in the $E000..$FFFF range (intermixed with portions of the p-code interpreter). The BIOS resides mainly in bank #2 of the $D000.$DFFF range with a small portion appearing in the $F800..$FFFF range. This section will ignore the RSP and BIOS portions and will concentrate on the p-code interpreter for Apple Pascal v1.1.

Zero Page Variables

The Apple Pascal p-code interpreter uses zero page extensively for temporary and permanent variable storage. Most importantly, zero page pointers are used to implement the p-machine registers including IPC, NP, KP, BASE, MP, JTAB, SEG, etc.

Some of the zero-page variables used by the version 1.1 p-code interpreter include:

$50,$51 BASE: p-machine BASE register.

$52,$53 MP: Markstack pointer (p-machine register).

$54,$55 JTAB: Jump table pointer (p-machine register).

$56,$57 SEG: Segment pointer (p-machine register).

$58,$59 IPC: Interpreter program counter (p-machine register).

$5A,$5B NP: New pointer (p-machine register).

$5C,$5D KP: Program stack pointer (p-machine register).

$5E,$5F Vars: Stachoice.

$5E, $5F BIG: used to hold "BIG" opcode parameters.

$60, $61 DIF: used during set and arithmetic operations.

$62, $63 PREVMP: used to hold MP register during static link traversal.

$64, $65 SUM: used during arithmetic operations.

$66, $67 SPTEMP: used to hold stack ptr.

$68, $69 SOURCE: used during block moves.

$6A,$6B DEST: Used for block moves, etc.

$6C,$6D MASK: Used in masking operations (i.e., sets).

$6E..$70 JMP () instruction: used for transferring control to one of the p-code routines.

$71..$73 JMP () instruction: used for transferring control to a CSP routine.

$74..up Temporaries used by the p-machine.

NOTE: The 6502 stack pointer is used as the evaluation stack pointer.

The Apple Pascal p-code interpreter consists of a main loop that fetches a p-code from memory and transfers control to a 6502 subroutine that emulates the actions of the specified p-code. After the routine is executed IPC is incremented by one, two, three or more (depending on the length of the p-code instruction) and control is returned to the main loop.

At the beginning of the p-code interpreter (at address $D000) is a table, 256 bytes long, containing the addresses of the 128 active p-code instructions (i.e., all p-codes except the SLDC instructions). Each address is two bytes long and points to the beginning of the routine used to handle the specific p-code. The p-codes, the address of the routine, and the address of the address of the routine appear in the following table.

P-CODE	(ADRS)	TABLE	P-CODE	(ADRS)	TABLE	P-CODE	(ADRS)	TABLE
ABI	D6BB	D000						
ABR	ECB2	D002	XJP	D59E	D058	NOP	D24D	D0AE
ADI	D6D9	D004	RNP	E33F	D05A	SLDL0	D2A9	D0B0
ADR	EAC2	D006	CIP	E253	D05C	″ 1	D2A9	D0B2
LAND	D56B	D008	CEQL	DDE8	D05E	″ 2	D2A9	D0B4
DIFP	DB57	D00A	CGEQ	DDE0	D060	″ 3	D2A9	D0B6
DVI	D839	D00C	CGTR	DDD8	D062	″ 4	D2A9	D0B8
DVR	EB5A	D00E	LDAP	D3AD	D064	″ 5	D2A9	D0BA
CHK	D87E	D010	LDC	D495	D066	″ 6	D2A9	D0BC
FLO	ED3F	D012	CLEQ	DD34	D068	″ 7	D2A9	D0BE
FLT	ED62	D014	CLSS	DDDC	D06A	″ 8	D2A9	D0C0
INN	DC55	D016	LOD	DE87	D06C	″ 9	D2A9	D0C2
INT	DB20	D018	CNEQ	DDD4	D06E	″ A	D2A9	D0C4
LOR	D57E	D01A	STR	D3DB	D070	″ B	D2A9	D0C6
MODI	D866	D01C	UJP	D267	D072	″ C	D2A9	D0C8
MPI	D742	D01E	LDP	DA1C	D074	″ D	D2A9	D0CA
MPR	EC55	D020	STP	DA72	D076	″ E	D2A9	D0CC
NGI	D6F1	D022	LDM	D4C8	D078	″ F	D2A9	D0CE
NGR	ECC0	D024	STM	D4F6	D07A	SLDO0	D318	D0D0
LNOT	D591	D026	LDB	D523	D07C	″ 1	D318	D0D2
SRS	DCCC	D028	STB	D53D	D07E	″ 2	D318	D0D4
SBI	D703	D02A	IXP	D9D9	D080	″ 3	D318	D0D6
SBR	EB09	D02C	RBP	E32A	D082	″ 4	D318	D0D8
SGS	DCBA	D02E	CBP	E2F9	D084	″ 5	D318	D0DA
SQI	D789	D030	EQUI	DF65	D086	″ 6	D318	D0DC
SQR	EC7D	D032	GEQI	DF37	D088	″ 7	D318	D0DE
STO	D47B	D034	GTRI	DF2F	D08A	″ 8	D318	D0E0
IXS	D948	D036	LLA	D2D4	D08C	″ 9	D318	D0E2
UNI	DB79	D038	LDCI	D29D	D08E	″ A	D318	D0E4
LDE	D401	D03A	LEQI	DF33	D090	″ B	D318	D0E6
CSP	E630	D03C	LESI	DF2B	D092	″ C	D318	D0E8
LDCN	D296	D03E	LDL	D2B6	D094	″ D	D318	D0EA
ADJ	DBE5	D040	NEQI	DF3B	D096	″ E	D318	D0EC
FJP	D25F	D042	STL	D2FA	D098	″ F	D318	D0EE
INCP	D987	D044	CXP	E2D4	D09A	SIND0	D461	D0F0
IND	D96B	D046	CLP	E2A1	D09C	SIND1	D467	D0F2
IXA	D99A	D048	CGP	E2BD	D09E	″ 2	D467	D0F4
LAO	D343	D04A	LPA	D8CD	D0A0	″ 3	D467	D0F6
LSA	D8E5	D04C	STE	D426	D0A2	″ 4	D467	D0F8
LAE	D44B	D04E	NOP	D24D	D0A4	″ 5	D467	D0FA
MOV	D557	D050	- - -	D1EF	D0A6	″ 6	D467	D0FC
LDO	D325	D052	- - -	D1EF	D0A8	″ 7	D467	D0FE
SAS	D907	D054	BPT	E82B	D0AA			
SRO	D369	D056	XIT	D6A0	D0AC			

Table 6-1: Addresses of p-code routines

Immediately following the p-code table comes a short table of addresses for CSP routines. Whenever the CSP p-code is executed, the byte following the CSP opcode is fetched, doubled, and used as an index into this table at address $D100. The entries in this table are:

CSP	(ADRS)	TABLE	CSP	(ADRS)	TABLE	CSP	(ADRS)	TABLE
IOC	EF04	D100	RSRVD		D11E	EXP	D1EF	D13C
NEW	D62F	D102	RSRVD	0000	D120	SQRT	D1EF	D13E
MOVL	E8A0	D104	RSRVD	0000	D122	MRK	D66B	D140
MOVR	E8A0	D106	RSRVD	0000	D124	RLS	D682	D142
EXIT	E784	D108	RSRVD	0000	D126	IOR	EEF9	D144
UREAD	F069	D10A	RSRVD	0000	D128	UBUSY	EF0F	D146
UWRT	F06E	D10C	LDS	E61C	D12A	POT	EDE5	D148
IDS	E63A	D10E	ULS	E626	D12C	UWAIT	EF1D	D14A
TRS	E640	D110	TNC	EDD0	D12E	UCLR	EFA5	D14C
TIME	E841	D112	RND	EDBB	D130	HLT	E833	D14E
FLCH	E6B2	D114	SIN	D1EF	D132	MEMAV	E904	D150
SCAN	E6F7	D116	COS	D1EF	D134			
USTAT	EF27	D118	LOG	D1EF	D136			
RSRVD	0000	D11A	ATAN	D1EF	D138			
RSRVD	0000	D11C	LN	D1EF	D13A			

Table 6-2: Addresses of CSP routines

Note that some of the routines in the CSP table are reserved for future use. Also, the transcendental and log routines are not implemented (D1EF is a jump to the unimplemented opcode error).

Immediately following the CSP routine address table is the p-interpreter startup location. The BIOS, after handling its own boot-up chores, jumps to this location when the Pascal system is booted up. There's a jump at this location that transfers control to a routine at address $F275. The routine at address $F275 copies itself down to address $6800 and then jumps to the routine beginning at location $6827 (thereby skipping the code that performed the transfer). The 1K of memory space freed by this transfer will be used by the system later on. This initialization code sets up BIOS variables, initializes the p-machine, loads in SYSTEM.PASCAL, and then transfers control to the main interpreter loop at address $D253. Following the initial jump are several utility subroutines, the interpreter main loop, and the p-code routines. These will be discussed on a routine-by-routine basis.

D155 – D170 GETBIG routine. This routine extracts a parameter from the code stream. If the byte immediately after the current p-code is positive then it is multiplied by two (to convert it to a word pointer in the range 0..$FE). If this byte is negative then the next two bytes are fetched and used as a two-byte word pointer.

D171 – D18F TRVSTAT routine. This routine traverses X static links where X is passed in the 6502 X-register. This is accomplished by replacing MP with the two bytes pointed at by MP "x" times.

D190 – D1AC CHKGDRP routine. Check to see if there is a pointer to a directory block present on the heap. If so, de-allocate the storage for it and return. Otherwise do nothing and return. A pointer to the directory block (2K) is stored at address $BDE6 and $BDE7. If it is zero, no directory block exists. If it is non-zero it is copied to the NP register (heap pointer) and then set to zero.

D1AD – D1B5 Interpreter relative relocation table. The first two bytes contain the address of the next two bytes. The second two bytes contain the address of the XEQERR routine, the third address is the address of the BIOS jump table, the fourth address is the address of the SYSCOM area, and the fifth address is the address of the zero page workspace.

D1B7 – D22D XEQERR routine. This routine is called whenever an execution error occurs. Location D1B7 is called if an invalid index is detected (i.e., array out of bounds). Location D1BB is called if an attempt is made to load a segment which isn't on the disk (no such segment). Location D1BF is jumped to if an attempt to exit from an uncalled procedure is made. Location D1C3 is called if a stack overflow occurs. Location D1DB should be called in the event of an integer overflow, but Apple Pascal doesn't check for integer overflow so this entry point is probably never jumped to. The p-code interpreter jumps to address D1DF if a division by zero is attempted. The routine at D1E3 is called if the user break key is pressed. D1E7 is called if a system I/O error occurs and D1EB is called if a user I/O error occurs. The p-code interpreter transfers control to location D1EF if an unimplemented p-code is encountered. If a floating point error occurs control is transferred to location $D1F3 and $D1F7 is called if a string too long error occurs.

After any of the above XEQERR routines are called control is transferred to the general XEQERR routine at address D1FB. At this point the stacks are reinitialized and the IPC is pointed at a CXP 0,2 instruction (which reinitializes the system) and control is transferred to the main interpreter loop (thus causing execution of the CXP 0,2 instruction).

D22E – D239 UPIPC3: Up the IPC register by three. Adds three to the IPC register and then transfers control to the main interpreter loop. Many three-byte p-code instructions jump here after the execution in order to bump the IPC and execute the next p-code.

D23B – D246 UPIPC2: Increments the IPC by two and jumps to the interpreter's main loop. This code is called by most two-byte p-code instructions.

D248 – D24C SLDC p-code routine. This short routine pushes the p-code fetched onto the p-machine evaluation stack (which is the 6502 hardware stack).

D24D – D251 UPIPC1: Increments the IPC by one. Most one-byte, and many two- and three-byte instructions jump here to return control to the interpreter main loop.

D253 – D25C Interpreter main loop: This short section of code fetches a p-code from the location pointed at by the IPC. If the high order bit of the p-code is zero, then control is transferred to location D248 (SLDC). Otherwise the p-code is multiplied by two and this value is used as an index into the table at address $D000. Control is transferred to the routine pointed at in this table.

D25F – D265 FJP p-code routine. This code emulates the p-machine false jump instruction. A word (two bytes) is popped off of the stack. If the low order bit of this word is equal to one then the FJP routine jumps to UPIPC2. Otherwise (if the low order bit of the word on TOS contained zero) control drops through to the UJP instruction which follows.

D267 – D293 UJP p-code routine. This code emulates the p-machine unconditional jump instruction. The byte immediately following the opcode is fetched. If it is positive then this value is added to the IPC and control is transferred back to the main loop. If the byte following the opcode is negative then control is transferred to the INJTAB routine at location $D279 where the minus value is used as an index into the jump table for the current procedure. The address in the jump table is subtracted from the address of the jump table and this value is placed in the IPC. Control is passed back to the main interpreter loop.

D296 – D29A LDCN p-code routine. The code at this address pushes the implementation-dependent value for NIL onto the stack. Since, on the 6502, NIL is represented by the value zero this routine pushes zero onto the evaluation (6502 hardware) stack. Control is transferred to the UPIPC1 location.

D29D – D2A6 LDCI p-code routine. This routine fetches the two bytes that follow in the code stream and pushes them onto the evaluation stack. The high order byte is pushed first, low order byte is pushed last. This leaves the low order byte of the value on the TOS.

D2A9 – D2B3 SLDLX p-code routine. Upon entering this routine the 6502 accumulator contains the opcode shifted to the left (multiplied by two). $A3 is subtracted from this value leaving a value in the range $35..$44. The word at address MP + Acc (where MP is the p-machine MP register and Acc is the 6502 accumulator) is pushed onto the evaluation stack.

D2B6 – D2D3 LDL p-code routine. This routine loads a local variable from the current activation record. It begins by fetching a "big" parameter immediately after the opcode (the JSR D155 at address D2D6) which returns the **byte** offset into the activation record. This byte offset is added with the MP register and the word pointed at by this sum is pushed onto the 6502 stack.

D2D4 – D2F9 LLA p-code routine. This routine is quite similar to the LDL routine above, except that the address of a local word, rather than the data at that address, is pushed onto the stack. It calls "GETBIG" in order to fetch the one or two byte parameter that follows the opcode. This value is returned in BIG (zpage location $5E). This value is added to MP (zpage location $52) and this sum is saved. Finally, the value 10 is added to this sum (ten is the size of the activation record minus two) and the result is pushed onto the stack.

D2FA – D317 STL p-code routine. This routine stores the data on the evaluation stack into the local activation record area. It fetches a "big" parameter with a call to "GETBIG", calculates the address of the data where TOS is to be stored (in the same manner as that used for LDL and LLA) and then stores the data on TOS at that location.

D318 – D324 SLDOX p-code routine. This routine loads one of the first 16 words of global storage onto the stack. This is a short (one-byte) instruction that allows quick access to any of the first sixteen words of storage in the main procedure. Upon entry the 6502 accumulator contains the SLDOX opcode times two MOD 256 (which is a value in the range $D0..$EF). $C4 is subtracted from this value (upon entry the carry is cleared, so although the actual instruction is SBC #$C3, the true value subtracted is $C4) to obtain an index in the range 12..28 which is used as an index off of BASE to obtain a pointer to the word to be pushed. The word pointed at by BASE plus this index is pushed onto the evaluation stack.

D325 – D342 LDO p-code routine. This routine is used to load a global variable onto the evaluation stack. It is virtually identical in operation to the LDL p-code except that the indexing is performed off of the BASE register instead of the MP register.

D343 – D368 LAO p-code routine. This routine is used to load the address of a global variable onto the evaluation stack. It is identical to the LLA instruction except that indexing is performed off the p-machine BASE register instead of the MP register.

D369 – D386 SRO p-code routine. This routine stores the data on the TOS into the global variable whose word offset follows the opcode. This routine is identical to the STL instruction except that indexing is performed off of the BASE register instead of the MP register.

D387 – D3AC LOD p-code routine. This routine loads a word from an intermediate level routine. It begins by fetching the number of lex levels to descend and then it calls a routine to drop down that many static links. Upon return the PREVMP register contains a pointer to the activation record of the procedure in mind. The "BIG" parameter immediately after the static link parameter is fetched and is added to the value in PREVMP. This value plus 10 is a pointer to the word desired. The Y register is loaded with 11 (which points at the high byte of the word to be pushed) and the two bytes comprising the desired word are pushed onto the 6502 stack.

D3AD – D3DA LDA p-code routine. This routine loads the address of some intermediate variable onto the stack. It begins, just like the LOD routine by fetching the number of lex levels to traverse and dropping down that many static levels (accomplished by calling the static link traversal routine). The offset into this activation record (a "BIG" parameter) is fetched and added to the value in the PREVMP register. Ten is added to the sum (the width of the mark stack control word) and the resulting sum (which is the address of the desired word) is pushed.

D3DB – D400 STR p-code routine. The STR routine pops the data on TOS and stores it into the intermediate variable whose lex level and offset are specified after the opcode. This instruction operates identically to LOD except that the data is popped off of the stack and stored into memory instead of vice versa.

D401 – D425 LDE (LoaD Extended) p-code routine. This routine loads a word from the activation record of an intrinsic unit. The byte immediately following the opcode is fetched at addresses $D401..$D406 and is left in the X-register. This is the segment number from which the word is to be fetched. The "BIG" parameter following the segment number is fetched with a call to GETBIG at address $D408. Once the BIG parameter is fetched it is added to the address of the desired segment which is fetched from the SYSCOM area by indexing off of SEGTABLE with the value in the X-register (the segment # times two). The word pointed at by this sum is pushed onto the stack at addresses $D41A..$D422.

D426 – D44A STE (STtore Extended) p-code routine. This routine is the exact converse of the LDE p-code described above. The only difference between the two routines is the fact that STE pops data off of the stack and stores it into main memory instead of pushing data onto the stack. The code from $D426..$D43E is virtually identical to the first 13 statements of the LDE routine. From $D43F to $D446 STE pops data off of the stack instead of pushing data onto the stack.

D44B – D466 LAE (Load Address, Extended) p-code routine. This routine calculates the address of a word within a different segment (in an identical manner to LDE and STE) and then pushes the address calculated onto the stack.

D467 – D47A SINDx (Short INDex and load) p-code routine. This routine handles the eight short indexed load routines (SIND0..SIND7). The opcodes for these routines (times two and MOD 256) are in the range $F0..$FE. This value is in the accumulator upon entry (and the carry is set). $F0 is subtracted from the value in the accumulator to normalize this to a value in the range $0..$E which is then transferred to the Y-register. This value will be used as the index. The word on TOS is popped off and stored into a zero page memory location. Then the (Zpage),y addressing mode is used to fetch the word specified by the SINDx instruction. A special entry point is provided for SIND0 because this instruction is emitted quite often by the Pascal compiler. This entry point at address $D46A assumes that the Y-register contains zero on entry (which it does) and avoids the SBC and TAY instructions at address $D467..$D469.

D47B – D494 STO (store indirect) p-code routine. This routine pops two words off of the stack and stores them into a pair of zero page memory locations ($74..$77). The first word popped off of the stack is stored at the memory location pointed at by the second word popped off of the stack.

D495 – D4C7 LDC (load multiple word constant) p-code routine. The UB parameter which follows the LDC instruction is fetched and saved in the X-register. This value is also incremented by one, multiplied by two, and then stored into memory location $74. This is the total number of bytes required by this instruction (n words at two bytes each plus the one byte UB value and the one byte opcode). Next the IPC is incremented by one if it is not on a word boundry. Certain 16-bit processors (such as the 68000) require that all 16-bit data be aligned on word boundries. Once this is accomplished, the next 'UB' words are read from the code stream and pushed onto the stack. Finally, the value saved in location $74 is added to the IPC and control is returned to the main interpreter loop.

D4C8 – D4F5 LDM (load multiple words) p-code routine. This routine begins by fetching the UB parameter that follows the opcode. This value (the number of words to push) is multiplied by two (to get the number of bytes to push) and then copied into a temporary location. Then the stack is checked to make sure that there is enough room on the stack to hold the data being pushed. If there is not, then a jump to the stack overflow routine is made. Assuming there was enough room on the stack, a pointer to the block of data to be pushed is popped off of the stack and saved into memory location $68. Finally, the UB words pointed at by locations $68 and $69 are pushed onto the 6502 hardware stack (p-machine evaluation stack).

D4F6 – D522 STM (store multiple words) p-code routine. This guy checks the UB parameter that follows to find out how many words are to be stored into memory. UB*2 is used as an index into the stack to find the pointer to the memory area where TOS is to be stored. The 'UB' words on TOS are popped and stored into the memory locations described by the above pointer. Finally, the pointer is removed from the stack and control returns to the p-machine's main loop.

D523 – D53C LDB (load byte) p-code routine. TOS contains an index into a byte array. TOS – 1 is a pointer to the base address of a byte array. TOS is added to TOS – 1 and the sum forms a pointer to the byte to be pushed. A zero (for the H.O. byte) is pushed followed by the byte pointed at by the above mentioned sum.

D53D – D556 MOV (move words) p-code routine. TOS (a pointer to a block of 'B' words) is popped and stored into locations $68 and $69. TOS – 1 (a pointer to a similar block of 'B' words) is popped and stored into locations $6A and $6B. Next, the 'BIG' parameter that follows the opcode is fetched by calling the GETBIG subroutine. Finally, the data pointed at by $68/$69 is moved to the block pointed at by $6A/$6B with a call to the block move routine.

D56B – D57D LAND (logical and) p-code routine. Two words are popped off of the stack, logically AND'ed with one another, and pushed back onto the stack.

D57E – D590 LOR (logical OR) p-code routine. The two words on TOS are popped, logically OR'ed, and the result is pushed.

D591 – D59D LNOT (logical NOT) p-code routine. The word on TOS is popped XOR'ed with $FF (inverted) and pushed back onto the stack.

D59E – D62E XJP (case jump) p-code routine. The jump index (on TOS) is popped and compared to the first word-aligned word following the XJP opcode. If TOS is less than this value, the IPC register is loaded with the address of the third word-aligned word following the XJP opcode and control is transferred to the main interpreter loop. If TOS is greater than or equal to W1, then it is compared to the second word-aligned word following the XJP instruction (W2). If TOS is greater than this value then the IPC is pointed at W3 and control is transferred to the interpreter main loop. Otherwise, the value (TOS – W1)*2 is used as an index into the table which immediately follows the W3 value. The table entry pointed at by this value is subtracted from the address of the table entry. This difference is loaded into the IPC and control is returned to the interpreter main loop.

D62F – D66A NEW p-code routine. This routine handles the Pascal NEW procedure. It begins by checking to see if space has been reserved on the stack for a directory. If so, the directory space is de-allocated. Next the NEW routine pops two words off of the evaluation stack. The first word is the size (in words) of the variable being allocated, the second word is the address of the pointer to the new variable. The value in NP (new pointer) is stored into the pointer variable and then the size value is added to the NP register. Finally, the NP and KP pseudo-registers are compared to make sure stack overflow has not occurred.

D66B – D681 MRK (mark stack) p-code routine. This routine checks to see if space was allocated on the top of the heap for the directory. If so, it is de-allocated. Next a word pointer is popped off of the stack and the NP register is copied into the word pointed at by this value.

D682 – D69F RLS (release stack) p-code routine. A word pointer is popped off of the TOS. The two bytes pointed at by this byte are loaded into the NP register and the directory pointer is set to NIL.

D6A0 – D6BA XIT p-code routine. This opcode stores the 6502 instructions "LDA $C08A" and "JMP ($FFFC)" at locations $0..$5 and then executes this code. This turns off the language card and simulates a reset.

D6BB – D6D8 ABI (absolute value, integer) p-code routine. This routine pops the value off of TOS. If it is positive, it gets pushed back onto TOS. If it is negative then the two's complement is taken and the positive value is pushed back onto the stack.

D6D9 – D6F0 ADI (add integers) p-code routine. The two words on TOS are popped, added, and the sum is pushed back onto the stack.

D6F1 – D702 NGI (negate integer) p-code routine. The word on TOS is popped, negated, and then pushed back onto the stack.

D703 – D71A SBI (subtract integers) p-code routine. The integer on TOS is subtracted from the integer on TOS-1 and the difference is pushed back onto the stack.

D71B – D742 Multiply routine. The integers (signed) at addresses $88..$8B are multiplied and the result is left in location $8C and $8D.

D742 – D788 MPI (multiply integers) p-code routine. Two integers are popped off of the stack. If they are both positive, or if they are of different signs, then the routine at address $D71B is called and the resulting product is pushed. If the values popped off of the stack are both negative then they are both negated and treated as though they were both positive.

D789 – D794 SQI (square integer) p-code routine. This routine duplicates the TOS and jumps the the MPI routine at address $D742.

D795 – D838 DVIMOD routine. This routine takes the 16-bit value in memory locations \$88 and \$89 and divides it by the signed integer in locations \$86 and \$87. The remainder (MOD) is left in locations \$88 and \$89, the quotient is left in locations \$8C and \$8D. Note that no check for underflow or overflow is made.

D839 – D865 DVI (divide integers) p-code routine. This routine pops two values off of the top of stack and calls the DVIMOD routine to divide TOS-1 by TOS. Upon return from DVIMOD, DVI checks to see if both the divisor and dividend were of the same sign. If they were not, then the positive quotient is negated. Lastly, the quotient is pushed back onto the stack and control is returned to the main interpreter loop.

D87E – D8CC CHK (check subrange) p-code routine. This code pops two words off of the stack and compares them to the new TOS value. If (TOS – 1) <= TOS – 2 <= TOS then control is transferred back to the main interpreter loop. Otherwise a runtime error (bounds violation) is forced.

D866 – D87D MODI (modulo integers) p-code routine. This routine is identical to DVI except the remainder is pushed back onto the stack.

D8CD – D8E4 LPA (load packed array pointer) p-code routine. This routine pushes the contents of the IPC **plus two** onto the evaluation stack. This pushes a pointer that points to the first character of the string (just past the length byte) that follows the LPA instruction. Once this is accomplished, the length byte (which immediately follows the LPA opcode) plus two is added to the IPC so that it points at the first p-code immediately following the string. Control is then returned to the main interpreter loop.

D8E5 – D906 LSA (load string address) p-code routine. This routine operates identically to the LPA opcode except that the address pushed onto the stack is the IPC value **plus one.** This pushes a pointer to the string (at the length byte) which immediately follows the LSA opcode. The IPC is moved beyond the string and control is returned to the main loop.

D907 – D947 SAS (string assign) p-code routine. On the top of stack are two words. The first is either a pointer to a source string or a single character. (If the high order byte is zero, then it is a single character, if it is non-zero then it is a pointer). The word on TOS – 1 is a pointer to a destination string. If TOS is a single character then the value one is stored at the address pointed at by TOS – 1 and the character is stored in the next consecutive address. If a string pointer is on TOS, then the length of that string (which is pointed at by the pointer) is compared to the UB value that follows the SAS opcode. If the length of the string is greater than this UB value a run-time bounds error occurs. Otherwise, the string pointed at by the pointer on TOS is stored into the string pointed at by TOS – 1. The IPC is incremented by two and control is transferred to the main interpreter loop.

D948 – D96A IXS (index string array) p-code routine. TOS contains an index into a string array. TOS – 1 is a pointer to a string. If TOS is outside the range 1..255 then give an execution error. If TOS is greater than the current length of the string give an execution error. Otherwise return to the main loop *leaving TOS and TOS – 1 on the stack.*

D96B – D986 IND (static index and load word) p-code subroutine. TOS is a pointer to a word structure. It is popped and added to the 'BIG' parameter that follows the IND opcode. The word pointed at by this sum is pushed onto the stack.

D987 – D999 INC (increment field pointer) p-code routine. The word on TOS is popped, added to the 'BIG' parameter that follows the opcode, and the resulting sum is pushed.

D99A – D9D8 IXA (index array) p-code routine. TOS is an integer index into an array whose base element is at TOS – 1. A 'BIG' parameter is fetched from the code stream, this is the size of each element of the array. This 'BIG' value is checked to see if it is two. If it is, the value on TOS is multiplied by two (by shifting it to the left) and then added to the base address. If the 'BIG' value is not two, then the value on TOS is multiplied by 'BIG' and the product is added to the base address. The sum is left on TOS.

D9D9 – DA1B IXP (index packed array) p-code routine. IXP is followed by two unsigned byte parameters in the code stream and there are two words of parameters on TOS. TOS is an integer index and TOS – 1 is the array base pointer. To begin with, the two UB values are fetched from the code stream and saved in temporary zero page locations. The high order bytes for these values are then zeroed. Next the integer index is popped off the stack and saved into a pair of zero page memory locations. Then DVIMOD is called to compute "index div UB1" and "index mod UB1". The quotient is shifted to the left to convert it from a word index to a byte index. This byte offset is added to the array base address (which is popped off of the stack). This sum points at the byte containing the bit field we are interested in. This byte pointer is pushed onto the stack. Next the field width, which is the value "index mod UB1", is pushed onto the stack. Finally the right bit number (computed by: rbn := UB2*(index mod UB1)) is pushed onto the stack.

DA1C – DA71 LDP (load packed field) p-code routine. LDP expects a three byte packed field pointer on the top of the stack. The byte on TOS is the right bit number, TOS – 1 is the field width, and the byte at TOS – 2 is a pointer to the byte where the structure is located. These three bits are popped and stored into zero page memory locations. The word pointed at by the pointer is loaded into memory locations $7E and $7F. If the right bit number is greater than eight, then location $7F is stored into location $7E and eight is subtracted from the right bit number (this performs a fast shift by eight). Next, the bits in location $7E and $7F are shifted to the right 'right bit number' times. This right justifies the field into locations $7E and $7F. Finally, the field width is multiplied by two and used as an index into a table of two-byte masks. Locations $7E and $7F are AND'ed with these two masks (to turn off the unnecessary high order bits). The result is pushed onto the evaluation stack.

DA72 – DAFA STP (store into a packed field) p-code routine. This instruction pops the word off the top of the stack and stores it into the packed field pointer which occupies the three words of storage immediately below the data on the stack. This routine begins by popping the data, right bit number, and field width pointer off of the stack. The data is then masked so that only the pertinent bits are retained. Next, the data is shifted so that data is properly aligned. Then a pointer to the word structure where this data is to be stored is popped off of the stack and the two words pointed at by this pointer are fetched. The bit positions where the data is to be stored is zeroed out and the data is OR'ed into this spot. Finally, the data is stored back into the memory word described by the pointer popped off of the stack.

DAFB – DB1D FIXSET routine. Most of the stack operations expect two sets to appear on the top of the stack. The stacks have the format:

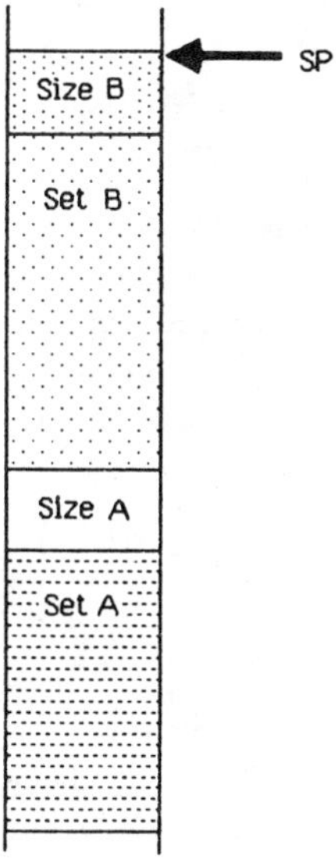

Figure 6-1

where 'size B' is on the top of stack and is the number of words in the set B (also on the stack). FIXSET pops size B off of TOS and stores it into locations $7C and $7D ($7D is always zero). Next a pointer to the 'size A' word is computed and this value is loaded into the 6502 accumulator. A pointer to the A set is stored into location $74 (only one byte is stored since it is known that the set is always in page one). Finally, the return address (which was popped and stored into locations $8C and $8D) is incremented by one, and control is returned to the calling procedure by jumping indirect through locations $8C and $8D.

DB20 – DB56 INT (set intersection) p-code routine. Set intersection is performed by AND'ing set B with set A. If the sets are not the same size, then the high order 'n' words of the resultant set are set to zero. This routine AND's the low order bytes of A with the low order bytes of B and stores the result back into A until 'n' words have been AND'ed together (where 'n' is the minimum of size A and size B). Finally, 'm' words of zero are pushed, where 'm' is the absolute value of the difference between size A and size B. Finally, the 6502 stack pointer is tweaked so that it points at the new set just created.

DB57 – DB78 DIF (Set difference) p-code routine. This routine logically negates set B and then AND's it into set A. After FIXSET is called, the X-register is loaded with the value min(size B, size A) and then this many bytes are taken from set B, inverted, and AND'ed with the corresponding byte in set A. If there are more entries in set A than set B, the high order entries are left untouched. Finally, the SP register is loaded with the pointer to set A and control is returned to the main loop.

DB79 – DBE4 UNI (set union) p-code routine. This routine compares the size of A with the size of B. If size A is greater than or equal to the size of B, then a short routine is executed which simply pops the B set off of the stack and OR's it with the A set. Control is returned to the main interpreter loop with the 6502 SP register pointing at the A set.

If the size of A is less than the size of B then a separate routine is called that OR's set A into set B, and then moves set B down over set A on the stack. If the size of B is zero, then A is simply returned.

DBE5 – DC54 ADJ (set adjust) p-code routine. A single UB-type parameter is fetched from the code stream. This byte contains the final size (in words) that the set on TOS must occupy. If the size of the set on TOS is equal to this value, then the ADJ routine promptly returns control to the main loop. If the size of the set on TOS is greater than this value, then the UB words on TOS are moved down over the extra words which are to be truncated.

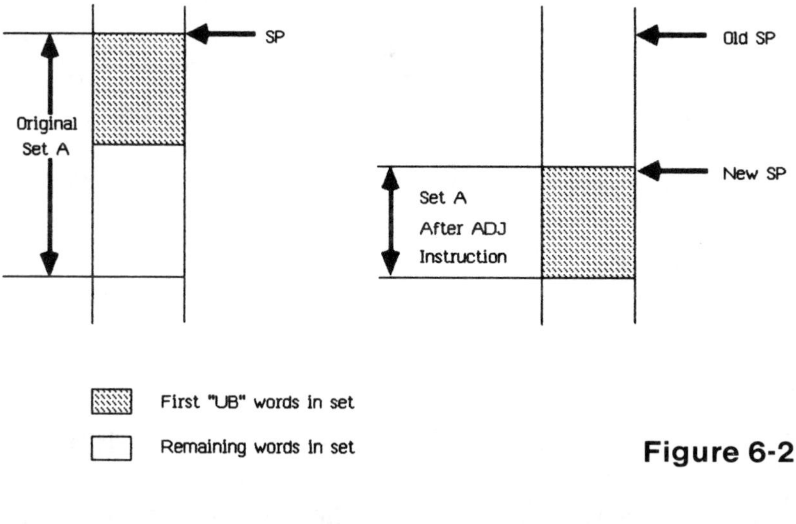

Figure 6-2

This is accomplished by the code at locations $DBFF..$DC19. First, the Y-register is loaded with a pointer to the last (high order) byte of the set which is to be kept. Next, the X-register is loaded with a pointer to the high order byte of the current set. Finally, the UB bytes pointed at by Y are transferred down to the set pointed at by the X-register and control is returned to the main interpreter loop.

If the size of the set on TOS is greater than UB, then control is transferred to location $DC1C. Here, the size of the set on TOS is checked to see if it is zero. If it is, this fact is noted, the SP register is modified accordingly, and control is transferred to the zero fill loop at location $DC47. If the size of the set on TOS is not zero, then it is moved downwards in memory in order to expand the size of the set. The area cleared out by this downward movement is zeroed out by the code at location $DC47. In either case, control is returned to the main interpreter loop at location $DC52.

DC55 – DCB9 INN (set inclusion) p-code routine. This routine expects the following data on TOS:

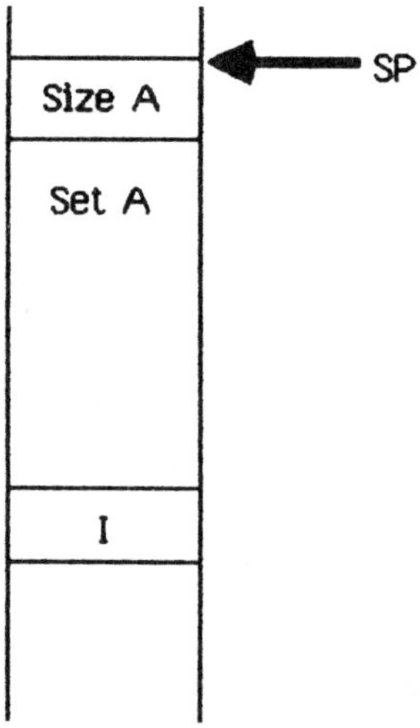

Figure 6-3

where size A is the size of the set A which immediately follows on the stack and I is an integer. I is divided by eight (by shifting) and I mod eight (by AND'ing) is also kept around. The value I DIV "8" is used as an index into the set A and the "I mod eighth" bit of this byte is checked. If this bit is one, then TRUE is pushed onto the stack in place of size A, so that generated by the first string assignment in the code stream.

DCBA-DCCB SGS (build singleton set) p-code routine. This code copies TOS and falls through to the SRS routine below.

DCCC-DDD3 SRS (build subrange set) p-code routine. Two words are popped off of the stack and stored into memory locations $7A..$7D. Replace these two words with the set [(low_range)..(high_range)]. First, check the low range and make sure it is not negative, give an execution error if it is. Next, make sure that the high range is less than 512. If not, cause a run-time error. If the high range is less than the low range, then push a null set onto the stack (which is accomplished by pushing two zeroes). Then the set consisting of zero bits up to the "low rangeth" bit is pushed, then between low range and high range one bits are pushed, and finally the size word is pushed onto the stack. The data from $DD92 to $DDD3 is a table containing the bit masks.

DDD4 – DE10 Comparison lead-in routine. This p-code routine handles the EQUxxx, NEQxxx, LEQxxx, LESxxx, GEQxxx, and GTRxxx routines. The individual entry points load the 6502 accumulator with a three bit value according to the test being made. The values in the accumulator are interpreted as:

BIT 0 = 1: TEST FOR EQUALITY
BIT 0 = 0: TEST FOR INEQUALITY

BIT 1 = 1: TEST FOR LESS THAN
BIT 1 = 0: TEST FOR NOT LESS THAN

BIT 2 = 1: TEST FOR GREATER THAN
BIT 2 = 0: TEST FOR NOT GREATER THAN

For example, the accumulator is loaded with one if the EQUxxx instruction is executed, four if the GTRxxx instruction is to be executed, and three if testing for less than or equal.

Once the accumulator is loaded with the appropriate value, control is transferred to location $DDEA where this comparison flag is saved into zero page location $6C. At this point, the second byte following the p-code is fetched. This byte determines whether a Boolean, string, set, or array operation is to be performed. If this value is two, then two REAL values are compared, if it is four, then two string values are compared, if it is six then Boolean values are compared, if eight then two sets are compared, if ten then two word arrays are compared, otherwise two byte arrays are compared.

DE12 – DE5F Byte and word comparisons. The compare byte entry point is at location $DE12, the compare word entry point is at $DE1E. Both call the GETBIG routine to fetch the one/two byte operand that follows in the code stream. The compare byte entry then divides locations $5E and $5F by two since the GETBIG routine multiplied them by two (thinking they were a word offset). Then the compare byte routine jumps into the compare word routine at location $DE23. The code between locations $DE23 and $DE5F pops two array pointers off of the stack and compares the arrays pointed at by these pointers. Upon determining that the arrays are equal or not equal, control is transferred to the code at location $DEC2 (if the arrays are equal), $DEC6 (if the array pointed at by TOS – 1 is less than the array pointed at by the pointer on TOS), or $DEBE (if the array pointed at by TOS – 1 is greater than the array pointed at by TOS).

DE64 – DEBD String comparison routine. This routine compares two strings whose pointers are found on TOS. It is somewhat complicated by the fact that if the high order byte of the pointer is zero then the string consists of a single character. If a single character is detected (for either pointer on the stack) then it is converted to a string by storing it into a zero page location and prefacing it with a length byte of one. The normal string pointer is set up to point at this zero page location. Locations $74 and $75 point at the first string (with locations $80 and $81 used for the single character string) and locations $76 and $77 point at the second string (with locations $7E and $7F used for a single character string).

Once the pointers to the strings are set up, the lengths of these strings are compared and the minimum string length is loaded into the X-register. Next the strings are compared until it is determined that they are not equal, or are equal through the length of the shortest string. If they are not equal, then control is passed to location $DEBE if string one is greater than string two, and to location $DEC6 if it is less than string two. If the two strings are equal through to the length of the shortest string, then the lengths are compared. If the lengths are equal, so are the strings. If the length of string one is greater than string two then control is passed to location $DEC6, if they are equal to location $DEC2, otherwise to location $DEBE.

DEBE – DED9 Push Boolean routines. Location $DEBE is jumped to if the comparison routine determines that item one is greater than item two. This guy pushes TRUE onto the stack if a GTRxxx, GEQxxx, or NEQxxx opcode was being processed, false otherwise.

Location $DEC2 is jumped to if the comparison routine determined that the two values being compared were equal. TRUE is pushed if the EQLxxx, GEQxxx, or LEQxxx was being processed.

Location $DEC6 is jumped to if the comparison routine determined that the first value being compared is less than the second value being compared. TRUE is pushed if the LESxxx, LEQxxx, or NEQxxx opcode was being processed. False is pushed otherwise.

The code at location $DEC8..$DEDB is common to all these routines. It is responsible for pushing TRUE or FALSE and determining which opcode caused the current state of affairs.

DEDC – DF15 REAL comparisons. This code pops two real values off of the stack and compares them. If the REAL value on TOS – 1 is less than the REAL value on TOS, then control is transferred to location $DEC6. If TOS – 1 is greater than TOS then control is transferred to location $DEBE. If TOS – 1 is equal to TOS then control is transferred to location $DEC2.

DF16 – DF2A Compare Boolean values. The word on TOS is popped, AND'ed with one, and compared to TOS – 1 after it is popped and AND'ed with one. If TOS – 1 is greater than TOS, control is transferred to location $DEBE; if they are equal, $DEC2; if TOS – 1 is less than, then a branch to location $DEC6 is made.

DF2B – DF98 EQUI, NEQI, LESI, LEQI, GTRI, and GEQI routines. These routines compare the two words on TOS and push true if the respective comparison holds, false otherwise. All these comparisons except EQUI are handled in a fashion similar to the comparisons above in that a three-bit value is saved and a single comparison routine is jumped to in the interest of saving code. The EQUI routine is handled separately, probably because it is called many more times than any other comparison. The entry points for these routines are:

LESI: $DF2B
GTRI: $DF2F
LEQI: $DF33
GEQI: $DF37
NEQI: $DF3B
EQUI: $DF65

DF9B – DFD4 Set comparison setup routine. This subroutine computes certain pieces of useful data for use by the set comparison routines. It returns the size of the set on TOS (set B) in locations $7C and $7D, the size of the set on TOS – 2 (set A) in locations $7A and $7B, the address of set B in location $76 (only one byte is required since the set is always in page one), the address of set A in location $74, the difference (size A – size B) in location $86, the minimum set size (i.e. min(sizeA,sizeB)) in location $7E, and the new SP value in location $80.

DFD5 – DFF1 Check remainder of set to make sure it contains zeroes. If the sets are of unequal length then this routine is called to make sure that zeroes are present in the high order bytes of the set. If set B is being checked, the entry point is location $DFD5. If set A is being checked, the entry point is location $DFDE. The X register contains the first byte on the stack to check for a zero.

DFF2 – E026 Set comparison routine. This subroutine is called to compare the sets on TOS. If they are equal, the carry is returned set. If they are not equal, the carry is returned cleared.

E027 – E03A Set compare jump table. It was determined that a set comparison is to be made. This short segment of code checks for SETEQL, SETNEQ, SETLEQ, or SETGEQ.

E03D – E042 Set equal routine. This routine calls the set comparison routine, and then jumps to the code that pushes true if the carry is set, false if the carry is clear.

E043 – E04E Set not equal routine. This code calls the set compare routine, complements the carry, and then jumps to the code to push TRUE or FALSE depending on the contents of the carry flag.

E04F – E069 Set less than or equal routine. This routine checks to see if A is a subset of B. If so, TRUE is pushed, otherwise FALSE is pushed.

E06A – E08A Set greater than or equal. This routine checks to see if B is a subset of A. TRUE is pushed if it is, FALSE is pushed otherwise. E08B – E09E Set compare exit point. All set routines exit to this code. The normal entry point is $E08C. If the carry is clear, FALSE is pushed. If the carry is set, TRUE is pushed.

E0A1 – E0BB CXP (call external procedure) p-code utility subroutine. This code fetches the segment number from the segment table at address $BD9E and stores it into the 'nextseg' register at addresses $82 and $83. It then jumps to some common procedure code (shared with the Normal procedure call subroutine) at address $E0D2.

E0BC – E0D1 Normal procedure call utility subroutine. This routine copies the current contents of the segment register into the 'nextseg' memory location. It also stores $FF into the segment number variable at address $86. This is used by the common code to differentiate between an external procedure and a normal procedure call.

E0D2 – E252 Common procedure code for the CXP and Normal procedure call subroutines. This code pushes return addresses, parameters, loads in segment procedures, etc. whenever a procedure or function is invoked.

E02D – E10A Sets up a pointer to the procedure attribute table in locations $7C and $7D.

E10B – E14B Check for an assembly language subroutine and call it if this is a 6502 machine code routine. Assembly language routines are denoted by the fact that the procedure number (pointed at by $7C and $7D) is zero. If this is an external procedure, then decrement the value at location ($BD1E + segnum*2). This value is used to determine if the code is to be left in memory. If this is an assembly routine, a return address is pushed onto the stack, the address of the assembly routine is stored into locations $90 and $91. Finally, a jump indirect through locations $90/$91 transfers control to the assembly routine.

E14E – E252 Handle a p-code subroutine invocation.

E159 – E1AA Set up pseudo registers and check for stack overflow. Jump to $E1AB if a stack overflow occurs.

E1B0 – E1B9 Push activation record onto program stack.

E1BA – E1DD Pop "parmsize" parameters off of the 6502 hardware stack and copy them onto the program stack. Then push the current value of the 6502 hardware stack pointer onto the program stack.

E1DE – E1FA The address of the p-code subroutine is computed and stored into the IPC register here. Addresses in the Apple Pascal p-machine are always self-relative. So the address contained in the procedure location entry in the procedure table is subtracted from the address of the table entry. This difference is the absolute address of the p-code routine to be executed.

E1FB – E250 Completion of p-code subroutine set up. This code initializes the JTAB register, the jump table, the MP register, the program stack pointer (to set up for any local variables), and copies the 'nextseg' value into the segment register. Control is then returned to the calling 6502 program by incrementing the return address (which was saved in locations $8E and $8F) and returning via a jump indirect instruction.

E253–E2A0 CIP (call intermediate) p-code routine (with special entry point at $E25C for CXP calls). First the procedure call subroutine is called to set up the stack, then this code looks into the procedure table to get at the dynamic links and it traverses the stack looking for the proper lex level to operate at. Once the dynamic links are properly set up, control is returned to the main procedure at which point the p-code subroutine begins execution.

E2A1 – E2BC CLP (call local procedure) p-code routine. This code fetches the procedure number from the code stream, calls the procedure invocation subroutine, patches the stack, and then returns control to the main interpreter loop for the execution of the p-code subroutine.

E2BD – E2D3 CGP (call global procedure) p-code routine. Identical to the CLP routine, except the BASE register is pushed onto the stack in place of the normal dynamic link.

E2D4 – E2F8 CXP (call external procedure) p-code routine. The CXP p-code routine fetches two parameters from the code stream. The first is the procedure number, the second is the segment number. If the segment number is not zero (a special case) then a subroutine is called to load the code from the disk onto the program stack (LOADSEG). Then the special entry point at $E0A1 is called to set up the system for the procedure call. Finally, the lex level is checked to see if it is less than or equal to zero. If it is, then this is a base external procedure and control is transferred to location $E302, otherwise this is an external intermediate procedure and control is transferred to location $E25C.

E2F9 – E329 CBP (call base procedure) p-code routine (special entry point at address $E302 for call external base procedure). This code fetches the procedure number and calls the procedure set-up routine (just like all the other calls) and then it pushes a copy of the BASE register on to the 6502 hardware stack. Then it patches all the links in the activation record so that the static and dynamic links point at the proper place. Finally, the stack pointer is copied into the BASE register and control is returned to the main interpreter loop.

E32A – E33E RBP (return from base procedure) p-code routine entry point. Get the pointer to the stack frame (6502 hardware) and load the 6502 SP register with this value. Next, pop the BASE value off of the stack and load this into the BASE register and the temporary BASE register. Then a jump to common code at location $E345 is made.

E33F – E344 RNP (return from normal procedure) p-code routine. This code reloads the 6502 stack pointer with the proper value and falls through to the common return code at $E445.

E445 – E3C5 Return from p-code procedure common code. This code is common to the RNP and RBP p-codes. First, the old value of the program stack pointer (KP) register is fetched off of the stack. Then the code from $E53D to $E371 fetches any function return value from the program stack and pushes it onto the evaluation stack. Finally, the code from location $E371 to $E3C5 reloads the SEGMENT, JTAB, IPC, MP, and other registers with their original values.

E3C6 – E3D6 This code computes an address by subtracting the data in location $90 and $91 from the word pointed at by these two locations. The address computed is stored into the procedure location variable at addresses $7C and $7D.

E3D7 – E416 Relocation subroutine. The value contained in the location pointed at by the procedure pointer ($7C) is fetched. This is the number of items to be relocated. Next, two is subtracted from the procedure pointer and this data is used as a self relative pointer to the relocation table. For each item to be relocated, the data pointed at by the self relative pointer at location $7C (procedure pointer) is relocated by adding the relocation value (in locations $88 and $89) to the value already there. This process is repeated until the table entries are exhausted. Every assembly language program loaded into the system is relocated by this routine at run-time.

E417 – E4A4 Read segment routine. This code reads in the external segment whose segment number is passed in the 6502 accumulator register. The segment directory is checked to find the drive and block numbers for this routine. First the unit is checked to make sure it is on line. If so, then the BIOS DISKREAD routine is called to read the code in from the disk.

E4A5 – E5F6 Load segment subroutine. This subroutine is called (if necessary) to load in a segment procedure. The segment number is passed in the 6502 accumulator. To begin with, an external procedure counter is checked to see if it is zero. If it is zero, then the segment procedure must be loaded from the disk. If it is not zero, then this is a (possibly indirect) recursive procedure call and the procedure is already in memory. If the segment procedure count is not zero, then it is incremented by one and the subroutine returns. The segment procedure count array is at location $BD1E.

The code from $E4BE to $E4DE checks to see if a p-code segment or a data segment is to be loaded from the disk. The code at locations $E4DF through $E4FD load the data segment, and the code from $E4FE to $E5F6 loads a code segment.

E5F7 – E61B Unload a segment subroutine. This code de-allocates the space used by a segment procedure. Then the procedure counter is checked to make sure it is zero. If it is not, then some recursive invocation of this routine is outstanding and the code cannot be removed from memory. Otherwise (assuming the segment procedure counter is zero) the stack is fixed up to de-allocate the space occupied by the external procedure.

E61C – E625 LDS (load segment) p-code routine. This guy pops the segment number off of the stack, gets it into the 6502 accumultor, and then calls the load segment subroutine. Upon return from load segment, control is returned to the main interpreter loop.

E626 – E62F ULS (unload segment) p-code routine. This routine pops the segment number off of the stack, calls the unload segment subroutine, and then returns control to the main interpreter loop.

E630 – E639 CSP (call special procedure) p-code driver routine. This code fetches the next byte in the code stream (the special routine opcode) multiplies it by two, and uses this as an index into the CSP table. This code is identical to the main interpreter loop except the indirect jump is at locations $71..$73.

E63A – E63F IDS (ID search) special driver routine. This code is a simple jump instruction to the actual IDS code at location $FF3F.

E640–E6B1 TRS (tree search) p-code routine. This code searches through a binary tree for an eight byte token. It is used by the compiler and other system routines for symbol table lookups and other general look-up schema. This function pops three words off of the TOS. The first word popped is a pointer to an eight byte target token. This is the character string TRS searches for in the tree. The second word popped is a pointer to a pointer variable. On return, the pointer is loaded with the address of the last node visted if a match was not found (this is required so that the right and left links of the binary tree can be modified by the calling routine). The third word popped off of the stack is a pointer to the root node of the tree structure. The tree always has the following structure:

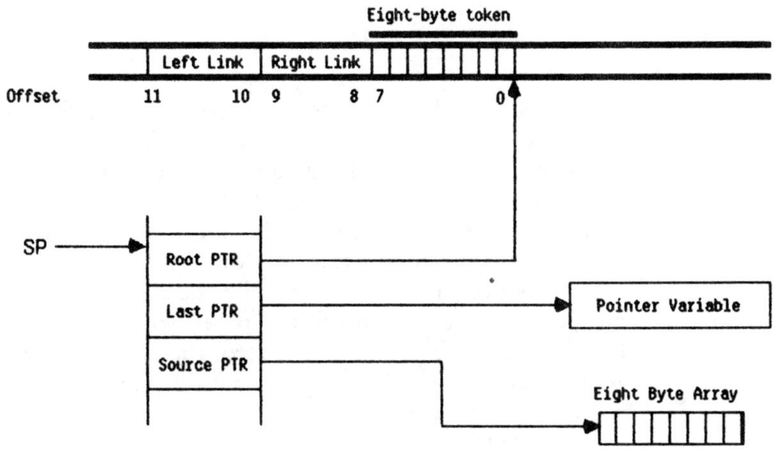

Figure 6-4

E6B2 – E6F6 FLC (fill character) p-code routine. The fill character routine expects the following data on the 6502 hardware stack:

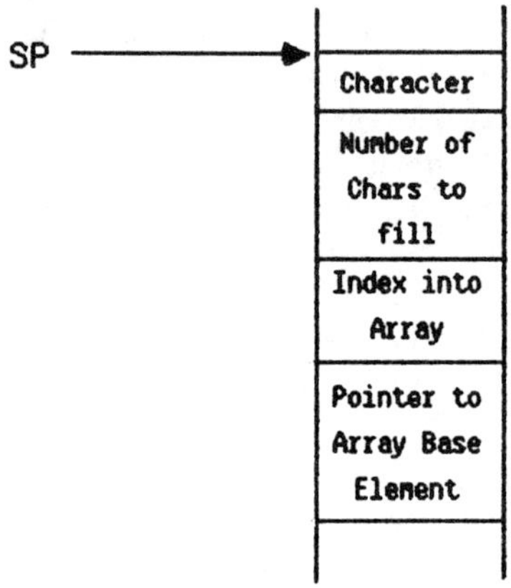

Figure 6-5

The character to be copied is popped off of the stack. Then the number of bytes to be filled is popped. If this number is negative, fill char immediately terminates (and removes the other parameters from the stack. If the number of bytes to be filled is positive, then the index and array base pointer are popped and added. Next, the X-register is loaded with the number of pages to be filled with the character and the program enters a loop that fills 'X' pages with the character. Finally, when the page count is zero, the remaining bytes are filled by loading the X-register with the low order byte of the count value and entering a second loop that fills less than 256 bytes.

E6F7 – E783 SCN (scan) p-code routine. The address and index of the source array are popped and added, the character is fetched, a Boolean flag (0 = "=", 1 = "<>") is popped, and the number of characters to check is popped. Next, the absolute value of the number of characters to search through is taken and this number is stored in locations $5E and $5F. Finally, the array is searched (for the specified number of characters) for the character specified. If it is found, the position in the array is returned. Otherwise, the original value is returned on the stack.

E784 – E82A EXIT (procedure EXIT) p-code routine. This p-code is executed whenever the Pascal EXIT statement is executed. It pops a procedure and segment number off of the stack. If this causes an exit from the operating system, then a jump to the XIT p-code routine is made. Otherwise for each lex level you are exiting, this code computes pointers to the activation record for each statically nested procedure and readjusts the stack to remove the activation record for the procedure(s) being exited.

E82B – E832 BPT (break point) p-code routine. This code gets a big parameter from the code stream and then returns to the main interpreter loop (i.e., it is a NOP).

E833 – E840 HLT (HALT) p-code routine. This code increments the program counter by two and jumps to the user-invoked execution error entry point.

E841 – E85C TIME p-code routine. Two pointers are passed on the 6502 hardware stack. TIME stores zeroes into the words pointed at by these pointers.

E85D – E89F MVR (move right) p-code routine. This routine performs a block move of bytes using decrementing pointers. This routine is jumped to from location $E8DB whenever the MOVERIGHT Pascal statement is executed.

E8A0 – E8DE Block move routine. This code is common to the MVR and MVL routines. It pops the required parameters off of the stack and stores them into zero page locations and then decodes the second opcode byte to determine whether a moveleft or moveright should be performed.

E8DD – E903 MVL (move left) p-code routine. This code performs a block move using incrementing pointers. The block move routine above drops through to this routine if it is determined that a moveleft is to be performed.

E904 – E928 MEMAVAIL p-code routine. If there is a valid directory pointer (at location $BDE6/$BDE7) then push the value MP – DIRP ($5C/D – $BDE6/7) Otherwise push the value MP – NP ($5C/D – $5A/B).

E929 – E956 Floating point pop routine. This utility subroutine pops a floating point number off of the stack and unpacks it. The X-register points at one of three floating point accumulators. The floating point work area is:

$74..$79: FP work area #1
$7A..$7F: FP work area #2
$80..$85: FP work area #3

Within each work area the first byte is reserved for the sign (bit 7 is zero for positive numbers, one for negative numbers), the second byte holds the exponent in bias 128 form, and the last four bytes in each work area form the exponent. All floating point calculations are carried out in this special "unpacked" form. When data is stored into memory, it is converted to a more compact "packed" form. The format of a packed floating point data element is:

Byte	Bits	Description
0	31..24	Sign (bit 7) and H.O. bits of exponent.
1	23..16	L.O. bit of exponent, and H.O. bits of mantissa
2	15..8	Middle bits of mantissa.
3	7..0	L.O. bits of mantissa.

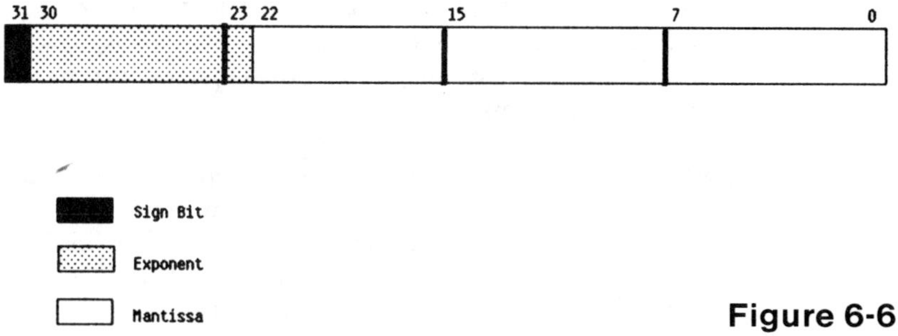

Figure 6-6

Since the packed floating point numbers are always normalized the H.O. bit of the mantissa is always one. Since this bit is always one (unless the value is zero) this bit is not kept around. It is used to hold the leftover bit of the exponent in the packed form. When the data is unpacked, the unpacking routine sets the H.O. bit of the mantissa.

The floating point pop routine pops a packed floating point value off of the evaluation stack, unpacks it, and stores the unpacked data into the floating point work area pointed at by the X-register.

E957 – E979 Floating point push routine. This routine performs the opposite function of the pop routine. It takes the floating point work area pointed at by the X-register, packs it, and pushes the packed result onto the evaluation stack.

E97A – E999 Bump exponent routine. This routine is called within the REAL addition and multiplication routines. If the carry is set, then the number is shifted to the right and the exponent is bumped up by one.

E99A – E9B9 FP Normalize routine. After any floating point operation the floating point value must be normalized. This is accomplished by shifting the mantissa to the left until a one appears in the H.O. bit. Each time the mantissa is shifted the exponent is decremented by one.

E9BA – E9D7 Round routine. This code rounds the floating point value in the third floating point work area. If a number lies exactly between two representable values, then it is rounded to the value with the least significant bit of zero.

E9D8 – EA12 FP Adjust routine. When adding or subtracting two floating point values the exponents must be the same. This routine scales the values in floating point work areas one and two so that they have the same exponent. This is accomplished by shifting the smaller value to the right and incrementing its exponent.

EA13 – EA38 FP addition subroutine. This routine aligns the values in FP work areas one and two, adds the mantissas, normalizes the result, rounds the result, and finally re-normalizes the result.

EA39 – EA71 FP Subtraction subroutine. This routine aligns, subtracts, normalizes, and rounds two floating point numbers.

EA72 – EA9D FP compare and swap routine. Compares the absolute values of the floating point numbers in the FP work area one (FPWA #1) and FP work area two (FPWA #2). If FPWA #1 is greater than FPWA #2, they are swapped and the carry is cleared. Otherwise the carry is returned set.

EAC2 – EB08 ADR (add REAL) p-code routine. Pops two floating point numbers off of the stack and adds them. If the signs are different, then the floating point subtraction routine is called instead.

EB09 – EB59 SBR (subtract REAL) p-code routine. Two floating point numbers are popped off of the stack and the FP subtract routine is called. If the signs are different then the FP add routine is called instead.

EB5A – EBE5 DVR (Divide REAL) p-code routine. This routine pops two floating point values off of the stack and stores them in the FP work area. Then it checks the first value popped off to see if it is zero. If it is, then a division by zero execution error is forced. If the first number was zero then zero is pushed onto the evaluation stack and DVR returns to the main interpreter loop. If neither number was zero the two exponents are subtracted to determine the exponent of the result. If an underflow occurs, a floating point error is forced, otherwise the FPWA#2 is divided by the FPWA #1 and the result is returned on the evaluation stack.

EBE6 – EC54 FP multiplication subroutine. This routine multiplies FPWA#1 by FPWA#2 and leaves the REAL result in FPWA#3.

EC55 – EC7C MPR (multiply REALs) p-code routine. This code pops two floating point values off of the stack, calls the FP multiplication subroutine, and then pushes FPWA#3 onto the evaluation stack.

EC7D – ECB1 SQR (square REALs) p-code routine. This code checks the REAL number on TOS to see if it is zero. If it is, then zero is returned. Otherwise the data on TOS is duplicated in FPWA#1 and FPWA#2, the FP multiply routine is called, and FPWA#3 is pushed onto the evaluation stack.

ECB2 – ECBF ABR (absolute value of a REAL number) p-code routine. This routine clears the H.O. bit of the exponent byte by shifting it to the left and then shifting it to the right.

ECC0 – ECDF NGR (Negate REAL) p-code routine. This routine inverts the sign bit in the exponent byte.

ECE0 – ED3E Float integer value. An integer value is on TOS. This routine pops it and converts it to a floating point value. The resultant floating point value is left in FPWA#3.

ED3F – ED61 FLO (float integer) p-code routine. This routine floats the integer value on TOS – 1. It accomplishes this by popping four bytes off of the TOS (there is always a real on TOS) and saving it in FPWA#1. Then a call to the float routine is made to float the integer left on TOS. Finally, the floating point value saved in FPWA#1 is pushed back onto the stack and this routine returns control to the main interpreter loop.

ED62 – ED6C FLT (float TOS) p-code routine. This routine simply calls the float routine and pushes the floating point value left in FPWA#3.

ED6D – EDBA Truncation/round routine. If location $86 contains zero, then the floating point number in FPWA#1 is truncated, otherwise it is rounded.

EDBB – EDCF RND (round REAL) p-code routine. The floating point number on TOS is converted to an integer and the result is pushed.

EDD0 – EDE4 TNC (truncate REAL) p-code routine. The floating point number on TOS is converted to an integer by truncation and the integer result is pushed.

EDE5 – EE0D POT (power of ten) p-code routine. TOS contains an integer. If it is greater than 38, zero (four bytes) is pushed onto the stack. Otherwise this value is used as an index into a table containing the floating point representations for the various powers of ten. The appropriate value is pushed.

EE0E–EECC Power of ten table. This table is an array [0.38] of REAL used by the POT p-code routine.

EECD – EEF8 Unit on-line check subroutine. This routine is passed a unit number in the 6502 accumulator and X-register. The unit specified is checked to make sure that it is valid and on-line. First, the value is checked to see if the H.O. bit is set. If it is not, then the unit number is checked to make sure it is in the range 1..12. If it is, this routine immediately returns to the calling procedure. Otherwise a run-time error (bad unit number) is forced.

If a user-defined unit number is specified (user-defined unit numbers are always in the range $80..$8F) then the unit table at address $FE82 is checked to see if the desired user-defined unit has been attached to the system. If so, this subroutine simply returns. If the unit is not in the system (denoted by a zero entry in the unit table) then a run-time error is forced by jumping to location $EEEF.

EEF9 – EF03 IOR (IORESULT) p-code routine. This p-code function pushes the value of IORESULT onto the stack. The IORESULT value is contained in memory locations $BDDE and $BDDF.

EF04 – EF0E IOC (IOCHECK) p-code routine. This routine checks IORESULT. If it is not zero a run-time error is caused.

EF0F – EF1C UBUSY (unitbusy) p-code routine. Since all I/O on the Apple II is synchronous, this routine does very little. It does check to make sure the specified unit is on-line and then pushes false onto the evaluation stack (since the unit will never be busy).

EF1D – EF26 UWAIT (unit wait) p-code routine. Since all I/O is synchronous, this routine does nothing more than pop the unit number off of the stack, make sure the unit is on-line, and return control to the main interpreter loop.

EF27 – EFA4 USTATUS (unit status) p-code routine. This code begins by popping unnecessary data off of the stack, massaging the stack so that it is in the format expected by the BIOS STATUS routines, and then transfers control to the appropriate BIOS subroutine.

EFA5 – F035 UCLEAR (unit clear) p-code routine. This code initializes the device specified by the word on TOS. The code at location $EFB4 handles user defined devices. The code between $EFBD and $EFC4 converts unit number seven to unit number eight (REMIN: is converted to REMOUT:) and the code at location $EFC5 determines whether a character oriented device or a block structured device is being accessed. Block structured devices are initialized by the code at $EFD0..$EFE1. The console is handled by the code at locations $EFEA..$F005. The printer initialization is handled by the code at addresses $F006..$F013. The remote units are initialized by the code at addresses $F014..$F01D. And the graphics unit is initialized by the code at address $F01E.

F036 – F068 Disk I/O subroutine. This code handles block structured I/O requests.

F069 – F06D UREAD (unit read) input entry point. This code loads the accumulator with zero and jumps to the unit I/O code at address $F070.

F06E – F06F UWRITE (unit write). This routine loads the accumulator with one and drops through to the unit I/O code at address $F070.

F070 – F210 UNIT I/O. This code handles the unitread and unitwrite functions of the Pascal operating system. This code modifies the parameters on the stack and dispatches the I/O request to the appropriate BIOS subroutine.

F213–FFFF Pascal O/S, BIOS hooks, and boot-time transient area. During the boot of the Pascal system this area contains the initialization code. Once initialization is complete, the Pascal reserved word table, ID search routine, and other various routines are loaded into this area.

D000–DFFF (second BANK). BIOS, IDS p-code routine and reserved word table.

This short description of the Apple Pascal p-code interpreter is far from perfect, nor is it quite complete. No attempt to describe the BIOS routines was made since these routines are the most likely to change in the event changes are made to the system. For more information on the BIOS, consult the chapter on the ATTACH-BIOS code.

Section Three

Modifying Apple Pascal

7
Modifying the Apple Pascal P-code Interpreter

The Apple Pascal P-code interpreter is written in 6502 machine code to insure that programs run fairly fast. As it turns out, the students who originally wrote the 6502 p-code interpreter were fairly inexperienced on the 6502 microprocessor chip. As a result of this inexperience, the p-code interpreter is not as optimal as it could be. If the 6502 interpreter were completely rewritten using better coding techniques an overall increase of 15-20% could be realized. That's almost as good as the 6809! While rewriting the Apple Pascal p-code interpreter you can also modify the interpreter to take advantage of special hardware like a clock/calendar board or possibly even a hardware floating point board like the CCS 9511 Arithmetic processor card, the DTACK Grounded 68000 board, or Lazer's 16032 board. While I cannot present a completely rewritten 6502 interpreter here, several examples will be presented (which actually work) that can be used as a template for rewriting additional portions of the interpreter.

There are several ways to rewrite the Apple Pascal p-code interpreter, you can patch the interpreter on the disk so that the modifications are loaded into memory every time the master disk is booted; you can patch the interpreter in memory by running a program that overlays the interpreter; or you can use a feature found in Apple Pascal 1.1 to attach drivers to the Pascal BIOS. I've used the latter method because it's the easiest to implement. The code I've written allows the use of the CCS Arithmetic card and the Mountain Computer Apple Clock in the Pascal system to provide additional features and performance improvement.

The program begins with four equates to define the status of the optional hardware. HASAPU should be equated to one if you have a CCS Arithmetic card in your system, it should be set to zero if you don't have such a device. APUSLOT defines the slot number where the CCS Arithmetic card can be found. This label should be equated to address $C080 + $n0 where "n" is the slot number of the APU. The next two equates, HASCLK and CLKSLOT, define the presence and slot number of the Mountain Computer Apple Clock. If you do not have a clock in your system you should set HASCLK to zero. One final note on the Apple Clock code: it only works with the Mountain Computer Apple Clock, it does not work with Mountain's CPS card or anybody else's clock card for that matter.

Following the special hardware equates come the p-machine register equates. The Apple Pascal p-machine's registers are emulated in zero page RAM at these locations. This locations will be used extensively by the interpreter patch code. Twelve temporary locations are also used by this code, they immediately follow the p-machine register equates.

Several locations within the interpreter itself are also of great importance. At location $D000 (in bank zero of the language card) the interpreter jump table can be found. This table consists of 128 addresses that point to routines for each of the 128 p-codes (excluding the SLDC p-codes). The easiest way to patch the interpreter is to simply overlay the address in the interpreter address table with a new address pointing at your replacement routine. The JMPTBL equate in the program listing provides the base address of the interpreter table so that certain addresses can be easily patched with the address of the replacement routine.

Once a p-routine has executed the necessary code to emulate its respective p-code, control is returned to the main interpreter loop by jumping to location $D23B or location $D24D. The code at location $D23B increments the IPC (interpreter program counter) by two and then fetches the next p-code from the opcode stream. The code at location $D24D increments the IPC by one and falls through to the opcode fetch section. There's also an entry point which increments the IPC by three and falls through, but it is not required by this code.

EXECERR and RANGERR are entry points into the interpreter which this code jumps to if an execution error or a range error occurs during the execution of the p-code. In particular, the RANGERR entry point is branched to if the CHK p-code detects data which is out of range. HNDLJTAB is an entry point into the middle of the interpreter which is taken in certain cases depending on the target address of a branch instruction. GBPARM is a subroutine which is called to fetch a variable-length address operand from the code stream.

Immediately following the equates is the initialization entry point for the interpreter patch routine. This code follows the "ATTACH-BIOS" specifications found in the manual distributed by the International Apple Core and reprinted in the appendix. This manual is also available from your local Apple club (assuming it is a member of the IAC), the Call – A.P.P.L.E club, or directly from the IAC. For additional info on the ATTACH–BIOS routines you should consult this manual or the appropriate chapter in p-Source.

The entry point for the initialization code checks the X-register to make sure it contains three. If the X-register contains a value other than three then the programmer/user is attempting to do some sort of I/O to this "device". Since these BIOS patches are not an I/O device driver, an IORESULT of nine (unit off-line) is returned to the user. If the x-register contains three then the p-system is performing an initialization call. Since this "device" is usually initialized at boot-time, the initialization entry condition is perfect for patching the p-code interpreter.

In order to patch the interpreter the RAM card must be write-enabled. This is accomplished by writing to location $C089 twice in succession. Once the RAM card is write-enabled the data from ADRSTBL is used to patch the interpreter address table. Each entry in the table contains four bytes. The first two bytes contain the address of the p-routine jump address in the interpreter jump table. The next two bytes contain the new jump address that points to a replacement routine. The jump table is terminated with a pair of zero bytes.

The first two routines I've enhanced are the p-machine ABI and NGI (integer absolute value and negate p-code) instructions. The original Apple Pascal code is shown in comments to give you an idea of how much improvement can be made to the p-code interpreter's code. The original authors of the 6502 p-code interpreter used the textbook method for taking the two's complement of a number: invert all the bits and add one. On the 6502, taking the two's complement of a sixteen bit value using this method is very inefficient. It's much quicker to simply subtract the value you wish to negate from zero (See "Signed Arithmetic on the 6502" in the May, 1983, issue of MICRO or "Using 6502 Assembly Language"). By reorganizing the code it was also possible to save a considerable amount of space by combining the ABI and NGI p-routines.

The next p-code routine I've included is a replacement for the ADI (add integers) opcode. The original Apple Pascal code (included in the comments) performs a lot of unecessary operations to add two integers. Not only does the new routine require less space but it also executes quite a bit faster. Like the ABI and NGI p-codes, ADI jumps to INCIPC to return control to the Apple Pascal p-code interpreter.

The code for the subtract p-code, SBI, is a little different than that for the ADI p-code. Unlike addition, which is commutative, the SBI routine must subtract the item on TOS-1 from the item on TOS. Therefore the code for SBI must be a little bigger, slower, and more complex than the ADI p-code routine.

The logical OR and logical AND instructions (LAND and LOR) p-routines follow. They are essentially identical to the ADI routine except, of course, the logical operation is performed instead of an addition.

The CHK p-code is emitted whenever you access an array element, use a value with range limitations, or perform any string operations. Essentially it performs two signed comparisons and causes an execution error if a value is out of range. The authors of the 6502 p-code interpreter used a rather bizzare method to compare signed values on the 6502. I've substituted a standard signed comparison routine which speeds up the operation of the CHK p-code. Speeding up the CHK p-code is important because it is frequently executed. The signed comparison comes straight out of "Using 6502 Assembly Language" (also see the May, 1983, issue of MICRO).

The Apple Pascal p-code interpreter uses a set of common subroutines for the p-codes GTRI, LEQI, GEQI, LESI, and NEQI. Combined with their non-standard method of comparing two's complement numbers these routines are very slow. The code in the program listing from address \$012A..\$01FC is a set of replacement routines for these integer comparisons. These routines were sped up by using individual routines for each comparison (instead of passing parameters to and from a common subroutine) and using the improved signed comparison routines. Unlike the other routines in this package which are shorter as well as faster, these routines are much longer than the equivalent routines in the p-code interpreter since the Apple Pascal p-routines use a common subroutine for most of the comparisons.

The next two routines in the interpreter patch package (MPI and DVI) require a CCS Arithmetic Processor card for proper operation. These routines replace the integer multiply and divide routines in the p-code interpreter with the hardware functions provided by the CCS card. Most readers will ask why I didn't include routines for the floating point operations as well as the integer operations. As it turns out, the Apple Pascal floating point format is a bit different from the AMD9511 format so a conversion routine is necessary. When I first wrote these routines I included a format conversion subroutine. Unfortunately, the dynamic range of the 9511 chip is limited to −10E−19 to +10E19 while the Apple Pascal system regularly uses values in the range −10E28 to +10E28 (especially during floating point I/O conversion) so the range limitation can cause some real problems. One last fix I tried was to call the software routines if there was a range problem and use the 9511 if the calculations fell within the precision of the 9511. The extra calculations required more time than the 9511 saved. Therefore I didn't include floating point routines in the p-code interpreter patch program listing.

The last routine included in the p-code interpreter patch program is the TIME routine. UCSD Pascal includes a special built-in TIME function that returns the current time in 60ths of a second. The TIME routine reads the Mountain Computer Apple Clock, converts the time value to 60ths of a second, and returns the time to the Pascal system. By setting the "HASCLOCK" Boolean variable to true in the SETUP program you will be able to write programs that can read the clock and take different actions depending upon the current time. Furthermore, with the TIME routine included in the interpreter the Apple Pascal compiler will report how slow it is running (usually around 330 lines/minute). Since there is no TIME routine provided in the current interpreter, comparing my version to Apple's is impossible.

In order to actually patch the interpreter using this routine you must assemble the program using the UCSD 6502 assembler (without using the ".ABSOLUTE" option) and change the codefile's name to "ATTACH.DRIVERS". Next you must put a copy of the "SYSTEM.ATTACH" program (provided by the IAC and available from your local Apple club or directly from the IAC) on the disk. Finally, you must create an "ATTACH.DATA" file using the program "ATTACHUD.CODE" (also provided by the IAC). Follow the directions supplied in the documentation for these programs (or see the chapter on the Apple Pascal BIOS in P-SOURCE) to create the "ATTACH.DATA" file. When it asks you what device number you want to attach your driver to you should respond "140" (unless you have attached some other user-defined device to this device number). When the ATTACHUD.CODE program asks you if you want the driver to be initialized at boot time you should answer "YES". This boot-time initialization performs the patch to the interpreter for you.

While only a few of the p-code routines were optimized here, most of the p-routines in the p-code interpreter can be improved somewhat. In particular the load and store operations should be optimized as much as possible since they're executed considerably more often than any other single opcode. Such experimentation will be left to the reader.

Listing 7-1

```
PAGE -   1  INTERP    FILE:INT.1.TEXT


0000|                                    .PROC   INTERP
Current memory available:    8644
0000|                       ;
0000|                       ;
0000|                       ;  Apple Pascal interpreter Patches.
0000|                       ;
0000|                       ;  (c) Copyright 1982, Lazer MicroSystems, Inc.
0000|                       ;      All rights reserved.
0000|                       ;
0000|                       ;      Conceived and written by Randall Hyde.
0000|                       ;      Date: 8/25/82
0000|                       ;
0000| 0001                  HASAPU          .EQU    1       ;Zero if no CCS card installed.
0000| C0F0                  APUSLOT         .EQU    0C0F0   ;Slot # of CCS APU card
0000| 0001                  HASCLK          .EQU    1       ;Zero if no Mountain Clock card.
0000| C0D0                  CLKSLOT         .EQU    0C0D0   ;SLOT # of Mountain Clock card.
0000|                       ;
0000|                       ;
0000|                       ; Interpreter variables
0000|                       ;
0000| 0050                  BASE            .EQU    50      ;p-code BASE register
0000| 0052                  MP              .EQU    52      ;Mark stack pointer
0000| 0054                  JTAB            .EQU    54      ;Jump table pointer
0000| 0056                  SEG             .EQU    56      ;Segment register
0000| 0058                  IPC             .EQU    58      ;p-code program counter
0000| 005A                  NP              .EQU    5A      ;Heap pointer
0000| 005C                  KP              .EQU    5C      ;Program stack pointer
0000| 005E                  BIGPARM         .EQU    5E      ;Value returned by GBPARM
0000|                       ;
0000| 0088                  MULTOP1         .EQU    88      ;Operands used by multiply.
0000| 008A                  MULTOP2         .EQU    8A
0000| 008C                  MULTOP3         .EQU    8C
0000|                       ;
0000|                       ;
0000|                       ; Temporary locations used by this code.
0000|                       ;
0000| 0000                  PTR             .EQU    0
0000| 0002                  OPCODE          .EQU    2
0000| 0004                  TEMP1           .EQU    4
0000| 0006                  TEMP2           .EQU    6
0000| 0008                  TEMP3           .EQU    8
0000| 000A                  TEMP4           .EQU    0A
0000|                       ;
0000|                       ;
0000|                       ; Interpreter locations.
0000|                       ;
0000| 0100                  STACK           .EQU    00100
0000| D000                  JMPTBL          .EQU    0D000   ;p-code address table
0000| D23B                  INCIPC2         .EQU    0D23B   ;Increment IPC by 2 and return.
0000| D24D                  INCIPC          .EQU    0D24D   ;Increment IPC and return.
0000| D1FB                  EXECERR         .EQU    0D1FB   ;Execution error.
0000| D1B7                  RANGERR         .EQU    0D1B7   ;Range error.
0000| D279                  HNDLJTAB        .EQU    0D279   ;Handle a jump in jump table.
0000| D155                  GBPARM          .EQU    0D155   ;Gets a big parameter
0000|                       ;
```

Listing 7-1 (continued)

```
PAGE -    2  INTERP     FILE:INT.1.TEXT

0000|                       ;
0000|                       ;
0000|                       ;
0000|                       ;  The following entry point corresponds to the protocol
0000|                       ;  described in the ATTACH-BIOS Pamphlet distributed by the
0000|                       ;  International Apple Core.
0000|                       ;  The Read, Write, and Status entry points fix the stack and
0000|                       ;  return.
0000|                       ;  The initialization code patches these routines into the
0000|                       ;  Apple Pascal p-code interpreter.
0000|                       ;
0000| E0 00                 ENTRY           CPX     #0          ;READ?
0002| F0**                                  BEQ     RWS
0004| E0 01                                 CPX     #1
0006| F0**                                  BEQ     RWS
0008| E0 04                                 CPX     #4
000A| D0**                                  BNE     INITCODE
000C|                       ;
000C|                       ; User program attempted to Read, Write, or check the status
000C|                       ; of this device.  Return a unit off-line error.
000C|                       ;
0006* 04
0002* 08
000C| A2 09                 RWS             LDX     #9
000E| 60                                    RTS
000F|                       ;
000F|                       ;
000F|                       ; INITCODE patches the Apple Pascal p-code interpreter to jump
000F|                       ; to these routines instead of the code in the language card.
000F|                       ;
000A* 03
000F| AD 89C0               INITCODE        LDA     0C089               ;Write enable RAM card
0012| AD 89C0                               LDA     0C089               ;by accessing $C089.
0015|                       ;
0015|                       ; Patch the interpreter p-code address table with pointers
0015|                       ; to the routines in this source file.
0015|                       ; The address table below consists of two word-pointer pairs.
0015|                       ; The first word is the address of the entry in the p-code
0015|                       ; intepreter address table, the next two bytes are the address
0015|                       ; of the corresponding routine in this source file.
0015|                       ;
0015| A2 00                                 LDX     #0
0017| BD ****               MOVEADRS        LDA     ADRSTBL,X           ;Get the address of the
001A| 85 00                                 STA     PTR                 ;entry in the p-code
001C| BD ****                               LDA     ADRSTBL+1,X         ;address table.
001F| 85 01                                 STA     PTR+1
0021| 05 00                                 ORA     PTR                 ;Done if zero.
0023| F0**                                  BEQ     ALLDONE
0025|                       ;
0025|                       ; If the pointer address is not zero, transfer the next two
0025|                       ; bytes to the address specified by the pointer saved in PTR.
0025|                       ;
0025| A0 00                                 LDY     #0
0027| BD ****                               LDA     ADRSTBL+2,X
002A| 91 00                                 STA     (PTR),Y
```

Listing 7-1 (continued)

```
PAGE -    3  INTERP    FILE:INT.1.TEXT


002C| C8                                   INY
002D| BD ****                              LDA     ADRSTBL+3,X
0030| 91 00                                STA     (PTR),Y
0032|                          ;
0032|                          ; Increment the index to the next pointer pair and repeat.
0032|                          ;
0032| E8                                   INX
0033| E8                                   INX
0034| E8                                   INX
0035| E8                                   INX
0036| 4C 1700                              JMP     MOVEADRS
0039|                          ;
0039|                          ;
0039|                          ; Once the patches are made, renable the RAM card and return
0039|                          ; control to the p-code interpreter/ SYSTEM.ATTACH programs.
0039|                          ;
0023* 14
0039| AD 80C0                  ALLDONE     LDA     0C080            ;Read enable RAM card.
003C| 60                                   RTS
003D|                          ;
003D|                          ;
003D|                          ; The following address table consists of several two-address
003D|                          ; pairs.  The first address of each pair is the address of
003D|                          ; of the table entry in the p-code interpreter.  The second
003D|                          ; address is the address of the p-code routine that is
003D|                          ; replacing the stock Apple routine.
003D|                          ;
002E* 4000
0028* 3F00
001D* 3E00
0018* 3D00
003D|                          ADRSTBL
003D| 00D0 ****                ABIADR      .WORD   JMPTBL,ABI       ;ABS(n) function.
0041| 04D0 ****                ADIADR      .WORD   JMPTBL+4,ADI     ;ADD integers.
0045| 2AD0 ****                SBIADR      .WORD   JMPTBL+2A,SBI    ;Subtract integers.
0049| 22D0 ****                NGIADR      .WORD   JMPTBL+22,NGI    ;Negate integer on TOS.
004D| 08D0 ****                LANDADR     .WORD   JMPTBL+08,LAND   ;Logical AND TOS.
0051| 1AD0 ****                LORADR      .WORD   JMPTBL+1A,LOR    ;Logical OR TOS.
0055| 10D0 ****                CHKADR      .WORD   JMPTBL+10,CHK    ;CHK subrange bounds.
0059| 88D0 ****                GEQIADR     .WORD   JMPTBL+88,GEQI   ;Test for integer >=.
005D| 8AD0 ****                GTRIADR     .WORD   JMPTBL+8A,GTRI   ;Test for integer >.
0061| 90D0 ****                LEQIADR     .WORD   JMPTBL+90,LEQI   ;Test for <=.
0065| 92D0 ****                LESIADR     .WORD   JMPTBL+92,LESI   ;Test for <.
0069| 96D0 ****                NEQIADR     .WORD   JMPTBL+96,NEQI   ;Test for <>.
006D| 42D0 ****                FJPADR      .WORD   JMPTBL+42,FJP    ;False jump.
0071| 72D0 ****                UJPADR      .WORD   JMPTBL+72,UJP    ;Unconditional jump.
0075|
0075|                                      .IF     HASAPU=1
0075|
0075| 1ED0 ****                MPIADR      .WORD   JMPTBL+1E,MPI    ;Integer multiply.
0079| 0CD0 ****                DVIADR      .WORD   JMPTBL+0C,DVI    ;Integer division.
007D|
007D|                                      .ENDC
007D|
007D|                                      .IF     HASCLK=1
```

Listing 7-1 (continued)

```
PAGE -    4  INTERP    FILE:INT.1.TEXT

007D|
007D| 12D1 ****          TIMEADR        .WORD   JMPTBL+112,TIME
0081|
0081|                                   .ENDC
0081|
0081| 0000                              .WORD   0
0083|                  ;
0083|                  ;
0083|                  ;
0083|                  ; Code to replace the Apple Pascal ABI and NGI instructions.
0083|                  ;
0083|                  ; Original Apple Pascal code:
0083|                  ;
0083|                  ;       ABI     PLA
0083|                  ;               TAX
0083|                  ;               PLA
0083|                  ;               BMI     $0
0083|                  ;               PHA
0083|                  ;               TXA
0083|                  ;               PHA
0083|                  ;               JMP     INCPC
0083|                  ;
0083|                  ;       $0      TAY
0083|                  ;               CLC
0083|                  ;               TXA
0083|                  ;               EOR     #0FF
0083|                  ;               ADC     #1
0083|                  ;               TAX
0083|                  ;               TYA
0083|                  ;               EOR     #0FF
0083|                  ;               ADC     #0
0083|                  ;               PHA
0083|                  ;               TXA
0083|                  ;               PHA
0083|                  ;               JMP     INCPC
0083|                  ;
0083|                  ;       NGI     PLA
0083|                  ;               XOR     #0FF
0083|                  ;               CLC
0083|                  ;               ADC     #1
0083|                  ;               TAX
0083|                  ;               PLA
0083|                  ;               XOR     #0FF
0083|                  ;               ADC     #0
0083|                  ;               PHA
0083|                  ;               TXA
0083|                  ;               PHA
0083|                  ;               JMP     INCIPC
0083|                  ;
0083|                  ;
0083|                  ; The improved code is:
0083|                  ;
003F* 8300
0083| BA               ABI            TSX                     ;Get the integer
0084| BD 0201                         LDA     STACK+2,X       ;on TOS.
```

Listing 7-1 (continued)

```
PAGE -   5  INTERP    FILE:INT.1.TEXT

0087| 10**                          BPL     ABIXIT          ;Is it positive?
0089|              ;
004B* 8900
0089| BA           NGI              TSX                     ;Negate integer
008A| 38                            SEC                     ;by subtracting it
008B| A9 00                         LDA     #0              ;from zero.
008D| FD 0101                       SBC     STACK+1,X
0090| 9D 0101                       STA     STACK+1,X
0093| A9 00                         LDA     #0
0095| FD 0201                       SBC     STACK+2,X
0098| 9D 0201                       STA     STACK+2,X
0087* 12
009B| 4C 4DD2      ABIXIT           JMP     INCIPC
009E|
009E|              ;
009E|              ;
009E|              ;  ADI- Add two integers on TOS.
009E|              ;
009E|              ;       ADI adds the integer at TOS-1 to the integer at TOS.
009E|              ;  Both items are popped and the sum is then pushed onto the
009E|              ;  p-machine evaluation stack.  The stack frame for this
009E|              ;  operation looks something like:
009E|              ;
009E|              ;  Before ADI:
009E|              ;
009E|              ;  ---------------
009E|              ;  |   value1    |
009E|              ;  |-------------|
009E|              ;  |   value2    |
009E|              ;  |-------------|
009E|              ;  | rest of the |
009E|              ;  |    stack    |
009E|              ;
009E|              ;
009E|              ;  After ADI:
009E|              ;
009E|              ;  -------------------
009E|              ;  | value1 + value2 |
009E|              ;  |-----------------|
009E|              ;  |  rest of stack  |
009E|              ;  |                 |
009E|              ;
009E|              ;     Since addition is commutative TOS can be popped and
009E|              ;  added to TOS-1 on the stack.  The original Apple (UCSD)
009E|              ;  code fails to take advantage of the fact that data on
009E|              ;  the stack can be accessed using the X index register.
009E|              ;  Apple's code pops TOS and stores it into some temporary
009E|              ;  zero page location, pops TOS-1, adds them, and pushes
009E|              ;  the result.
009E|              ;
009E|              ;
009E|              ;   Original Apple Pascal code:
009E|              ;
009E|              ;       ADI     PLA
009E|              ;               STA     TEMP
```

Listing 7-1 (continued)

```
PAGE -   6  INTERP    FILE:INT.1.TEXT

009E|                    ;             PLA
009E|                    ;             STA      TEMP+1
009E|                    ;             PLA
009E|                    ;             TAY
009E|                    ;             PLA
009E|                    ;             TAX
009E|                    ;             TYA
009E|                    ;             CLC
009E|                    ;             ADC      TEMP
009E|                    ;             TAY
009E|                    ;             TXA
009E|                    ;             ADC      TEMP+1
009E|                    ;             PHA
009E|                    ;             TYA
009E|                    ;             PHA
009E|                    ;             JMP      INCIPC
009E|                    ;
009E|                    ;  Improved code:
009E|                    ;
0043* 9E00
009E| BA                 ADI           TSX
009F| 18                               CLC
00A0| 68                               PLA                     ;Add TOS to
00A1| 7D 0301                          ADC      STACK+3,X      ;TOS-1 and leave
00A4| 9D 0301                          STA      STACK+3,X      ;result on TOS.
00A7| 68                               PLA
00A8| 7D 0401                          ADC      STACK+4,X
00AB| 9D 0401                          STA      STACK+4,X
00AE| 4C 4DD2                          JMP      INCIPC
00B1|                    ;
00B1|                    ;
00B1|                    ; SBI- Subtract integer on TOS-1 from integer on TOS.
00B1|                    ;
00B1|                    ;
00B1|                    ; Before:
00B1|                    ;
00B1|                    ; ________________
00B1|                    ; |     TOS      |
00B1|                    ; |--------------|
00B1|                    ; |    TOS-1     |
00B1|                    ; |--------------|
00B1|                    ; | rest of stack |
00B1|                    ;
00B1|                    ;
00B1|                    ; After:
00B1|                    ;
00B1|                    ; ________________
00B1|                    ; | (TOS-1) - TOS |
00B1|                    ; |--------------|
00B1|                    ; | rest of stack |
00B1|                    ;
00B1|                    ;
00B1|                    ;    Subtraction is a little more complicated than addition
00B1|                    ; because subtraction is not commutative.  The data on TOS
00B1|                    ; must be subtracted from the data on TOS-1.  This means
```

Listing 7-1 (continued)

```
PAGE -   7  INTERP    FILE:INT.1.TEXT

00B1|                        ; the data on TOS cannot be popped off of the stack until
00B1|                        ; the subtraction operation is complete.
00B1|                        ;
00B1|                        ;
00B1|                        ; Original Apple code:
00B1|                        ;
00B1|                        ;       SBI     PLA
00B1|                        ;               STA     TEMP
00B1|                        ;               PLA
00B1|                        ;               STA     TEMP+1
00B1|                        ;               PLA
00B1|                        ;               TAY
00B1|                        ;               PLA
00B1|                        ;               TAX
00B1|                        ;               TYA
00B1|                        ;               SEC
00B1|                        ;               SBC     TEMP
00B1|                        ;               TAY
00B1|                        ;               TXA
00B1|                        ;               SBC     TEMP+1
00B1|                        ;               PHA
00B1|                        ;               TYA
00B1|                        ;               PHA
00B1|                        ;               JMP     INCIPC
00B1|                        ;
00B1|                        ; Improved code:
00B1|                        ;
00B1|                        ;
0047* B100
00B1| BA                     SBI             TSX
00B2| 38                                     SEC
00B3| BD 0301                                LDA     STACK+3,X       ;Get TOS and
00B6| FD 0101                                SBC     STACK+1,X       ;subtract it from
00B9| 9D 0301                                STA     STACK+3,X       ;the value on TOS-1
00BC| BD 0401                                LDA     STACK+4,X       ;The result is left
00BF| FD 0201                                SBC     STACK+2,X       ;on TOS-1
00C2| 9D 0401                                STA     STACK+4,X
00C5| 68                                     PLA                     ;Remove TOS so that
00C6| 68                                     PLA                     ;TOS-1 becomes TOS.
00C7| 4C 4DD2                                JMP     INCIPC
00CA|                        ;
00CA|                        ;
00CA|                        ; LAND- Logical AND.
00CA|                        ;
00CA|                        ;  The logical AND operation IS commutative, therefore
00CA|                        ;  the new code is very similar to that for the ADI
00CA|                        ;  p-code routine.
00CA|                        ;
00CA|                        ;  Original Apple code:
00CA|                        ;
00CA|                        ;       LAND    PLA
00CA|                        ;               STA     TEMP
00CA|                        ;               PLA
00CA|                        ;               STA     TEMP+1
00CA|                        ;               PLA
```

Listing 7-1 (continued)

```
PAGE -   8  INTERP    FILE:INT.1.TEXT

00CA|                         ;              TAX
00CA|                         ;              PLA
00CA|                         ;              AND     TEMP+1
00CA|                         ;              PHA
00CA|                         ;              TXA
00CA|                         ;              AND     TEMP
00CA|                         ;              PHA
00CA|                         ;              JMP     INCIPC
00CA|                         ;
00CA|                         ; Improved code:
00CA|                         ;
004F* CA00
00CA| BA                      LAND           TSX
00CB| 68                                     PLA
00CC| 3D 0301                                AND     STACK+3,X
00CF| 9D 0301                                STA     STACK+3,X
00D2| 68                                     PLA
00D3| 3D 0401                                AND     STACK+4,X
00D6| 9D 0401                                STA     STACK+4,X
00D9| 4C 4DD2                                JMP     INCIPC
00DC|                         ;
00DC|                         ; LOR- Logical OR.
00DC|                         ;
00DC|                         ;
00DC|                         ;  Logical OR is also commutative, therefore it's
00DC|                         ;  easy to perform the LOR operation.
00DC|                         ;
00DC|                         ;  Original Apple code:
00DC|                         ;
00DC|                         ;
00DC|                         ;       LOR    PLA
00DC|                         ;              STA     TEMP
00DC|                         ;              PLA
00DC|                         ;              STA     TEMP+1
00DC|                         ;              PLA
00DC|                         ;              TAX
00DC|                         ;              PLA
00DC|                         ;              ORA     TEMP+1
00DC|                         ;              PHA
00DC|                         ;              TXA
00DC|                         ;              ORA     TEMP
00DC|                         ;              PHA
00DC|                         ;              JMP     INCIPC
00DC|                         ;
00DC|                         ; Improved code:
00DC|                         ;
0053* DC00
00DC| BA                      LOR            TSX
00DD| 68                                     PLA
00DE| 1D 0301                                ORA     STACK+3,X
00E1| 9D 0301                                STA     STACK+3,X
00E4| 68                                     PLA
00E5| 1D 0401                                ORA     STACK+4,X
00E8| 9D 0401                                STA     STACK+4,X
00EB| 4C 4DD2                                JMP     INCIPC
```

Listing 7-1 (continued)

```
PAGE -    9  INTERP     FILE:INT.1.TEXT

00EE|
00EE|
00EE|                                          .INCLUDE        INT.2
00EE|                          ;
00EE|                          ;
00EE|                          ; CHK- bounds checking routine.
00EE|                          ;
00EE|                          ;   The CHK p-code routine checks to make sure
00EE|                          ; that (TOS-1) <= (TOS-2) <= (TOS).  (TOS) and
00EE|                          ; (TOS-1) are popped, (TOS-2) is left on the stack.
00EE|                          ; Since these three values are are signed 2's
00EE|                          ; compliment integers, a signed comparison must be
00EE|                          ; used.  Apple's code does perform a signed comparison,
00EE|                          ; but the method used is quite bizarre.  The code replacing
00EE|                          ; the CHK p-code routine uses the standard method for
00EE|                          ; signed comparisons (see "Using 6502 Assembly Language"
00EE|                          ; by Randall Hyde, Chapter Six).
00EE|                          ;
00EE|                          ;
00EE|                          ; Original Apple code:
00EE|                          ;
00EE|                          ;      CHK     PLA
00EE|                          ;              STA     TEMP1
00EE|                          ;              PLA
00EE|                          ;              STA     TEMP1+1
00EE|                          ;              PLA
00EE|                          ;              STA     TEMP2
00EE|                          ;              PLA
00EE|                          ;              STA     TEMP2+1
00EE|                          ;              TSX
00EE|                          ;              LDA     STACK+1,X
00EE|                          ;              STA     TEMP3
00EE|                          ;              LDA     STACK+2,X
00EE|                          ;              STA     TEMP3+1
00EE|                          ;              EOR     TEMP2+1
00EE|                          ;              BMI     $0
00EE|                          ;              LDA     TEMP2+1
00EE|                          ;              CMP     TEMP3+1
00EE|                          ;              BCC     $2
00EE|                          ;              BNE     DORNGERR
00EE|                          ;              LDA     TEMP3
00EE|                          ;              CMP     TEMP2
00EE|                          ;              BCS     $2
00EE|                          ;              BCC     DORNGERR
00EE|                          ;
00EE|                          ;      $0      LDA     TEMP3+1
00EE|                          ;              BMI     DORNGERR
00EE|                          ;
00EE|                          ;      $1      LDA     TEMP1+1
00EE|                          ;              EOR     TEMP3+1
00EE|                          ;              BMI     $2
00EE|                          ;              LDA     TEMP3+1
00EE|                          ;              CMP     TEMP1+1
00EE|                          ;              BCC     $3
00EE|                          ;              BNE     DORNGERR
```

Listing 7-1 (continued)


```
00EE|                      ;               LDA     TEMP
00EE|                      ;               CMP     TEMP3
00EE|                      ;               BCS     $3
00EE|                      ;               BCC     DORNGERR
00EE|                      ;
00EE|                      ;      $2       LDA     TEMP1+1
00EE|                      ;               BPL     DORNGERR
00EE|                      ;      $3       JMP     INCIPC
00EE|                      ;   DORNGERR    JMP     RANGERR
00EE|                      ;
00EE|                      ; The improved code is:
00EE|                      ;
0057* EE00
00EE| 68                   CHK             PLA
00EF| 85 04                                STA     TEMP1
00F1| 68                                   PLA
00F2| 85 05                                STA     TEMP1+1
00F4| 68                                   PLA
00F5| 85 06                                STA     TEMP2
00F7| 68                                   PLA
00F8| 85 07                                STA     TEMP2+1
00FA| BA                                   TSX
00FB| BD 0101                              LDA     STACK+1,X
00FE| 85 08                                STA     TEMP3
0100| BD 0201                              LDA     STACK+2,X
0103| 85 09                                STA     TEMP3+1
0105|                      ;
0105|                      ; Check to see if TOS >= TOS-2
0105|                      ;
0105| A5 04                                LDA     TEMP1
0107| C5 08                                CMP     TEMP3
0109| A5 05                                LDA     TEMP1+1
010B| E5 09                                SBC     TEMP3+1
010D| 30**                                 BMI     CHK1
010F| 50**                                 BVC     CHK2
0111| 4C B7D1              ERROR1          JMP     RANGERR
0114|                      ;
010D* 05
0114| 50FB                 CHK1            BVC     ERROR1
0116|                      ;
0116|                      ; Now check to make sure than TOS-2 >= TOS-1
0116|                      ;
010F* 05
0116| A5 08                CHK2            LDA     TEMP3
0118| C5 06                                CMP     TEMP2
011A| A5 09                                LDA     TEMP3+1
011C| E5 07                                SBC     TEMP2+1
011E| 30**                                 BMI     CHK3
0120| 70EF                                 BVS     ERROR1
0122| 4C 4DD2              ITSGOOD         JMP     INCIPC
0125|                      ;
011E* 05
0125| 50EA                 CHK3            BVC     ERROR1
0127| 4C 4DD2                              JMP     INCIPC
012A|                      ;
```

Listing 7-1 (continued)

```
PAGE -  11  INTERP    FILE:INT.2.TEXT

012A|                         ;
012A|                         ; Integer comparisons.
012A|                         ;
012A|                         ;   The integer comparisons which follow compare the signed
012A|                         ; integer on (TOS-1) with the signed integer on (TOS).  TRUE
012A|                         ; (which is the value $01) is pushed if the comparison
012A|                         ; operation holds,  FALSE is pushed otherwise.  In either
012A|                         ; case, the two operands on TOS are popped before TRUE or
012A|                         ; FALSE gets pushed.
012A|                         ;
012A|                         ;   This code offers two optimizations over Apple's code.
012A|                         ; First of all, standard signed comparisons were used instead
012A|                         ; of Apple's funny method for performing signed comparisons.
012A|                         ; Second, individual routines were used instead of one routine
012A|                         ; with a lot of extra tests.  This helped increase the
012A|                         ; execution time of the individual routines at the expense of
012A|                         ; a larger piece of code.  The code for EQUI is not included
012A|                         ; here since the routine in the Apple p-code interpreter is
012A|                         ; fairly optimal.
012A|                         ;
012A|                         ;
012A|                         ;   Note: after a sixteen bit compare of the form:
012A|                         ;
012A|                         ;             LDA     VALUE1
012A|                         ;             CMP     VALUE2
012A|                         ;             LDA     VALUE1+1
012A|                         ;             SBC     VALUE2+1
012A|                         ;
012A|                         ;   The V flag is equal to the N flag if VALUE1 >= VALUE2
012A|                         ;   The V flag is not equal to the N flag if VALUE1 < VALUE2
012A|                         ;
012A|                         ;  Assuming that VALUE1 and VALUE2 are signed, 16-bit,
012A|                         ;  2's compliment numbers.
012A|                         ;
012A|                         ;
012A|                         ;
012A|                         ; GTRI- compares TOS-1 to TOS and push TRUE if TOS-1 > TOS.
012A|                         ;
012A|                         ;
012A|                         ;  Note: this routine actually checks to see if TOS < TOS-1
012A|                         ;        which is functionally the same comparison.
012A|                         ;
005F* 2A01
012A| BA                      GTRI        TSX
012B| 68                                  PLA
012C| DD 0301                             CMP     STACK+3,X
012F| 68                                  PLA
0130| FD 0401                             SBC     STACK+4,X
0133| 30**                                BMI     GTRI0
0135| 50**                                BVC     PSHFLS0
0137|                         ;
0137|                         ; At this point N <> V so TOS < TOS-1 (which means
0137|                         ; that (TOS-1) > TOS.
0137|                         ;
0137| A9 00                   PSHTRU0     LDA     #0
```

Listing 7-1 (continued)

```
PAGE -  12   INTERP     FILE:INT.2.TEXT

0139| 9D 0401                              STA      STACK+4,X
013C| A9 01                                LDA      #1
013E| 9D 0301                              STA      STACK+3,X
0141| 4C 4DD2                              JMP      INCIPC
0144|                   ;
0133* 0F
0144| 50F1              GTRI0              BVC      PSHTRU0
0146|                   ;
0146|                   ; At this point N = V so TOS >= TOS-1.
0146|                   ;
0135* 0F
0146| A9 00             PSHFLS0            LDA      #0
0148| 9D 0301                              STA      STACK+3,X
014B| 9D 0401                              STA      STACK+4,X
014E| 4C 4DD2                              JMP      INCIPC
0151|                   ;
0151|                   ;
0151|                   ;
0151|                   ;
0151|                   ; LEQI- Push true if TOS-1 <= TOS.
0151|                   ;
0151|                   ;   Note: This code actually checks to see if TOS >= TOS-1
0151|                   ;         which is functionally the same comparison.
0151|                   ;
0063* 5101
0151| BA                LEQI               TSX
0152| 68                                   PLA
0153| DD 0301                              CMP      STACK+3,X
0156| 68                                   PLA
0157| FD 0401                              SBC      STACK+4,X
015A| 30**                                 BMI      LEQI0
015C| 50**                                 BVC      PSHTRU2
015E|                   ;
015E|                   ; At this point N <> V so TOS >= TOS-1
015E|                   ;
015E| A9 00             PSHFLS2            LDA      #0
0160| 9D 0301                              STA      STACK+3,X
0163| 9D 0401                              STA      STACK+4,X
0166| 4C 4DD2                              JMP      INCIPC
0169|                   ;
015A* 0D
0169| 50F3              LEQI0              BVC      PSHFLS2
016B|                   ;
016B|                   ; At this point N = V so TOS >= TOS-1
016B|                   ;
015C* 0D
016B| A9 01             PSHTRU2            LDA      #1
016D| 9D 0301                              STA      STACK+3,X
0170| A9 00                                LDA      #0
0172| 9D 0401                              STA      STACK+4,X
0175| 4C 4DD2                              JMP      INCIPC
0178|                   ;
0178|                   ;
0178|                   ;
0178|                   ; GEQI Checks to see if TOS-1 >= TOS.
```

Listing 7-1 (continued)

```
PAGE -  13  INTERP    FILE:INT.2.TEXT


0178|                    ;
005B* 7801
0178| BA                 GEQI          TSX
0179| BD 0301                          LDA     STACK+3,X
017C| DD 0101                          CMP     STACK+1,X
017F| BD 0401                          LDA     STACK+4,X
0182| FD 0201                          SBC     STACK+2,X
0185| 30**                             BMI     GEQI0
0187| 50**                             BVC     PSHTRU1
0189|                    ;
0189| 68                 PSHFLS1       PLA
018A| 68                               PLA
018B| A9 00                            LDA     #0
018D| 9D 0301                          STA     STACK+3,X
0190| 9D 0401                          STA     STACK+4,X
0193| 4C 4DD2                          JMP     INCIPC
0196|                    ;
0185* 0F
0196| 50F1               GEQI0         BVC     PSHFLS1
0187* 0F
0198| 68                 PSHTRU1       PLA
0199| 68                               PLA
019A| A9 01                            LDA     #1
019C| 9D 0301                          STA     STACK+3,X
019F| A9 00                            LDA     #0
01A1| 9D 0401                          STA     STACK+4,X
01A4| 4C 4DD2                          JMP     INCIPC
01A7|
01A7|                    ;
01A7|                    ; LESI- Pushes TRUE if TOS-1 < TOS.
01A7|                    ;
0067* A701
01A7| BA                 LESI          TSX
01A8| BD 0301                          LDA     STACK+3,X
01AB| DD 0101                          CMP     STACK+1,X
01AE| BD 0401                          LDA     STACK+4,X
01B1| FD 0201                          SBC     STACK+2,X
01B4| 30**                             BMI     LESI0
01B6| 50**                             BVC     PSHFLS3
01B8|                    ;
01B8| 68                 PSHTRU3       PLA
01B9| 68                               PLA
01BA| A9 01                            LDA     #1
01BC| 9D 0301                          STA     STACK+3,X
01BF| A9 00                            LDA     #0
01C1| 9D 0401                          STA     STACK+4,X
01C4| 4C 4DD2                          JMP     INCIPC
01C7|                    ;
01B4* 11
01C7| 50EF               LESI0         BVC     PSHTRU3
01C9|                    ;
01B6* 11
01C9| 68                 PSHFLS3       PLA
01CA| 68                               PLA
01CB| A9 00                            LDA     #0
```

Listing 7-1 (continued)

```
PAGE -  14  INTERP    FILE:INT.2.TEXT

01CD| 9D 0301                         STA     STACK+3,X
01D0| 9D 0401                         STA     STACK+4,X
01D3| 4C 4DD2                         JMP     INCIPC
01D6|                  ;
01D6|                  ;
01D6|                  ; NEQI- Pushes TRUE if TOS-1 <> TOS.
01D6|                  ;
006B* D601
01D6| BA               NEQI           TSX
01D7| 68                              PLA
01D8| DD 0301                         CMP     STACK+3,X
01DB| D0**                            BNE     PSHTRU4
01DD| 68                              PLA
01DE| DD 0401                         CMP     STACK+4,X
01E1| D0**                            BNE     PSHTRU5
01E3|                  ;
01E3| A9 00            PSHFLS4        LDA     #0
01E5| 9D 0301                         STA     STACK+3,X
01E8| 9D 0401                         STA     STACK+4,X
01EB| 4C 4DD2                         JMP     INCIPC
01EE|                  ;
01DB* 11
01EE| 68               PSHTRU4        PLA
01E1* 0C
01EF| A9 01            PSHTRU5        LDA     #1
01F1| 9D 0301                         STA     STACK+3,X
01F4| A9 00                           LDA     #0
01F6| 9D 0401                         STA     STACK+4,X
01F9| 4C 4DD2                         JMP     INCIPC
01FC|                  ;
01FC|                  ;
01FC|                  ;
01FC|                  ;
01FC|                  ;  The FJP and UJP instructions are another couple of p-codes
01FC|                  ;  that can benefit from a little optimization.
01FC|                  ;
006F* FC01
01FC| 68               FJP            PLA
01FD| 4A                              LSR     A
01FE| 68                              PLA
01FF| B0**                            BCS     JMPIPC2
0201|                  ;
0073* 0102
0201| C8               UJP            INY                     ;Set Y-reg to one.
0202| 18                              CLC
0203| B1 58                           LDA     (IPC),Y
0205| 30**                            BMI     JMPJTAB
0207| 65 58                           ADC     IPC
0209| 85 58                           STA     IPC
020B| 90**                            BCC     JMPIPC2
020D| E6 59                           INC     IPC+1
020F|                  ;
020B* 02
01FF* 0E
020F| 4C 3BD2          JMPIPC2        JMP     INCIPC2
```

Listing 7-1 (continued)

```
PAGE -  15   INTERP    FILE:INT.2.TEXT

0212|                     ;
0205* 0B
0212| 4C 79D2             JMPJTAB        JMP     HNDLJTAB
0215|
0215|
0215|                                    .LIST
0215|                                    .IF           HASAPU=1
0215|
0215|                     ;
0215|                     ; APU functions.
0215|                     ;
0215|                     ;   These guys are only implemented if the HASAPU label is
0215|                     ;   equated to one. If order for this code to function
0215|                     ;   properly you must have a CCS arithmetic
0215|                     ;   card installed in the slot defined by APUSLOT.
0215|                     ;
0215|                     ;
0215|                     ;   Do the integer stuff first:
0215|                     ;
0215|                     ;   MPI- Multiply the two integers on TOS.
0215|                     ;
0077* 1502
0215| 2C F1C0             MPI            BIT     APUSLOT+1       ;Wait 'til FPU ready.
0218| 30FB                               BMI     MPI
021A|                     ;
021A| 68                                 PLA
021B| 8D F0C0                            STA     APUSLOT
021E| 68                                 PLA
021F| 8D F0C0                            STA     APUSLOT
0222| 68                                 PLA
0223| 8D F0C0                            STA     APUSLOT
0226| 68                                 PLA
0227| 8D F0C0                            STA     APUSLOT
022A| A9 6E                              LDA     #6E             ;9511 MUL opcode
022C| 8D F1C0                            STA     APUSLOT+1
022F|
022F| 2C F1C0             $0             BIT     APUSLOT+1
0232| 30FB                               BMI     $0
0234| AD F0C0                            LDA     APUSLOT
0237| 48                                 PHA
0238| AD F0C0                            LDA     APUSLOT
023B| 48                                 PHA
023C| 4C 4DD2                            JMP     INCIPC
023F|                     ;
023F|                     ;
023F|                     ; DVI- Divide integer on TOS-1 by integer on TOS.
023F|                     ;
007B* 3F02
023F| 2C F1C0             DVI            BIT     APUSLOT+1
0242| 30FB                               BMI     DVI
0244| 68                                 PLA
0245| A8                                 TAY
0246| 68                                 PLA
0247| AA                                 TAX
0248| 68                                 PLA
```

Listing 7-1 (continued)

```
PAGE -  16  INTERP    FILE:INT

0249| 8D F0C0                         STA    APUSLOT
024C| 68                              PLA
024D| 8D F0C0                         STA    APUSLOT
0250| 8C F0C0                         STY    APUSLOT
0253| 8E F0C0                         STX    APUSLOT
0256| A9 6F                           LDA    #6F            ;Divide integers opcode
0258| 8D F1C0                         STA    APUSLOT+1
025B| 2C F1C0         $0              BIT    APUSLOT+1
025E| 30FB                            BMI    $0
0260| AD F0C0                         LDA    APUSLOT
0263| 48                              PHA
0264| AD F0C0                         LDA    APUSLOT
0267| 48                              PHA
0268| 4C 4DD2                         JMP    INCIPC
026B|                 ;
026B|                 ;
026B|                                 .ENDC
026B|                 ;
026B|                                 .IF    HASCLK=1
026B|                 ;
007F* 6B02
026B| AD D3C0         TIME            LDA    CLKSLOT+3      ;Get 10ths of a second
026E| 29 0F                           AND    #0F            ;and convert them to
0270| 0A                              ASL    A              ;60ths of a second by
0271| 85 08                           STA    TEMP3          ;multiplying by 6.
0273| 0A                              ASL    A
0274| 65 08                           ADC    TEMP3          ;CLC from ASL above
0276| 48                              PHA                   ;Save 10ths of a second.
0277|                 ;
0277|                 ; Get the seconds value and multiply it by 60.
0277|                 ;
0277| AD D3C0                         LDA    CLKSLOT+3
027A| 29 F0                           AND    #0F0
027C| 85 04                           STA    TEMP1
027E| 85 08                           STA    TEMP3
0280| AD D2C0                         LDA    CLKSLOT+2
0283| 85 05                           STA    TEMP1+1
0285| 85 09                           STA    TEMP3+1
0287| AD D1C0                         LDA    CLKSLOT+1
028A| 85 06                           STA    TEMP2
028C| 85 0A                           STA    TEMP4
028E| AD D0C0                         LDA    CLKSLOT+0
0291| 29 1F                           AND    #1F
0293| 85 07                           STA    TEMP2+1
0295| 85 0B                           STA    TEMP4+1
0297|                 ;
0297|                 ; At this point locations TEMP3..TEMP4+1 contain the time
0297|                 ; multiplied by 16.
0297|                 ;
0297|                 ;  Make it times 32.
0297|                 ;
0297| 06 08                           ASL    TEMP3
0299| 26 09                           ROL    TEMP3+1
029B| 26 0A                           ROL    TEMP4
029D| 26 0B                           ROL    TEMP4+1
```

Listing 7-1 (continued)

```
PAGE -  17  INTERP    FILE:INT

029F|                    ;
029F|                    ; Add in the time multiplied by 16, 8, and 4 to create
029F|                    ; the value TIME*60.
029F|                    ;
029F| A2 03                         LDX    #3
02A1| 46 07              DIVDLOOP   LSR    TEMP2+1
02A3| 66 06                         ROR    TEMP2
02A5| 66 05                         ROR    TEMP1+1
02A7| 66 04                         ROR    TEMP1
02A9| 18                            CLC
02AA| A5 04                         LDA    TEMP1
02AC| 65 08                         ADC    TEMP3
02AE| 85 08                         STA    TEMP3
02B0| A5 05                         LDA    TEMP1+1
02B2| 65 09                         ADC    TEMP3+1
02B4| 85 09                         STA    TEMP3+1
02B6| A5 06                         LDA    TEMP2
02B8| 65 0A                         ADC    TEMP4
02BA| 85 0A                         STA    TEMP4
02BC| A5 07                         LDA    TEMP2+1
02BE| 65 0B                         ADC    TEMP4+1
02C0| 85 0B                         STA    TEMP4+1
02C2| CA                            DEX
02C3| D0DC                          BNE    DIVDLOOP
02C5|                    ;
02C5|                    ; Get the 10ths of a second value and add it in.
02C5|                    ;
02C5| 18                            CLC
02C6| 68                            PLA
02C7| 65 08                         ADC    TEMP3
02C9| 85 08                         STA    TEMP3
02CB| 90**                          BCC    $0
02CD| E6 09                         INC    TEMP3+1
02CF| D0**                          BNE    $0
02D1| E6 0A                         INC    TEMP4
02D3| D0**                          BNE    $0
02D5| E6 0B                         INC    TEMP4+1
02D7|                    ;
02D7|                    ; Now store the time in the locations pointed at by
02D7|                    ; TOS and TOS-1.
02D7|                    ;
02D3* 02
02CF* 06
02CB* 0A
02D7| 68                 $0         PLA
02D8| 85 04                         STA    TEMP1
02DA| 68                            PLA
02DB| 85 05                         STA    TEMP1+1
02DD| 68                            PLA
02DE| 85 06                         STA    TEMP2
02E0| 68                            PLA
02E1| 85 07                         STA    TEMP2+1
02E3| A0 00                         LDY    #0
02E5| A5 08                         LDA    TEMP3
02E7| 91 04                         STA    (TEMP1),Y
```

Listing 7-1 (continued)


```
02E9| A5 0A                              LDA     TEMP4
02EB| 91 06                              STA     (TEMP2),Y
02ED| C8                                 INY
02EE| A5 09                              LDA     TEMP3+1
02F0| 91 04                              STA     (TEMP1),Y
02F2| A5 0B                              LDA     TEMP4+1
02F4| 91 06                              STA     (TEMP2),Y
02F6| 4C 3BD2                            JMP     INCIPC2
02F9|
02F9|                                    .ENDC
02F9|                    ;
02F9|                    ;
02F9|                                    .END
```

8
Attaching Your Own Devices to the Pascal BIOS

Modifying the Apple Pascal BIOS

When Apple Pascal was first released, many Apple owners were shocked to learn that Apple Pascal only supported devices that were manufactured by Apple or were completely hardware compatible with Apple's device (which was quite rare). After numerous complaints, Apple modified the operating system in version 1.1 to allow foreign peripheral cards to operate with the Pascal system.

The official document describing how to interface "foreign" devices to the Apple Pascal system is:

ATTACH-BIOS for Apple II Pascal 1.1

written by Barry Haynes. It is reprinted in the appendix. This manual provides enough information that the advanced user can write his own drivers for the Pascal system. I will use several concrete examples here to help solidify the use of the ATTACH-BIOS routines and the FIRMWARE protocol for attaching devices to the Apple Pascal system version 1.1

I/O Overview

The Apple Pascal system supports four levels of I/O. These I/O levels are grouped into a hierarchy as follows:

Pascal High Level I/O (including READLN, WRITELN, GET, and PUT).

These routines are written in Pascal and are the main reason I/O is so slow in the Pascal CS.

↓

Pascal low-level I/O. Includes the BLOCKREAD, BLOCKWRITE, UNITREAD, UNITWRITE, UNITCLEAR, and UNITSTATUS routines.

BLOCKREAD and BLOCKWRITE are written in Pascal, so they tend to run quite slowly. The UNITxxx calls all have their own p-codes so they run fairly fast.

↓

RSP (Run time support package). These routines, written in 6502 assembly language, are called by the interpreter code for the UNITxxx routines. The RSP checks the legality of the parameters passed by the UNITxxx routines, reformats the calls for the BIOS routines, and performs certain code translations (like expanding the DLE (blank compression) characters, adding linefeeds to carriage returns, check for EOF, etc.).

↓

BIOS level. This is the lowest level of I/O. This is the point that you attach your drivers to.

Figure 8-1

There are two standard methods used to attach a driver to the Pascal system. You can use the "SYSTEM.ATTACH" method to load your driver into RAM at boot time, or you can use a special "FIRMWARE" protocol on the interface card ROM on your peripheral device.

The "SYSTEM.ATTACH" method has the advantage that it is easy to reconfigure the system at will. Since the drivers are in RAM bugs can be fixed easily simply by updating a disk. Furthermore, you aren't restricted to 256 bytes to 2K of code for your driver. Theoretically a driver using the "SYSTEM.ATTACH" method could be up to 32K long. There are three principle disadvantages to the "SYSTEM.ATTACH" method. First, every byte of RAM utilized by the driver is subtracted from the user's available RAM. So although you can write drivers 32K long, doing so would severely limit the amount of memory left for running application programs. Second, the "SYSTEM.ATTACH" method slows the boot process down by several seconds. This is a minor annoyance, but the average Pascal user will certainly notice it at boot time. Finally, if the driver is rather large, or the user loads a bunch of drivers into memory at once, an eight kilobyte block of memory from locations $2000 to $3FFF must be left unused in the event the user needs to use HIRES graphics. To prevent memory contention the person attaching a driver to the system must allow for the HIRES page or serious trouble may develop if an attempt to use HIRES graphics is made. This 8K is totally wasted if the user never uses HIRES graphics. Luckily, most drivers are rather small and the user rarely loads in more than one driver, so this problem shouldn't occur very often.

The "FIRMWARE" protocol has the advantage that it is instantly recognized at boot time, doesn't use up any user RAM, and doesn't create any memory contention problems (unless it's poorly written). The firmware protocol suffers from two main disadvantages: it requires ROM (and the associated support circuitry) which is certainly more expensive than a diskette, and if a bug is found in the software, updates are very costly. A final (and possibly fatal) disadvantage is that you are limited to a maximum of 2 1/4 kilobytes of space for the driver without resorting to exotic bank switching techniques.

Creating Drivers Using the "SYSTEM.ATTACH" Method

To use the "SYSTEM.ATTACH" method you **must** obtain a copy of the ATTACH-BIOS disk from your local Apple club, the Call – A.P.P.L.E user's group, or the International Apple Core (IAC). This diskette includes the ATTACH-BIOS documentation mentioned previous in addition to the SYSTEM.ATTACH and ATTACHUD.CODE programs required to use the SYSTEM.ATTACH method to attach user devices to the Pascal system.

To use the SYSTEM.ATTACH method you must include three files on your boot diskette: the "SYSTEM.ATTACH" program provided on the ATTACH-BIOS disk, an ATTACH.DRIVERS file containing the 6502 assembly language drivers for your device, and the ATTACH.DATA file that holds certain information for the user defined device drivers. The ATTACH.DATA file is created using the ATTACHUD.CODE (attach user device) program found on the ATTACH-BIOS disk. During the boot process the SYSTEM.ATTACH program is the first program executed (even before SYSTEM.STARTUP). This program reads the ATTACH.DRIVERS and ATTACH.DATA files and patches the user device drivers into the operating system.

User defined device drivers **must** be written in 6502 assembly language using the Pascal Assembler. They cannot use the ".ABSOLUTE" option since they are relocated as they are loaded into the system at boot time. All drivers must be assembled separately (if you are attaching more than one driver to the system) and may not contain any external references. The driver must be completely self-contained. If you need to create an ATTACH.DRIVERS file with more than one driver you must assemble the files separately and link them together using the Pascal librarian program.

Each driver uses the following organization:

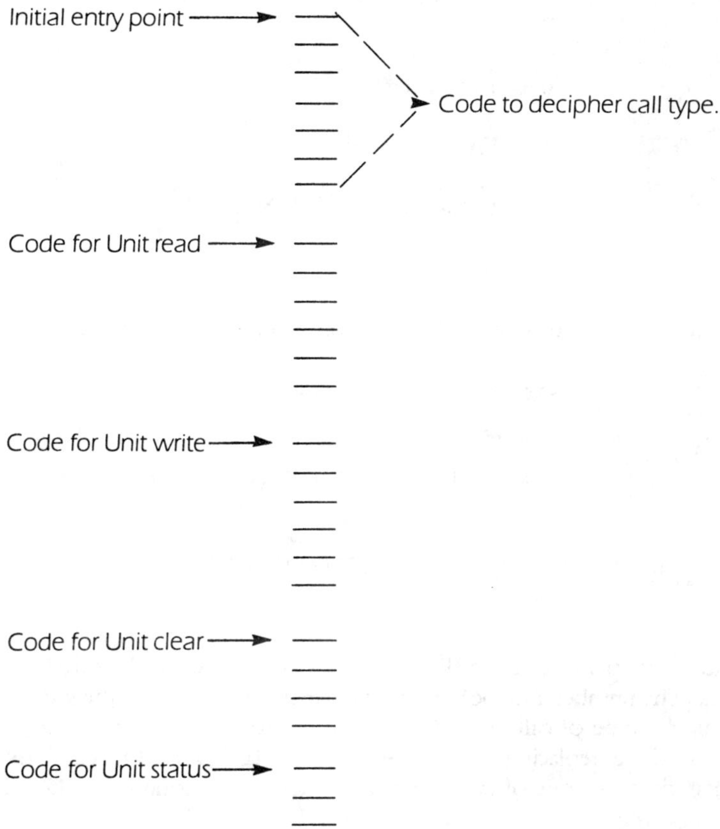

Figure 8-2

Whenever a user-defined I/O device is referenced the RSP JSR's to the initial entry point in the user device driver. The initial entry point must figure out what type of I/O operation is being requested based on the contents of the X-register. Upon entry into the user device driver the X-register is decoded as follows:

0 → Read operation

1 → Write operation

2 → Initialization call (UNITCLEAR)

3 → Status call.

A code segment to handle this decision making process might be:

```
               If XREG < 2 it must be 1,
ENTRY     CPX     #0
          BEQ     USERREAD
          CPX     #2
          BCC     USRWRITE ;If XREG < 2 it must be 1.
          BEQ     USERINIT ;If XREG = 2
;
;
; At this point you must be performing a UNITSTATUS
; operation.
```

Additional parameters to these routines are passed on the 6502 hardware stack. The number and meaning of the parameters passed on the stack depends upon the type of call being made (read, write, init, or status) and whether this is a driver replacing the CONSOLE:, REMIN:, REMOUT:, PRINTER:, a disk drive, or one of the user defined devices (unit numbers 128..143).

Replacing the CONSOLE: Driver

The CONSOLE: driver requires considerable care in its implementation. First of all, a special entry point must be made for the console check routine that handles the type ahead buffer. Second, due to the interaction between the Apple's keyboard and the rest of the system there are special initialization steps which must be taken.

For the CONSOLE: driver, the Accumulator is used to pass the character read or written to the console device, the Y-register contains the UNIT number (usually unit numbers one and two are attached to the console driver, but you can hook the PRINTER: and REMxxx: devices to this driver as well. The Y-register will let you decode which device is requesting I/O), and the X-register contains the operation desired. On exit the Accumulator passes the data (if this is a read operation) back to the calling routine and the X-register contains the IORESULT (zero if no error).

The entry points for the CONSOLE: driver should look something like:

```
CONCHK   JMP     CONSCHK
ENTRY    CPX     #0
         BEQ     CONREAD
         CPX     #2
         BCC     CONWRITE
         BEQ     CONINIT
;
;
; CONSTATUS goes here
;
```

The CONSCHK routine should check the console input device and see if a character is available. If it is, then the character should be read and buffered up in the type ahead buffer. The normal entry point for the CONSOLE: driver is located three bytes after the start of the driver routine. Therefore, there's just enough space at the beginning of the driver for a single JMP instruction to the console check routine. The normal driver code should immediately follow the JMP to the console check subroutine.

CONSOLE: read and write calls only have the return address sitting on the hardware stack. All data passed to and from the routines is passed in the 6502 registers. Init and status pass parameters to the driver routine on the stack (as well as in the registers). If the X-register contains two then the call is an initialization call and the data passed on the stack is:

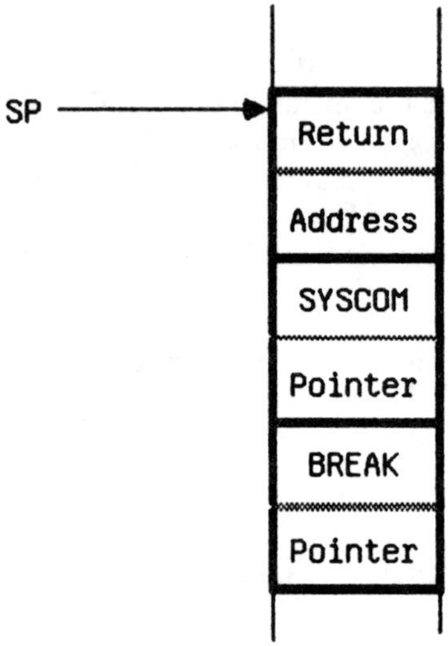

Figure 8-3

As usual, the 6502 return address is sitting on the top of the hardware stack. This return address **must** be popped off of the stack and saved in a couple of temporary locations. The next two bytes on the stack form a pointer to the system's communication area (SYSCOM). It is the responsibility of the CONSOLE: init routine to pop this pointer off of the stack and save it in locations $F8 and $F9. Immediately above the SYSCOM pointer lies the pointer to the break vector. The console routine must jump to this location whenever the break key is pressed (currently shift-control-P on the Apple II; shift-control-2 on the Apple //e). This address should be popped and stored into locations $BF16 and $BF17. Once the break and syscom vectors have been popped and stored the init routine should push the return address back onto the stack, load the X-register with zero (no error), and execute an RTS instruction. A typical CONSOLE: status routine might look something like:

```
CONINITPLA
          STA       TEMP
          PLA
          STA       TEMP+1
          PLA
          STA       ØF8
          PLA
          STA       ØF9
          PLA
          STA       ØBF16
          PLA
          STA       ØBF17
          LDA       TEMP+1
          PHA
          LDA       TEMP
          PHA
          LDX       #Ø
          RTS
```

Note that the low order byte is popped off of the stack before the high order byte is popped.

The CONSOLE: status routine, just like the CONSOLE: init routine, expects to find three words of data sitting on the stack. The word on the top of stack is the 6502 return address (which must be popped and saved). Immediately above the return address is the "control word". The control word uses the following format:

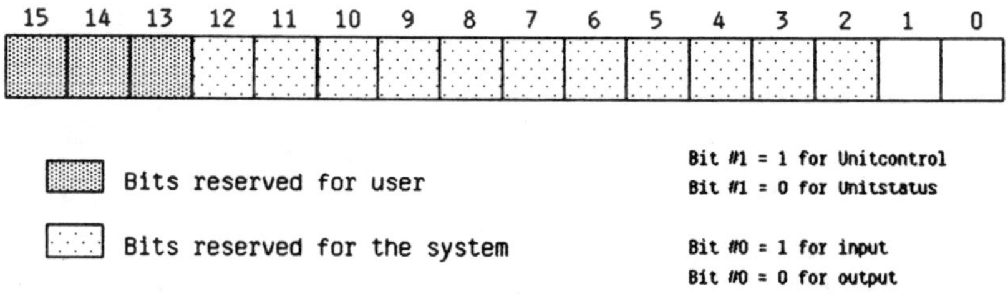

Figure 8-4

If bit number zero is one then the status of the CONSOLE: input is being checked. If bit number zero is zero then the output status is being checked. Bit number one is used to determine the type of call. If bit number one is zero, then a unitstatus call is being made. If bit number one is one, then a unitcontrol call is being made. Bits two through twelve are reserved for use by the system and bits thirteen through fifteen are reserved for the user.

The next byte on the stack is a pointer to the status record. If a unitstatus call is being made, then the CONSOLE: status routine should return the number of characters buffered in the direction specified. For example, if this is an input status request you should return the number of characters currently buffered in the typeahead buffer in the word pointed at by the third word on the stack. If you have not implemented a type-ahead buffer then you should return one if a console character is ready and zero if no character is ready. If an output request is being made you should return the number of characters being buffered in the output direction. If you haven't implement a "printer" buffer on the CONSOLE: output you should store zero in the word pointed at by the status record pointer. An example of a CONSOLE: status routine is:

```
CONSTAT         PLA
                STA             TEMP
                PLA
                STA             TEMP+1
                PLA
                STA             CNTRLWRD
                PLA
                STA             CNTRLWRD+1
                PLA
                STA             STATREC
                PLA
                STA             STATREC+1
;
                LDA             CNTRLWRD
                AND             #2
;Check for UNITCONTROL
                BNE             UCNTRL
;
; Unit status here.
;
                LDA             CNTRLWRD
                LSR
;Check L.O. bit
                BCC             OUTSTAT
                LDY             #Ø
                LDA             NUMINBUF
;Get # of chars in buffer
                STA             (STATREC),Y
                INY
                LDA             #Ø
                STA             (STATREC),Y
                JMP             XITSTAT
;
OUTSTAT         LDY             #Ø
                TYA
                STA             (STATREC),Y
```

```
;No output buffer
                INY
                STA          (STATREC),Y
;
XITSTAT         LDA          TEMP+1
                PHA
                LDA          TEMP
                PHA
                LDX          #0
;No errors
                RTS
;
;
; NOTE: Unit control is totally defined by the user.
;
```

Input data received from the console device must be returned with the H.O. bit cleared since Pascal uses the seven-bit ASCII code. Output data **may** contain bytes which have their high order bits set. Your output routine should interpret this data and act accordingly. If your output device requires seven bit ASCII data then you should strip the H.O. bit. If your output device responds to certain codes in the range \$80..\$FF then you should pass the data unchanged.

The RSP (run-time support package) will send both upper and lower case to the console output device. If it cannot handle lower case your driver must map lower case to upper case. This is accomplished using the code:

```
LC2UC     CMP     #"a"
          BCC     $0
          AND     #0DF
$0
```

The CONSOLE: output routines must recognize, and respond, to certain characters in a predefined fashion. The requirements are:

a) CR (HEX 0D) A carriage return should move the cursor to the beginning of the current line. It must **not** move the cursor down a line.

b) LF (HEX 0A) A line feed should move the cursor to the next line but it should not change the horizontal position. If the cursor is on the last line of the screen when the LF is transmitted, the screen should scroll up one line and the bottom line should be cleared.

c) BELL (HEX 07) If possible, a sound should be made (preferably a beep) when this character is received. If a sound cannot be made the BELL character should be ignored.

d) SP (HEX 20) A space character should move the cursor one position to the right, overwriting the data the cursor is currently on top of. If the cursor is in the last column of the current line then the CONSOLE: driver should leave the cursor in its current position after placing a space at the cursor position. If the cursor is in the last column of the last line on the screen then the screen should not scroll and the cursor should be left in the last column as above. These are the most desirable actions. In reality, any attempt to write beyond the last column on the display is undefined and almost anything is allowed. Keep in mind, however, that user programs often attempt to write beyond the last column so your driver should be rather robust about handling this situation.

e) NULL (HEX 00) When a null character is sent to the screen it should be ignored. If possible, you should delay the amount of time required to print a normal character on the screen.

f) All printable characters (HEX 20..7F) should be treated exactly like the SP character.

g) The Apple Pascal Operating System Reference manual contains a discussion of the special characters and how they must be treated on pages 199-216. You should consult this manual for additional details.

Additional CONSOLE: input requirements:

a) The RSP handles echoing characters to the console. The characters typed at the keyboard should **not** be echoed to the screen by your driver.

b) The start/stop character (usually control-S, but it is redefinable) must be detected and processed by CONCK. The program should loop in CONCK until either the start/stop character is received again or the break character is received. Locations $F8 and $F9 in zero page point at the SYSCOM area. The start/stop character is located at this location plus 85. To access the start/stop character you would use the code:

```
LDY #85
LDA ($F8),Y
```

The start/stop character should never be returned to the RSP.

c) The flush character (offset 83 from the beginning of SYSCOM) will stop all echoing to the console until a second flush character is received. CONCK must detect the flush character and set a flag to tell the console output routine to ignore characters while the flag is set. If a system reset occurs or the break key is encountered, the flush flag should be reset. Flush should only stop output to the console, other processing should continue. The flush character, like the start/stop character, must not be returned to the RSP.

d) The break character should cause CONCK to jump to the location whose address is stored in locations $BF16 and $BF17. This location is stored in locations $BF16 and $BF17 by the console init routine. Offset from syscom for the break character is 84.

e) The type-ahead buffer must be maintained by the CONCK routine. Every time the CONCK routine is called it should check the Apple's keyboard to see if a character is available. If a key has been pressed it should be stored into the type-ahead buffer. When the console read routine is called characters should be taken from the type ahead buffer and returned to the RSP.

For more information on the requirements of the CONSOLE: driver consult pages 199–216 of the Apple Pascal v1.1 Operating System Reference Manual.

Replacing the PRINTER: Device (Unit 6)

The Apple Pascal operating system supports a listing device called PRINTER:. This unit is reserved for a hardcopy listing device for use in listing programs and for data output from within programs. The PRINTER: device is automatically attached to the system during the boot sequence if the BIOS determines that an Apple Parallel interface, communications card, or "firmware" card is present in slot number one. If you do not have one of the Pascal-compatible cards in slot one, or you wish to run your printer out of another slot, you will need to re-write the printer driver and attach it to unit number six.

The PRINTER: driver follows standard driver protocols, the first byte(s) of the driver routine must contain the first instruction of the initial entry code. Upon entry into the PRINTER: driver your code must check the X-register to determine what type of call (read, write, init, or status) the current invocation happens to be.

If a write operation is being performed the character to be written to the PRINTER: device is passed in the 6502 accumulator. Therefore care must be taken in the initial entry code to preserve the 6502 accumulator in the event this is a write operation. The interpreter and RSP filter out and transform certain character like the blank compression codes and the EOF character. The RSP also adds line feeds to carriage returns automatically for you. If your printer must have an entire line of data transmitted at once, your driver must buffer the data up and transmit it once a CR-LF sequence is received.

The Pascal system assumes that the printer responds to three ASCII characters: CR, LF, and FF (carriage return, line feed, and form feed). The CR character should simply move the printhead to the beginning of the **current** line. It must not perform an automatic line feed. If your printer forces a CR-LF sequence whenever a CR is encountered you should filter out the LF that follows the CR character (or use the line feed program found on APPLE 3:). The FF (form feed) character should advance the printer to the top of the next page and position the print head at column one of the first line on the new page. If your printer hardware doesn't support the FF character you should attempt to emulate this feature in software by counting output lines. If this isn't feasible, print a CR followed by one or two LF characters upon receipt of a form feed character.

The PRINTER: init entry point should perform any necessary hardware initialization, clear any characters buffered up (if you have a buffered printer interface for example), and output a CR-LF sequence to the printer. As with all driver routines, the IORESULT code should be returned in the X-register.

The input entry point for the PRINTER: driver should normally return with a completion code of three in the X-register. If your PRINTER: device can be read, then the character should be returned in the 6502 accumulator with the X-register containing zero if an I/O error didn't occur.

The PRINTER: status call pushes two words onto the stack before transferring control to the PRINTER: driver. The stack setup is identical to the CONSOLE: stack set up. Your PRINTER: status routine should return the number of bytes buffered in the first word of the status record. Make sure you check the direction of this request (especially if your printer driver is output only) in the control word before returning any value. If you cannot determine this value then return zeroes in the first word of the status record. Don't forget to push the return address back onto the stack and load the X-register with the I/O completion call before executing an RTS instruction.

Replacing the REMOUT: and REMIN: Drivers (Units 7 & 8)

The REMOTE: unit was originally intended for data communication purposes via an RS-232 interface device. However any device, be it modem, speech synthesizer, or whatever you've got, can be attached to the REMIN: and REMOUT: drivers. The only restriction is that the REMOTE: device should be capable of handling ASCII data (as opposed to pure binary data) since the RSP massages the data sent to the REMOTE: device. Blank compression codes are expanded, EOF is handled by the system, and line feeds are appended to carriage returns. If your device cannot handle line feeds after a carriage return then your driver must strip any line feed which immediately follows a return out of the output stream.

Parameters are passed to the REMOTE: driver in a fashion identical to that for the PRINTER: driver. Data is passed to REMOUT: in the 6502 accumulator, data is returned from REMIN: in the accumulator, init requires no parameters (except IORESULT in the X-register upon return), and the remote status call passes its data on the stack and is handled in a fashion identical to that of the PRINTER: and CONSOLE: drivers.

Attaching Drivers to Block Structured Devices (Units 4,5,9..12)

The block devices (units 4, 5, 9, 10, 11, and 12) are typically reserved for disk or similar devices. The UCSD/Apple Pascal system assumes the disk device is a zero-based consecutive array of 512-byte logical blocks. All Apple Pascal disks must conform to this logical structure regardless of their actual physical structure. The driver must convert this Pascal block number to the track/sector values required by the specific hardware. This scheme allows a wide variety of devices to be attached as a disk driver to the Pascal system.

The attached driver, due to the way the system operates, cannot be the boot device. You must continue to boot off of the Apple's 5 1/4" floppy disk. Vendors or users who want to boot off of some device other than an Apple drive should contact Apple vendor support for additional instructions.

The Apple Pascal system accesses the disk using the UNITREAD and UNITWRITE routines. When accessing a block structured device five parameters are passed to the block device driver: a unit number, a control word, a buffer address, a byte count, and a block number. For read and write calls the stack looks something like:

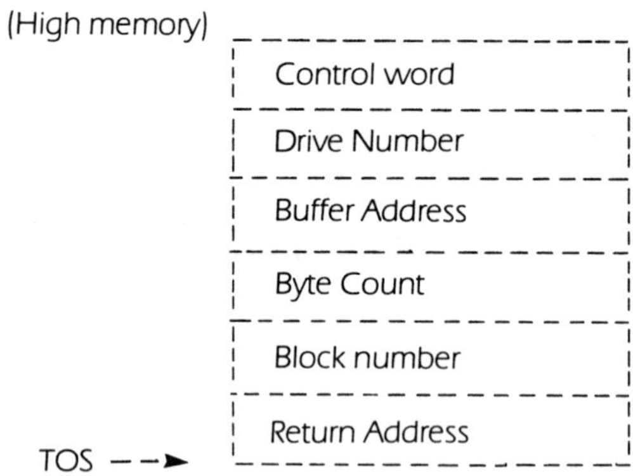

Figure 8-5

As usual the return address must be popped and saved while the other parameters are popped and saved. The unit number is passed in the 6502 accumulator. The drive number found on the stack is a drive number for Apple's 5 ¼″ floppy disk drives and should be ignored.

The disk init routine has no parameters other than the unit number in the 6502 accumulator. Any hardware/software initialization required should be performed during this call.

The stack setup for the status entry is identical to that for CONSOLE:. Status requests should return the following in the status record:

Word1: Number of bytes buffered in the direction asked for. Return zero if you have no way of checking.

Word2: Number of bytes per sector.

Word3: Number of sectors per track.

Word4: Number of tracks per disk.

When a unitwrite is performed to the disk drive with a byte count that is not an even multiple of 512 bytes, you are allowed to write out a full block of 512 bytes if that is convenient. However, if a unitread is being performed you are **not** allowed to read a full block into the memory buffer if the byte count is less than 512. Attempting to do so may wipe out variables and code on the Pascal stack. If the byte count MOD 512 is not equal to zero you will have to buffer the last sector read into a local data area and move the last portion of data into the buffer using a 6502 move routine.

Attaching User Defined Devices to the BIOS (Units 128-143)

Units 128-143 are reserved totally for user-defined applications. Their usage is totally user-defined except that parameters are passed to the user device exactly like the block structured devices. This allows you to connect a disk drive or similar device to the system. Examples of several device drivers appear in the listings.

Attaching Your Drivers to the System

Apple Pascal v1.1 supports a special boot-up protocol to handle attaching user defined devices to the BIOS. As you probably recall, Apple Pascal executes the "SYSTEM.STARTUP" program before control is returned to the user at the system level. This allows the programmer to create a "turnkey" system that automatically executes a program when the system is booted. Attaching drivers to the system is handled in a similar fashion. A special program, "SYSTEM.ATTACH", is executed when the system is booted (even before "SYSTEM.STARTUP" is executed). SYSTEM.ATTACH reads two files on the disk, "ATTACH.DATA" and "ATTACH.DRIVERS", and then patches the operating system with the user defined drivers kept in ATTACH.DRIVERS. The ATTACH.DATA file contains information used by SYSTEM.ATTACH to determine which drivers are to be patched. The previous sections in this chapter described how write the device driver; organizing these drivers on the boot diskette is all that remains to be done in order to make your driver functional.

The first step to place the SYSTEM.ATTACH program on your boot diskette. SYSTEM.ATTACH is found on the ATTACH-BIOS diskette distributed by the International Apple Core. You **must** obtain a copy of this diskette in order to attach your own drivers to the system. When SYSTEM.ATTACH executes it reads the two files ATTACH.DRIVERS and ATTACH.DATA.

ATTACH.DRIVERS contains the 6502 code for your driver programs. If you wish to attach more than one driver to the system you must assemble the files separately and combine them into a single file using the LIBRARY program found on the Apple3: diskette. Typically you would copy your first driver into slot #0 of the ATTACH.DRIVERS file, your second driver would be copied into slot #1, etc.. This facility lets you attach drivers written by other vendors to your drivers as well as combine drivers written by different vendors into a single ATTACH.DRIVERS file.

The ATTACH.DATA file is read by the SYSTEM.ATTACH program to determine what drivers must be patched into the system. ATTACH.DATA is created by executing the ATTACHUD.CODE (attach user device) program found on the disk distributed by the International Apple Core. After X)ecuting ATTACHUD.CODE you will be given the prompt:

```
Apple Pascal Attachud [1.1]
Enter name of attach data file:
```

You should respond with the name of the **output** file followed by return. Unless you already have an ATTACH.DATA file on the disk and you don't want to delete it you should enter ATTACH.DATA to this prompt. This will cause the ATTACHUD.CODE program to write the data out to the ATTACH.DATA file for you. If you make some sort of error while entering data into the ATTACHUD program ATTACHUD will prompt you to re-enter the data.

The next two prompts will ask you if your driver can reside in the HIRES graphics pages. First you will be asked if your driver(s) will ever use the $2000..$3FFF (page one) HIRES page. If you answer no then SYSTEM.ATTACH will assume that the driver can be loaded into the HIRES graphics page. The second question asks you if if the driver will ever be used with the HIRES page two memory buffer. Answering no will inform the SYSTEM.ATTACH program that your driver can be loaded into the $4000..$7FFF memory range.

Answering no to either of these questions will allow the SYSTEM.ATTACH program to load your drivers into the HIRES graphics memory buffers. This can produce disastrous results if the user attempts to use HIRES graphics while your drivers are in memory. On the other hand, if you answer yes to these questions and HIRES graphics are never used, eight to sixteen kilobytes of user memory will be removed from the system.

This is a considerable chunk of memory to lose to an already-starved system. Careful thought must go into the answer of this question. Perhaps you should create **two** systems: one for an execute-only environment where you will be executing programs using the Turtle Graphics package; and one for systems which will not be using the graphics system. It should be pointed out that most drivers are quite small and will never be big enough to encroach on the HIRES memory space anyway. But keep in mind that if you attach several drivers, especially drivers from different vendors, your drivers may go beyond the (approx.) four kilobyte limit.

The next question you will be asked is the name of the driver. The name you should enter is the name of the assembly language program. This is the name following the .PROC pseudo opcode at the beginning of your driver program. If you hit return at this point the ATTACHUD program will terminate without creating the ATTACH.DATA file. After you enter the driver name you will be asked which unit numbers should refer to the specified device driver. Valid unit numbers are 1, 2, 4..12, and 128..143. Entering a number outside this range will produce an error message. Attempting to attach a character oriented unit (1, 2, 6, 7, or 8) to a to the same driver a block oriented device is attached to also produces an error message.

The next question ATTACHUD asks you is if you would like the unit to be initialized at boot time. If you answer yes, the init entry point will be called by the SYSTEM.ATTACH program. If you answer no then the call to UNITCLEAR (which calls then init entry point) will not be made.

After answering yes or no to the initialization question you will be asked if you want another unit number to refer to this device driver. This allows you to connect two units to the same device driver. For example, if your software makes considerable use of the PRINTER: unit and you wish to install your software on a system without a printer you could attach unit number six (the printer) to the CONSOLE: unit so that all output goes to the screen instead of the printer (which would cause a unit offline error). If you answer yes to this question you will be asked the number and whether or not you want it initialized. If you already told the system to initialize the driver there's no sense in having it re-initialized here.

When you answer no to the “another unit number” question you will be asked if you want the driver to start on a certain byte boundry. If your driver needs to be byte-aligned you should answer yes, normally you should simply answer no.

Finally you will be asked if you want to attach another driver to the system. If you answer yes the program will be repeated, otherwise the program will terminate saving your data file to diskette. Each driver you attach must be present in the ATTACH.DRIVERS file. The individual drivers must be linked together using the LIBRARY program as previously mentioned.

Appendix
ATTACH-BIOS Document for Apple II Pascal 1.1

By Barry Haynes
Jan 12, 1980

This document is intended for Apple II Pascal internal applications writers, Vendors and Users who need to attach their own drivers to the system or who need more detailed information about the 1.1 BIOS. It is divided into two sections, one explaining how to use the ATTACH utility available through technical support and the other giving general information about the BIOS. It is a good idea to read this whole document before assuming something is missing or hasn't been completely explained. This document is intended for more advanced users who already know a fair amount about I/O devices and how to write device drivers. It is not intended to be a simple step by step description of how to write your first device driver, nor does it claim to be a complete description of all there is to know about the Pascal BIOS.

The Apple Pascal UCSD system has various levels of I/O that are each responsible for different types of actions. It was divided at UCSD into these levels to make it easy to bring up the system on various processors and also various configurations of the same processor and yet have things look the same to the Pascal level regardless of what was below that level. The levels are:

LEVEL	TYPES OF IO ACTIONS
Pascal	READ & WRITE BLOCKREAD & BLOCKWRITE UNITREAD & UNITWRITE UNITCLEAR UNITSTATUS
RSP (Runtime Support Package)	This is part of the interpreter and is the middle man between the above types of I/O and the below types of I/O. All the above types are translated by the compiler and operating system into UNITREAD, UNITWRITE, UNITCLEAR and UNITSTATUS if they are not already in that form in the Pascal program. The RSP checks the legality of the parameters passed and reformats these calls into calls to the BIOS routines below. The RSP also expands DLE (blank suppression) characters, adds line feeds to carriage returns, checks for end of file (CTRL C from CONSOLE:), monitors UNITRW control word commands, makes calls to attached devices if present, echoes to the CONSOLE:.
BIOS (Basic I/O Subsystem)	This is the lowest level device driver routines. This is the level at which you can attach new drivers to replace or work with the regular system drivers and also attach drivers for devices that will be completely defined by you.

I. RECONFIGURING THE BIOS TO ADD YOUR OWN DRIVERS USING THE ATTACH UTILITY

INTRODUCTION

With the Apple Pascal 1.1 System (both regular and runtime 1.1), there is an automatic method for you to configure your own drivers into the system. This method requires you to write the drivers following certain rules and to use the programs ATTACHUD.CODE and SYSTEM.ATTACH provided through Apple Technical Support. At boot time, the initialization part of SYSTEM.PASCAL looks for the program SYSTEM.ATTACH on the boot drive. If it finds SYSTEM.ATTACH, it Xecutes it before Xecuting SYSTEM.STARTUP. SYSTEM.ATTACH will use the files ATTACH.DATA and ATTACH.DRIVERS which must also be on the boot disk. ATTACH.DATA is a file the developer will make using the program ATTACHUD. It tells SYSTEM.ATTACH the needed information about the drivers it will be attaching. ATTACH.DRIVERS is a file containing all the drivers to be attached and is constructed by the developer using the standard LIBRARY program. The drivers are put on the Pascal Heap below the point that a regular program can access it. They do take away Stack-Heap (= to the size of the drivers attached) space from that available to Pascal code files but this should not be a problem unless the drivers are very large or the code files very hungry in their use of memory. Since these drivers are configured into the system after the operating system starts to run, this method will not work for configuring drivers for devices that the system must cold boot from. Some of supporting code in the RSP, boot and Bios may make the task of bringing up boot drivers easier though. The advantages to this kind of setup are:

1. Software Vendors can use the ATTACHUD program to put their own drivers into the system at boot time. This will be invisible to the user.
2. There can be no problems losing drivers due to improper heap management since the drivers are put on the heap by the operating system and before any user program can allocate heap space.
3. This method does not freeze parts of the system to special memory locations since it enforces the clean methodology of using relocatable drivers.

USING ATTACHUD

ATTACHUD.CODE will ask you questions about the drivers you want to attach to the system. It makes a file called ATTACH.DATA which tells SYSTEM.ATTACH which drivers to attach to the system, what unit numbers to attach them to and other information. The options covered by ATTACHUD are:

1. A driver can be attached to one of the system devices, then all I/O to this device (PRINTER: for example) will go to this new driver. In the case of a new driver for a disk device the user will have to specify which of the 6 standard disk units will go to this new driver. This will allow replacement of standard drivers with custom ones without having to restrict the I/O interface to UNITREAD and UNITWRITE as is the case with option 2.

2. A driver can be attached to one of 16 userdevices. I/O to these will be done with UNITREAD and UNITWRITE to device numbers 128-143.

3. A method will be included to allow the attached driver to start on an N byte boundry. The driver writer will be responsible for aligning his code from that point.

4. More than one unit can be attached to the same driver. This way only one copy of the driver resides in memory and I/O to all the attached units goes to this one driver. It is up to the driver to decide which unit's I/O it is doing. How this is done is explained below.

5. The initialize routine for any attached driver can be called by SYSTEM.ATTACH after it has attached the driver and before any programs can be Xecuted.

6. In case any of your programs use the Hires pages, you can specify in ATTACHUD that drivers must not be put on the heap over these areas. Your drivers would have to be quite large before they could possibly overlap the Hires pages.

Follow through this example of a session with ATTACHUD where the options available are completely described. First Xecute ATTACHUD:

You will be given the prompt:

> Apple Pascal Attachud [1.1]
> Enter name of attach data file:

This is asking for what you want the output file from this session with ATTACHUD to be called. You could call it ATTACH.DATA or some other name and then rename it to ATTACH.DATA when you put it on the boot disk with SYSTEM.ATTACH.

If you ever get a message of the form:

> ERROR => some error
> Try again (RETURN to exit program):

then just retype what was requested on the previous prompt after deciding what mistake you made while typing it the first time.

The next prompt is:

> These next questions will determine if attached drivers can reside in the hires pages. It will be assumed they can for the page in question if you answer no to the prompt for that page.
> Will you ever use the (2000.3FFF hex) hires page?

Followed by:

> Will you ever use the (4000.5FFF hex) hires page?

You should answer yes to the question for a particular Hires page if you will ever be running a program that uses that Hires page while the drivers are Attached. You don't want the possibility of your driver residing in the Hires page if that page will be clobbered by one of your programs. After answering the Hires questions you will be asked the following questions once for each driver you will be attaching:

> What is the name of this driver? This must be the .PROC name in its assembly source (RETURN to exit program):

This must be the name of one of the drivers in the ATTACH.DRIVERS that will be used with this ATTACH.DATA. The length of this name must not be more than 8 characters. After entering the name you will be asked:

> Which unit numbers should refer to this device driver?
>
> Unit number (RETURN to abort program):

You must enter a unit number in the range 1,2,4..12,128..143 or will be given an error message. You cannot attach a character unit (CONSOLE:, PRINTER: or REMOTE:) to the same driver as a block structured unit and if you try you will be given the message:

> You can't attach a character unit and a block unit to the same driver. I will remove the last unit# you entered. Type RETURN to continue:

If you don't get the above error, you will be asked:

> Do you want this unit to be initialized at boot time?

A yes response will put the unit number just entered on a list of units that SYSTEM.ATTACH will call UNITCLEAR on after attaching all the drivers. This gives you a way to have the system make an initialize call on your attached unit at boot time. A no response will mean that no boot time init call will be made on this unit to the driver you just attached.

You will be eventually asked:

> Do you want another unit number to refer to this device driver?:

A yes response will get you to the Unit number prompt again and a no response will get you to the prompt:

> Do you want this driver to start on a certain byte boundary?

A yes here will give you more prompts:

```
The boundry can be between 0 and 256.
    0=>Driver can start anywhere.(default)
    8=>Driver starts on 8 byte boundary.
    N=>Driver starts on N byte boundary.
  256=>Driver starts on 256 byte PAGE boundary.
Enter boundary (RETURN to exit program):
```

And the last line of the prompt will repeat until you enter a boundary in the correct range. The boundary refers to the memory location where the first byte of the driver is loaded. If your driver needs to be aligned on some N byte boundary you can assure it will be using this mechanism. if you know how the driver's origin is aligned, You can align internal parts of your driver however you want. Finally you will get to the prompt:

```
Do you want to attach another driver?
```

And if you answer Yes to this you will return to the 'What is the name of this driver' prompt and answering No will end the program, saving the data file you have made.

THE DRIVER

Drivers must be written in assembly using the Pascal Assembler. They must not use the .ABSOLUTE option, so the drivers can be relocated as they are brought in by the system. Each driver must be assembled separately with no external references. When all drivers are assembled, use the LIBRARY program (in the same way you would use it to put units into a library) to put all the drivers in one file. Name this file SYSTEM.DRIVERS. See further explanation of making SYSTEM.DRIVERS below.

Considerations for all drivers:

1. Study the examples below as certain information is only documented there.

2. Refer to the Apple II Pascal memory map below and you will see that parts of the interpreter and BIOS reside in the same address range and are bank-switched. The system automatically folds in the BIOS for drivers added using ATTACH. Most of these drivers will have to make calls to CONCK if they want type ahead to continue to work properly. CONCK is the BIOS routine that monitors the keyboard. See the example drivers below to be sure you are doing this correctly. You cannot call CONCK through the CONCK vector at BF0A (see BIOS part of this document) because this call would go through the same mechanism used to get to your driver and the return address to Pascal would be lost.

3. All attached drivers must be written with one common entry point for read, write, init and status. The driver will use the Xreg contents to decide which type of I/O call this is and jump to the appropriate place within it's code. The Xreg is decoded as follows:

   0 -->read (no bits set)
   1 -->write (bit 0 set)
   2 -->init (bit 1 set) { The Pascal statement
   UNITCLEAR(UNITNUMBER); makes an init call
   for unit UNITNUMBER }
   4 -->status (bit 2 set)

4. The drivers must also pop a return address off the stack, save it and later push it to do a RTS when the driver is finished. All other parameters must be removed from the stack by the driver. For all calls, the return address will be the top word on the stack.

5. SYSTEM.ATTACH will make a copy of the normal system jump vector (the vector after the fold) and put this on the heap. There will be a pointer to this vector at 0E2. Your drivers can use this vector to get to the normal system drivers for device numbers 1..12. See example below.

6. All drivers must pass back a completion code in the X register corresponding to the table on page 280 of the 1.1 "Apple II Apple Pascal Operating System Reference Manual".

7. In references below to parameters passed on the stack, all parameters are one word parameters so they require two bytes to be popped from the stack by the driver.

8. Control word format for Unitread & Unitwrite

bits	15..13	12..6	5	4	3	2	1..0
	user defined functions	reserved for future expansion	type B chars	type A chars	nocrlf	nospec	reserved for future expansion

type B	=0	==>System will check for CTRL S & F from CONSOLE: during the time of this Unitio call.
	=1	==>System will not check for CTRL S & F during this Unitio.
type A	=0	==>If using Apple Keyboard, system will check for CTRL A, Z, K, W & E from CONSOLE: during the period of this Unitio.
	=1	==>System will not check for the chars during this Unitio.
nocrlf	=0	==>line feeds are added to carriage returns by the Interpreter.
	=1	==>no line feeds are added ...
nospec	=0	==>DLE's (blank suppression code) are expanded on output and the EOF character is detected on input.
	=1	==>nothing special is done to DLE's on output and EOF on input.

default setting for all control word bits = 0.

9. Control word format for UNITSTATUS

bits	15..13	12..2	1	0
	user defined	reserved for future	for purpose	direction

direction = 0 = = >Status of output channel is requested
= 1 = = >Status of input ...
purpose = 0 = = >Call is for unit status
= 1 = = >Call is for unit control

10. These are the new vectors and routines added to the BIOS to make attach work. The RSP, bootstrap, and readseg were also modified to allow for attaches.

```
UDJMPVEC ;Jump vector for user devices, offset=0 => unattached
         ;device. The correct addresses are initialized by
         ;SYSTEM.ATTACH . See locations section of BIOS part below
         ;for pointers to this vector.
              JMP Ø ;Unit 128
              JMP Ø ;Unit 129
              .
              .
              .
              JMP Ø ;Unit 143

DISKNUM ;If high byte=FF then
        ; device is not a disk drive
        ;else
        ; if high byte=Ø then
        ; device is a regular disk drive and low byte=drive #
        ; else
        ; driver for this disk drive has been attached by
        ; SYSTEM.ATTACH and the driver address is stored in this
        ; word. (Driver address has to be the address-1 for RTS in
        ; PSUBDR to work correctly, remember this for ATTACH.
        ; PSUBDR is listed below.)
        ;See locations section of BIOS part below for pointers to
        ;this vector.
             .WORD ØFFFF ;Unit #1
             .WORD ØFFFF ;Unit #2 (ATTACH would modify the words
             .WORD ØFFFF ;Unit #3 for units 4,5,9..12 if a
             .WORD Ø     ;Unit #4 different disk driver were
             .WORD 1     ;Unit #5 attached to any of them)
             .WORD ØFFFF ;Unit #6
             .WORD ØFFFF ;Unit #7
             .WORD ØFFFF ;Unit #8
             .WORD 4     ;Unit #9
             .WORD 5     ;Unit #10
             .WORD 2     ;Unit #11
             .WORD 3     ;Unit #12
```

```
UDRWIS ;Routine to get to an attached driver through UDJMPVEC
       ;Assume unit# in Areg & operation to be performed in Xreg.
       ;See the jump vector in the BIOS sections to see how you
       ;get to this routine.
            STA TT1
            AND #7F ;Clear top bit of unit#
            STA TT2 ;Make address in UDJMPVEC table
            ASL A ;Address=Areg*3 + base of table
            CLC
            ADC TT2 ;Now we have (Areg*3).
            ADC #JVECTRS ;Add in low byte of base of table having
            STA TT2 ;no carry problem with only 16 UD's.
            LDA #Ø
            ADC JVECTRS+1 ;JVECTRS is a word pointing to the base
                                          ;of UDJMPVEC.
            STA TT2+1
            LDA TT1
            JMP @TT2

PSUBDR ;Routine to get to an attached driver through DISKNUM
            ;We assume on entry, Areg=unit#, Yreg=DISKNUM
            ;offset & Xreg=the command to be performed by the
            ;substituted disk driver.
            ;See the jump vector in the BIOS sections to see how
            ;you get to this routine.
            STA TT1 ;Save unit#.
            LDA DISKNUM-1,Y ;Store MSB of driver address.
            PHA
            LDA DISKNUM-2,Y ;Store LSB of driver address.
            PHA LDA TT1 ;Restore unit# to Areg.
            RTS ;Jump to substituted driver. This assumes
                ;the driver address in DISKNUM =
                ;(ADDRESS OF DRIVER)-1 for the RTS to work
```

Special Considerations when Attaching Drivers for the System Devices, Unitnumbers 1..12.

A. Character Oriented Devices (Pass the character to be read-written in the A-register and make Bios calls one character at a time from RSP level. On entry, the unit number will be in the Y register in case you wanted to attach all character oriented devices to the same driver). If you attach REMOTE: & or PRINTER: to the same driver as CONSOLE:, all will have their jump vectors pointing to the start of the driver + 3 bytes. See further discussion on this below.

Units 1 & 2 (CONSOLE: and SYSTERM:)

1. These must both go to the same driver.

2. The system CONCK routine will be patched to jump to the start of the driver. The CONCK routine gets characters entered at the keyboard and fills the type ahead buffer. See the example CONSOLE: driver below.

3. Because of item 2, the entry point for normal calls (not CONCK calls) to the attached driver will be 3 bytes beyond the start of the driver.

4. The interpreter takes care of expanding blank suppression codes (DLE's), echo to the screen, EOF (the end of file character), and adding line feeds to every carriage return. Your driver doesn't need to do this.

5. CONSOLE: read and write have only the return address on the stack. The stack for CONSOLE: init looks like:

POINTER TO BREAK VECTOR	(This should be stored at location BF16..BF17 by CONSOLE: init.)

POINTER TO SYSCOM (This should be stored at location F8..F9 by CONSOLE: init.) (Also at init time, the Flush and Start/Stop conditions should be set to normal and the type-ahead queue should be emptied.)

RETURN ADDRESS <--TOS (top of stack)

The stack for CONSOLE: status looks like:

POINTER TO STATUS RECORD
CONTROL WORD
RETURN ADDRESS <--TOS

6. A status request should return, in the first word of the status record, the number of characters currently queued in the direction asked for. This is the number of characters in the type-ahead buffer. If no type-ahead is being used then output status should always return a 0 and input status a 1 if a char is waiting to be read, otherwise a 0.

7. Since we are using 7 bit ASCII codes, the CONSOLE: read routine should zero the high order bit of all characters it reads from the keyboard and passes back to Pascal (to the RSP). The CONSOLE: write routine should transfer all 8 bits as received from the RSP since many devices use 8 bit control codes.

8. The RSP will send both upper and lower case chars to the CONSOLE: write routine. The write routine should map the lower to upper if the device cannot handle lower case.

9. **CONSOLE: Output Requirements:**

A. CR (0D hex) A carriage return should move the cursor to the beginning of the current line.

B. LF (0A hex) A line feed should move the cursor to the next line but not change the column position. If the cursor is on the last line on the screen when a line feed is sent, the rest of the screen should scroll up one line and the bottom line be cleared.

C. BELL (07 hex) A sound should be made if possible when the CONSOLE: gets 07. If making a sound is not possible then ignore the 07.

D. SP (20 hex) Place a space at the current cursor position overwriting whatever is there. Move the cursor to the next column. If the cursor is on the last column of a line, it is best if the cursor stays where it is after the space fills that position. If the cursor is on the last column of the last line on the screen, it is also best if the cursor remains in that position and the screen does not scroll. These are the prefered actions of the cursor at end of line & end of screen; in the strict sense, the actions of the cursor in these circumstances are undefined.

E. NUL (00 hex) When a Null is sent to the CONSOLE: from the RSP, the CONSOLE: should delay for the ammount of time required to write one character but the state of the screen should not change.

F. All printable characters should be written to the screen and the cursor should move in the same way it does for SP.

G. See the discussion on pages 199-215 in the 1.1 Operating System Reference Manual for further requirements and information.

10. **CONSOLE: Input Requirements:**

A. The RSP takes care of echoing characters to the screen typed from the CONSOLE: keyboard. (below items optional The Start/Stop, Flush & Break chars are redefinable; see 9G above for more info.)

B. The Start/Stop character is detected by CONCK and is used to stop all processing until the character is received a second time. When the character is received (see 9G above for more info) one should loop in CONCK continuing to process other characters until:

1. the S/S char is received again
2. the Break char is received

In case 1, the suspended processing should continue as it was before the first S/S was typed. Action needed for the Break char is described below. The S/S char is never returned to the RSP and CONSOLE: type-ahead, if implemented, should continue during the suspended state. Offset from SYSCOM to this char is 85 decimal. (This and the next 2 chars are redefinable by the Setup program and SYSCOM is the system area that keeps track of this info. The pointer to the start of SYSCOM is passed to the CONSOLE: init routine and is stored at F8..F9 hex.)

C. The Flush character will stop all output and echoing to the CONSOLE: until it's second occurEnce (see 9G above). CONCK detects this and must set a flag to tell the CONSOLE: output routine to ignore characters while the flag is set. If the CONSOLE: is re-initialized or a Break char is received, the flush state should be turned off. Flush is never returned to the RSP. Flush only stops CONSOLE: output, other processing continues. Offset from SYSCOM to this char is 83 decimal.

D. The Break char should cause CONCK to jump to the location stored at BF16. This location is also passed to the CONSOLE: init routine which stores it at BF16. The break char is never returned to the RSP and it should remove the system from Stop or Flush mode if it is in either mode. Offset from SYSCOM to this char is 84 decimal.

E. Type-ahead should be implemented in CONCK by storing characters typed at the keyboard in a queue until they are requested by a CONSOLE: read from Pascal. When the queue fills, further characters should be ignored and a bell sounded when they are typed. The length of the queue should be at least 20 characters.

11. For more information on CONSOLE: requirements, see pages 199–216 of the 1.1 Operating System Reference Manual.

Unit 6 (the PRINTER:)

1. The interpreter takes care of expanding blank suppression codes (DLE's), EOF (the end of file character), and adding line feeds to every carriage return.

2. PRINTER: read,write and init have only the return address on the stack. PRINTER: status has the same items on the stack as CONSOLE: status. PRINTER: init should cause the PRINTER: to do a carriage return and a line feed and throw away any characters buffered to be printed. No form feed should be done.

3. For status, return in the first word of the status record the number of bytes buffered in the direction asked for; if this cannot be determined by your PRINTER:, return a 0.

4. The PRINTER: write routine must buffer a line and send it all at once if your PRINTER: can only receive data that way.

5. Line Delimiter characters:

A. CR (hex 0D) A carriage return should cause the PRINTER: to print the current line and return the carriage to the first column. An automatic line feed should not be done by the PRINTER: driver when it reads a CR.

B. LF (hex 0A) The RSP will send line feeds to the PRINTER: driver after each carriage return. This should cause the PRINTER: to advance to the next line. If the PRINTER: must also do a carriage return when it is given a line feed, then this is O.K.

C. FF (hex 0C) This should cause the PRINTER: to move the paper to top of form and do a carriage return. If top of form is not possible on your PRINTER:, do a carriage return followed by a line feed.

6. It is assumed that input cannot be received from the PRINTER:. See the BIOS section for a discussion of how to get input from the PRINTER:. Normally, trying to get input from the PRINTER: should return completion error code #3.

Units 7 (REMOTE: in) & 8 (REMOTE: out)

1. These must both go to the same driver.

2. The interpreter takes care of expanding blank suppression codes (DLE's), EOF and adding line feeds to every carriage return.

3. Same stack setup as the PRINTER:.

4. Status should return in first word of status vector the number of bytes buffered for the direction specified in the control word, 0 if you have no way to check.

5. This unit is supposed to be an RS-232 serial line for many different applications so it is necessary that it transfer the data without modifying it in any way. The transfer rate default is 9600 baud.

6. It would be nice if the input to REMOTE: could be buffered in the same way input to the CONSOLE: is but this is not an absolute requirement.

7. REMOTE: init should set up the REMOTE: device so it is ready to read and write.

B. Block Structured Devices
Units 4 (the boot unit),5,9,10,11,12.

1. These units are assumed to be block structured devices, the drivers for these units must do their own Pascal Block to Track-Sector conversions.

   The UCSD system assumes the disk device is a 0-based consecutive array of 512 byte logical blocks. All UCSD Pascal disks must have this logical structure no matter what their actual physical structure or size are. The physical allocation schemes for information on different types of disks are arranged with sectors that are of various sizes that depend on the hardware of the particular disk device used. The driver must convert the Pascal block # to the appropriate track & sector # of where that block is stored on it's disk device. This could be a floppy or hard disk or some other type of device. It doesn't really matter, so long as your driver maps the Pascal Block to the correct place and continues to do so for the length (byte count) required for the UnitIO operation.

   The Pascal system uses logical blocks 0 & 1 for its bootstrap code. These logical blocks should not be used for anything else and should therefore only be available to Pascal through direct UNITREAD & UNITWRITE operations and not accessable by the system through any other means. This document will not attempt to describe the boot sequence & does not attempt to give you enough information to attach another driver or device to unit #4: so you can cold boot from that unit. When a UNITWRITE is done to disk where the byte count MOD 512 is not equal to 0 (this means the last block included in the write would be partially written to according to the byte count), it is undefined whether garbage is written into the remaining part of this last block. So you may write a whole block anyhow if that is more efficient and the Pascal system will not suffer any bad consequences.

   When a UNITREAD is done from a disk you are not allowed to overwrite into the unused part of the last block (if there is an unused part due to byte count MOD 512 <> 0). You must only send the number of bytes asked for because you could clobber memory having some other valid use if you wrote extra bytes. You will have to buffer the last sector inside your disk read routine then transfer exactly the number of bytes from this last sector needed to add up to the total bytes requested.

2. The unit number will always be in the A register.

3. The stack setup for read and write is:

   CONTROL WORD (The MODE parameter mentioned in the
   1.1 Language Ref Manual on page 41)
   DRIVE NUMBER
   BUFFER ADDRESS
   BYTE COUNT
   BLOCK NUMBER
   RETURN ADDRESS <--TOS

   For init there is only the return address on the stack and for status the setup is the same as for the CONSOLE:.

4. Status requests should return the following in the status record:

   word1:Number of bytes buffered in the direction asked
   for in the control word. Return 0 if you have no
   way of checking.
   word2:Number of bytes per sector.
   word3:Number of sectors per track.
   word4:Number of tracks per disk.

C. Other
Unit 3

1. This unit has no meaning for the Apple II system except that UNITCLEAR on this unit sets text mode.

Considerations when attaching drivers for user defined devices numbers 128-143.

These unit numbers are provided for you to do whatever you want with them. you can define what they do except for the following protocols.

1. Follow the considerations for all drivers listed above.
2. The unit number will always be in the A register.
3. The stack setup for read and write is:

CONTROL WORD
DRIVE NUMBER
BUFFER ADDRESS
BYTE COUNT
BLOCK NUMBER
RETURN ADDRESS <--TOS

For init there is only the return address on the stack and for status the setup is the same as for the CONSOLE:.

This is a sample driver for a user defined device

```
         ;Locations 0..35 hex may be used as pure temps. One
         ;should never assume these locations won't be clobbered
         ;if you leave the environment of the driver itself.
         ;("leaving" includes calls to CONCK).

CONCKADR .EQU 02

         ;Only one .PROC may occur in a driver, each driver to be
         ;ATTACHED must be assembled separately using the Pascal
         ;assembler and can have no external references.

         .PROC U128DR

         STA TEMP1 ;Save Areg contents (unit#)
         PLA
         STA RETURN
         PLA
         STA RETURN+1
         TXA ;Use the X reg to tell you what kind of
                      ;call this is.
         CMP #2
         BEQ INIT
         CMP #4
         BEQ STATUS
         CMP #0
         BEQ PMS
         CMP #1
         BEQ PMS

         ;Could have error code here
         JMP RET
```

```
PMS PLA ;Get the parameters
        STA BLKNUM
        PLA
        STA BLKNUM+1
        PLA
        STA BYTECNT
        PLA
        STA BYTECNT+1
        PLA
        STA BUFADR
        PLA
        STA BUFADR+1
        PLA
        STA UNITNUM ;Also in TEMP1
        PLA
        STA UNITNUM+1 ;Should always be Ø
        PLA
        STA CONTROL
        PLA
        STA CONTROL+1
        TXA
        BNE WRITE

READ JSR GOTOCK
         ;Your driver's code for a read
         ;(If more than one unit were attached to this driver,
         ;this code could jump to various places depending on the
         ;contents of the Areg stored in TEMP1)
         JMP RET

WRITE JSR GOTOCK
        ;Your driver's code for a write
        JMP RET

        ;If you wanted to call CONCK whenever your device did a
        ;read for write, you would use this routine:
CKR .WORD CONCKRTN-1
GOTOCK LDY #55. ;Offset to address of CONCK
         LDA @ØE2,Y
         STA CONCKADR
         INY
         LDA @ØE2,Y
         STA CONCKADR+1
         LDA CKR+1 ;Set it up so you return to CONCKRTN after
         PHA ;the CONCK call.
         LDA CKR
         PHA
         JMP @CONCKADR ;Jump to CONCK
CONCKRTN RTS ;Return to caller.

INIT ;Your driver's code for init
         JMP RET

STATUS PLA
         STA CONTROL
         PLA
```

```
          STA CONTROL+1
          PLA
          STA BUFADR ;Address of status record.
          PLA
          STA BUFADR+1
          ;Your driver's code for status

RET LDA RETURN+1
          PHA
          LDA RETURN
          PHA
          LDA TEMP1
          RTS

RETURN .WORD 0 ;Can't use 0 page for these since we leave
TEMP1 .WORD 0 ;our environment when going to CONCK.
CONTROL .WORD 0
UNITNUM .WORD 0
BUFADR .WORD 0
BYTECNT .WORD 0
BLKNUM .WORD 0

.END
```

This is a sample driver for a CONSOLE: driver replacement

```
ROUTINE .EQU 02
TEMP1 .EQU 04

          .PROC CKATCH
          JMP CONCKHDL ;SYSTEM.ATTACH will patch the start of CONCK
                       ;to jump here when you attach a driver to
                       ;the CONSOLE:.

                       ;We are not popping the return address from
                       ;the stack cause we'll return from the
                       ;system routine we call from this driver.
          STA TEMP1 ;All the read,write,init and stat calls will
                         ;jump here (the starting address of your
                         ;CONSOLE: driver+3).

          STY TEMP1+1
          TXA
               ;This example shows you how to have your
               ;own code for the CONSOLE: as well as using
               ;the system CONSOLE: routines. If you want
               ;to replace the system routines completely,
               ;you need to pull the return address here.
```

```
          BEQ READ
          CMP #1
          BEQ WRITE
          CMP #2
          BEQ INIT
          CMP #4
          BEQ STATUS

          ;Error code here

READ ;Your driver's code for a read

          LDY #1 ;offset to address of CONSOLE: read in
                 ;the copy of the jmp vector made by
                 ;SYSTEM.ATTACH. See the jump vectors in the
                 ;BIOS section below to see how we get the
                 ;offsets.

          BNE GET
          ;You would have a JMP RET here (see example for user
          defined
          ;device) if you were not using the system CONSOLE:
          routines
          ;as well.

WRITE ;Your driver's code for a write
          LDY #4
          BNE GET

INIT ;Your driver's code for init
          LDY #7
          BNE GET

STATUS ;Your driver's code for status
          LDY #43.

GET LDA @ØE2,Y ;At E2 is a pointer to the copy of the
                        ;jump vector made by SYSTEM.ATTACH before
                        ;it was modified to attach your drivers.

          STA ROUTINE
          INY
          LDA @ØE2,Y
          STA ROUTINE+1
          LDY TEMP1+1 ;Restore registers
          LDA TEMP1
          JMP @ROUTINE ;Go to the original CONSOLE: driver for
                        this
                        ;I/O command. You will return from there;
                        the
                        ;BIOS is already folded in due to the way
                        your
                        ;driver was attached by SYSTEM.ATTACH.
```

```
CONCKHDL PHP ;Duplicate the 1st three instructions of CONCK
         PHA ;as they were patched by SYSTEM.ATTACH to jump
         ;TXA below  the 1st instruction of this driver.

         ;Here you can put the code for your own part of CONCK(you
         ;may want to check some additional device like a keypador
         ;something or you may want to replace the system CONCK
         ;routine alltogether. If you do this, you must save therest
         ;of the machine state and return it when you are finished.
         ;See example below.

         TYA ;Save Yreg contents for a second.
         PHA

         ;This code gets us to the system CONCK routine.
         CLC
         LDY #55. ;Offset to the address of system CONCK in the
                      ;copy of the original jmp vector.

         LDA @ØE2,Y
         ADC #3 ;Add 3 so you enter right after the three
                      ;instructions you duplicated at CONCKHDL.
         STA ROUTINE
         INY
         LDA @ØE2,Y
         ADC #Ø
         STA ROUTINE+1
         PLA ;Restore Yreg.
         TAY
         TXA ;Last of CONCK instructions SYSTEM.ATTACH
                      ;overwrote with the jmp to the start of
                      ;this driver.

         JMP @ROUTINE ;Goto system CONCK and return from there.

         .END
```

Here is another alternative for the CONCKHDL part of the above program

```
CKRTN .WORD CONCKRTN-1
CONCKHDL ; 1.If you don't care about type-ahead, this could be
         ; simply the following code (assuming your CONSOLE:
         ; read gets a character directly from your CONSOLE:
         ; device whenever it is called) :

----------------------------------------------------------------
         PHP
         INC RANDL ;RANDL is a permanent word at BF13 used in
                   ;the built in random function.
         BNE $1
         INC RANDH ;RANDH
         $1 PLP
         RTS
----------------------------------------------------------------

         ; 2.If you want type-ahead, this code should check to
         ;see if there is a character available and stuff it into
         ;a type-ahead buffer.
         ; 3.If you are using this with the regular CONCK (extra
         ;keypad to check for statistics for example), then you can
         ;do it this way.

----------------------------------------------------------------
         PHP ;Save state of machine
         PHA
         TXA
         PHA
         TYA
         PHA

         ;Put your driver's part of CONCK here (gives your driver
         ;priority)

         LDA CKRTN+1 ;Set up things to return from reg CONCK
         PHA
         LDA CKRTN
         PHA
         PHA ;Push garbage to account for other pushes done
         PHA ;in first three bytes of CONCK

         CLC ;Setup to call CONCK
         LDY #55. ;Offset to the address of system CONCK in the
         ;copy of the original jmp vector.

         LDA @0E2,Y
         ADC #3 ;Add 3 so you enter right after the three
                   ;instructions you duplicated at CONCKHDL.
         STA ROUTINE
         INY
```

```
LDA @0E2,Y
ADC #0
STA ROUTINE+1
            ;In this example we don't have to worry about
            ;the machine state here as we are restoring
            ;it after we call CONCK

JMP @ROUTINE ;Goto system CONCK and return to CONCKRTN

CONCKRTN PLA ;Restore state of machine
         TAY
         PLA
         TAX
         PLA
         PLP
         RTS ;Return to the guy who called CONCK.
```

Making ATTACH.DRIVERS

1. Xecute the standard 1.1 LIBRARY program.

2. The output code file should be ATTACH.DRIVERS or could be named somethine else and renamed ATTACH.DRIVERS when you put it on the boot disk.

3. For the Link code file use the code file of your first driver.

4. Copy its slot #1 into slot #0 of ATTACH.DRIVERS.

5. As long as you have more drivers to add, use N(EW to get another Link code file and copy it's slot #1 into slots #2,3,...15 of ATTACH.DRIVERS.

6. When done, type 'Q' then 'N' followed by a RETURN for the notice. See the 1.1 Operating System Reference Manual for further info on the LIBRARY program.

The Workings of SYSTEM.ATTACH

If it is on the boot disk, SYSTEM.ATTACH is Xecuted by the operating system (both regular 1.1 and runtime 1.1) before SYSTEM.STARTUP. The 1.1 runtime system will use a runtime version of SYSTEM.ATTACH.

The error messages that can be generated by SYSTEM.ATTACH are:

1. ERROR =>No records in ATTACH.DATA
2. ERROR =>Reading segment dictionary of ATTACH.DRIVERS3
3. ERROR =>reading driver
4. ERROR =>A needed driver is not in ATTACH.DRIVERS
5. ERROR =>ATTACH.DATA needed by SYSTEM.ATTACH
6. ERROR =>ATTACH.DRIVERS needed by SYSTEM.ATTACH

If all goes well attaching drivers, SYSTEM.ATTACH will display nothing unusual in the regular boot sequence except for extra disk accesses and anything done in the init calls to any of the attached devices.

II.BIOS

This section explains things in the BIOS area that are extensions and modifications that were added to Apple Pascal version 1.1 that were different or not there at all in Apple Pascal version 1.0 (UCSD version II.1).

1. The disk routines have been modified to handle interrupts (So interrupt driven devices could be attached to 1.1 Pascal) if they are being used. To use interrupts, one would have to attach an interrupt driver, then patch the IRQ vector (FFFE hex) to point to this driver. The Pascal system is defined to come up with interrupts turned off so, once the driver is brought in and the IRQ patched, interrupts must be turned on. The driver's init call could patch the IRQ and turn on interrupts. The disk routines save the current state of the system and turn interrupts off only during crucial time periods, the state of the system is returned during non crucial time periods so interrupts can be handled. This has not been tested at this time, so there is no data concerning the maximum interrupt response time delay.

2. The control word parameter in UNITREAD and UNITWRITE was not passed on to the BIOS level routines from the RSP level. This has been done in 1.1 to allow the changes to the control word listed below under special character checking and also so user defined units or attached Pascal units can use the user defined bits of the control word.

3. IORESULTS 128-255 are available for user definition on user defined devices.

4. UNITSTATUS has been implemented in the Apple II Pascal 1.1 system. This works for the Pascal system units as described in the ATTACH part of this document. For user defined units, Unitstatus can be used for whatever necessary.

   Unitstatus is a procedure that can be called from the Pascal level in the same way Unitread can. It has three parameters:

   1. unit#.
   2. pointer to a buffer. (any size buffer you want of type Packed Array of Char)
   3. control word.

When you make a Unitstatus call from Pascal, the call should look like:

UNITSTATUS(UNITNUM,PAC,CONTROL);

Where UNITNUM & CONTROL are integers and PAC is a Packed Array of CHAR or a STRING and may be subscripted to indicate a starting position to transfer data to or from. See further information on what Unitstatus is defined to do for the various devices in the ATTACH part of this document.

The control word will tell the status procedure for a particular unit what information about the unit you want. Bit 0 of this word should equal 1 for input status and 0 for output status. Unitstatus is implemented with bit 1 of the control word 1 meaning the call is for unit control. When this bit =0 the call is for unitstatus. In all cases bits 2-12 are reserved for system use and bits 13-15 are available for user defined funtions.

An entry in the jump vector has been made for each of the system Unitstatus calls, i.e. CONSOLESTAT,PRINTERSTAT, REMOTESTAT,etc.. Unitstatus calls to a user defined device (128-143) will all go through the same jump vector location.

5. The handling of CTRL-C by the Apple bios was non standard in 1.0. The UCSD BIOS definition specifies that a CTRL-C coming from REMOTE: or the PRINTER: should be placed in the input buffer and then no more characters should be received. Our bios did fill the buffer with nulls including the place where the CTRL-C was to go. Apple Pascal's BIOS now conforms to the standard definition, where the null filling of the buffer is done only when CTRL-C comes from the CONSOLE: (#1:).

6. The unitio routines can be accessed from assembly procedures by pushing the correct parameters on the stack and using the jump vector to get to the BIOS routine. A seperate document needs to be written describing how this is done and pointing out the problems doing it in the case of the CONSOLE:,SYSTERM:,PRINTER: & REMOTE: units. These problems are concerned with the special character handling done in the RSP for these units. The assembly procedures calling the pascal drivers for these units would either have to repeat portions of the RSP code themselves or not get the special character handling provided by the RSP. Calling the CONSOLE: init routine requires pointers to syscom and the break routine to be passed on the stack. These pointers are now stored in a fixed location so assembly routines wanting to call coninit can get at them. See the locations section.

7. Suppression of Special Character Checking.

   Special characters in the Pascal system are of three types:

   A. Chars used to control the 40 character screen. These are ctrl-A,Z,W,E & K.

   B. Pascal system control chars for general CONSOLE: use. These are ctrl-S & F.

C. Types A & B are checked for by the CONCK funtion in the bios. There are other special chars checked for in the RSP. These are ctrl-C, DLE, and CR (line feeds are automatically appended to CR). With UNITREAD and UNITWRITE the automatic handling done by the Pascal system of these characters can be turned off. To turn off DLE expansion and EOF checking give bit 2 of the control word a value of 1. The automatic adding of line feeds to carriage returns can be suppressed by setting bit 3 of the control word to 1.

A way was needed to suppress special handling for types 'A'&'B'. This can now be done in two ways. First, the control word of UNITR/W will turn off checking for type 'A' control chars if bit 4 is set and will turn off checking for type 'B' chars if bit 5 is set. In this mode, the special char handling will only be turned off during that particular unitio. This will be be done for you in the RSP by setting bits in a byte 'SPCHAR' at location BF1C. The CONCK routine will look at bit 0 of SPCHAR and if set will not look for the type 'A' chars; if bit 1 is set, it will not look for the type 'B' chars. If you set these bits in the SPCHAR yourself instead of letting the RSP do it through the unitio control word, then the associated special character checking will be turned off until you reboot or reset the bits again. When special char checking is turned off, the chars are passed back to the Pascal level like all other chars would be. You can use these added features to redefine the system special chars in a particular application program or to just disable them.

8. The EOF char (ctrl-C) causes a lot of problems in the Pascal system. The cause of the problems is that the editor looks for this character to end many of it's editing modes. The editor has it's own getchar routine which reads each character the user enters from SYSTERM:. When reading from SYSTERM: instead of the CONSOLE:, the EOF char is passed back as any other character but it still ends the current call to unitread. The editor echoes each char to the CONSOLE: itself until it comes to ctrl-C. The operating system and the filer both use the getchar routine in the operating system. This routine is defined to re-init the system if it gets a ctrl-C from the CONSOLE: and it reads from the CONSOLE:, not SYSTERM:. You

must be sure not to end responses with control-C except for the cases (in the editor only) that are supposed to end with control-C. See the 1.1 Operating System Reference Manual.

9. The bios card recognizing section has been enhanced to recognize a new 'FIRMWARE' type card. This card will allow OEM's to have their drivers in their own firmware on the card. Routines have been added to allow for init,read,write & status calls to this new type card. This protocol has been documented and is attached as an appendix to this document.

10. As you can see, the Pascal system memory usage is scattered all over the 64k space. The Apple II was not designed with a stack machine, like the Pascal P-machine, in mind. We don't need any more constraints fixing certain pieces of the system to certain EXACT places. To make the best use of the space we have, we must have the ability to move things around. To achieve this goal, we intend the following:

    A. To stop people from writing things that peek here and poke there and expect things to stay exactly where they were for future versions.

    B. Various people need space for patch areas and other purposes. All programs have to be written so this space does not have to be in a permanent fixed location if this is at all possible. The areas reserved for system use are filling up fast, we need to avoid using them. You can get space dynamically using NEW but you must be careful that this space stays around for the whole time you need it. If you are attaching a driver, you can get buffer space in the driver by using .WORD or .BLOCK in the Assembler. This space can be accessed from outside the driver if you know the offset to the start of this space from the start of the driver. This method could even be used to get space below the heap by attaching a driver to one of the user defined devices that is a large .BLOCK and is only used as a buffer. You can get the address of this buffer (of a driver) from the jump vector that has a pointer to the driver. Pointers to all the jump vectors are in zero page, see the locations section below.

C. The jump vector will have a fixed order for version 1.1 and future versions. The order is the same as in the old version 1.0 with the new entrys added to the bottom. The setup for the jump vector and getting into the BIOS is different than the old 1.0 system. Here is how the new system is set up with the fixed order for the jump vector:

```
;----------------------------------------------------
;
; MAIN BIOS JUMP TABLE CALLED FROM INTERPRETER
; (FOLLOWED BY REAL JUMP TABLE AT FIXED OFFSET)
; RSP CALLS COME TO THIS JUMP VECTOR
;
;----------------------------------------------------
BIOS JSR SAVERET ;CONSOLE READ ;Jump vector before fold.
            JSR SAVERET ;CONSOLE WRITE
            JSR SAVERET ;CONSOLE INIT
            JSR SAVERET ;PRINTER WRITE
            JSR SAVERET ;PRINTER INIT
            JSR SAVERET ;DISK WRITE
            JSR SAVERET ;DISK READ
            JSR SAVERET ;DISK INIT
            JSR SAVERET ;REMOTE READ
            JSR SAVERET ;REMOTE WRITE
            JSR SAVERET ;REMOTE INIT
            JSR SAVERET ;GRAFIC WRITE
            JSR SAVERET ;GRAFIC INIT
            JSR SAVERET ;PRINTER READ
            JSR SAVERET ;CONSOLE STAT
            JSR SAVERET ;PRINTER STAT
            JSR SAVERET ;DISK STAT
            JSR SAVERET ;REMOTE STAT
KCONCK JSR SAVERET ;To get to CONCK from CONCKVEC
            JSR SAVERET ;USER READ For UDRWIS
                                  ;USER WRITE
                                  ;USER INIT
                                  ;USER STAT
            JSR SAVERET ;For PSUBDR
            JSR SAVERET ;IDSEARCH
                .
                .
                .

;------------------------------------
;
; THIS JUMP TABLE MUST BE OFFSET
; FROM BIOSTBL BY EXACTLY $5C.
; SYSTEM.ATTACH MODIFYS THIS JUMP
; VECTOR TO POINT TO ATTACHED DRIVERS
; FOR THE STANDARD SYSTEM UNITS.
;
;------------------------------------
```

```
BIOSAF JMP CREAD ;Jump vector after fold.
            JMP CWRITE
            JMP CINIT
            JMP PWRITE
            JMP PINIT
            JMP DWRITE
            JMP DREAD
            JMP DINIT
            JMP RREAD
            JMP RWRITE
            JMP RINIT
            JMP IORTS ;Do nothing for GRAFWRITE.
            JMP GRAFINIT
            JMP IORTS ;Do nothing for PRINTER: read.
            JMP CSTAT
            JMP ZEROSTAT ;For PRINTER: stat, pop params & store 0
                               ;in 1st buffer word.
            JMP DSTATT
            JMP ZEROSTAT ;For REMOTE: stat, pop params & store 0
                                         ;in 1st buffer word.
            JMP CONCK
            JMP UDRWIS ;Routine to get to user defined devices, see
                       ;ATTACH part of document for
                       ;description of
                       ;this routine.
            JMP PSUBDR ;Routine to get to drivers that are
                       ;substituted
                       ;for the standard Pascal disk
                       ;units 4,5,9..12.
                       ;See ATTACH part of document for
                       ;description of
                       ;this routine.
            JMP IDS

;----------------------------------------
;
; STRIP LOCAL RETURN ADDR,
; STRIP PASCAL ADDR AND SAVE IN RETL,RETH
; PLACE "GOBACK" ON RETURN STACK
; THEN RESTORE LOCAL RET ADDR & RETURN
; MEANWHILE UNFOLD BIOS INTO DXXX
;
;----------------------------------------
SAVERET STA TT1 ;SAVE A REG
            PLA
            CLC
            ADC #05A ;ADD OFFSET TO JUMP TABLE (BIOSAF)
            STA TT2 ;LOCAL RET ADDR
            PLA
            ADC #0
            STA TT3
            PLA
            STA RETL ;PRESERVE PASCAL RETURN
            PLA
            STA RETH
            .IF RUNTIME=0
```

```
          LDA ØC083 ;UNFOLD BIOS INTO DXXX
          .ENDC
          LDA TT1 ;RESTORE A-REG
          JSR SAVRET2 ;PUTS "GOBACK" ON STACK
;--------------------------------------
;
; FOLD INTERP INTO DXXX
; THEN RETURN TO PASCAL VIA
; RETURN ADDR SAVED IN RETL,RETH
;
;--------------------------------------
GOBACK STA TT1 ;SAVE A-REG
          LDA RETH
          PHA
          LDA RETL
          PHA
          .IF RUNTIME=Ø LDA ØC08B ;FOLD INTERP INTO DXXX
          .ENDC
          LDA TT1
          RTS ;AND BACK TO PASCAL

SAVRET2 JMP
TT2 ;JUMP INTO JUMP TABLE (BIOSAF)
```

D. In zero page are two words pointing to the base of the two jump vectors (before and after the fold). These are stored in PERMANENT locations that had a value of 0 in the old 1.0 release and were not used by the system (see locations section). Applications needing to patch the jump vectors can store the offset from the vector base in the Y reg and use indirect indexed addressing to do the patch. The application will need to have the vector base locations for the old release hardcoded in as the base pointer for the old 1.0 release will be 0. If you want to write an application that works with 1.0 and 1.1 and future versions, you know if the zero page vector pointers are 0 it's the 1.0 system otherwise it's 1.1 or a future version which will use the same protocols as 1.1 as described in this document.

   It is important that any application patching the jump vector temporarily then returning it to its original value get the original value from the vector itself before the patch and put it in a storage location. When the vector needs to be restored to it's original state, use this storage location for it's original value. The patches should be done in this manner so the applications doing the patches will always return the system to it's original state no matter what past, present or future Pascal version it is patching.

E. For CONSOLE: init to be used from assembly routines the locations of SYSCOM and the BREAK routine have to be available. The CONINIT routine requires these on the stack. Pointers to SYSCOM and BREAK will be stored by the interpreter boot in a PERMANENT location in the BF00 page (see locations section).

F. Since the old 1.0 release, the code to jump to the CONCK routine has been set up at location BF0A. Anyone wishing to get to the CONCK routine should do a JSR BF0A as this will always get them there no matter where the CONCK routine really is. The keypress function has been changed to conform to this new convention but it will use the old convention if it is working from within an old system. Do not try to get to CONCK in this way from within an ATTACHED driver as you will loose your return address to Pascal. See ATTACH part of this document for how to get to CONCK from an attached driver.

G. There is now a version byte so one can tell which version (1.0, 1.1, etc.) of Apple Pascal he is working with. There is also a flavor byte to tell one which flavor of this version he has (regular, runtime, runtime without sets, etc.). (see locations section)

11. Whenever SYSTEM.ATTACH is used, it will make a copy of the original BIOS jump vector (the after fold vector that has the actual driver addresses in it) and put this below the heap with the drivers that are attached. It will leave a pointer to this copy of the vector at location 00E2. You can use this vector in you drivers to get to the standard Apple drivers for any device. This way you can define a driver that does something above and beyond the standard Apple driver yet this new driver can still make use of the standard Apple driver. See the ATTACH part of this document for more information.

12. In the RSP are two vectors that tell the RSP what is legal (input &-or output) for a particular character orientated device (CONSOLE:, REMOTE: & PRINTER:). For example it tells the RSP that it is illegal to read from the PRINTER:. If you wanted to ATTACH a PRINTER: driver so you could read from the PRINTER:, you would have to change this vector. 00E4 points to the READTBL

vector and 00E6 to the WRITTBL vector. Let's take the READTBL for an example:

```
READTBL ;table of routine addresses to be called when
        ;writing to that unit (disk I/O does not use
        ;this table).
        ;an entry=0 means that the operation is illegal
        ;for that unit.
              .WORD BIOS+CONREAD ;unit 1
              .WORD BIOS+CONREAD ;unit 2
              .WORD 0 ;unit 3
              .WORD 0 ;4 & 5 are disk units
              .WORD 0
              .WORD 0 ;6 is PRINTER:
              .WORD BIOS+REMREAD ;unit 7
              .WORD 0 ;8 is rem write which has
              ;an address in the WRITTBL
```

Here BIOS refers to the base of the jump vector before the fold and CONREAD is the offset off the base of that vector to get to the jump to the CONSOLE: read routine (for CONSOLE: read the offset is 0, for CONSOLE: write it's 3, etc). The value for BIOS is the pointer stored in location 00EC mentioned in the locations section below.

Locations

These are the locations of new system permanents mentioned in this document, all pointers are set up by the system and are stored low byte first. Do not modify what is stored in these pointers (except for SPCHAR if you want to suppress special character checking) since the system uses this information too. These locations are defined to have the same function & remain in the same place for future versions of Apple II Pascal.

```
BF1C SPCHAR (To control special chars)
BF1D IBREAK (Set by boot in interp for assembly calls to CONINIT)
BF1F ISYSCOM ( "  " )
BF21 VERSION (1 byte Version # of system, =2 for the new release,
                    0 for the old 1.0 release)
BF22 FLAVOR (This byte tells which flavor [runtime,regular,
                    etc.] of this VERSION you are dealing with)
                    The encoding is:
```

```
                 1 -->regular system runtime versions:
                 2 -->LC-ALL (LC- means no language card)
                 3 -->LC-no sets
                 4 -->LC-no floating point
                 5 -->LC-no sets or floating point
                 6 -->LC+ALL
                 7 -->LC+no sets
                 8 -->LC+no floating point
                 9 -->LC+no sets or floating point
                 This flavor byte is Ø in the old 1.0 release.

BFCØ-BFFF BDEVBUF (Area for non Apple boot devices, like the CORVUS)
ØØE2 ACJVAFLD (Pointer to ATTACH copy of the original Jump Vector
              after the fold)
ØØE4 RTPTR (Pointer to READTBL)
ØØE6 WTPTR (Pointer to WRITTBL)
ØØE8 UDJVP (Pointer to user device jump vector)
ØØEA DISKNUMP (Pointer to disknum vector)
ØØCC JVBFOLD (Pointer to jump vector before fold)
ØØEE JVAFOLD (Pointer to jump vector after fold)

FFF6 (Version word which = 1 for version 1.Ø and
                         = Ø for version 1.1
     This version word should not be used at runtime
     to tell which version you have. For that use the
     version byte mentioned above. This word should only
     be used by software that wants to see which
     SYSTEM.APPLE it is dealing with by looking at the
     contents of this word in the SYSTEM.APPLE file
     when it is not loaded in memory)

FFF8 (Start vector)
FFFA (NMI non maskable interrupt vector)
FFFC (RESET vector)
FFFE (IRQ interrupt request vector)
```

The locations and code in the 1.0 'PRELIMINARY APPLE PASCAL GUIDE TO INTERFACING FOREIGN HARDWARE' BIOS document are not the same for Apple Pascal 1.1 and that document clearly stated we would not commit ourselves to keeping them the same.

Pascal 1.1 Firmware Card Protocol

One major problem with Apple Pascal 1.0 is the way it deals with peripheral cards. It was set up to work with the four peripheral cards that Apple supported at the time of its release (the disk,communciations,serial and parallel cards) and had no mechanism for interfacing any other devices. Since Apple as well as many other vendors continue to produce new peripherals for the Apple][, a new protocol was designed and implemented in the Pascal 1.1 BIOS which allows new peripheral cards to be introduced to the system in a consistent and transparent fashion. The new protocol is called the "firmware card" protocol since the BIOS deals with these cards by making calls to their firmware at entry points defined by a branch table on the card itself. The new protocol fully supports the Pascal typeahead function and KEYPRESS will work with firmware cards used as CONSOLE devices. The following paragraphs describe the firmware card protocol in full detail.

A firmware card may be uniquely identified by a four byte sequence in the card's $CN00 ROM space. Location $CN05 must contain the value $38 and location $CN07 must contain $18. Note that these are identical to the Apple Serial Card. A firmware card is distinguished from a serial card by the further requirement that location $CN0B must contain the value $01. This value is called the "generic signature" since it is common to all firmware cards. The value at the next sequential location, $CN0C, is called the "device signature" since it uniquely identifies the device.

The device signature byte is encoded in a meaningful way. The high order 4 bits specify the class of the device while the low order four bits contain a unique number to distinguish between specific devices of the same class. The appendix to this document defines some device class numbers; in any case vendors should contact Apple Technical Support to make sure they use a unique number for their device signature. Although the device signature is ignored by the 1.1 BIOS, it may be used by applications programs to identify specific devices.

Following the 2 signature bytes is a list of four entry point offsets starting at address $CN0D. These four entry points must be supported by all firmware cards. They are the initialization, read, write and status calls. The BIOS takes care of disabling the $C800 ROM space of all other cards before calling the firmware routines.

The offset to the initialization routine is at location $CN0D. Thus, if $CN0D contains XX, the BIOS will call $CNXX to initialize the card. On entry, the X register contains $CN (where N is the slot number) and the Y register contains $N0. On exit, the X register should contain an error code, which should be 0 if there was no error. This error code is passed on to the higher levels of the system in the global variable "IORESULT". Registers do not have to be preserved.

The offset to the read routine is at location $CN0E. On entry, the X register will contain $CN and the Y register will contain $N0. On exit, the A register should contain the character that was read while the X register contains the IORESULT error code. The A and Y registers do not have to be preserved.

The offset to the write routine is at location $CN0F. On entry, the A register contains the character to be written while the X register contains $CN and the Y register contains $N0. On exit the X register should contain the IORESULT error code (which should be 0 for no error). The A and Y registers do not have to be preserved.

The offset to the status routine is at location $CN10. On entry, the X register contains $CN and the Y register contains $N0 while the A register contains a request code. If the A register contains 0, the request is "are you ready to accept output?". If the A register contains 1, the request is "do you have input ready for me?". On exit, the driver returns the IORESULT error code in the X register and the results of the status request in the carry bit. The carry clear means "false" (i.e., no, I don't have any input for you), while the carry set means true. Note that the status call must preserve the Y register but does not have to preserve the A register.

Thus, sample code for the first few bytes of a firmware card's $CN00 space should look something like:

```
BASICINIT BIT $FF58 ;set the v-flag
                BVS BASICENTRY always taken
IENTRY SEC ;BASIC input entry point
                DFB $90 (code for BCC
OENTRY CLC ;BASIC output entry point
                CLV
                BVC BASICENTRY ;Always taken
```

```
;
; Here is the Pascal 1.1 Firmware Card Protocol Table
;
                DFB $01 ;Generic signature byte
                DFB $41 ;Device signature bye
;
PASCALINIT DFB >PINIT ; > means low order byte
PASCALREAD DFB >PREAD ;offset to read
PASCALWRITE DFB >PWRITE ;offset to write
PASCALSTATUS DFB >PSTATUS ;offset to status routine
```

The above code fulfils all the requirements for both the BASIC and Pascal 1.1 I/O protocols. The routines PINIT, PREAD, etc, are probably jumps into the card's $C800 space which is already properly enabled by the BIOS. The reason the $CN00 space was chosen for the protocol (as opposed to the $C800 space) is that the BASIC protocol requires that all cards have $CN00 ROM space while some smaller cards may not need any $C800 ROM space.

The firware card protocol includes 2 optional calls that do not have to be implemented but would be kind of nice. The BIOS checks location $CN11 to determine if the optional calls are present; if that location contains a $00 then the BIOS thinks the calls are implemented. Thus if your card does not implement the optional calls, you should ensure that $CN11 contains a non-zero value. The two optional calls are a control call pointed to by $CN12 and an interrupt handler call pointed to by $CN13.

The control call entry point is specified by the offset at $CN12. On entry, the X register contains $CN, the Y register contains $N0 and the A register contains the control request code. Control requests are defined by the device. On exit the X register should contain the IORESULT error code.

The interrupt poll entry point is specified by the offset at $CN13. On entry, the X register contains $CN and the Y register contains $N0. The interrupt poll routine should poll the card's hardware to determine if it has a pending interrupt; if it does not it should return with the carry clear. If it does, it should handle the interrupt (including disabling it) and return with the carry set. Also, the X register should contain the IORESULT error code which should be 0 if there was no error. An interrupt polling routine must be careful not to clobber any zero page or screen space temporaries.

The control and interrupt requests are not implemented in the Pascal 1.1 BIOS but it would be nice to support them if possible as they may be implemented in later versions of the Pascal BIOS as well as other forthcoming operating system environments for the Apple][.

Note that the firmware card signature is a superset of the Apple serial card signature as recognized by the Pascal 1.0 BIOS. This allows a firmware card to function with both Pascal 1.0 and Pascal 1.1. If a card wishes to work with Pascal 1.0 as a "fake" seral card, it must provide an input entry point at $C84D and an output entry point at $C9AA. Note that since Pascal 1.0 will think the card is a serial card, typeahead and KEYPRESS capabilities will be lost.

Additional Notes

1. The Pascal RSP expects the high order bit of every ASCII character it receives from the Console read routine to be clear. The RSP will not do this for you; you must ensure the high bit of all text your card passes to the RSP from the console read routine is clear.

2. Zero page locations $00 to $35 may be used as temporaries by your firmware, as are the slot 0 screen space locations ($478,$4F8, etc.). In general, peripheral card firmware should be as conservative as possible in their memory usage, preserving zero page contents whenever possible. An interrupt polling routine must not destroy these or any other memory locations.

3. Location $7F8 must be set up to contain the value $CN, where N is the slot number, if your card utilizes the $C800 expansion ROM space. The BIOS does not do this for you; his must be done if you want your card to function in an interrupting environment.

4. The firmware card status routine should be as quick as possible, as it may be called from within the I/O polling loops of many other peripherals if your card is being used as the console device. In no case should the status routine take longer than 100 milliseconds.

5. A firmware card in slot 1 is automatically recognized as the volume "PRINTER:". A firmware card in slot 2 is automatically recognized as the volumes "REMIN:" and "REMOUT:". A firmware card in slot 3 is automactically recognized as the volumes "CONSOLE:" and "SYSTERM:".

APPENDIX

The following numbers correspond to device classes used in the device signature code. Make sure you contact Apple Technical Support to ensure that you have a unique device signature code.

0 -- reserved
1 -- printer
2 -- joystick or other X-Y input device
3 -- I/O serial or parallel card
4 -- modem
5 -- sound or speech device
6 -- clock
7 -- mass storage device
8 -- 80 column card
9 -- Network or bus interface
10 -- Special purpose (none of the above)

11 through 15 are reserved for future expansion

Additional Information

1. The type ahead buffer is located at $Ø3B1 hex and is $4E hex in length. It is implemented with a read pointer (RPTR at BF18 hex) and a write pointer (WPTR at $BF19 hex). At CONSOLE: init time, these should both be set to Ø. When a character is detected by CONCK, the WPTR is incremented then compared with $4E. If it is equal to $4E, it is set to $Ø (this is a circular buffer). Then the WPTR is compared with RPTR and if they are equal the buffer is full. If the buffer is not full, the character is stored at $Ø3B1 + the value in WPTR.

   When removing a character from the type ahead buffer, use the following sequence. Compare the RPTR with WPTR and if they are equal, the buffer is empty and you must wait until a character is available from the keyboard. If they are not equal, increment the RPTR and compair it to $4E. If it equals $4E, set it to $Ø. Now get the character from location $Ø3B1 + the value in RPTR.

If you are implementing your own type ahead, you can do it however you wish. This information is made available in case you want to check for input from another device as well as the standard system CONSOLE: and have characters from that device be put in the system type ahead buffer.

2. The example drivers in this document did not show the setting of the IORESULT in the X register. This would be done in the code specific to your driver and should allways be set to something (Ø if there are no errors). If there are errors, set it as described elsewhere in this document and the Pascal Manuals.

3. For further information, see the newest edition of the Apple II Reference Manual.

4. These listings from the BIOS are included to show you how we implemented certain system drivers. You cannot rely on the locations of these to stay in the same place in the BIOS in future releases of Apple II Pascal nor can you rely on the routines themselves staying the same. They are only included as examples and to give you information that may not be documented elsewhere. This is not a complete BIOS listing so you may find references to routines or locations that are not included in this listing. The only locations that will be sure to remain the same for future releases are those mentioned in the LOCATIONS section above. We are against you poking the BIOS yourself to change or overwrite any of these routines. We did not include this information so you could poke the BIOS. If you do modify the BIOS, it is completely at your own risk! We have provided the ATTACH utility so you can add your own drivers the system without poking the BIOS and this is the way it should be done! If you have special requirements that are not solved by ATTACH, please contact Apple Technical Support.

```
;--------------------------------------
;
; ZERO PAGE PERMANENTS
;
;--------------------------------------
FIRST .EQU ØFØ ;START ZERO PAGE USE
BAS1L .EQU FIRST ;SCREEN 1 PTR
```

```
BAS1H .EQU FIRST+1
BAS2L .EQU FIRST+2 ;SCREEN 2 PTR
BAS2H .EQU FIRST+3
CH .EQU FIRST+4 ;HORIZ CURSOR, Ø..79
CV .EQU FIRST+5 ;VERT CURSOR, Ø..23
TEMP1 .EQU FIRST+6
TEMP2 .EQU FIRST+7
SYSCOM .EQU FIRST+8 ;2 BYTES PTR TO SYSCOM AREA

;---------------------------------------
;
; BFØØ PAGE PERMANENTS
;
;---------------------------------------
CONCKVECTOR .EQU ØBFØA ;4 BYTES
SCRMODE .EQU ØBFØE
LFFLAG .EQU ØBFØF
NLEFT .EQU ØBF11
ESCNT .EQU ØBF12
RANDL .EQU ØBF13
RANDH .EQU ØBF14
CONFLGS .EQU ØBF15
BREAK .EQU ØBF16 ;2 BYTES
RPTR .EQU ØBF18 ;1 BYTE
WPTR .EQU ØBF19 ;1 BYTE
RETL .EQU ØBF1A
RETH .EQU ØBF1B
SPCHAR .EQU OBF1C ;ØØ MEANS DO ALL SPECIAL CHARACTER CHECKING
                  ;Ø1 MEANS DON'T CHECK FOR APPLE SCREEN STUFF
                  ;Ø2 MEANS DON'T CHECK FOR OTHER SCREEN STUFF
IBREAK .EQU ØBF1D ;INTERP STORES BREAK & SYSCOM ADR HERE FOR
ISYSCOM .EQU ØBF1F ;USER ROUTINES TO GET AT
VERSION .EQU ØBF21 ;VERSION OF SYSTEM SET TO 2 FOR APPLE 1.1
FLAVOR .EQU ØBF22 ;SEE TABLE IN INTERP BOOT
SLTTYPS .EQU ØBF27 ;BF27..ØBF2E
XITLOC .EQU ØBF2F ;INTERP INITS THIS TO LOCATION OF XIT
           ;FORTRAN PROTECTION USES BF56..BF7F
           ;VENDOR BOOT DEVICES CAN USE BFCØ..BFFF

;---------------------------------------
;
; MISCELANEOUS PROGRAM EQUATES
;
;---------------------------------------
BUFFER .EQU Ø2ØØ ;TEMP HSHIFT BUFFER (OVERLAPS DISK BUF)
CONBUF .EQU Ø3B1 ;78 CHAR TYPE-AHEAD BUF
CBUFLEN .EQU Ø4E ;78 DECIMAL
NCTRLS .EQU 14. ;# CTRL CHARS IN TABLE
SIGVALUE .EQU 1
BYTEPSEC .EQU 256. ;DISK INFO FOR DISKSTAT
SECPTRAK .EQU 16.
TRAKPDSK .EQU 35.
UDJVP .EQU ØE8 ;Ø PAGE JUMP VECTOR POINTER LOCATIONS
DISKNUMP .EQU ØEA
JVBFOLD .EQU ØEC
JVAFOLD .EQU ØEE
```

```
HCMODE .EQU ØE1 ;THESE TWO BYTES USED FOR HIRES STUFF
HSMODE .EQU ØEØ

JVECTRS .WORD UDJMPVEC
            .WORD DISKNUM
            .WORD BIOS
            .WORD BIOSAF

;---------------------------------------
;
; HARD RESET INITIALIZATION
;
;---------------------------------------
START CLD ;SET HEX MODE
            SEI ;MAKE SURE INTERRUPTS ARE OFF.

;---------------------------------------
;
; CLEAR ALL MEMORY Ø TO BFFF
; (RUN-TIME SYSTEM:Ø TO TOPMEM + BF PAGE);
;
;---------------------------------------
            LDA #Ø
            STA ZEROL
            STA ZEROH
            TAY
            TAX
ZERLP STA (ZEROL),Y ;WRITE A BYTE OF Ø
            INY ;BUMP POINTER
            BNE ZERLP ;LOOP TILL NEXT PAGE
            INC ZEROH ;BUMP MSB POINTER
            INX
            .IF RUNTIME=1
            CPX #TOPMEM ;DONE CLEARING MEM?
            BNE $1
            LDX #0BF ;CLEAR BF PAGE
            STX ZEROH
$1: CPX #0C0
            BNE ZERLP
            .ELSE
            CPX #0C0 ;DONE CLEARING BFXX?
            BNE ZERLP
            .ENDC

;----------------------
;
; CHECKSUM PROMS ON EACH SLOT
; TO FIND OUT WHO'S OUT THERE
;
; SUM TWICE TO TELL IF CARD THERE
; IF SUMS DONT MATCH THEN NO PROM IS THERE
; IF MS BYTE OF SUM=Ø THEN NO PROM IS PRESENT
;
;----------------------
```

```
            LDY #0C7 ;POINT TO SLOT 7 PROM
NXTCRD STY CKPTRH ;(CKPTRL=Ø FROM MEM CLEAR)
            JSR CKPAGE ;16 BIT SUM IN X,A
            STA CHECKL
            STX CHECKH ;SAVE FOR MATCH
            JSR CKPAGE ;SUM AGAIN
            CPX #Ø ;WAS MSB ZERO?
            BEQ NOPROM ;YES NO PROM ON CARD
            CMP CHECKL ;LSB MATCH?
            BNE NOPROM ;NO, NO PROM ON CARD
            CPX CHECKH
            BNE NOPROM ;MSB DIDNT MATCH
            BEQ SKIPIORTS ;ALWAYS TAKEN

 ;----------------------------
 ;
 ; TABLE OF CNØ5 AND CNØ7 BYTES OF EACH CARD
 ;
 ;----------------------------
CNØ5BYTS .BYTE ØØ3,Ø18,Ø38,Ø48
CNØ7BYTS .BYTE Ø3C,Ø38,Ø18,Ø48

 ;----------------------------
 ;
 ; NOW THAT WE KNOW A CARD IS THERE,
 ; EXAMINE CNØ5 AND CNØ7 BYTE TO
 ; DETERMINE WHICH CARD IT IS
 ;
 ; SET CARDTYPE AS FOLLOWS:
 ; Ø=CKSUM NOT REPEATABLE OR MSB=Ø
 ; 1=CKSUM REPEATABLE,CARD NOT RECOGNIZED
 ; 2=DISK CARD (BYTE Ø7= Ø3C)
 ; 3=COM CARD (BYTE Ø7= Ø38)
 ; 4=SERIAL (BYTE Ø7= Ø18)
 ; 5=PRINTER (BYTE Ø7= Ø48)
 ; 6=FIRMWARE (BYTE Ø7= Ø48)
 ;-----------------------------
SKIPIORTS LDX #5 ;4 TYPES OF CARDS
NXTYP LDY #5 ;CHECK BYTE CNØ5 OF CARD
            LDA (CKPTRL),Y
            CMP CNØ5BYTS-2,X ;MATCH TABLE?
            BNE TRYNXT ;NO, TRY NEXT IN LIST
            LDY #7
            LDA (CKPTRL),Y ;TEST CNØ7 BYTE
            CMP CN07BYTS-2,X ;MATCH TABLE?
            BEQ STOR ;BOTH MATCHED, CARD RECOGNIZED
TRYNXT DEX ;BUMP TO NEXT IN LIST
            CPX #2 ;TRY ALL TYPES IN LIST
            BCS NXTYP ;IF NOT IN LIST,FALL THRU WITH X=1
STOR CPX #4 ;IS IT A SERIAL CARD?
            BNE STOR1
            LDY #ØB
            LDA (CKPTRL),Y
            CMP #SIGVALUE
            BNE STOR1
            LDX #6
```

```
STOR1 LDY CKPTRH
            TXA
            STA SLTTYPS-0C0,Y
NOPROM LDY CKPTRH
            DEY ;BUMP TO NEXT LOWER SLOT
            CPY #0C0 ;SLOTS 7 DOWNTO 1 DONE?
            BNE NXTCRD ;LOOP TILL 7 SLOTS DONE
                                ;LEAVE WITH Areg:=0
;----------------------------------------
;
; SET UP CONCK VECTOR FOR KEYPRESS FUNCTION
;
;----------------------------------------
            BEQ $2 ;ALWAYS BRANCHES
$1 JSR KCONCK ;HERE ARE THE 2 INSTRUCTIONS TO BE TRANSFERRED
            RTS
$2 LDY #3 ;TRANSFER 4 BYTES TO BF0A
$21 LDA $1,Y
            STA CONCKVECTOR,Y
            DEY
            BPL $21

            ;SET UP JUMP VECTOR POINTERS IN 0 PAGE
            LDY #7
$3 LDA JVECTRS,Y
            STA UDJVP,Y
            DEY
            BPL $3

;----------------------------------------
;
; SET SCREEN MODE ETC
;
;----------------------------------------
            LDA #80
            STA HCMODE
            LDA 0C051 ;SET TEXT MODE
            LDA 0C052 ;SET BOTTOM 4 GRAFIX
            LDA 0C054 ;SELECT PRIMARY PAGE
            LDA 0C057 ;SELECT HIRES GRAFIX
            LDA 0C010 ;CLEAR KEYBOARD STROBE
            JSR FORM ;ERASE SCREEN
            JSR INVERT ;PUT CURSOR ON SCREEN
            JSR DRESET ;DO ONCE ONLY DISK INIT
            LDA SLTTYPS+3 ;WHAT CARD IN SLOT 3?
            LDY #030 ;SLOT 3
            JSR GENIT ;SET BAUD IF COM OR SER THERE
            CPX #0 ;WAS AN EXTERNAL CONSOLE THERE?
            BNE STARTUP ;NO,USE APPLE SCREEN
            LDA #4
            STA SCRMODE ;SET BIT 2 FOR EXT CON
STARTUP JMP JPASCAL ;FOLD IN INTERP AND START PASCAL
```

```
;------------------------
;
; SUB TO CHECKSUM ONE PAGE
;
CKPAGE LDA #0
            TAX ;CLEAR SUM
            TAY ;CLEAR INDEX
CKNX CLC
            ADC (CKPTRL),Y ;ADD BYTE
            BCC NOCRY
            INX ;INC HI BYTE IF CARRY
NOCRY INY ;BUMP INDEX
            BNE CKNX ;SUM 256 BYTES
            RTS ;RETURN SUM IN X,A AND Y=0


;-------------------------------------------------------------
;
; BIOS HANDLERS FOR LOGICAL AND PHYSICAL DEVICES.
;
;-------------------------------------------------------------


;-------------------------------------
;
; CONSOLE CHECK FOR CHAR AVAIL
; STATUS AND ALL REGS PRESERVED
; IF CHAR AVAIL,PUT IN CONBUF AND INC WPTR.
;
; WARNING...THIS ROUTINE ALSO CALLED FROM DISK ROUTINES
;
;-------------------------------------
CONCK PHP
            PHA
            TXA
            PHA
            TYA
            PHA
RNDINC INC RANDL ;BUMP 16 BIT RANDOM SEED
            BNE RNDOK
            INC RANDH
RNDOK LDA SLTTYPS+3 ;WHAT CARD IS IN SLOT 3?
            CMP #3 ;IS IT A COM CARD?
            BEQ COMCK ;YES,GO CHECK IT
            CMP #4 ;IS IT A SERIAL CARD?
            BEQ JDONCK ;YES,IT CANT BE TESTED
            CMP #6
            BEQ FIRMCK
TSTKBD LDA 0C000 ;TEST APPLE KEYBOARD
            BPL JDONCK ;NO CHAR AVAIL
            STA 0C010 ;CLEAR KEYBD STROBE
            AND #07F ;MASK OFF TOP BIT
            TAX ;See if checking for apple special chars is
            LDA SPCHAR ;turned off.
            ROR A
            BCS NOTFOLP2 ;Jump if so
            TXA
```

```
            CMP #11. ;CTRL-K?
            BNE NOTK
            LDA #05B ;YES,REPLACE WITH LEFT SQR BRACKETT
NOTK CMP #1 CTRL-A?
            BNE NTTAB
            JSR HTAB ;YES,TAB NEXT MULT 40
            LDA CONFLGS
            AND #0FE
            STA CONFLGS ;CLEAR AUTO-FOLLOW BIT
            JMP DONECK
NTTAB CMP #26. ;CTRL-Z?
            BNE NOTFOL ;NO,PUT CHAR IN BUFFER
            LDA CONFLGS
            ORA #1
            STA CONFLGS ;SET AUTO-FOLLOW BIT
            BNE DONECK ;BR ALWAYS


COMCK LDA 0C0BE ;CHAR AVAIL?
            LSR A
            BCC DONECK ;NO CHAR AVAIL
            LDA 0C0BF ;GET CHAR FROM UART
GOTCHAR AND #07F ;MASK OFF BIT 7
NOTFOL TAX
            LDA SPCHAR ;See if console special char checking is
                                    ;turned off.
            ROR A
NOTFOLP2 ROR A
            BCS NFMI1 ;Jump if so
            TXA
            LDY #055
            CMP (SYSCOM),Y ;STOP CHAR?
            BNE NOTSTOP
            LDA CONFLGS
            EOR #080
            STA CONFLGS ;YES,TOGGLE STOP BIT (BIT 7)
JDONCK JMP DONECK

FIRMCK LDA #1
            LDY #030
            JSR FIRMSTATUS
            BCC DONECK
            JSR FREAD1
            JMP GOTCHAR

NOTSTOP DEY
            CMP (SYSCOM),Y
            BNE NOTBRK
            LDA CONFLGS
            AND #03F
            STA CONFLGS ;CLEAR FLUSH&STOP BITS
            .IF RUNTIME=0
             JMP TOBREAK
            .ELSE
             JMP @BREAK ;BREAK OUT
            .ENDC
```

```
NOTBRK DEY  CMP (SYSCOM),Y ;FLUSH?
            BNE NOTFLUS
            LDA CONFLGS
            EOR #040
            STA CONFLGS ;TOGGLE FLUSH BIT (BIT 6)
            JMP DONECK

NFMI1 TXA
NOTFLUSH LDX WPTR
            JSR BUMP
            CPX RPTR ;BUFFER FULL?
            BNE BUFOK
            JSR BELL
            JMP DONECK ;BEEP&IGNORE CHAR
BUFOK STX WPTR
            STA CONBUF,X ;PUT CHAR IN BUFFER
DONECK BIT CONFLGS ;IS STOP FLAG SET?
            BPL CKEXIT
            JMP RNDINC ;LOOP IF IN STOP MODE

CKEXIT PLA
            TAY
            PLA
            TAX
            PLA
            PLP
            RTS ;ELSE RESTORE STAT AND ALL REG AND RETURN
BUMP INX ;BUMP BUFFER POINTER WITH WRAP-AROUND
            CPX #CBUFLEN
            BNE BMPRTS
            LDX #0
BMPRTS RTS


;------------------------------------
;
; INITIALIZE CONSOLE:
;
;------------------------------------
CINIT PLA
            STA TEMP1 ;SAVE RETURN ADDR
            PLA
            STA TEMP2
            PLA
            STA SYSCOM ;SAVE PTR TO SYSCOM ARE
            PLA
            STA SYSCOM+1
            PLA
            STA BREAK ;SAVE BREAK ADDRESS
            PLA
            STA BREAK+1
            LDA TEMP2
            PHA ;RESTORE RETURN ADDR
            LDA TEMP1
            PHA
```

```
            LDA RPTR ;FLUSH TYPE-AHEAD BUFFER
            STA WPTR
            LDA CONFLGS
            AND #03E
            STA CONFLGS ;CLEAR STOP,FLUSH,AUTO-FOLLOW BITS
            JSR TAB3 ;NO,HORIZ SHIFT FULL LEFT
CINIT2 LDA #0 ;CLEAR IORESULT
            RTS ;AND RETURN

;-----------------------------------
;
; READ FROM CONSOLE:
; KEYBOARD,COM OR SERIAL CARD IN SLOT 3
;
;-----------------------------------
CREAD JSR ADJUST ;HORIZ SCROLL IF NECESSARY
            LDY #030 ;SLOT 3
            LDA SLTTYPS+3 ;WHAT TYPE OF CARD?
            CMP #4 ;IS IT A SERIAL CARD?
            BNE CREAD2 ;NO,CONTINUE
            JSR RSER ;YES, READ IT
            AND #7F ;MASK OFF TOP BIT
            RTS
CREAD2 JSR CONCK ;TEST CHAR
            LDX RPTR
            CPX WPTR
            BEQ CREAD ;LOOP TILL SOMETHING IN BUFFER
            JSR BUMP
            STX RPTR ;BUMP READ POINTER
            LDA CONBUF,X ;GET CHAR FROM BUFFER
            LDX #0 ;CLEAR IORESULT
            RTS ;AND RETURN TO PASCAL

;-----------------------------------
;
; INITIALIZE PRINTER:
; PRINTER IS ALWAYS IN SLOT 1
; IT MAY BE A PRINTER,COM,OR SERIAL CARD
;
;-----------------------------------
PINIT LDY #010 ;SLOT 1 ; 010
            LDA SLTTYPS+1 ;WHAT CARD IN SLOT 1?
            CMP #5 ;PRINTER CARD?
            BEQ CLRI01 ;YES,NO INIT NEEDED
GENIT CMP #4 ;SERIAL CARD?
            BEQ ISER ;YES, INIT SER CARD
            CMP #3 ;COM CARD?
            BEQ ICOM ;YES,INIT COM CARD
            CMP #6
            BEQ FIRMINIT
            LDX #9 ;NONE OF ABOVE,OFFLINE
            RTS

FIRMINIT PHA
            JSR SER1
            LDY #OD
```

```
FVEC1 LDA (TEMP1),Y
            STA TEMP1
            LDY 6F8
            PLA
            JMP @TEMP1

;--------------------------------
;
; INITIALIZE REMOTE:
; REMOTE IS ALWAYS IN SLOT 2
; IT MAY BE A COM OR SERIAL CARD
;
;------------------------------
RINIT LDA SLTTYPS+2 ;WHAT CARD IN SLOT 2?
            LDY #020
            BNE GENIT ;BR ALWAYS TAKEN

;--------------------------------
;
; INIT COM CARD, Y-ONO
;
;-------------------------------
ICOM LDA #3 ;MASTER INIT
            STA OC08E,Y ;TO STATUS
            LDA #21.
            STA OC08E,Y ;SET BAUD ETC
CLRIO1 LDX #0 ;CLEAR IORESULT
            RTS ;AND RETURN

;------------------------------
;
; INIT SERIAL CARD, Y=ONO
;
;-------------------------------
ISER JSR SER1 ;ASSORTED GARBAGE
            JSR OC800 ;SET UP SLOT DEPENDENTS
CLRIO3 LDX #0 ;CLEAR IORESULT
            RTS ;AND RETURN

;---------------------
;
; ASSORTED SERIAL CARD SET-UP
;
;------------------------------
SER1 STY 06F8 ;STORE NO
            TYA
            LSR A
            LSR A
            LSR A
            LSR A
            ORA #OCO
            TAX ;MAKE OCN IN X
            LDA #0
            STA TEMP1
            STX TEMP2 ;SET UP INDIRECT ADDRESS
            LDA OCFFF ;TURN OFF ALL C8 ROMS
```

```
            LDA (TEMP1),Y ;SELECT C8 BANK
            RTS

;--------------------------------
;
; WRITE TO CONSOLE:
; VIDEO SCREEN,COM OR SER CARD IN SLOT 3
;
;--------------------------------
CWRITE JSR CONCK ;CONSOLE CHAR AVAIL?
            BIT CONFLGS ;IS FLUSH FLAG SET?
            BVS CLRIO ;YES,DISCARD CHAR & RETURN
            TAX ;SAVE CHAR IN X
            LDY #030 ;SLOT 3;010
            LDA SLTTYPS+3 ;WHAT KIND OF CARD?
            CMP #3 ;COM CARD?
            BEQ WCOM ;YES WRITE TO COM CARD SLOT 3
            CMP #4 ;SERIAL CARD?
            BEQ WSER ;YES,WRITE TO SER CARD SLOT 3
            CMP #6
            BEQ WFIRM
            TXA ;ELSE RESTORE CHAR & SEND TO SCREEN
VIDOUT STA TEMP1 ;SAVE CHAR FOR LATER
            JSR INVERT ;REMOVE CURSOR
            LDY CH
            JSR VOUT2 ;DO THE BUSINESS
            JSR INVERT ;RESTORE THE CURSOR
CLRIO LDX #0 ;CLR IORESULT
            RTS ;RETURN FROM VIDOUT

WFIRM TXA
            PHA
            LDA #0
            JSR IOWAIT
            JSR SER1
            LDY #0F
            JMP FVEC1

;--------------------------------
;
; WRITE TO SERIAL CARD, Y=ONO,CHAR IN X
;
;--------------------------------
WSER JSR CONCK ;CONSOLE CHAR?
            TXA
            PHA ;SAVE CHAR ON STACK
            JSR SER1 ;ASSORTED GARBAGE
            PLA
            STA 05B8,X SET UP DATA BYTE
            JSR 0C9AA ;SEND IT (SHOUT)
            LDX #0
            RTS
;--------------------------------
;
; WRITE TO REMOTE:, CHAR IN A
;
;--------------------------------
```

```
RWRITE TAX ;SAVE CHAR
            LDA SLTTYPS+2 ;WHAT CARD IN SLOT 2?
            LDY #020
            BNE GENW2 ;BR ALWAYS TAKEN

;---------------------------------
;
; WRITE TO PRINTER CARD SLOT1, CHAR IN X
;
;---------------------------------
WPRN JSR CONCK ;CONSOLE CHAR AVAIL?
            LDA 0C1C1 ;TEST PRINTER READY
            BMI WPRN ;LOOP TILL READY
            STX 0C090 ;SEND CHAR
CLRIO2 LDX #0
            RTS

;---------------------------------
;
; WRITE TO COM CARD, Y-QNO,CHAR IN X
;
;---------------------------------
WCOM JSR CONCK ;CONSOLE CHAR?
            LDA 0C08E,Y ;TEST UART STATUS
            AND #2 ;READY?
            BEQ WCOM ;NO,WAIT TILL READY
            TXA
            STA 0C08F,Y ;SEND CHAR
            LDX #0
            RTS

;---------------------------------
;
; WRITE TO PRINTER:, CHAR IN A
;
;---------------------------------
PWRITE TAX ;SAVE CHAR IN X
            LDA LFFLAG ;TEST LINE-FEED FLAG
            BPL LFPASS ;PASS IF BIT7=0
            CPX #10. ;IS IT A LINE-FEED?
            BEQ CLRIO ;YES,IGNORE
LFPASS LDY #010 ;SLOT 1
            LDA SLTTYPS+1 ;WHAT KIND OF CARD?
GENW CMP #5 ;PRINTER CARD?
            BEQ WPRN ;YES WRITE TO PRINTER CARD
GENW2 CMPL#4 ;SERIAL CARD?
            BEQ WSER ;YES WRITE TO SER CARD
            CMP #3 ;COM CARD?
            BEQ WCOM ;YES WRITE TO COM CARD
            CMP #6
            BEQ WFIRM
OFFLINE LDX #9
            RTS
```

```
;------------------------------
;
; READ FROM REMOTE:
;
;------------------------------
RREAD LDA SLTTYPS+2 ;WHAT CARD IN SLOT 2?
            LDY #020
GENR CMP #4 ;SERIAL CARD?
            BEQ RSER ;GET FROM SER CARD
            CMP #3 ;COM CARD?
            BEQ RCOM ;GET FROM COM CARD
            CMP #6
            BEQ RFIRM
            BNE OFFLINE ;CARD NOT RECOG

;--------------------------------
;
; READ FROM COM CARD, Y=NO
;
;--------------------------------
RCOM JSR CONCK ;CHECK FOR CONSOLE CHAR
            LDA 0C08E,Y ;TEST UART STATUS
            LSR A ;TEST BIT 0
            BCC RCOM ; WAIT FOR CHAR
            LDA 0C08F,Y ;GET CHAR
            LDX #0
            RTS

RFIRM LDA #1
            JSR IOWAIT
FREAD1 JSR SER1
            PHA
            LDY #0E
            JMP FVEC1

;------------------------------
;
; READ FROM SERIAL CARD, Y =0NO
;
;-------------------------------
RSER JSR CONCK ;CONSOLE CHAR AVAIL?
            JSR SER1 ;ASSORTED GARBAGE
            JSR 0C84D ;GET A BYTE (SHIFTIN)
            LDA 05B8,X ;GET BYTE 0678+SLOT
            LDX #0
            RTS
FIRMSTATUS PHA
            JSR SER1
            LDY #10
            JMP FVEC1

IOWAIT JSR CONCK
            PHA
            JSR FIRMSTATUS
            PLA
            BCC IOWAIT
            RTS
```

Index

A

ABI p-code 232, 353
ABI p-code routine 321
ABR p-code 260
ABR p-code routine 345
Absolute value 232, 260
Accessing data at the bit level 22
Accessing elements of a multi-word structure 184
Accessing elements of a record 186
Accessing fields in different variants 20
Accessing global variables within an intrinsic unit 192
Accessing individual bits in an integer 24
Accessing intermediate variables 64
Accessing locations adjacent to an array 44
Accessing parameters by turning off range checking 44
Accessing real variables 84
Accessing record elements 88
Accessing string variables 88
Activation record 152, 177
Addition 94
ADDR function 44
Address of a parameter 44
ADI p-code 234, 354
ADI p-code routine 321
ADJ p-code 86, 87, 282
ADJ p-code routine 327
ADR p-code 262
ADR p-code routine 344
Advantages of pointer variables 32
Allocating space for a dynamic variable 226
Allocating storage for permanent variables 28
Allocating storage on the heap 32
AMD9511 355
Apple keyboard port 32
Apple Pascal's memory allocation scheme 28
Arithmetic and logical instructions 232
Arithmetic negation 94
Arithmetic overflow 234, 240
Array allocation 85
Array index checking 66
Array storage allocation 41
Assigning one string to another 208
Assigning real constants 64
Assigning two data types to the same physical location 22
Assigning values to a set variable 25
ATTACH-BIOS diskette 392
ATTACH.BIOS 152, 375
ATTACH.DATA 356, 392
ATTACH.DRIVERS 356, 392
Attaching drivers to block structured devices 390
Attaching user drivers to the system 392
ATTACHUD.CODE 356, 393

B

B 153
Backwards address allocation 41

Backwards allocation 62
BASE 152, 307
Base procedure 152
BASE register 168, 170, 172
Bell character 386
Big parameter 153
Binary Boolean operators' code 94
Binary operator 234
BIOS 311
BIOS hooks 348
Bit arrays 25
Bit correspondences within a set 25
Block move subroutine 341
Boosting Pascal's execution speed 59
Boot-time transient area 348
BPT p-code routine 341
Break character 387
Break-even point on the case statement 68
Building a singleton set 284
Building a subrange set 286
Bump exponent routine 343
Byte and word comparisons 330
Byte array comparisons 294
Byte array handling 202

C

C Programming Language 44
Carriage return character 385
Case jump instruction 304
CASE statement 93
CBP p-code routine 336
CCS Arithmetic card 351, 355
CGP p-code 98
CGP p-code routine 335
Character assignments 89
Check for a 6502 subroutine 334
Check for a stack overflow 334
Checking a value to see if it is within range 248
Checking an array index 248
Checking array indices 42
Checking for I/O errors 67
CHK p-code 42, 86, 88, 248, 354
CHK p-code routine 322
CHKGDIRP routine 312
Choosing the REPEAT UNTIL loop over the FOR loop 91
Choosing the While loop over the FOR loop 91
CHR 94
Clearing bits 24
CLP p-code 98
CLP p-code routine 335
Code generated by arithmetic operators 94
Code generated by functions and operators 94
Code generated for complex expressions 95
Code generated for expressions in Apple Pascal 94
Code generated for set operations 86
Code generated for the CASE statement 68, 93
Code generated for the IF/THEN/ELSE statement 68
Code offset value 76
Code offsets 74
Commenting tricks 45
Comparison lead-in routine 329
Compiled program performance 59
Compiler functions 95
Compiler messages 67
Compiler range checking options 43
Completion of p-subroutine set up 335
Computing a power of ten 274
Computing the address of an array element 85
CONCAT function 96
CONSCHK routine 381
CONSOLE driver requirements 385
CONSOLE init and status calls 381
CONSOLE read and routine calls 381
CONSOLE status routine 381
Constant loads 154
Contiguous case values 68
Converting a REAL value to an integer value 256
Converting an integer to a floating point value 252, 254
COPY function 97
Copying NP into a pointer variable 228
Creating a pointer to a field within a record 214
Creating portable programs 32
CROSSREF program 63
CSP p-code 96, 226, 256, 258

CSP p-code routine 338
CXP and normal procedure routine, common code 334
CXP p-code 96, 97, 98
CXP p-code routine 336
CXP parameters 98
CXP utility subroutine 333

D

Data offsets 74
Data or code offsets 74
DB 153
Debugged programs and the RANGECHECK option 66
Debugging Pascal Programs 15
Debugging Pascal run-time errors 76
Debugging run-time errors 76
Declaring string sizes 65
Declaring variables in separate statement 63
DECODE disassembler 61, 83, 95, 98, 142
DELETE procedure 97
Determining the address of a data structure 44
Determining the bounds of memory in use 36
DIF p-code 87, 294
DIF p-code routine 326
Directly reading the Apple's keyboard 37
Disassembling an integer into four nibbles 22
Disassembling an integer into hi- and low-order bytes 22
Disk directory 224
Disk I/O subroutine 348
Dividing two integers 244
Division 94
Don't care byte 153
DUMPCODE disassembler 83, 95
Duplicating string constants 65
DVI p-code 244, 355
DVI p-code routine 322
DVIMOD routine 322
DVR p-code 272
DVR p-code routine 344
Dynamic frequency analysis 71
Dynamic memory allocation 35
Dynamic variable allocation 19, 224
Dynamic variables 152, 224
Dynamic vs. static optimization 70

E

Echoing characters 386
EFJ p-code 300
EQU p-code 251
Equal false jump instruction 300
EQUI p-code 92, 250
EQUI routine 332
Evaluation stack 151, 154
eX)ecuting a program 28
EXECERR 352
EXIT p-code routine 341
Extended loads and stores 190

F

False jump instruction 298
Field width 218
Finding free memory in Apple Pascal 36
FIRMWARE protocol 375, 377
First 127 words of variables 64
First 16 words of storage in a procedure 61
FIXSET routine 325
FJP p-code 90, 92, 298
FJP p-code routine 314
FLC p-code routine 340
FLO p-code 254
FLO p-code routine 345
Float integer value routine 345
Floating point addition routine 344
Floating point adjust routine 344
Floating point comparison routine 344
Floating point multiplication routine 345
Floating point normalize routine 343
Floating point pop routine 342
Floating point push routine 343
Floating point round routine 344
Floating point subtraction routine 344
FLT p-code 252
FLT p-code routine 346
Flush character 387
FOR loop "phantom" variables 90
FOR loop code generation 90

Function calls 98
Function return values 98

G

GDIRP 224, 226, 228, 230
Generating one byte loads 63
GEQ p-code 251
GEQI p-code 250, 354
GEQI routine 332
GETBIG routine 312
Global loads and stores 168
Global variables 61, 152
GTR p-code 251
GTRI p-code 280, 354
GTRI routine 332

H

HEAP 32, 152, 224
HIRES graphics 377, 393
HLT p-code routine 341

I

IDS p-code routine 338, 348
IF . . . THEN . . . ELSE code
  generation 92
Immediate loads 154
INC p-code 214
INC p-code routine 323
Increasing the performance of Pascal
  programs 59
Incrementing a field pointer 214
IND p-code 184, 186
IND p-code routine 323, 328
Index subscript checking 42
Indexing into a packed array 214
Indexing into a string array 210
Indexing into an array 216
Indirect loads and stores 184
Indirect, indexed loads 186
Information provided on a
  compiled listing 73
Initializing an array to zero 69
INN p-code 87, 94, 288
INSERT procedure 97
Inside the p-code interpreter 307
Instruction formats 152
Instruction parameters 152
INT p-code 87, 292
INT p-code routine 325
Integer addition 234
Integer comparisons 250
Integer division 244
Integer modulo 246
Integer multiplication 240
Integer operations 232
Integer overflow 242
Integer subtraction 238
Intermediate loads and stores 176
Intermediate variables 176
Internally used strings 65
Interpreter jump table 352
Interpreter main loop 313
Interpreter program counter 151
Interpreter relative relocation table 312
Intrinsic segments 95
Intrinsic units 190
IOC p-code routine 347
IOR p-code routine 347
IORESULT 353
IO_ERROR routine 67
IPC 151, 307
IPC register 206, 296
IXA p-code 85, 216
IXA p-code routine 323
IXP p-code 218
IXP p-code routine 324
IXS p-code 210
IXS p-code routine 323

J

JTAB 151, 307
JTAB register 296
Jump table 151, 296
Jumps 296

K

KP 152, 307

L

LAE p-code 192

LAE p-code routine 317
LAND p-code 276, 354
LAND p-code routine 319
LAO p-code 84, 85, 86, 87, 88, 96, 172
LAO p-code routine 316
LDA p-code 180
LDA p-code routine 316
LDB p-code 96, 202
LDB p-code routine 319
LDC p-code 84, 196
LDC p-code routine 318
LDCI p-code 86, 158
LDCI p-code routine 314
LDCN 156
LDCN p-code routine 314
LDE p-code 190
LDE p-code routine 317
LDL p-code 162, 176
LDL p-code routine 315
LDM p-code 87, 198
LDM p-code routine 318
LDO p-code 84, 85, 170, 176
LDO p-code routine 316
LDP p-code 222
LDP p-code routine 324
LDS p-code 97
LDS p-code routine 338
LENGTH function 96
LEQ p-code 251
LEQI p-code 90, 91, 250, 354
LEQI routine 332
LES p-code 251
LESI p-code 250, 354
LESI routine 332
LIBRARY program 395
Line feed character 385
Line feed insertion after carriage return 388
List option 73
Listing a compiled program 73
LLA p-code 164
LLA p-code routine 315
LNOT p-code 280
LNOT p-code routine 320
Load constant NIL 156
Load global word 170
Load intermediate address 180
Load intermediate variable 176
Load local address 164
Load segment routine 337
Loading a global variable onto the stack 168
Loading a packed array address 220
Loading a string address onto the stack 206
Loading a word from an intrinsic unit 190
Loading an element from a packed field 222
Loading and storing data 61
Loading data from a byte array 202
Loading intrinsic units off the disk 95
Loading local variables onto the evaluation stack 160
Loading real and set constants onto the stack 196
Loading real and set variables onto the stack 198
Loading the address of a local variable onto the stack 164
Loading the address of an array element onto the stack 216
Loading the address of an intermediate variable 180
Loading values onto the evaluation stack 154, 158
Local loads and stores 160
Local procedures 98
Local variables 152
LOD p-code 176, 177
LOD p-code routine 316
Logical AND and OR operations 354
Logical AND function 25
Logical AND operations 276
Logical comparisons 282
Logical negation 94, 280
Logical NOT operation 280
Logical operations 276
Logical OR function 25
Logical OR operation 278
LONG integer routines 97
LONGINT intrinsic unit 95
LOR p-code 278, 354
LOR p-code routine 319
Low level data manipulation 16
LPA p-code 220
LPA p-code routine 322
LSA p-code 88, 95, 96, 206

LSA p-code routine 322
LSI-11 microprocessor 88

M

Maintaining programs 45
MARK procedure 228
Mark stack pointer 152
Maximizing code usage 64
MC68000 88, 351
MC6809 351
Mechanical optimizations 59
MEMAVAIL 36
MEMAVAIL p-code routine 342
Memory allocation 28
MODI p-code 246
Modifying the address contained within a pointer 36
Modifying the Apple Pascal BIOS 375
Modifying the Apple Pascal p-code Interpreter 351
Modulo 94
Mountain Computer Apple Clock 355
Mountain Computer Apple Clock card 351
Mountain Computer CPS card 351
MOV p-code 88, 212
MOV p-code routine 319
MOVELEFT 75
Moving a block of words 212
MP 152, 307
MP register 160, 164, 172, 177
MPI p-code 240, 321, 355
MPR p-code 268
MPR p-code routine 345
MRK p-code 228
MRK p-code routine 320
Multiple word loads and stores 196
Multiplication 94
Multiply p-code routine 321
Multiply routine 321
MVL p-code routine 342
MVR p-code routine 341

N

Negating an integer 236
Negating real values 264
NEQ p-code 251
NEQI p-code 250, 354
NEQI routine 332
NEW 19, 32, 152
NEW p-code 226
NEW p-code routine 320
New pointer 152
NFJ p-code 302
NGI p-code 236, 353
NGI p-code routine 321
NGR p-code 85, 264
NGR p-code routine 345
NIL 156, 224, 226, 228, 230
Non-contiguous case values 68
Non-integer comparisons 251
Non-portable tricks 20
Non-segmented procedure calls 98
NOP p-code 88, 89, 95, 96
NOT 94
Not equal false jump instruction 302
NP 152, 307
NP register 228, 230
NS16032 351
Null character 386

O

Observing the action of the NEW procedure 35
Obtaining the address of a REAL array element 216
Obtaining the address of a SET array element 216
Obtaining the address of a STRING array element 216
Obtaining the Pascal stack pointer value 36
ODD 94
ODD function 276, 280
Offset into a procedure 73
One's complement operation 280
One-byte instructions for loading and storing data 61
One-time initialization 71
Optimization techniques 15
Optimizing parameter data 63
Optimizing a program to make it compact 63

Optimizing array and subrange accesses 66
Optimizing compiler generated code 15
Optimizing for speed 70
Optimizing I/O instructions 67
Optimizing IF and CASE statements 67
Optimizing loops 71
Optimizing real variable accesses 64
Optimizing string accesses 65
ORD function 94, 276, 280
Overriding the automatic initialization of pointers 32
Overwriting pointer values 36

P

p-code assemblers 61
p-code disassemblers 60, 61
p-code subroutine call 334
p-machine 151
p-machine HEAP 152
p-machine registers 307
Packed field pointer 218, 222, 224
Parameter allocation 41
Pascal disk logical structure 390
Pascal Tools II 60, 98
Passing an array by value 75
Passing global variables by reference 172
Passing parameters by reference 44
Patching the p-code interpreter 353
PDQ disk utility 98, 145
PDQ Pascal utilities 61
PEEK 15, 36
PEEKing and POKEing various data structures 37
Performing input or output to a file 67
Phantom variables 96
Pinpointing the location of a run-time error 76
Placement of variables within a program 61
Pointer variable usage 89
Pointer variables 32
Pointers to integers 35
POKE 15, 36
Pop parameters off 6502 stack 335
Popping values off the evaluation stack 166
POS function 96
Positioning the editor at a specific line in a program 73
POT p-code 274
POT p-code routine 346
Power of ten table 346
PRED 94
Preventing the emission of the CHK p-code 248
Printable characters 387
Printer init entry point 388
Printer input entry point 388
Printer status entry point 389
Printer write operation 388
Printing an integer in hex format 22
Problems with pointer variables 32
Problems with the CASE statement 68
Procedure and function calls 304
Procedure call routine 334
Procedure calls 98
Procedure dictionary 151
Procedure lex level 73
Procedure number 73
Procedure segment number 73
Program stack 28
Program stack pointer 152
Push activation record 334
Push Boolean routine 331
Pushing a block of words onto the stack 196
Pushing the address of a string constant onto the stack 206
Pushing the address of an element of a packed array 218
Pushing the address of an intrinsic unit variable 192

R

RANGERR 352
RBP p-code 85
RBP p-code routine 336
Read segment routine 337
Real addition 262
REAL comparison routine 331
REAL comparisons 276
Real division 272
Real multiplication 268

Real operations 252
Real subtraction 266
Record and array allocation 40
Record and array handling instructions 212
Record and word array comparisons 294
Reducing the size of, and speeding up a program 61
Referencing array variables 42
Referencing variables as one of three data types 27
Registers 151
RELEASE 152, 224
Releasing storage allocated by MRK 230
Relocation routine 337
REPEAT . . . UNTIL code generation 91
Replacing the console driver 380
Replacing the PRINTER: driver 387
Replacing the REMIN and REMOUT drivers 389
Reserved word table 348
Resetting bits 24
Re-using record fields 16, 17
Reverse Polish notation 95
Right bit number 218
RLS p-code 230
RLS p-code routine 321
RND p-code 256
RND p-code routine 346
RNP p-code routine 336
Round routine 346
Rounding a real value 258
RSP 385
Run time support package 142

S

SAS p-code 89, 95, 208
SAS p-code routine 323
SB 153
SBI p-code 238, 354
SBI p-code routine 321
SBR p-code 266
SBR p-code routine 344
Scalar variable allocation 61
SCN p-code routine 340
SEG 151, 307
Segment procedures 28, 98, 152
Segments reserved for the system 74
Selectively setting or clearing bit patterns 25
Selectively turning the range checking on or off 43, 66
Self relative pointers 296
Set adjust 282
Set assignments 86
Set compare jump table 333
Set comparison routine 333
Set comparison setup routine 332
Set comparisons 294
Set difference 86, 294
Set difference operator 26
Set equal routine 333
Set equality operator 26
Set greater than or equal routine 333
Set inclusion 94
Set inclusion operator 26
Set inclusions 86
Set inequality operator 26
Set intersection 86, 292
Set intersection operator 25
Set less than or equal routine 333
Set membership 288
Set membership operator 26
Set not equal routine 333
Set operations 86, 282
Set remainder check routine 333
Set type implementation 25
Set union 86, 290
Set union operator 25
Setting bits 24
Setting several bits with a single assignment 25
SETUP program 355
SGS p-code 284
Shared allocation in Apple Pascal 15
Short load word indirect, indexed 184
Short store local 166
Shrinking Pascal programs 59
Signed byte 153
Similarities between Pascal and BASIC 28
Simulating PEEK and POKE 36
SIND p-code 184
SIND p-code routine 317
Sixteen-bit microprocessors 88
Size of the CASE table 68

SLDC p-code 85, 86, 87, 88, 97, 154
SLDC p-code routine 313
SLDL p-code 63, 160
SLDL p-code instruction 61
SLDL p-code routine 314
SLDO p-code 63, 83, 89, 92, 94, 168
SLDO p-code instruction 61
SLDO p-code routine 315
SP 151
SP register 204
Space available for user programs 28
Space character 386
Speed of the CASE statement 68
Speeding up a program vs. shrinking it 70
SQI p-code 242
SQI p-code routine 321
SQR p-code 270
SQR p-code routine 345
Squaring an integer 242
Squaring real values 270
SRO p-code 83, 87, 89, 94, 174
SRO p-code routine 316
SRS p-code 286
Stack pointer 151
Start/stop character 386
Static analysis 154
Static frequency analysis 70
Static links 177
STB p-code 204
STE p-code 194
STE p-code routine 317
STL p-code 166
STL p-code routine 315
STM p-code 84, 85, 86, 200
STM p-code routine 319
STO p-code 90, 188
STO p-code routine 318
Storage requirements for Pascal variables 38
Store a global word 174
Store a word into an intrinsic unit 194
Store data indirect 188
Storing a block of words 200
Storing data into a byte array 204
Storing data into a packed field 224
Storing data into an intermediate variable 182
Storing data into an intrinsic unit's global area 194
Storing often used constants in a variable 64
Storing real and set values 200
Storing top of stack into a local variable 166
STP p-code 224
STP p-code routine 325
STR p-code 182
STR p-code routine 317
STR procedure 95, 97
String address high order byte 89
String comparison routine 330
String comparisons 276
String handling functions 95
String handling instructions 206
String optimizations 65
Strings in Pascal 206
Subtraction 94
SUCC 94
SYSCOM 224, 382
SYSTEM.ATTACH 356, 377, 392
SYSTEM.STARTUP 392

T

Taking the absolute value of an integer 232
Testing bits 24
TIME 355
TIME p-code routine 341
TNC p-code 256
TNC p-code routine 346
Top of stack arithmetic 232
Transferring a block of words to a similar structure 212
Treating a word as a set or a Boolean array 26
Treating Boolean values as integers 276
Treating integers as Boolean values 276
Tricks with the case variant 19
TRS p-code routine 339
TRUNC function 256
Truncating a REAL value 256
Truncation routine 346
TRVSTAT routine 312
Turning off the range checking 66
Turning the I/O checking on or off 67
Turning the range checking off 43
Two's complement 236

Two-byte load and store instructions 64
Type ahead buffer 387
Type transfer functions 276

U

UB 153
UB values 208
UBUSY p-code routine 347
UCLEAR p-code routine 347
UCSD Pascal version IV.0 154
UJP p-code 90, 91, 92, 93, 297
UJP p-code routine 314
ULS p-code routine 338
Unary operators 232, 258, 280
Unconditional jump instruction 297
Understanding the operation of the p-machine 59
UNI p-code 87, 290
UNI p-code routine 326
Unimplemented opcode 311
Uniquely indentifying a procedure 74
UNIT 152
UNIT I/O routine 348
Unit on-line check routine 346
UNITCLEAR 394
UNITREAD 390
UNITWRITE 390
Unload segment routine 338
Unsigned byte 153
UPIPC1 313
UPIPC2 313
UPIPC3 313
UREAD input entry point 348
User hardware drivers 152
Using better algorithms 70
Using FILLCHAR to initialize arrays 69
Using two variant fields simultaneously 21
USTATUS p-code routine 347
UWAIT p-code routine 347
UWRITE output entry point 348

V

Value Range error 43
Variable address assignment 37
Variable declaration order 63
Variable definitions and the size of a program 61
Variable definitions and the speed of a program 61
Variable length instructions 162
Variable storage 152
Variant records 16
Variant storage allocation 17

W

Wasted space in Pascal records 19
When not to pull tricks 44
WHILE loop code generation 91

X

XEQERR routine 312
XIT p-code routine 321
XJP p-code 93, 304
XJP p-code routine 320

Z

Zeroing integer arrays 69
Zeroing real variables 69
Zeroing record variables 69
Zeroing set variables 69
Zeroing user defined scalars 69